Paul Stump contributes features on music and popular culture to *The Sunday Telegraph, The Wire, Harper & Queen, The Guardian* and *The New Statesman. Unknown Pleasures* is his second book and he is currently writing a history of bubblegum music.

By the same author
The Music's All That Matters: A History of Progressive Rock

unknownpleasuresaculturalbiographyofRoxyMusicpaulstump

THUNDER'S MOUTH PRESS
NEW YORK

Published in the United States by Thunder's Mouth Press
841 Broadway, 4th Floor
New York, N.Y. 10003

First published in Great Britain by Quartet Books Limited in 1998
A member of the Namara Group
27 Goodge Street
London W1P 2LD

Library of Congress Cataloging-in-Publication Data

Stump, Paul.
    Unknown pleasures : a cultural biography of Roxy Music / by
Paul Stump.
       p.   cm.
    Originally published: London : Quartet Books, 1998.
    Discography: p. 346
    Includes bibliographical reference (p. 329) and index.
    ISBN 1-56025-212-X
    1. Roxy Music (Musical group) 2. Rock musicians—England
Biography. I Title.
    ML421.R68S78   1999
    782.42166'092'2—dc21
    (B)   99-30296
                                                     CIP

Phototypeset by FSH, London

Distributed by Publishers Group West

Manufactured in the United States of America

'In 1972 style was something you climbed over in a muddy field to get to a pop festival. Then along slinked Roxy Music' Patrick Humphries, *Record Hunter* magazine, 1992

CONTENTS

PREFACE: JUST FOR A CHANGE, THIS BIT'S IMPORTANT

When I was about eight years old I thought that Bryan Ferry was French. Or German. Or Italian, or something. And that gave him style, as did anything European to my childlike eyes. The first time I heard him sing ('These Foolish Things', probably), I thought he sounded like Tom's impression of Charles Boyer in the *Tom and Jerry* cartoons, and I won't deny he made an indelible impression. In fact, I remember how crestfallen I felt when, five years later, through the medium of one of those deflationary schoolyard enlightenments of the kind that more usually divulge the real identity of Santa Claus, I discovered that Bryan Ferry was a Geordie, just like Bob

Ferris and Terry Collier out of *The Likely Lads*. Somehow, Ferry never again appeared in quite the same cognac-coloured light when I realized that he used phrases like 'why-aye, man, pet'. Instead of 'Here's looking at you, kid' (which was what a hipster like him *should* have said — and indeed did say, on the song '2HB'), it would *actually* be 'Here's looking at you, kidda'. A shame, that. But he was still something to see in that tuxedo, especially to a kid whose too-small tank tops were home-knitted from royal-blue Wendy wool.

Ferry's subtle integration of an unspoken 'continental' demeanour or inflection into his voice and presence was, back then, enough to ratchet up his interest value and invest him with an air of mystery. Not just for me — for everyone. The very words 'continental' and 'European', when applied to things in the 1970s, connoted superiority. This owed something to a combination of an end to the post-war British boom and the durability of all those Euro-myths that so nourished British culture from the first nudge-nudging accounts of the *Folies Bergère* to 1960s spy capers and beyond — louche Latins, the Blue Train and the Orient Express, naughty French maids, Virna Lisi and Belmondo and Zizi Jeanmaire, Marlene Dietrich, Gitanes — all appeared irresistibly *other*. Europe was still very special, psychologically and physically distant.

Maybe it was something to do with that Charles Boyer quaver, but Ferry's power to suggest an adult world of experience pulled my emotional development up by its bootstraps. The music too, familiar yet alien, boppy yet harmonically diffuse, added an extra layer of mystery and suggestiveness. Just what were these guys about?

It's taken until now for me to try to answer that question — what it meant to me, what it meant to others, what it meant to the girls — and boys — who sent their knickers to Bryan Ferry (or to Brian Eno, or to Paul Thompson, or to Andy Mackay, or to Phil Manzanera — they all had their followings). Few acts, apart perhaps from David Bowie — and for similar reasons — provoke such a complex emotional response and stimulate fans on so many different levels as did Roxy Music in their pomp. This book intends to explain some of the magic.

I don't believe for one instant that any book about Roxy Music can avoid dealing with the issues they dealt with — metropolitan rather than hippie-idyllic leisure; the phenomena of stardom, celebrity and wealth and what they meant; the role of the pop star in the media; pornography; fashion and, of course, sex. And so I've dealt with all of them as best I can.

During the writing of this book, I attempted to contact as many members of Roxy Music as possible. Unfortunately, and for various reasons, no member was willing to be interviewed, and requests for the manuscript to be checked by Bryan Ferry's management were also turned down. As a result, the book is based on material already in the public domain and has been added to with sundry personal reminiscences from several of those who knew the band personally and professionally.

This book deals extensively with the environment in which Roxy Music thrived, for the simple reason that for Roxy Musc, unlike nearly all of their contemporaries, their inspiration was intimately connected to the times in which they existed — or more specifically, the times in which their chief songwriter and image consultant, Bryan Ferry, lived. And so I make no apologies for diversions into sex, dandyism, pornography — Roxy Music, as I have pointed out, is as much a quality as a band, and we love or remember or cherish a feeling/an allusion/an image as much as the band and the musicians in it and the notes they played. It is that conception of Roxy Music that I believe has helped preserve their memory and that I believe needs study. The music and the biography take precedence, of course, but extraneous factors cannot be ignored.

At this point I must thank Johnny Rogan for his book *Style with Substance: Roxy's First Ten Years*. He will, I am sure, be the first to admit that his book is not always good literature, but it is a first-class piece of journalism, telling the story of the band in a punchy, imaginative and no-nonsense manner with warmth, economy and drive. It provided me with an ideal historical framework around which to fit my own interpretation of the band and their significance. To those who discern similarities between this book and Johnny Rogan's, I can only say that this owes more to his hard work than my own. For fans of the band, I can also unhesitatingly recommend Rex Balfour's surprisingly informative (if unflaggingly sycophantic) *The Bryan Ferry Story*, as well as Eric Tamm's splendidly detailed *Brian Eno: His Music and the Vertical Colour of Sound*.

I have loosely followed Rogan's own simple chronological approach – although I have omitted discussion of Brian Eno's post-Roxy Music career within the band narrative itself and have devoted a long chapter to his life and music, along with a shorter one dealing with the music of both Andy Mackay and Phil Manzanera. My reasons for expending so many words on Eno are outlined in more detail at the beginning of Chapter 9, but suffice to say here that his music shares so many stylistic influences with Roxy Music that its development bears close study when compared to and contrasted with that of his former employers.

This book owes its creation largely to Ged Parsons, but would under no circumstances have been written in the form you see before you without the heroic and frankly bearded assistance of John Bland, who will henceforth be known only as SuperGeordie II (honourable mention here also for *Mrs* SuperGeordie II, Deanne, who had to put up with him attending to my phone calls and/or neuroses and/or manuscript and not to her or Peter). Considerable credit also accrues to Andy Aliffe; Paul Schutze, Paul Evans; Roger Eno and family; the ever-reliable Mark Paytress of *Record Collector* for his invaluable Phil Manzanera material; Paul Higgs for many books; the staff of the National Sound Archive and the British Library, London; Robert Wyatt; Stella, Jeremy, Lindy and Sarah at Quartet, without whom life would be a drag; Tim of No-Man; Steve Harris of *Hi Fi News*; Rob Ayling at Voiceprint; Mike Stobbie; Michael and Isabelle at the

Niederhaus; Christelle Chaigne; Pete Sinfield; Jon at Namara; Phil James; Simon Hopkins; my sister Emma Stump and folks Rowan and Nicki; Stephanie and Tom at the *Blue Goose*; Mike Barnes; Ian and Wieke; Hans-Joachim Roedelius and family; the constituent members of Roxy Music, whose creativity has made this book simultaneously such a bane and such a beauty to work on; John Goodwin at Virgin Records; and most of all to Alquimía, who is always there even when she isn't.

INTRODUCTION

Bryan Ferry (or SuperGeordie, as he is frequently known north of the River Wear) is one of the most recognizable faces in British pop music and his band Roxy Music one of the most talked-about acts in the genre's history, both during their existence (1971–83) and since. Nevertheless, despite much critical applause and spot-evaluation in the conventional avenues of rock discussion and mythology (the rock press, TV, etc.) and also in the fledgeling field of rock academia and popular cultural studies, Roxy Music remain a mercurial quality. They have lain unbiographized since the publication of two largely fan-biased books about them in 1982 following their tenth anniversary as a performing unit. Nothing, however, has been thus far produced to act as a concordance of the many reasons and theories as to why this band were both so consistently entertaining and so important, nothing to collate the many and varied opinions on one of popular music's most infuriatingly unclassifiable acts.

Their greatness – or otherwise – cannot be ascertained and without an appraisal incorporating biographical and analytical approaches. It is a task too important to be left to the conventional methods of rock biography. Roxy Music demand a cultural biography to enable them to be remembered as more than just another nobodica of animatronic rocker waxworks at the Trocadero.

Roxy Music, for all their initially lurid explicitness and good-time Glam attire, their Champagne Charlie image and dolly-bird mascots, were an enigmatic crew. They wooed teenyboppers by the thousand, appeared on the five-hundredth *Top of the Pops* (negatives exist of Ferry et al. schmoozing with Tony Blackburn, Noel Edmonds and Pan's People) having racked up yet another impeccably crafted Top Ten hit, yet, in an era when the personnel of singles charts and album charts were often mutually exclusive, they appealed to campus rock fans also. Out in sheepskin-coat land, the studenty fundamentalists of rock fandom in 1970s Britain had few qualms about nicking Roxy Music LPs from their younger sisters and filing them alongside those of Led Zeppelin, Pink Floyd and Tangerine Dream.

In an era when rock music was judged according to how deeply it reflected some 'other' quality, how profoundly it was informed by truth, justice or beauty, Roxy Music, along with David Bowie, were pioneering a postmodern outlook whereby artifice became the handmaiden of artistry. Roxy Music dealt in the youthful currency of transience, of instantaneous gratification and stinging loss, and the articulation of same in the emotional cadences of pop music. Yet they achieved it all in a peculiarly adult fashion, readable on several musical and cultural levels. Serious and trivial aspects were never so successfully and so seamlessly joined in the work of any other UK rock act. Music was, for Roxy Music, a disposable, adolescent pop moment of meaningless dissolution, but also a means to the end of creating new art. The panache and experimentalism they brought to that creative process meant they could never be lumped with conveyor-belt bubblegum producers such as Mickie Most, Mike Chapman and Nicky Chinn (although a few commentators tried).

This approach could not have contrasted more strongly with that of their Progressive rock contemporaries, whereby sophistication was to be sought only through a gnostic, exclusive, initiate musical culture which related more to high art than low art. What Progressive musicians disdained in pop – melody, beat, soul and above all dedication to visual image – Roxy Music greedily made their own, subjecting these qualities to formal transmogrifications and elisions as clever in their way as anything achieved in purely musical terms by the likes of Yes and Soft Machine. Roxy Music had real pop energy but also experimentalist curiosity – as their live performances show – and their combination of rock and pop voicings is unequalled.

This fixation with pop inevitably threw into question the predominantly masculine mores of contemporary rock discourse, quite apart from the sexual ambiguities suggested by Roxy Music's wardrobe. After all, pop in the 1970s was for girls and rock for boys. Roxy Music, however, were recognizably rockers when they played live but they didn't *dress* like rockers – they harnessed single-stud chic to Pop Art, mixing and matching styles from the 1920s to the 1950s. Pop trappings – they were fond of old rock and roll and soul voicings – were tantamount to a surgically implanted limpness of the wrists. But on the other hand these were conspicuously heterosexual lads – save for Eno, apparently a roaring and unashamed queen (until the linen got dirty and hung out). Nobody could be quite sure what Roxy Music were or intended to be, but they were certainly massively successful.

They embodied a peculiar decadence unique to its time – the 1970s – and commented sharply and satirically on it, both accommodating and standing proud of the decade's stop-start sexual revolution(s) which saw the spotlight on sex switch away from Soho and Carnaby Street and the campus and into suburban bedrooms. Roxy Music's records mirrored this – that the libido was not simply a plaything of bohemians but of everyone, as an immortal luxury and extravagance of all classes, of slumming glamour pusses and/or aspirant wife-swappers.

Their abandonment of their more experimental early music led to their discovery by an affluent constituency of older fans by the time of their mid-1970s trial separation. Punk may have passed them by during that period of 'devolution' in 1976–8 when Ferry, Manzanera and Mackay were attending to solo projects, but while Roxy Music's resplendent decadence was a target for Punk, it had also incubated many of the themes hatched by Punk. Roxy Music's evident aesthetic detachment from the exigencies of the times might have jarred, but the band's dedication to cataloguing and exploring the phenomena of *jouissance* and hedonism, albeit articulated in a luxuriant, consumerist vernacular, won them many Punk admirers. It tallied with Punk's attention to buyable delirium, sexual deviancy, postmodern surface, the dislocating promotion of artifice over meaning. There were differences of degree: Punk sex, for example, was all about bedsits and winded mattresses, Roxy Music sex was golden showers on heart-shaped waterbeds. But the concern with sex and sexuality as component of identity was the same.

Such concerns with the dissolute and fleeting were incorporated into a new manner of evaluating and practising rock production and consumption by a new breed of Punk-vanguard musicians and critics, sworn enemies of rockist universals and fundamentals The subsequent valorization of style over substance enabled Roxy Music – who always had substance to burn – to survive as a creative force into the 1980s.

In the 1970s, they had been out of touch with the public mood but in touch with private moods. In the 1980s, they found themselves bewildered heralds of a public mood, with the coalescence of a new, stylized and sequinned Me Generation from London's clubland, from Annabel's, Tramps, Stringfellows and Blitz, in a world which took more imagistic and musical cues from Roxy Music than perhaps from any other pop act.

This book intends to ask two questions: how did Roxy Music come to be so important and how did their pose end up taking over the country's youth? As usual, seeking the answers to such questions leads us out of the capital and into England's provinces — specifically, to its colleges of higher education.

1: THE MAKING OF SUPERGEORDIE

ROCKISM – THE POP SIXTIES

Since the publication in 1987 of Frith and Horne's fine (if ideologically skewed) book *Art into Pop*, the true function of the art school in British rock and pop music has finally been accorded the credit it deserves. A tribute to this peculiarly British institution – which inculcated in several generations of young creatively minded people a self-confidence to express themselves artistically – was long overdue. Through pop music, the majority of those energies were expended in a creative realm outside the fine arts; but the point is that they were ignited within the post-war British art school, and so these institutions became unrivalled avatars of youth culture. The common mythology of their role in society has been best summed up by the possibly apochryphal statement, 'Art school was somewhere they put you when they didn't know what else to do with you.'

John Lennon was maybe the most famous of pop's art school graduates; Keith Richard and Mick Jagger may have been playground chums at Maypole County Primary but their musical partnership was struck up thanks to Keith's attending art school. Art schools – in theory and, more often than not, in practice – impressed on young minds the validity, the *paramountcy*, of self-expression, the permissibility of using the world around them as simultaneous palette and template. They were official institutions which, for the unsporty, the four-eyed, the wallflower, the weirdo, *legitimized* daydreaming, detachment and obeisance to a private imaginary realm. There the romantic notion of the creative genius, unique and irresistible, was promulgated to an impressionable adolescent audience.

In the 1950s, however, when conventional art instruction (both in method and course content) began to wilt under the influence of continental and American modernism, the pedagogic tradition became inculcated with values that were diametrically opposed to bourgeois existence and to bourgeois means of conceptualizing the world. Central to the importance of the art school thereafter were its foregrounding of anti-bourgeois themes and thought processes to petit-bourgeois and/or working-class youth, and its making real a career choice which eschewed teleological notions of hard material labour equalling reward. The petit-bourgeois art school experience, in short, pitted traditional English values of thrift and hard work and application against values of material and spiritual absolution which were antithetical.

Also central to the art school experience of the 1950s and 1960s was the introduction to the British fine arts of Pop Art. Popularly (and mistakenly) assumed to be just another American import, another cultural concession to GI hegemony, Pop Art was taken to be an insidious highbrow piece of slumming, a new exemplar of the US's hedonistic and valueless emptiness, which defamed decency as shamelessly as Marilyn Monroe, the Bomb, Elvis and McCarthy. The fact that

Pop Art facetiously upheld all these concepts and more to be inspirational only goaded its critics further.

Pop Art was in fact originally a British invention and was perhaps, more than any other form of graphic artistic expression, an engine of pop musical creativity; and Roxy Music were, indisputably, the most visible and memorable of the many musical acts for whom Pop Art was an inspiration. They were certainly the pop act which handled the raw material of Pop Art with the greatest sensitivity, finesse and (requisite) cynicism.

Bryan Ferry's early years are a case in point. His formative art education was an object lesson of the process by which Pop Art came to have such a say in the production, the performance and ultimately the consumption of much British pop music of the 1970s and beyond.

Ferry was born in Washington, County Durham, in the north-east of England, on 26 September 1945. Washington is now a nondescript and somewhat oppressive town, a knot of abandoned collieries and slagheaps in the middle of what was once one of Europe's most famous coalfields – the whole black stain clotted around England's main north–south road artery, the A1. In Ferry's childhood, as had been the case for generations, coal dominated the town and the landscape. Coal dictated monoculture; coal was economy, polity and society; the whole town depended on the pits. The pits gave life, with social clubs, unions and the Labour Party all drawing their lifeblood from miners. The pits also took life away, with pneumoconiosis, roof-falls, faulty winches.

Ferry's father, Frederick, had been brought up on hill-farms and had won trophies for horse-drawn ploughmanship, but in the 1930s he moved to the more remunerative environment of the Washington collieries, where he tended ponies at the pithead. Wages were reasonable and, after the inauguration in 1947 of the National Coal Board, employment steady. He met his wife, Mary Ann, in Washington, and wooed her with a cart drawn by a horse with a flower behind its ear. 'He was a bit of a throwback,' remembers Ferry, 'which is why I loved him so much.'[1]

The Ferrys, a family of six, maintained a dignified if straitened proletarian existence. Ferry's childhood, as the third of four children, was frugal, but not destitute. 'Very poor,'[2] is as far as Ferry has gone in estimating his earliest circumstances. Holidays were unheard of; television arrived – ten shillings a week from Radio Rentals – only when Newcastle United reached the 1951 FA Cup Final – but, that said, it arrived everywhere else in Newcastle that day also.*

Nothing seems to have been said or done to deflect him from an early interest in the visual arts and in cinema, although his parents encouraged him in his schoolwork, hoping to see him scale the professional heights – a putative teacher, lawyer or doctor.

The cinema was one of Washington's few non-coal-related entertainments. Not many boys with any regard for their own safety or the attentions of their peers evinced much of an interest in things cultural beyond the silver screen, but Ferry seems to have been less involved with the cinema as social locus – a place for picking up and petting – than as an aesthetic experience. 'Whenever I saw a movie I'd really live it, and if it was sad I'd cry,'[3] he told an interviewer. Furthermore, Ferry recalls being uninterested in sport – a courageous choice for a schoolboy on soccer-addled Tyneside. Indeed, accounts of his early life seem to suggest an almost comical stereotype of popular myth, the delicate, sensitive boy born into the world of the unfeeling and ignorant horny-hands, taking their belt indiscriminately to all that they do not understand. The image has mushroomed mightily in popular culture, from the days of the dying industrialist berating his aesthete son in Kipling's *The Mary Gloster* to the very contemporary 1950s patriarch with his whippets cursing his London-bound son for a woolly-woofter.

*Newcastle beat Blackpool 2–0.

Johnny Rogan recounts in his biography that Ferry could be seen 'wandering the streets of Washington with his head in the air and a vacant expression on his face'.[4] Whether this was in fact, as he somewhat gratuitously continues, an 'attempt to emulate the Romantic image of Shelley or Keats' is harder to fathom. Ferry's interests were almost exclusively concerned with the graphic arts, and in the autumn of 1964 he started a BA Fine Arts course at Newcastle University. 'I wanted to get my degree,' he commented later, 'because as a kid I had been conditioned to the whole working-class thing of education – or sport – being the only ways of salvation or escape into a better...life. Self-improvement was a strong motivating force.'[5] As it had been for many millions of working-class people before him – and the liberal social economy still operating in 1960s Britain maintained the impetus of that improving culture, initially pioneered by philanthropic Victorians, in the shape of council-run adult education classes, local libraries and full grants for higher education. The escape routes many dreamed of were still open.

FERRY AND MUSIC

Ferry may have entertained dreams of artistic bohemia and creative epiphanies in garrets, but such success, whether in the fine arts or the cinema, was many years away, with un-believably hard work and possibly unbelievable disappoint-ment in between. By 1963, however, another escape route was opening up – pop music. This was the Beat Boom summer, a musical convulsion of guitars and hormones which saw young men throughout Britain climbing on to stages and beginning to change the face not just of popular music but of popular culture itself. The lure, of course, was the very ordinariness of the people who were causing such hysteria – those Beatles! Why, they could be (and were duly billed as) the boys next door. And the Stones! God, if losers like that could make it, anyone could. And so everyone tried. Anywhere with enough room for four musicians resounded to Beat groups.

Industrial cities in particular felt the force, and every town in the country now had to have its own homologue of the Cavern Club, a sounding-board of local resonances. From this Babel someone would emerge triumphant, the naturally selected, the town's unanimous delegate to the Beat revolution, through which, it was imagined, local boys could change the world.

In Newcastle the hub of the hysteria was the Club-a-Go-Go. The Club-a-Go-Go's contribution to the Beat Boom was the Animals, a band of low morals and high professionalism whose muscular and dissolute music – an uncompromising broth of rock and roll, soul and r'n'b – was perhaps the most individually distinctive Beat music (save that of the Beatles) and easily the most raucously down-home. The sweatbox from which they emerged ensured that. Nobody gave half-measures on stage at the Club-a-Go-Go and escaped with their lives.

Testimonies of the time, of the place, evoke the razor-edged world of ballroom tension described in Gordon Burn's *Alma Cogan*, with its 'ripe ponging crush of hot-eared young men who looked like their fathers and full-blown, over-talced young women who looked like their mothers'.[6] Newcastle, a tough town honed by mining and maritime manual labour, didn't take its entertainment, whether brawls or Beat groups, lightly.

Ferry's putative decadence might be expected to have risen above this musical proletarianism, but, as he once assured an interviewer with perhaps a little too much emphasis, 'I spent my youth hanging out in really seedy pool halls with the Teds.'[7] Loyalty to working-class roots has always been a touchy subject with Ferry, but available evidence contends that his distance from the masses – then and latterly – was and is not as great as is publicly assumed.

There wasn't much mileage in spending all one's time on Tyneside as a proxy Chatterton – it would have cut no ice with the girls, for a start. But Ferry became a musician – or at least a singer, which approximated to the same thing – in 1963, when a friend from a local cycling club talked him into singing for a club band called the Banshees who hawked their way around the Sunderland working-men's-club circuit, churning out good-time standards to keep the brawlers and boozers happy. Ferry recalls his family's reaction: 'My mother was modern and understood what I was doing. She would watch *Top of the Pops* and say, "You must get something out. This is all rubbish, you know. All rubbish."'[8]

Ferry's interest in music was subsidiary to his other passions, but was active enough. The Ferrys owned a piano, but their son got off to a bad start with it:

'My first piano lesson, which I had when I was five years old...I can remember coming home with my little music case and sitting down and playing this scale. My sister, who was a great pianist, then came in and started teasing me and saying, "No, you don't do it like that, you do it like this!" She then sat down and started playing Beethoven's *Moonlight Sonata* very well. I got so angry I started punching her and never took another piano lesson.'[9]

His Aunt Enid, when baby-sitting, introduced him to standard tunes with her collection of 78s, which included performances by the Ink Spots, Billy Eckstine and Nat King Cole. 'My first introduction to real music,' is how Ferry remembers the experience.[10] Later, he sneaked peeks at copies of the *Melody Maker* that he delivered on his paper round, and before he was ten he rushed through the streets of Washington clutching an autograph book to meet his hero Johnny Ray, the lachrymose American crooner who was visiting the town to rediscover his roots.

Such affinities wouldn't have won Ferry many admirers, at least among boys. Ray, a *kitschmeister* of melodrama, turned on the copious waterworks while performing, to the orgasmic delight of millions of female followers. Whether faked or real, Ray's confessional extravaganzas were, ostensibly, girls' stuff, as was Guy Mitchell, Ferry's other hero, whom he went to see perform in Newcastle. Ferry also remembers being moved at Newcastle's Theatre Royal by a touring performance of Puccini's *La Bohème*.

Ferry's other musical passion was jazz. He progressed to Chris Barber (first concert seen, shy in the company of his Uncle Billy) and Ken Colyer (first record bought), explored the influences on those two artists and then set about a thorough investigation of the output of Charlie Parker. Other loves included the Modern Jazz Quartet, and Norman Granz's Jazz At The Philharmonic concerts at Newcastle City Hall. He was also allowed to sit in on 'Duke Ellington Evenings' given by his elder sisters and a gramophone for their friends, during which suitable homage was paid to the master's finest recordings.

Ferry, although not immune to the charms of rock and roll – he had seen Bill Haley and His Comets bring chaos to Tyneside, after winning tickets in a Radio Luxemburg competition (they arrived on the day the young Ferry was due to sit his 11-plus exam), admired Chuck Berry, Fats Domino and Elvis, and had a special affection for Little Richard – was more of a black music purist. Apart from jazz, well catered for in Newcastle at the legendary Gray's club, he fell under the spell of classic r'n'b, of Bobby Bland, of Wilbert Harrison, of the Sue Records and Chess Records import scene. By 1963, after his baptism-of-fire stint with the Banshees – from which he had fortuitously emerged without broken teeth or spirit – he determined to enhance his appreciation of soul music by performing it himself, and to this end he assembled a group of fellow Newcastle University students into an eight-piece band, the Gas Board. This last featured a brass section comprising a formidable four saxophones and trumpet which at one stage included a young Mike Figgis, who would go on to direct such hit movies as *Leaving Las Vegas*. Bland and Harrison cover versions featured heavily, not least Harrison's showstopper 'Let's Work Together', later reworked by Ferry in 1976 as 'Let's Stick Together'. At some stage, however, Ferry and the band parted company. Figgis would go on record as saying that Ferry was fired because 'he wasn't a good soul singer; he had that [vocal] tremble'.[11] Ferry denied it, and told a reporter that he left due to the increasingly intolerable amounts of time that organizing and performing in the band occupied during periods otherwise reserved for study. He had not been prepared, he said hotly, to drop out and go professional like the rest of the musicians. 'How dare he say that?' Ferry stormed, in a rare display of naked public petulance. 'It's fucking rude, isn't it?'[12]

One early fan of the Gas Board was Gordon Sumner, a.k.a., Sting, who remembers them as 'very good. Ferry was just the same as he is now, really.'[13]

By 1965, however, r'n'b was becoming increasingly ghettoized. The slicker, *whiter* Detroit soul sound of Motown was winning plaudits and sales at the cost of the ballsier Memphis and Chicago schools, and it was only in tiny loyalist cells, such as Ferry's, or in diehard Mod strongholds, that an audience remained for 'original' r'n'b.

The pop revolution – of harmony, structure and melody – occasioned by the Beatles was moving on as the whims of the Fab Four changed and other currents took hold. The stylisms of soul – traditional, formulaic riffs, unabashed commercialism, show-business trappings, sartorial precision – were frowned upon in an increasingly subjectivized youth culture in which self-expression was the Holy Grail. Soul was, for increasing numbers of young people, an expression not of today but of yesterday, a hollow creation of corporate US capital, a dumbed-down dead end which regimented true black modes of expression into white show-business straitjackets (a misnomer, of course, but an easy one to fall for). The Gas Board, who dressed in bobbysox, white Levi's, initialled baseball shirts and sneakers, were, like their music, a brazen celebration of the cheap commercial Americana which youth culture increasingly came to see as the artistic arm of culturally imperialistic US corporate evil. Suits, liveries and uniforms of any sort became ciphers for uptightness, for individual repression and denial.

Ferry never understood this posture, preferring to accommodate US culture. There exists a wonderful 1967 photograph of him dressed in a dapper midnight-blue suit, leaning insouciantly on the fender of a grandiose Studebaker, his car of choice. Taken by his friend Nick de Ville, it was used to illustrate an exhibition of Ferry's fine art at neighbouring Durham University in the summer of 1967. (The low-riding gas-guzzler on the tarmac beneath sunny Californian trees was in fact moored next to a railway cutting in Newcastle and was an old banger that had cost £60 and would respond only to jump-starts.)

Ferry was a trendsetter at the Newcastle University Fine Art Department. He and a group of friends, including Tim Head and Nick de Ville, moved into studios in Eslington Terrace in nearby Jesmond. 'We thought we were very cool,' said Ferry of his circle, 'and all the others very square. They were the corduroy and Gauloises-smoking brigade. We were into button-down shirts, the Beach Boys, Jackson Pollock – this much more happening, American thing.'[14] Ferry – who, at the age of fourteen, had been working on Saturdays in Jackson's Haberdasher's on Northumberland Street, Newcastle – now bought his threads from Marcus Pryce's shop in Newcastle. Pryce was one of the instrumental designers in the history of Mod. Naturally enough, then, the Gothic excesses of psychedelia largely passed Ferry by. If anything, hippiedom sharpened his admiration for those willing to kick against it, and one of his fondest musical memories, oft-quoted, is a concert given by the touring package of Stax artists in Newcastle in 1967. This was a Pauline vision, 'just seeing Steve Cropper and Booker T and so on in their best stage suits'.[15] It recalled the formal rectitude, the discipline, the *dignity* of those Norman Granz Jazz At The Philharmonic sessions that had so thrilled him a decade before. That night Ferry thought there had to be something musical he could create 'that would have been as much me as that [was] them'.[16] Ferry, sartorially dazzled as much as musically transported, decided to become a professional musician – despite his parents' dismay ('they thought I was crackers'[17]) – and hitchhiked down the A1 to London.

Not that the years of study at Newcastle had been wasted; indeed, they had been valuable to the point where they now not only furnished Ferry with sufficient graphic skills to survive, should his musical aspirations fail, but also offered him a specific artistic outlook which became an instinctive informant of his musical inspirations. And it is here that Richard Hamilton enters the Roxy Music story, for although Hamilton is not a musician, no biography of the band can afford to overlook his massive influence upon them.

RICHARD HAMILTON

Hamilton was born in London in 1922 and his background was similar enough to Ferry's to imply an instinctive rapport between the two men. Hamilton had, according to his autobiography, no 'formal education' but learned to draw in LCC classes at Southwark and Millbank, prior to taking life classes at Westminster Tech and St Martin's. In 1938 he was accepted into the Royal Academy, a notable achievement. War interrupted this swift ascent, and he got work as a draughtsman and a 'jig–and–tool designer' until after the cessation of hostilities to avoid conscription. Shortly afterwards he was expelled from the Academy, along with some colleagues, for open insubordination, mocking the antediluvian regime of the principal, the arch-reactionary Sir Alfred Munnings, and in particular his own tutor, Thomas Monnington, a monstrous man given to such aesthetic observations as, 'They're [Cézanne and Picasso] not even good honest Frenchmen, just a lot of fucking Dagoes.'[18]

Next was the Slade, where Hamilton began teaching in 1953. His first contact with Newcastle University – to which he commuted from London every week – was when he co-ordinated an exhibition by students there entitled 'Man,

11

Machine and Motion', which showcased his love of photography. Victor Pasmore was moved to intimate to Hamilton that while he liked the exhibition as a whole, he'd have liked it more 'if it hadn't been for all those photographs'.[19]

Hamilton was friendly with a loose-knit group of young artists at the Institute of Contemporary Arts who from 1952 had met regularly under the rubric of the Independent Group to discuss the aesthetics of mass production, from automobile styling to pop music. Among them were Eduardo Paolozzi, John McHale, Peter Reyner Banham and Lawrence Alloway, and they were united in a boggled fascination with the syntax of mass communications, as shown in a 1956 Whitechapel Gallery exhibition featuring much of their work, 'This is Tomorrow'.

Hamilton's contribution, a collage of kitsch American images, while not pioneering (Paolozzi had produced a similar collage for a private group meeting in 1952), stole the show. It was entitled *Just What is It That Makes Today's Homes So Different, So Appealing?* The content of the frame was bold enough: a muscleman holding a giant lolly called 'Tootsie'; a raddled stripper with nipples masked by coy sequins; a 'painting' which was in reality a frame from a cheapo magazine, *Young Romance*; and a clutter of consumer durables. These household luxuries would go on to become iconographic in Hamilton's work in succeeding years; *She* (1958–60) takes its cue from advertising material for household appliances.

A natural articulacy enabled Hamilton swiftly to become Pop Art's chief spokesman. While Alloway coined the quotable 'Fine/Pop Art continuum' – with Picasso at one end and Elvis at the other – Hamilton had a louder voice and a more elegant pen to articulate this as-yet-undefined movement.

In the Whitechapel catalogue, Hamilton wrote, 'We reject the notion that tomorrow can be expressed through the formal presentation of rigid formal concepts. Tomorrow can only extend the range of the present body of visual experience.'[20] The following year, he issued the first serious attempt to outline Pop Art's *raison d'être*: 'popular (designed for a mass audience); transient (short-term solution); expendable (easily forgotten); low-cost; mass-produced; young (aimed at youth); witty; sexy; gimmicky; glamorous; and, last but not least, Big Business'.[21]

In short, the opposite of everything that conventional art and artistic attitudes stood for. Hamilton was quite aware of this, writing:

Pop Fine Art [is a] profession of approbations of mass culture, therefore also anti-artistic. It is positive Dada, creative where Dada was destructive. Perhaps it is Mama − a cross fertilisation of Futurism and Dada which upholds a respect for the culture of the masses and a conviction that the artist in 20th century urban life is inevitably a consumer of mass culture *and* [my italics] potentially a contributor to it.[22]

Hamilton impressed his students no end. Irrespective of his reputation, his Levi's and Havanas suggested uncommon approachability. Radio producer John Walters later remembered that the walls of his office were covered by a life-sized Brigitte Bardot cut in weekly parts from the pages of the magazine *Reveille*. To Ferry, Hamilton was a man who ensured that everyone tried that little bit harder. English Pop Art, which, contrary to popular myth, preceded the American variant by several years, proved both a crowd-pleaser and a lucrative cultural export in the 1960s. David Hockney became hot property in New York; Peter Blake wowed London. Robert Fraser, Hamilton's dealer, befriended the Beatles and the Rolling Stones, and was among Mick Jagger's co-detainees after the infamous police raid on the singer's London home in 1967. Photography, whose placid, unflinching rendering of any image and the possibility of its infinite reproduction lent Pop Art so much of its distinctiveness, became a fashionable, even sexy occupation. But while older heads tended to dismiss Pop

Art and the counterculture as mutually nutritive manifestations of the whole 1960s cultural malaise, Pop Art found little common ground with many countercultural elements, and specifically rock music.

From 1966 onwards, Pop Art and rock music famously began to deny, distance or subordinate their Americanisms. This was partly due to the whims of the Beatles – for their whims were the word – and partly due to disparate elements in the US, notably the pioneering auteurism of Bob Dylan, which helped hasten the decisive transfer of responsibility for pop musical composition from the corporate clutches of the Brill Building, Tin Pan Alley and the Kasenetz-Katz tune-smiths and into the hands of the artists themselves. A lust for rootsiness, for authenticity, for *echt*, found an echo first in blues revivalism, then folk revivalism. In short, in anything unadorned, anything but Gene Pitney, Neil Sedaka, Debbie Reynolds, the *Tonight Show*, which were already being seen as tools of US hegemony and as dangerous as the megadeath merchants, the Nixons, Goldwaters, Rockefellers.

Shibboleths and sacred cows were ripe for slaughter. The counterculture's rejection of the late twentieth century's 'modern' condition – urbanity, capital, regimentation, the implication of the urban environment of mass-production in world-war mass-production of death – ignited a longing for a utopia which explicitly denied the trappings of modernity. Suits and ties (what became known as 'uptight' chic), mass production, admass, popular cultural utterance from Liberace to Andy Williams, were out, encouraging the fascination for the explicitly arcane and the exotic which so characterized psychedelic culture. Britain merely wilted in the counter-cultural wake, and Hesse, Hokusai and Holman Hunt became as much a part of the lives of hippies in Hammersmith as they were in Haight-Ashbury.

Pop Art was groovy enough (parents and teachers didn't like it), but it was not *quite* what the head doctor ordered. It did posit an enjoyably subversive take on culture, sweeping away divisions between 'fine, applied and manufactured art';[23] it declared that anything could be a work of art. But it also represented a dangerous liaison with materialism, with the admass horrors the counterculture were trying to subvert and destroy. In the words of critic Mario Amaya, Pop Art eschewed

> direct experience and primary emotion...for the manu-factured, gift-wrapped feeling, shiny and new...these artists are not painting about 'life' itself so much as about an ad-mass attitude to a way of living, as experienced through certain idioms...such art, by its very nature, is transitory. Its freshness, its excitement, its uniqueness, depend on quick change, newness for its own sake, the expendable, the gimmicky, the cheap, the mass-produced, the deliberately offensive or ugly; in fact, all the things which we have been taught to abhor in a work of art.[24]

This jarred with the total lifestyle revolution proposed by the hippie project. Their revolution was meant to last; Pop Art, on the other hand, celebrated transience, disposability. Its artists did not see for ever, on clear days or otherwise. They did not sentimentalize, romanticize or beautify – another bone of contention with the Panglossian meliorism of much counter-culture thought. Pop Art's obsession with the metropolis – specifically, with the twin art capitals of New York and London – was perhaps its most obvious point of departure from the essentially anti-urban hippies and their world.

The most perfunctory overview of rock culture in the late 1960s tells us all there is to know. More than any other mode of countercultural expression, rock and pop were aggressive subscribers to the anti-metropolitan idyll, the exploration of interior and exterior worlds divorced from the modern capital. Rock art became a mélange – sometimes inspired, often risible – of Day-Glo-pulsing surrealism, roller-coaster Jugendstil swirls and Toy-Town Pre-Raphaelitism. Rock music became confessional, subjective, *white*, ransacking every other musical style it could get its hands on, like a trolley-dashing kid in a sweetshop. Traditions of form, melody and precision were summarily trashed. The art school dance ended violently, and instead of hully-gully and mambo, young musicians turned off, tuned out and dropped into sarabandes and gavottes. Pop Art's cool and calculated approach would find it rough-going; and as with art, so with music. Things were going to be taken seriously from now on – even fun, even play-power, was a serious business. For some, anyway. Others, like Bryan Ferry, had different plans.

2: IDEAS MEN (1970–72)

THE METROPOLITAN DREAM

Countless millions of words have poured forth about London in the 1960s, whether from red-eyed nostalgics or their cynical successors, both endorsements and condemnations. Whatever its merits, it is indisputable that London was, in contemporary vernacular, a happening place. Always possessed of a capital's unique geographic and social magnetism, it became in the 1960s a kind of Delphi of youth culture, a magical, oracular place where the means of hastening the unbuttoning of British society were to be found. Britain had become a younger place, and it got younger nowhere faster than in London.

From all over the country the young came, often in groups, sometimes alone, and most of them had some kind of musical ambition. Everywhere Britain, grumpy and uncertain after war and rationing, was emerging into a kind of stunted social and emotional liberation, but if you were young enough and couldn't wait to discover what the outcome of that process would be, you got your butt to London. Some hitchhiked (like

Ferry), some hired Transit vans, some stole cars, some stowed in lorries, some came by coach, some by train.

The key concept of the 1960s, particularly in London, was *mobility*. If you wanted to move jobs, you could. If you wanted to move house, you could. If you wanted to move out of one life into another, you could. London was the nexus for these latter (real and imagined) migrations. 'I always knew,' Ferry told Caroline Coon in 1975, 'that I wouldn't be there [in Washington] for the rest of my life. I felt sort of blessed.'[1] Ferry confessed to the same interviewer that he 'went through a period of resenting' his parents for being poor and 'unintellectual'.[2] Creditably, Ferry also acknowledged the conceit of these statements. 'They always,' he conceded, 'stressed the importance of education as the key to freedom.'[3]

Ferry, well educated already, was about to be re-educated in London's university of life. Like so many other products of the art school environment, the mystique of Bohemia and the dissolution of parental and other social restrictions suggested by London seemed irresistible. It seductively promised attainment of the ideal artistic milieu in which there were no hard and fast rules governing what one could say and do – save financial ones, of course.

London indeed offered a febrile and creative environment at the end of the 1960s, but this was mainly due to the fact that so much of the hippie project had failed to materialize. London's main attribute at the end of the 1960s was that it was precisely *not* the socialized hippie utopia many of the counter-culture's movers and shakers had planned and/or predicted. There were still so many jams to be kicked out – weekend hippies, acid casualties, skinheads, Trotskyite fratricide, pigs remaining obstinately un-offed. This, however, probably contributed to the artistic ferment that was abroad. There was a sense of disorientation, of lost threads, missed opportunities, obscured hopes charging an atmosphere that was still boldly liberating but lacking shape or identity. It was a zeitgeist whose immateriality welcomed attempts to change it.

For example, the counterculture regarded the likes of Andy Williams and Lauren Bacall butterflying around Carnaby Street and the Apple boutique saying things like 'far out' as the absolute antithesis of far-outness. The revolution had definitely been postponed when such things were happening. But the fiction between what was and what should be – especially evident in the pages of Jonathon Green's magnificent oral history of the period, *Days in the Life* – created a climate of jealousy, paranoia, resentment and naked competition which, of course, helped produce some of the greatest rock music ever. The Baroque decadence of the artistic life most art school refugees dreamed of, however, tended to materialize merely as squalid squats, World's End penury, scuffles with skins on the last tube home.

THE MAGNIFICENT FIVE

Most of the good and bad of London is mirrored in the pre-Roxy Music lives of the band's members, all of whom converged on the capital's countercultural scene around the same time.

In fact, Ferry's initial sojourn in London was probably as harshly unrewarding as anything he had ever faced before in his life. Having fortuitously discovered that his stylistic affectations had an audience on Tyneside in spite of the pop world turning Day-Glo, Ferry found London quite a different proposition. 'I've always liked nice things,' he once told *Melody Maker*.[4] He hadn't been able to afford many in Newcastle, but he did have the admiration of his peers. He didn't even have that in London, just a luxury-free flat in Kensington. With the determined self-reliance of the English blue-collar classes, Ferry knuckled down to work. Regular employment, at least, was one commodity not in short supply. Ferry bummed around, drove vans, restored antiques and finally found a job at the Mary Boon Secondary School for Girls in Hammersmith, teaching ceramics to teenagers. He was not unqualified for such a post, being able to boast not only his Fine Arts degree but also exhibitions of his own ceramics at the Piccadilly and Thomas Gibson Fine Art galleries. He proved to be a less than ideal pedagogue, however — 'If they wanted to talk about their boyfriends, we talked about their boyfriends,' he remembered later. 'If they brought records in, I'd play them.'[5] Ferry's feet-up approach won him considerable popularity, but crucially not with the educational authorities, who sacked him at the end of 1970.

Throughout his two years in London, Ferry had been toying with pop music and had begun, fitfully, to find his métier. 'I already knew what I wanted to do. I was rushing home each night to write songs.'[6] He'd kept in touch with an old colleague from the Gas Board days, Graham Simpson, who had lent him a stand-up piano to polish his skills. The instrument also allowed him to experiment with composition and self-instruction in musical theory. Later he bought a harmonium for £5 in order to be able to play sustained chords and elaborate on his compositional method. Simpson suggested that the two try to pool their talents and make some money in a band.

London in 1970 was a musical termitarium — a cursory glance at contemporary issues of *Melody Maker* reveals endless columns of small ads bearing Kensington and Chelsea phone numbers. Bands seeking bassists, bassists seeking bands; name drummers, freaky organists, spacy sitar players; pied pipers, bagpipers; accordionists, harpsichordists. Unfortunately, Ferry never managed to square himself with the rock business and remained unplugged from the underground grapevine. He simply didn't know any rock musicians. In the end, sympathetic to Simpson's ideas, he advertised for a keyboard player. He didn't get one but he did get Andy Mackay.

Mackay, who was born in London on 23 July 1946, was a grammar-school boy from the inner-city district of Westminster who had once nurtured dreams of becoming a classical woodwind virtuoso and had been a cathedral chorister. He wasn't just one of a string of applicants, anonymous behind a contact number, but was put in touch with Ferry by a mutual friend from Newcastle, the artist Tim Head. When Mackay arrived, however, he brought with him not only an oboe but the brass neck to tell Ferry that he (Mackay) couldn't actually play keyboards that well. He could, however, he added, contribute a lot to the sound of the new band with his oboe and saxophone work. It's hard to tell whether it was Mackay's chutzpah or the possibility that Stax-freak Ferry was thrilled with the idea of having a hard-blowing saxman with avant-garde sidelines in his putative band, but Mackay got the nod immediately. It proved to be one of the most propitious decisions of Ferry's life, and that was due less to Mackay's own musical talents and artistic outlook than those of a close friend of his, Brian Peter George St Baptiste de la Salle Eno, a balding, effeminate, convent-educated talker from East Anglia.

Both Mackay and Eno boasted impressive avant-garde credentials and had met at Reading University during a concert of experimental music. They discussed their mutual attraction to the form and briefly even considered forming a band, tentatively to be called Brian Iron and the Crowbars.

Mackay's classical leanings had been Beat-boomed out of him and he'd taken his saxophone talents into a local r'n'b band, Nova Express, as well as putting in a stint in the National Youth Jazz Orchestra. Classical theory didn't entirely disappear, however. Mackay concerned himself with the most iconoclastic genre of all, twentieth-century post-serialism, notably the subversive anti-musical works of the American composer John Cage. This led him to participate in some 'very pretentious' 'happenings' at Reading. 'We would sit in silence for a long time, someone would climb up a stepladder, someone would make some funny electronic noises…'[7]

It was a shared interest in Cage's work that cemented the friendship between Mackay and Eno, who, although they drifted apart briefly (Mackay went to Rome to teach English), met up again by chance on a London tube train. This was around the time that Mackay was auditioning in Kensington for Ferry and Simpson and was currently the owner of a recently purchased synthesizer. The technically minded Eno was intrigued enough to be drawn gradually into the orbit of Ferry's new line-up.

Eno's initial visibility in Roxy Music and his subsequent perennial association with its name has probably led to his contribution to the band being slightly overestimated, but it would be fair to say that in terms of impressing the band on the public's collective consciousness his contribution was second only to Ferry's – and this without the ability to play a note on a conventional musical instrument.

A postman's son, Eno was born in Woodbridge, Suffolk, on 15 May 1948. Like Ferry, his initial interests had focused on painting, but a short exposure to the regime at Ipswich College of Art forced a rethink. Eno was too garrulous, it seemed, for the disciplined, contemplative life of the 'true artist'. But fortunately for him, he found a kindred spirit among the staff, much as Ferry had found Hamilton.

Roy Ascott's behavioural psychology-based approach which sought to unleash creativity in his pupils whether or not it chimed with conventional artistic techniques, had a galvanic effect on Eno, who suddenly realized his hyperkinetic thought processes and lively social life were perfectly compatible with artistic creation, although Ipswich was not quite what he expected.

'I guess that we were all united by one idea – that art school was the place where you would be able to express yourself, where the passionate and intuitive nature that you felt raged inside you would be set free and turned into art. As it happened, we couldn't have been more wrong. The first term at Ipswich was devoted entirely to getting rid of these silly ideas about the nobility of the artist by a process of complete and relentless disorientation. We were set projects that we could not understand, criticized on bases that we did not even recognize as relevant.'[8]

Ascott recommended that his pupils experimented with role-reversals in which they acted contrary to their instincts, a process which meant Eno sublimating his garrulity for the good of works in progress. 'I had to try and execute everyone else's ideas,' he told Iain MacDonald in a long two-part interview for *New Musical Express* in 1977, 'not make a fuss, not try to dominate the proceedings.'[9] Ascott's classes became wildly diversionary; one particularly excitable girl was tied to a chair, another taught herself to walk the tightrope in class, and Eno at one stage parked himself on a porter's trolley, demanding that anyone wanting him to do something must first wheel him to the place where the task had to be carried out.

'Rarely,' writes Eric Tamm, 'did [Eno] work on making pictures for their own sake; he found himself too impatient to finish a canvas.'[10] Eno's social instincts led him to explore the creative dynamics of group efforts, among them 'scores for panting', in which four different people would be told to paint canvases according to instruction but without being allowed to interact or confer. He later told an interviewer:

'I did a whole series that involved more than one person doing the painting. In one, I would give four people identical instructions of the type, "make the canvas such-and-such square, make a mark 14 inches from the top right-hand corner, and then measure a line down at 83 degrees and find a point here" and so on. Each instruction built on the one before. If there was any error, it was compounded throughout the picture. I ended up with four canvases that were clearly related but different from each other, and they were stuck together to make one picture.'[11]

This investigation of random conflicts and/or compacts of imagination and inspiration could also be found in the *outré* world of the British avant-garde composer Cornelius Cardew (1936–81). His workshops in London invited non-musicians to work improvisationally alongside trained performers – including, interestingly, one Andy Mackay – in increasingly free-form scores, of which *The Great Learning*, a nine-hour cantata based on Tibetan texts, is probably the most ambitious and best known. Cardew was pure 1960s, a sentient totem of the possible in art, a charismatic icon of just how far and how fast artistic expression could be pushed. He was a hero of the counterculture's intellectual wing, and Eno was sufficiently enamoured of his work to become a member of his Scratch Orchestra, a unit comprised entirely of non-trained players.

Unfortunately his passion for music – or at least Cardew's conception thereof – and the travelling expenses incurred hoovered up his grant money and Eno was forced to leave Ipswich and take up a less financially demanding course at Winchester, where the licence and indulgence of Ascott's classes were absent.

Eno had in the meantime discovered the wonders of multi-track tape recorders. These, he found, could be used to create a form of music he could (he imagined or hoped) call his own. It was, contrary to accepted wisdom, hardly a breakthrough in compositional technique – Schaeffer and Stockhausen had been aware of the potential of magnetic tape since the early 1950s – but it kept Eno happy.

He had first used the technology at Ipswich; his first composition was the sound of him hitting a metal lampshade and then altering the speed of the tape. Sound sculptures followed, one featuring a vertical cylinder and loudspeaker, with the vibrations caused by the sounds passing through the speaker and randomly moving a number of objects placed on top of the speaker into different patterns. Eno also hung loudspeakers on trees in a local park and simultaneously piped different music through them. In 1966 he sent a composition to John Cage; it was returned with a cyclostyled thank-you letter which, while obviously a stock reply, none the less pleased the young Eno.

So inspired was he by this low-tech breakthrough that he sat down and dashed off a privately published treatise, *Music for Non-Musicians*, in 1968. He performed his own works publicly to small audiences and also took on more ambitious material by experimental composers such as Christian Wolff and Tom Phillips (who at one point would live next door to Eno). Eno would perform under the auspices of the Merchant Taylors Simultaneous Cabaret, a typically self-conscious piece of avant-garde epigonism. Eno's first public performance of any music was LaMonte Young's notorious *X for Henry Flint*, a piece in which the performer is instructed to perform a single, unspecified sound repetitively for however long takes his or her fancy. Eno responded to the challenge with cheerful childishness, bashing large clusters of notes on a piano with his forearms for the best part of an hour, with the added complication of playing each cluster precisely once every second. He devoured the avant-garde, specifically the more dangerous, confrontational avant-garde of European modernism, the Theatre of the Absurd, Dada, Futurism and Surrealism. Situationism was a factor too in Eno's musical environment – Situationist art, like Pop Art, sought (albeit in very different fashion) to eliminate all sentiment from art and reinvent bourgeois notions of beauty and value.

Such anarchy was the counterculture's clenched artistic fist – somewhat limp it may have been, but it asked more questions about social revolution and change than the 'classical' artistic heritage of psychedelia. It also persuaded Eno to revise his view of rock music, notably on contact with the music of the Velvet Underground and the auto-destructive performances and discourse of the Who. The Velvets were the accredited dark side of the rock project, an elemental force few smiled upon save in the most cultist and avant-garde circles. Their legendary status rests almost as much on the fact that hippies disliked them as on the merits of their output. Their undiluted pessimism, expounded both lyrically and through an immediately recognizable and uncompromising instrumental rawness, made them a bum trip, and to conventional ears their music was just acid rock played by schoolkids.

As Eno told Iain MacDonald, that Velvets never pretended to be able to play their instruments; they were pure antimatter, negative energy, hollow laughter in the urban dark. Like the Warhol paintings they are forever associated with, they meant nothing, apart from the commodification of life and the essential absurdity of artistic praxis. 'I found this very interesting,' Eno has remarked. Together, the Velvets and the Who showed that 'it was possible to occupy an area between fine art sensibility and popular art, and have the ambiguity work'.[12] Eno's aspiration was a music marrying their approach with Afro-American music's sensuousness.

Eno's life hadn't been entirely devoid of popular musical input beforehand. He grew up in East Anglia, one of the greatest concentrations of American Forces personnel in the United Kingdom. The local cafés' jukeboxes kept the young Eno's ears open to the latest waxings from America and Eno's sister visited the PX store and would 'come back with all these really very interesting records that you never heard in England otherwise'.[13] As Tamm points out, 'It was a musical environment [if not a geographical one] strikingly similar to that of the young Beatles' Liverpool, where sailors brought the latest American records.'[14] This enabled Eno to supplement his normal listening diet of 'feeble, weedy British pop music...really boring'[15] with American music 'full of menace and strangeness. I listened to Chuck Berry, Little Richard, Bo Diddley...I used to sing too...African music, in the middle of the English countryside.'[16] 'Martian' music is one term Eno has used to describe the foreignness of the music he heard emanating from the strange expatriate culture of the GI-settled East Anglia.[17] Doo-wop seemed

'magical...just *beautiful*. I had never heard music like this, and one of the reasons that it was beautiful was because it came without a context. It plopped from outer space, in a sense. Now, in later life I realize that this removal of context was an important point in the magic of music.'[18]

Other influences were the 'lush, soft, silky' timbre to the voices of the Ray Conniff Singers and English hymns such as 'Jerusalem' played on a player-piano.[19]

The genre of rock didn't magically divulge wonders to him – there was no revolution in Eno's head – but in his final year at Winchester he did at least decide, with fellow student Anthony Grafton, to start up a heavy rock band called Maxwell Demon. (This, incidentally, had to be fitted in between Eno's duties as President of the Students' Union, another testament to his indefatigable clubbability and gift for networking.)

After Winchester, Eno threw in his lot with his peers and took the obligatory road to London. There he paid the necessary dues – artists' commune, lousy band (admittedly the purposely incompetent crypto-Situationist classical combo the Portsmouth Sinfonia), dead-end job. Then came the meeting with Andy Mackay and Bryan Ferry.

'I'll never forget the sight of Brian lugging this enormous, German industrial tape recorder up the stairs,' Ferry remembered later.[20] Few who witnessed the embryonic sessions of what would later become Roxy Music in those first few months of 1971 would forget what they heard. Mackay blew great flourishes of Stax riffs, Ferry pedalled fit to bust on his harmonium, Simpson kept time on bass, and Eno manipulated the resultant row by means of his technology. It was still a matter of ideas rather than songs, textures rather than arrangements, but Ferry's songwriting ability and pop sensibility, honed throughout his sojourn in London, began slowly to emerge, a musical centrepiece around which others could weave their magic. The best dynamic in the band was between Ferry, who brought order, and Eno, who brought disorder.

Curiosity followed curiosity, and still the band remained

aloof from contemporary rock culture, next turning to the American-born classical timpanist Dexter Lloyd to add his own talent, but Ferry was by now a confident enough composer to conceive of a possible commercial future for his line-up. Lloyd was replaced by a conventional rock drummer, the first jobbing pop man they had called on.

Paul Thompson, born on 13 May 1951, was another Geordie, from the shipbuilding town of Jarrow. He had accrued a modest reputation from a few sessions in Billy Fury's backing band, as well as keeping body and soul together at the back of no-hope rock outfits the Urge and Smokestack. A drummer of imposing physicality and metronomic precision, a tub-thumper of power and no-frills urgency, the prosaic and proletarian Thompson may have seemed antithetical to the band's cerebral aspirations, but he stayed with them until near the end and is perhaps one of the most unsung figures in British pop history. When Mackay told Michael Bracewell in 1997 that 'it was important to Roxy Music that there was one band member who was non-intellectual, very physical and just drummed',[21] it simultaneously emphasized both dormant truth and accepted untruth. Thompson was by no means the gormless grunt behind the cymbals so often portrayed – had he been so, he would never have stayed in such a volatile and experimental environment as Ferry's embryonic band and worked so enthusiastically with its members on their solo projects – indeed, of all the members of Roxy Music, Thompson played on the most sessions organized by the others.

He'd started playing as a professional at the age of seventeen in home-town clubs with a band that also included singer/songwriter John Miles. Prior to this, he had moonlighted from his day job in a Jarrow shipyard to drum on the Tyneside circuit by night. Moving to London, he answered Ferry's *Melody Maker* ad after the aforementioned jobs, and 'this voice answered the phone. It wasn't a Geordie voice, but he recognized mine. Bryan never had an accent. I asked him why once and he said, "Ah well, you can't really read Shakespeare with a Geordie accent."[22]

There seemed to be something magnetic about Ferry. So far everyone who had turned up to rehearse had stayed; Ferry later compared the constituting of the band to the formation of the Magnificent Seven.[23] Eno's compelling personality helped, of course, this was a band that, despite a zero reputation in music, were obviously going places. Eclectic they may have been, but Ferry's increasing command over the direction of the music, allied to the arrival of Thompson's failsafe pulse, meant that the music was taking shape. Ferry 'wanted to do something very clever…but very passionate as well'.[24] What he and his colleagues were now aiming to create recalled nothing so much as Richard Hamilton's defence of good Pop Art: 'The elements hold their integrity because they are voiced in different plastic dialects within the unified whole',[25] a process which is all too evident on Roxy Music's first groundbreaking, eponymous album. The culture looked favourable also. In the fashion-conscious circles in which Ferry moved, nostalgia was in, particularly nostalgia for the 1940s and Ferry's beloved 1950s; even better, *Vogue* magazine was writing perplexedly in 1971 of 'fashion anarchy'[26] in young London. This was music to Ferry's ears. The world might just be ready for what he and his friends were playing.

For the time being, however, Roxy Music were Roxy. They were variously otherwise – Locarno, Gaumont and Rialto – but would have stayed Roxy had Ferry not discovered that an American band had issued an album in the UK in 1970 and copyrighted the name. A change was required. '"Odeon" wouldn't have worked,' Ferry reflects. 'We made a list of about twenty names for the group. We thought it should be magical or mystical but not mean anything.'[27] The cinematic connection was therefore deliberate; empty glamour, commodified escapism, an affectionate homage to Ferry's own childhood, when he'd boggled from the stalls in Washington at the grandeur and glitz of the screen. 'Roxy' became 'Roxy

Music', superficially a lazy cop-out but actually, as Rogan points out, 'The name now suggested a distinct type of music that was inextricably linked to...the visual appeal of the cinema.'[28]

Next in the masterplan – for Ferry was by now very obviously 'designing' a future for himself, much in the vein of Warhol and his Factory superstars – came the recruitment of a guitarist to further their pop credentials. Roger Bunn, once of undistinguished plodders Enjin, was on the scene long enough in the summer of 1971 to contribute to some demos, but as Ferry approached his goal of constructing his own pop vision, the more finicky and perfectionist he got. He returned to the small-ads columns, placing a request – as one did then – for a 'way-out' guitarist.

The most promising respondent was Phil Manzanera, another musician who had been through the mill of London's floundering counterculture. The son of a Spanish-Cuban mother and an English father whose work as a BOAC representative required him and his family to spend long spells in Latin America ('Quite literally our man in Havana,' one friend of Manzanera has said[29]). Manzanera was born Philip Targett Adams in London on 31 January 1951. He had learned guitar in the Cuban capital – acoustic guitar at six, electric at eight – playing through Colombian and Cuban folksongs his mother taught him, as well as memorizing Chuck Berry riffs from a *Teach Yourself* pack he'd sent off for. The young Manzanera was a passionate devotee of pop music and once, when the family had moved on to Caracas, he became the first child in town to own a Beatle wig.

His father died when Manzanera was fifteen, and the family returned to England. The young Manzanera developed easy musical facility on bass, drums and above all guitar, forming a band of professionals in the south London suburb of Dulwich at the age of seventeen which included friends Charles Hayward (drums) and Bill McCormick (bass), as well as the erstwhile Soft Machine vocalist, guitarist and all-round space-case Daevid Allen. His connections to the flourishing if precariously paying avant-garde and free-jazz scene in London, allied to the boys' precocious delight in the music of Frank Zappa and the Velvet Underground, ensured that their names swiftly became known but that their wallets emptied even more swiftly.

Under the name Quiet Sun they established a reputation as musically accomplished experimentalists, dedicated to musical complexity and 'being just about the most listener-unfriendly band in London' (according to one eyewitness),[30] for whom every technical advance probably meant one fewer listener. That they spent most of their time below the bill to their friend Robert Wyatt's band Symbiosis (a part-time sideline for the Soft Machine drummer/vocalist and probably one of his least distinguished endeavours) at shoebox clubs and indifferent campus halls testifies to their lack of progress. Moreover, the fact that their keyboard player left to become a maths teacher speaks silent volumes about the kind of music they believed in. Manzanera got out while he was behind and unwillingly subsided into nine-to-five at a travel agency, but he soon found himself hankering again after music. Browsing through *Melody Maker*, he saw Ferry's ad and replied.

The audition took place in the house Mackay and Ferry shared in Battersea. 'I played them my tape, which they hated, but we got on very well. I'd bump into them at gigs, things like Steve Reich at the Queen Elizabeth Hall.'[31]

Manzanera was struck most of all by Ferry's evident indifference to technical display – a rarity in late 1971, when rock music was investing musical virtuosity with increasingly improbable value. Manzanera's recollections betray the overt pop angle that was now apparent in the new band's music. 'The minute I heard [Bryan's tapes], I told him I thought that they were going to be really big,' Manzanera told the *NME*. 'And he probably thought, God, what a greasy freak.'[32] Jamming on Carole King numbers was, for Manzanera, a considerable relief from Quiet Sun, 'where we were playing insane 17/8 things [time signatures] at ridiculous speeds all the time. I rediscovered my melodic sense, in a word.'[33]

Manzanera's assessment of Ferry was a good one: 'What really impressed me was the pulse of Bryan's songs. On one hand they sounded mere amateurish constructions but they worked in this incredible way that sounded like Reich's experimental music.'[34] In one smart phrase Manzanera summarized his take on the Ferry writing method: 'working around the black notes until a form was created'.[35]

Unfortunately for Manzanera, however, Ferry promptly torpedoed his hopes, jumping at the chance of signing David O'List.

O'List was a considerable talent among rock guitarists whose career had been in freefall since being fired from the Nice after one album and then playing various and uncredited depping assignments for Pink Floyd when Syd Barrett's demons got the better of him. By 1971 it was predicted that O'List was heading the same way, his gifts undermined by overwork, overindulgence and lack of accommodation from other musicians. He was a player of speed and sensitivity, of fiery improvisational and textural ability, whose unsung reputation since disguises a massively innovative musician. For Ferry he offered two priceless qualities: dexterity and, much more importantly, cachet.

At first acquaintance, O'List's style must have seemed ideal for the band's sound: visceral enough to be exciting, bluesy enough to be propulsive, off-the-wall enough to be playful and interesting. But, more importantly, his name alone would help exalt the band's status for a public as yet oblivious to their existence.

With a generosity rarely seen at the bottom of the rock pile, Ferry kept faith with the jilted Manzanera and insisted that he stay in the band as assistant road manager. Manzanera showed similar good grace in not telling Ferry where to shove his job and stayed on — gratefully and, as he would later discover, fortuitously.

But if Ferry thought that O'List was the name to tempt the punters and the moneymen, he was sadly mistaken. Schlepping his band's demo tapes around London, he was greeted with either scepticism, indifference, belly laughs or outright hostility. 'Yes, it's the sound of the future, old boy – so you'd best come back next year,' was the general refrain. Everyone seemed to find a different fault, everyone a different quality, testament to the music's eclectic freshness and its craftsmanlike excellence but ultimately unprofitable and unhelpful. Virgin Records, then in the process of establishing their Manor Studios in Oxfordshire, gave the band the once-over on the say-so of boss Richard Branson. Engineer Tom Newman recalls:

> 'They came down and set up and started playing. And, to be honest, I thought they were fucking garbage. They sounded disjointed, and Bryan didn't sound as though he could sing. Of course, I was looking at them the wrong way, really. I should have looked at them for what they were – an artistic statement, if you like. But that wasn't the way I thought then, and I thought they were awful.'[36]

ON THE TOWN

Perplexed, Ferry took the decision of taking his fledgeling band on the road – at least some of the way.

Rogan's prognosis that Ferry wished to avoid the 'rock and roll route' of overgigging at an early stage in a business where 'familiarity breeds contempt' is a somewhat simplified but believable argument,[37] and one which Ferry has never denied. The band's attempt at manufacturing an image for themselves was an undertaking to be treated seriously. To invest too much of their fate in the hands of others at this stage would threaten their ability to refine the all-important Roxy Music mystique. As Rogan puts it, if the band were to be forced to gig, they would choose not only their own venues but also, as far as was practicable, the audience to watch them.[38]

Having made his face and name known on the rock circuit with the signing of O'List, Ferry organized some impromptu gigs for the band in November 1971, while the rejection letters fluttered around them like confetti; there may have been as much a morale-maintaining aspect to this sudden decision as anything. Instead of pounding the road, Ferry hawked his band around his own circle of artistic friends, announcing that they would be performing 'at private functions only'. Ferry even finagled a gig at the Tate Gallery on one occasion. It was a decision that minimized risk – if the audience didn't like them there wouldn't be a riot, they'd get paid and it would be valuable live practice. Also, it helped spread the word and magnify the image of Roxy Music as something different, something exclusive, a consumer durable of pop music. A pop artefact, in short.

Ferry, little daunted, plugged on, and the tapes kept going into the post. One was addressed to Richard Williams, a young feature writer at *Melody Maker*, and in effect that magazine's only genuine journalistic contact with Progressive and experimental rock music.

It certainly wasn't professional in any sense. Parts of it had things overlaid on the tape so that you'd be hearing two things at the same time. Several of the tracks, like 'The Bob: Medley' were vaguely recognizable on the first album. It seemed like people mucking around – and there was this bloke in the middle of it who wanted to be a pop singer.[39]

Williams perceived a band unafraid to think the unthinkable. He immediately drew mental parallels with Pop artists and their heretical admiration of material and commercial objects in a fine art context. 'I felt that the person who'd written this stuff was obviously very intelligent – just from his handwriting on the box,' he says.[40] Intrigued, he rang Ferry's contact number, arranged a meeting and the two got together, hitting it off immediately. 'Most people's interests,' observed Williams, 'went from B. B. King to Jimi Hendrix, so it was nice to meet someone who talked about Charlie Parker and Ethel Merman and the Velvet Underground, and in November 1971, *nobody* listened to the Velvet Underground. Maybe about three people in London, and he was one of them.'[41]

Williams enthused in the next *Melody Maker*: 'Personally, I've never felt so excited about a new band before. They haven't got a manager, they haven't got an agent and they haven't got a recording contract. But mark my words, within a matter of months they'll be bloody enormous.'[42] Whether Ferry had craftily persuaded Williams to so shamelessly advertise their availability or whether Williams was sufficiently in love with the music to sell the band off his own bat is uncertain. But the response was swift, with Radio One's John Peel-hosted show *Sounds of the Seventies* booking the band. A hurriedly arranged date at Oxford Street's 100 Club was also set up within the week.

The 100 Club was little more than a hole of insalubriousness and feedback, but its name oozed undeniable prestige. The occasion was duly noted and Roxy Music became, if not great white hopes, then at least names to watch.

Suddenly, after months of lassitude, false starts and half-hopes, the band were slogging like pros, despite the fact that all of them still held down other jobs. Ferry and Mackay taught, the former part-time, the latter full-time as a music teacher at Holland Park Comprehensive. Mackay was also responsible for wheels, organizing the transport by commandeering an ancient Austin van from his father. Equipment was packed inside and, occasionally, on the roof. Mackay recalled, 'I would be picked up from school and we would change into the flashest clothes we had.'[43] At this stage, 'flash' meant little – the costumes came later, with the money.

Thompson humped hods on a building site for his living and would turn up covered in dust and still wearing wellington boots, to 'play like a demon',[44] becoming encrusted in sweaty filth.

Ferry, for all his his calm authority and helmsmanship of the band's fortunes, was as yet a gauche stage performer and remained at one side of the stage.

He wasn't quite confident enough to stand in the centre and sing. Eno was mixing the sound and also playing the synthesizer, so he would actually be in the middle of the audience – if there was one. Then, in the middle of the stage, there was this kind of black hole, where one or other of us might venture a solo.[45]

One with few compunctions about so doing was O'List, and Williams remembers him as a featured soloist, a role which would be increasingly diminished within the band with the passage of time.

TAPES ON, O'LIST OUT

The band's first duties of 1972 were with the BBC. In a milieu which purportedly shunned notions of hierarchy and prestige, Peel's show was the most prestigious outlet for Progressive and experimental music, and was an important base camp for those on their way up. Peel's producer was one John Walters, who judged the submitted tapes along with his boss, had attended Newcastle University himself and had actually taken the same fine art course as Ferry. While there he had played with the Monty J. Young Jazzmen at a concert which, it transpired, Ferry had seen and enjoyed. Situation defused, they discussed the tape. 'I was quite impressed...the vocalist was really interesting,' Walters later recalled. 'Which was a bit of a relief, as I had no idea then that it was Bryan singing.'[46]

The first BBC session the band recorded was committed to tape in several sessions on 4 January 1972 at Studio T1, Kensington House, under the production supervision of John Muir, and comprised five tracks, 'The Bob: Medley', 'Would You Believe', 'Remake/Remodel', 'If There is Something' and 'Sea Breezes', all previews of début-album material.

According to engineer Bill Anthony:

'Despite the strange lashed-up control room the band seemed happy with this session. I remember Eno asking us about phasing effects machines. He was really into gadgets, and the only way then to get a really good flanging or phasing effect was to play back two recordings of the sound you wanted to phase off separate tape recorders and knock one slightly out of phase with the other by rubbing your finger against the flange of the tape reel. At the BBC, we never had the time to attempt such convoluted techniques. Consequently we had acquired a little box which attemped to simulate such phasing effects automatically. It didn't work very well, but it was all that was around, and I remember giving Eno the details.'[47]

Reactions to the broadcast – on 21 January – were favourable. The tapes are of good quality and contain performances that are not only surprisingly accomplished for a band which, according to Phil Manzanera, were still mostly – save for O'List – at the 'inspired amateur'[48] stage, but excitingly funky too. There is a wonderful balls-out, seat-of-the-pants audacity about it all, even if the production is unsympathetic to Ferry's vocals, rendering him, at quieter moments, as a somewhat anaemic John Lennon clone. It also subdues the textural tensions which would emerge on later recordings – both at the BBC and for record releases – so that on occasion Roxy Music, save for the bubbles and squeaks of Eno's gadgetry, sound disappointingly threadbare in their arrangements. These are, however, tapes which deserve public exposure.

They certainly convinced Peel and Walters, who invited the band back to the studio in the early summer for a second session. In all, Roxy Music would cut five sessions for the Corporation between January 1972 and March 1973.

This first session, however, also saw the first crisis of the band's young career: David O'List's increasingly eccentric behaviour. 'When the band came into the control room to listen back to the mix,' remembers producer John Muir, 'I asked "Where's Dave?" "In the studio," they said, and there he was, lying flat on his back.'[49]

Officially, O'List's problem with the band was 'musical', and it is true that his style was only incidentally compatible with Roxy Music's – to get the best out of him meant giving him the soloing space that the songs were not designed for and which Ferry found distasteful and tiresome. But, additionally, O'List had hang-ups on the drug front. At the most important gig of the band's life thus far, an audition for EG Management in Wandsworth, O'List and Thompson, according to most accounts, had a stand-up fist fight.

Thompson demurs: 'A disagreement. And he never wanted me in the band anyway.'[50] So whether punches were thrown or not, O'List was retained on sufferance for a short while longer and then, his behaviour and reliability unimproved, he was sacked and Manzanera asked to join officially as guitarist. At first Manzanera, then still a part-time roadie, was asked to join as sound-mixer. Manzanera thanked Ferry but raised the footling objection that he didn't know the first thing about mixing. 'Don't worry,' said Ferry. 'Eno'll show you how.' And he did.[51] Manzanera continues:

'So I went down to this derelict house in Notting Hill, and basically it had been a ruse to get me in and test me out. But I'd sussed this and learned all the stuff, so I could play it all straight off. It was only years later that they let on that it had been a complete set-up – and I let on that I knew.'[52]

Manzanera felt 'scared' at first being in the band:

'I knew it was going to be incredibly successful and I wanted to be in it. All the guys – except for Paul – were four years older, so they'd all been to university... The same week I joined Roxy I turned down an offer to go to university. But they'd already been at art school or university and seemed incredibly sophisticated...they had bank accounts! It was like having elder brothers. I sort of looked up to them and felt very secure...'[53]

The next stage was management. Ferry's calculations and chutzpah had already contrived a sellable music, but what was needed now was astuteness, energy, belief, professionalism and, above all, nous.

Rock management was, at the time, a shambles of corruption, naked greed and exploitation, in which the rock boom was preyed upon by the blithely moral-free, usually in the persons either of tight-arsed and tight-walleted refugees from show business and/or hippies with an eye for the main chance in the mould of Richard Branson. It speaks volumes for Ferry's presence of mind in crisis that he laid such faith in perhaps the one firm whose business practices were marked by a degree of respect for the artist – that firm being EG Management.

ENTHOVEN, GAYDON AND FENWICK

Ferry could have aimed higher and thought bigger, but could hardly have found better than EG. This selection was partially informed by the favourable impression he'd gained a year earlier when he'd auditioned for the vacant vocalist's chair in King Crimson. 'This was when we desperately needed a singer after Greg Lake had departed for ELP,' Crimson's lights, synthesizer and production man, Pete Sinfield, remembered later. 'Robert Fripp and I quite liked Bryan – we didn't think he was a great singer, he had this rather strained vibrato, but we liked his bashful attitude.'[54]

Ferry failed that one, but won new acquaintances in EG bosses David Enthoven and Mark Fenwick. In addition to the cultishly angular Prog rock of Crimson, EG had also hit pay dirt by signing pomp superstars Emerson, Lake and Palmer (not least through Lake's erstwhile membership of Crimson) and, most importantly, teenybop idol Marc Bolan and his metal-boogie vaudeville act T. Rex.

Enthoven and Fenwick were, in rock-management terms, like gentlemen as opposed to players, 'doing this for a hobby, old boy...they had their Harley-Davidsons...they were like public-school hell's angels, with their leather jackets and cowboy boots'.[55] They too were casualties of the 1960s, weekend hippies irradiated by the fallout after the dream exploded. They were not unique but rather a specialized, sophisticated and enlightened outgrowth of an increasingly infesting breed of middle-class pop entrepreneurs. George Melly's redoubtable *Revolt into Style* talks about 'ex-public-school layabouts who'd been sitting on their arses up and down the King's Road for a decade wondering what to do with the only talent most of them had – an instinct for style'. Melly was writing about the producer and impresario Tony Secunda, but could also have been alluding to EG's creators. 'Some became criminals, some hustled at the fringes of the art world, some went into advertising, some married heiresses. For those who'd hung on, pop was the answer – a simple world without precedents or an established hierarchy...prepared to accept any fantasy as a potential and profitable reality.'[56]

According to Robert Fripp, who also claims that Ferry 'took Roxy Music into EG at my recommendation',[57] EG was created simultaneously with his band King Crimson on 13 January 1969, the name being derived from the surnames of Enthoven and John Gaydon, the two founders of the firm. Gaydon had left by 1971 and Enthoven was to follow him in 1977, but, as Fripp writes, 'the relationship established in 1969 between EG and King Crimson, based on trust, mutual involvement, participation and sharing in the costs and rewards of our work together, was unlikely, idealistic, remarkable and worked', and the presence in the organization of the main players from Roxy Music and the King Crimson constellation – Ferry, Eno, Fripp and Bill Bruford – remained constant until internal wranglings and exploitative dealings within EG dissipated the sense of community in the 1980s.

Fripp goes on:

The quality of [the] agreement with musicians/ management/businessmen as partners rather than parties with opposing interests – distinguished the first phase in the life of EG from that of probably any other comparable managerial relationship of that time and helped make it an exceptional company; respected and admired in the business, and the home of some influential music.[58]

Nevertheless, EG's initial suggestions dissatisfied Ferry. Drop the sidemen, they whispered to him, and we'll make you a star. Balking at this – if anyone was going to make Bryan Ferry a star, it would be Bryan Ferry – Ferry stood firm, persuading the firm that he came as an indissoluble part of an entire package. It would, he insisted, be worth EG's while to have Roxy Music audition for them. Whether by accident or design, this audition took place in a decommissioned 1930s cinema in Wandsworth, south London.

Enthoven wasn't immediately sold. Only after hearing the band's demo tapes was he fully convinced and then he immediately elected to try to sell the putative Roxy Music phenomenon to a company much like his – young, dynamic, progressive in artistic and business affairs, and willing to put money where mouths were. This was Island Records, one of the chief English Progressive independent labels since its late 1960s launch. Unpromisingly, they had already turned Ferry down once. This time, however, the band had Enthoven, and a secret weapon.

Enthoven later went on record as saying that Roxy Music 'completely blew me away. It's only happened twice. Once when I first saw King Crimson, and the second time was when I heard this Roxy tape.'[59] But just as crucially, the visuals impressed too: 'Bryan presented the visuals and how they [the and] were going to present themselves. Very avant-garde. Very left-field.'[60] At the time, the only acts overtly concerned with the visual aspect of stage performance and personal packaging were teenybop outfits where visuals were not the band's concern at all but their management's. In the counterculture and in rock, innate distrust of glitz and glamour lived on; it was read as part of the exploitative formula of traditional show business, with the hucksters in control, not the musicians. Roxy Music, and Bowie, were setting out in 1972 to prove them wrong.

EG signed the band and within a week tried to resell them to Island. This time, Dave Betteridge, Island's marketing chief, liked what he heard and loved what he saw. Tim Clark, one of the company's PR personnel, was smitten and played the tape to his colleagues in a desperate attempt to convince them of Roxy Music's potential.

He played the tape to the entire senior staff but 'just about everybody around the table thought it was dreadful,' remembers Clark. 'I said to Chris Blackwell [the company chairman], "What do you think, Chris?" And he sat there and didn't say anything. We thought that that was it, the rest of the people around the table had won the day.'[61] Next day, Enthoven visited Island's offices with the planned cover artwork. Blackwell took one look at it, turned to an astonished Clark and said briskly and eagerly, 'Got them signed yet?'[62]

3: THE VERB 'TO ROXY' (1972)

KARI-ANN ON THE COVER

The only place that visuals counted in early 1970s rock was album sleeve art, which was already a thriving artistic sub-genre. What was so special about Roxy Music's album sleeve art that sold a hard-headed honcho like Blackwell on a band whose music had inspired little more than ambivalence in him?

The cover of *Roxy Music* is probably one of the most immediately recognizable artefacts in rock music, one of the most radically innovative and influential images in the genre's history. It was not, however, that the cover-girl usage of the wantonly pouting Kari-Ann Moller – sprawled so broadly across the cover that she might have been spread with a butter knife, and in colours so saccharine that just to look at them made the teeth ache – was *in itself* a breakthrough. What made the cover of *Roxy Music* so special was the incongruity of what it connoted at the time within its rock context.

Girls in varying states of undress had, contrary to subsequent critical (and Ferry-derived) discourse, been used to sell records for years, often in postures much more provocative than Moller's. Throughout the 1960s records of easy-listening music and of the lighter shades of jazz (George Shearing, Jackie Gleason) had been plastering lightly clad cheesecake across LP covers. But Roxy Music's use of Kari-Ann broke ground because it broke *rock* ground. 'Pictures of pretty girls had been used to sell everything else…so why not rock music?'[1]

Strange as it may seem, Ferry was correct. This was, after all, 1972, when album sleeve art's coming of age was being conducted in rigorously figurative terms – surreal montages, airbrushed fantasyscapes. T'n'A was, for now, not on the agenda. Instead, sleeve designers were fixated on maintaining the fiction of rock as art, diminishing the product's 'productness', minimizing all odours of 'commerciality'. The very fact that girls smouldered only on the records in the record collections of parents was something that challenged young album-buyers – were these guys for real, or just very clever? Thus was the entire artistic palette of Roxy Music's career established.

There were also noises of disapproval from a feminist movement, newly freeing itself from the libertarian cul-de-sac of hippie free love, which had seen through the era's let-it-all-hang-out *laissez-faire* attitudes to nudity and sexuality as so much masculine exploitation. That Ferry did not invoke the spirit of the Pop artists Anthony Donaldson, Tom Wesselmann and Peter Phillips, also renowned for their work with the concept of the pin-up girl, as artistic defence is a mystery.

Moller was a former girlfriend of both Rolling Stone Keith Richard and hairdresser superstar Vidal Sassoon. By 1972 she had married the painter Rufus Dawson and had a burgeoning reputation as a model. Most of her work was done at St Martin's College of Art. With these circles being Ferry's preferred hang-out rather than the down-at-heel precincts of rock, it was perhaps inevitable that such an imagistic tack would be taken. This was to be rock as art, but rock as commerce as well. For the next few years, Roxy Music would go all out to ripple the lines of distinction between the two. They would also insist on quality in so doing, Ferry asking clothes designer Antony Price and art director Nick de Ville to come on board.

It's now a rock commonplace that the conception and design of the sleeve for *Roxy Music* took longer and cost more than the fortnight and £5,000 required to actually lay down the tracks for the LP itself. A second true mythology is that *Roxy Music* genuinely was the first time that an album had credited couturiers, stylists and photographers. 'Fashion,' declared Price later, 'saw music as sweaty and disgusting. Music saw fashion as snooty.'[2] As he was well aware when uttering those words, *Roxy Music* changed all that.

Ferry had designed the first Roxy Music logo – a naïve little drawing of a plane trailing a 'Roxy Music' banner over a Manhattan skyline. Now he determined to co-ordinate every single phase of the development of the first album's cover. 'I felt it as my role as the artist to do it,' he has said. 'I was never much into the idea of the group as a totally democratic thing. I was all for throwing ideas in…[but] my solution was to have a singular image on the cover.'[3] A picture of one girl, Ferry reasoned, would shift more units than a picture of six men (maybe he'd underestimated his own and Eno's potential sex appeal). Whatever, it was his first serious graphic art project for two years.

The cover girl, he and Price decided, would be a Busby Berkeley-style pin-up. Price, fresh out of the Royal Academy, was 'obsessed with the ultimate Jayne Mansfield female…vastly different to all these hooray waifs stoned out of their heads in little see-through frocks'.[4] This further distanced Roxy Music from 'the now' of 1972, further dared their followers to accompany them into the world of admass and exploitative marketing which, for rock, was imagistic no-go territory, save for clumsy ironic satire and/or outright crude condemnation.

Rock, after all, pretended to transcend the admass, Walter

Benjamin's age of mechanical reproduction. That world, of course, included the world of fashion, whose entire artistic syntax of the time Roxy Music were keen to exploit, as the climate favoured such thinking. As Peter York writes, the early 1970s had seen a 'Return of Elegance', a 'Back to the Classics' spirit, rich-girl/jet-set looks, *Le Style Anglais*.[5] Price was after styling men with 'shorn-off hair, with ears showing and quiffs. What I was into is commonplace now but was wacky art college taste then. The 50s thing hadn't happened yet. Fashion is always on to it first, music comes along much later.'[6] But this by no means meant a homogeneous and wholesale revival of one 'look' – it meant mixing and matching. In the case of *Roxy Music*, it meant Nick de Ville's 1950s 'postcards' of the band, the pin-up posture, framing and decoration of Moller's physique, and Ferry's purloining of the typeface of the album from Wyndham Lewis.

THE INTERGALACTIC COUNCIL

A form was being meticulously created, a form slick and sellable. The recruitment of Dr Simon Puxley as publicist to the band assured that this process would become slicker still. This would be one of the swishest and most knowing pieces of rock and roll marketing ever seen.

But Roxy Music's reputation was already kindling in spite of the publicity. Even the *Radio Times*, scarcely noted for its affiliations with anything resembling youth culture in the early 1970s, let alone its seedier backwaters, as then typified by the likes of Roxy Music, wrote gushingly of the band:

> Quite simply, Roxy Music are destined to save the world, though the articulate, atmospheric songs of Bryan Ferry, the lunatic pre-recorded tapes of Captain Eno [sic], the honky sax of Andy Mackay, the sparkling lamé uniforms...Be the first on your block to discover one of next year's sensations.[7]

This provides an interesting insight into the early formation of critical attitudes towards Roxy Music, attitudes which would later raise blood pressures within the critical fraternity and the music business as a whole. Eno's shiny frills and flounces were, at this stage, the only real grabber for the newcomer, yet the resemblance to the attire of glitter bands like Slade and Sweet was enough to offend some sensibilities. Scrutiny of contemporary stage film and stills reveals a band which, while free of the lank locks and frayed atrocities sported by most of their contemporaries, possessed a notably undemonstrative wardrobe. There were shiny boots – particularly comely at Lincoln, where the band played their first official gig in May 1972 – but that was all. The advance from Island was what brought the outlandish gear out of the closet; for instance, it is hardly likely that bricklayer Thompson would have been able to afford his rig-out on the building-site wages he was earning before Island paid the band their advance.

'We were always aware of the fact that it would motivate interest in both the press and in the audience at the time,'[8] said Ferry to a later interviewer.

He also commented later, 'Besides, I have always identified more with Otis Redding and the Modern Jazz Quartet...and they always revelled in the performance aspect.'[9] They were also fastidious as to their on-stage garb, Ferry could have added.

Ferry metamorphosed from sharp economy – the baseball jackets and white Levi's of the Gas Board era – to the come-hither black eyeliner, shark-fin quiff and lurid tiger-skin jacket which immortalized him in his earliest Roxy Music phase by their famous appearance on-stage at the Royal College of Art in 1972.

He recalled:

'In the early days we were so desperate for success, in the first year or so I mean, because we wouldn't have carried on doing it or maybe we'd have stopped without it. We

wouldn't have given up our day jobs if we hadn't wanted to
make a living out of it. We were going on-stage thinking
that on-stage was for dressing and making up – to intensify
the whole experience. And maybe we'd have been afraid of
going on-stage, being looked at by an audience, in our
everyday clothes. Then we'd have been ourselves and not
extensions of ourselves.'[10]

In effect, then, Roxy Music were presenting the look and
sound of pop music, and popular culture as flux, as elastic, as
relative. The much-vaunted Futurism and 1950s aspects of the
grotesque outfits into which Antony Price shoehorned the
band for the inside of *Roxy Music*'s gatefold cover were neither
really futuristic nor 1950s in derivation.

What they best approximated to was a hybrid of sartorial
comments on both concepts – a stab designers long ago might
have made at coming up with costumes for a band a quarter
of a century in the future. They even perhaps recalled the Man
of the Future from the pages of 1930s *Vogue*, glowingly
tunicked, head haloed with steel antennae. Galvanized gloss
and sparkle were the visual ciphers of the future. Ferry, to this
end, adopted a glitter-epauletted claret tunic, Mackay duly
appeared in a petrol-blue figure-hugging spangled top,
Manzanera in scarlet sequins with diamanté Fabergé-style
lenses attached to his Price-designed 'insect' sunglasses, which
were not entirely unlike pairs sported by jazz trumpeter Miles
Davis at the time. Even the rhythm section, traditionally
subsidiary, didn't escape the makeover: Graham Simpson was
squeezed into a shiny, honey-coloured vest and Paul
Thompson was a treat in a jumpsuit of mirror-ball-glistening
royal blue.

More significantly, the wings and louvres of these and later
Ferry costumes owe substantial debts to *Flash Gordon* and
1930s B-movie science fiction of the kind most members of
the band would have sat through at one time or another (the
cinematically mesmerized Ferry in particular). Witness

Manzanera's sleeves and, more significantly, Mackay's white jumpsuit (he would later sport clumsy white moonboots onstage); both seem like novice pilots of the future, trainee Dan Dares.

'Our costumes,' remembers Brian Eno, 'were quite deliberate takes on those Fifties visions of space nobility – the masters of the Galactic Parliament and so on.'[11] This was streamline fashion, future casual, airstream chic, a look which the art historian Robert Hughes has dubbed 'Deco and Fins'.[12] It is expressive of the aestheticized speed and confidence of optimistic public design in the 1930s and 1940s, of the Chrysler Building, of Henry Dreyfuss's bullet-nosed steam locomotives of 1937 and Norman Bel Geddes' flying-wing planes, a machinery of dreams made futuristic flesh that kept inter-war America hoping for a brighter tomorrow. This was the design that dominated the 1939 World's Fair (motto: "See tomorrow – now!"), the design that 'launched a thousand rocketships into the future'.

The tiger-skin/leopard-skin rigs of Ferry and Eno connoted access to that other last frontier of that lost era: delinquent decadence, luxury, penthouse sex, the promiscuous atmosphere of Sally Bowles's Berlin. It was a look that seduced easily and swiftly, and seduced a very particular type.

As Richard Williams recalled, 'They had weird audiences. They had girls wearing skirts, pillbox hats and veils. Just like the New Romantics. It was an…élite corps, a supporters' club.'[13]

MUSIC, ROXIED

But even a band as image-conscious as this paid court to their musical duties. Strikingly, there was no hierarchy of priorities with the music and the image. Williams once remarked that only when he saw Roxy Music play at the 100 Club did he realize how perfectly image and music fitted together. They complemented, rather than detracted from, each other.[14] It wasn't all about sequins and Velvet Underground comparisons, though it might have initially appeared that way.

The key word was eclecticism, but also important was how Roxy Music used that quality. Eclecticism is not simply the use of many sources; it is to be judged, rather, on how those sources are used once they are brought into contact. Manzanera says of the stage act, 'We'd start off with "Memphis Soul Stew" and then we'd go into this heavy thing, "The Bob: Medley", about the Battle of Britain with synthesizers and sirens. We had everything from King Curtis to the Velvet Underground to systems music to 50s rock and roll.'[15] This approach was laid bare from the very first bar of the debut album, with 'Remake/Remodel' and its baton-charging, climactic codas, featuring outtakes from 'C'mon Everybody' (Manzanera), 'Day Tripper' (Simpson) and the Valkyrie motif from Wagner's *Die Walküre* (Mackay).

Eno's contribution was to ensure that the flux remained mobile; his synthesizer and tape work kept the textures volatile. Although charged with this important task, and a naturally outgoing person, Eno remained off-stage for some early Roxy Music performances, hunched over his controls like a benign gremlin or a deranged grease-monkey, fitting all the parts together in the wrong order and having no end of fun doing it. He would, for example, sometimes burst into song and enjoy seeing the audience wheel around to find a backing vocalist in their midst. Manzanera in particular was subjected to Eno's pranks with balance and texture, when his monitor would start playing back at him notes he had no knowledge of. Only then would he look up to see a grinning Eno manipulating the sound from the back of the room. The signal would be divided on to separate recorders and played back at different delays – clearly Eno had learned fast from the counselling he'd picked up at the BBC session in January.

The nature of Roxy Music's experimentation depended on the endearing vagaries of a decidedly low-tech set-up, even in the studio. For Manzanera:

'A lot of that stuff was essentially played live and expanded upon with the Heath Robinson approach...a lot of "The Bob" was improvised on the spot. Everyone brought their individual ideas and expertise to the melting pot but it was all still based on the practicality of playing and recording and capturing sounds. In other words, it's not using the studio as an instrument. By the time you get to "Avalon" 90 per cent of it was being written at the studio.'[16]

That's a debatable point, as another comment by Manzanera himself contends. The studio was very much an instrumental part of Roxy Music's conception, even at this early stage. On 'Chance Meeting' Manzanera was required to play normally on to a backwards-running tape.

'When that failed dismally I tried feedback, which meant playing so loud I couldn't hear Bryan singing, only the chord changes. Eno likes that a lot, that kind of random approach to recording. For instance, taping one track then sticking another one over the top without listening to the first one.'[17]

Eno has since expressed misgivings about his methodology of random overdubbing, although the somewhat primitive approach of the band, merely relying on machinery to overdub on to live performances and play-throughs of songs, couldn't have helped, as Eno would discover later in his own endless odyssey through the world of sound generation and recording. At the time of the first album he, like the rest of the band, was a relative greenhorn in the studio. Thompson, thanks to Billy Fury, was the only member with any experience whatsoever of a professional recording studio. Manzanera later expressed surprise that any material had been recorded at all.[18] Corners were cut; pedals were used to control tape speeds. The bombs exploding on 'The Bob' were white noise from a VCS3 synthesizer, and for the motorbike on 'Virginia Plain' a real bike was taped. The approach would get better only by degrees; even on the following album, a trick credited as 'butterfly echo' involved applying Sellotape to the capstan of a tape recorder to destabilize the tape passing over it and induce tone wobble.

But somehow *Roxy Music* was recorded, at Command Studios, Piccadilly, London, with Andy Hendriksen engineering and Pete Sinfield producing (a team which would later go on to work with such Prog-rock eminences as Premiata Forneria Marconi [PFM] and Emerson, Lake and Palmer). Sinfield, whose production has been the subject of some unfair barbs in later years, says:

'It wasn't perfect. But this was a band trying lots of new things, or newish things. They were inexperienced, there wasn't much money or time available, and they recorded it as cheaply as they possibly could. We just got in there every day and did what we could. Some pretty strange things, actually, with Eno there doing these ridiculous things like chopping up sounds with his VCS3 synthesizer. Which is what I'd been trying to do a couple of years earlier with King Crimson, so I'm in no position to laugh.'[19]

Of *Roxy Music*, Ferry has since said, somewhat surprisingly, 'If the first album had gone without a trace I would have been so brought down that I wouldn't have made the second one.'[20] Whether or not this bears out the contemporary sneers of many of his peers, who saw Roxy Music as a bunch of unmusical dilettantes, a tissue of hype and tinsel wholly unsuited to and unrepresentative of the brave new world of rock music, is a moot point. But the question is superfluous; *Roxy Music* was a success, critically and commercially, and went on to become, like its sister single, 'Virginia Plain', one of the definitive moments in British pop music history.

Reading the praise lavished on the records is like reading a slew of dictator's birthday cards, so unanimous is it. Perhaps most perceptive is the opinion ventured by *Rolling Stone* magazine. This was a brave move in a country where almost nobody had heard of the band and those who had were more than sceptical: '*Roxy Music* was the album we weren't ready for.'[21] Richard Williams, the man who had effectively introduced them to Britain's rock cognoscenti in the pages of *Melody Maker*, was entitled to laud his protégés with I-told-you-so satisfaction in his own columns, but if anything the review in rival paper *New Musical Express* went even further: 'The answer to a maiden's prayer...' it panted, 'the best first album I can ever remember.'[22]

Age has not withered the enthusiasm. In 1985 James Truman of the *Face* could write: 'Trashing the idea of art-derived rock as something portentous and humourless, the songs Ferry wrote for Roxy were witty, literate, original, innovative and driven by the ambiguity of being simultaneously heartfelt and ironic. That is, they were clever beyond belief.'[23]

Max Bell, writing about the band's 1979 album, *Manifesto*, harked back wistfully: 'The first Roxy Music album was... special, fine-art English rock; the 50s, the 60s and the deadened 70s all rolled up into one immediate wham. Suddenly, Roxy Music proved that fashion was fun – we were all dressed up with somewhere to go.'[24]

Perhaps the best single summary of the album is Eno's, who described it as 'having about twelve different futures on it',[25] each offering rock music a new blueprint.

Roxy Music is prefaced by an anonymous crowd scene, a cocktail party heard as the listener approaches through the hall, while underneath it all something nasty and doomy seems to stir, not unlike the undercurrents swishing beneath Brian Eno's Ambient recordings a decade later. The observant will note that somewhere in the room a transistor radio is playing the bass line from the track that's about to start, an effect startlingly reproduced on an album by US fusion duo Pat Metheny and Lyle Mays during the opening of their 1981 album *As Falls Wichita So Falls Wichita Falls*. The bass-heavy sound is shattered by the tinkling kitsch of Ferry's good-time 'joanna', itself barged out of the way by stomp-along good-time rock timbre, a kind of heavy-metal hooray-Henryism. This would all be quite straightforward if it were not for the chordal anomalies of the piece and the lack of a chorus (Ferry would later claim that all his best compositions lacked a chorus)[26] and the torrential Coltraneisms of Mackay's tenor saxophone swooping over the chords. And then there are the lyrics – love object as digital sequence (CPL 593H),* love object as car/consumer durable. Ferry has never been drawn on the comparisons begged by this song – is his beloved a car, or is she being compared to one? It is inviting to imagine so, especially when one considers Hamilton paintings like *Hommage à Chrysler Corp.* (1958). 'Remake/Remodel' is actually inspired by a Derek Boshier painting of the same name from 1962, but the concentration of that painter's early work on astronautics and the deliberate neologisms and ambiguities of the words suggest something else.

The author prefers to believe that the CPL 593H sequence is a red herring, an intentional and playful piece of arbitrary diversion, although it is harmless to conjure images of a loved one as being something not unique and irreplaceable, but actually entirely replicable.

The fact that Roxy Music songs lacked the metric and thematic developmental complexity of contemporary Progressive rock music – for example, that of King Crimson, Gentle Giant, Yes or Genesis (all then in the process, incidentally, of creating some of their finest music) – does not belittle Roxy Music's brand of innovation. Here we must call upon the musicologist Allan F. Moore and his highly erudite analysis of *Roxy Music*.

Moore argues that the most distinctive feature of the album is the 'total domination of open-ended harmonic patterns' (he

---

*Apparently, the CPL 593H registration number was that of a car owned by a girl Ferry had met – and fancied – at the 1971 Reading Festival.

cites the 'simplistic dorian I#3 – VII – V#3 – IV' of 'Ladytron' and 'the chromatic aeolian I – #VII#3 – VI – I' of 'Chance Meeting' as examples – for the uninitiated, these are sequences of chords which do not 'close', that is assume a circular and consonant pattern in the listener's mind). Moore continues, 'It is almost as if Ferry's fingers have found a random triadic sequence on the keyboard, over which he starts to spin a frequently discongruent vocal line.'[27] This echoes Manzanera's early estimation of Ferry's compositional method of 'working around the black notes until a form was created'.

Moore rightly concentrates on the surface textures of this first album and their relation to the underlying compositional structures, together with the mutual relationship operative between them.

The traditional instrumental relationships are frequently and subtly overturned. Ferry's piano style is remarkable for its simplicity; frequently just repeated triads or open fifths, allowing Paul Thompson's kit to play a more adventurous role than normal. 'Chance Meeting' dispenses with the kit altogether, the rhythmic layer being provided by a Jerry Lee Lewis piano style executed at an exceedingly slow pace, while the bass spends much of its time at the very top of its range.[28]

Moore also emphasizes Eno's contribution: 'The virtuosic utilization of extraneous sounds as a form of atmosphere moved far beyond previous examples.'[29] True, the effects of mortar and machine-gun fire and sirens in 'The Bob: Medley' are a little hackneyed (the song is an impressionistic tribute to wartime Britain), but as the whole hangs together so well it proves just how important texture has become to the overall musical conception of the LP. There are moments of obvious beauty: the introduction to 'Ladytron', with its tapes and oboe, the woodwind lines carrying on into pentatonic arabesques over mellotron chords, the Debussyan figurations on electric piano which prefigure '2HB', and the chromatic hesitations which underscore Ferry's plaintive, neurotic, halting delivery of the verses of 'Chance Meeting'. There is bristling violence too, Manzanera's guitar treatments enhancing the nerve-jangling pain of that same piece, and Mackay's galloping oboe triplets, acting as a quirky anchor in the treble range, which contribute so much to the sound of the accompanying single, 'Virginia Plain'.

But to return to Eno, Moore states categorically, 'It is the environment Eno creates that gives the music its particular aura...Eno's filling of the textural centre allows the band to dispense with rhythm guitars and keyboards, whose normal role in rock is to fill those central textural holes.'[30]

Manzanera has spoken half-deprecatingly of the 'inspired amateurism' of the sessions, yet there is musical magic aplenty, the discipline as impressive as the freedom.[31] The short, punchy sections for Manzanera and Mackay to improvise in in 'Ladytron', for example, could have encouraged them to pack in as much fleet-fingered self-indulgence as possible; the fact that they do not and manage to choose such graceful forms of filling the space allotted to them is a testament to their musicianship as much as to any high-speed grandstanding.

Listen also to the shuffles and syncopated grace-notes of Thompson's apparently simple vamping backing for '2HB', and, as Moore points out, the rhythm section play a crucial role in the relationship between texture and structure, a relationship that Ferry would later overlook at cost to the music.

Moore begins by highlighting the 'modally obscure bass pattern...in which "wrong" notes predominate'[32] which backs Ferry's vocal on 'Sea Breezes' as a prelude to praising Thompson and Simpson in particular. 'Sea Breezes', he writes, features Thompson playing 'a highly varied counterpoint with the bass beat, eschewing [his] own normal timekeeping function'.[33] He goes on:

The album's most interesting textures seem to hinge on Graham Simpson's idiosyncratic use of chromatic walking lines and high registers. His departure...resulted in less interesting textures on subsequent albums. This powerful bass/kit relation is also found toward the end of the second third of 'If There is Something', as Ferry's protestations of 'love' reach their peak and the song's emptiness, beneath the kit/bass surface, is realized.[34]

Elsewhere, Moore writes that rich surfaces on *Roxy Music* often 'hide the most minimal of structures, thus delivering a rich metaphor for glam rock itself'.[35]

Then there were Ferry's vocals, a flawed high baritone with a vibrato which grew more pronounced the longer and louder the note grew (witness 'I would swim all the oceans blue', from 'If There is Something'). Johnny Rogan's assertion that Ferry's voice was 'unstylized' doesn't quite fit with his perfectly legitimate observation that Ferry approached singing 'like an actor learning a part and on cetain songs he would consciously attempt to mimic a particular singer for extra effect. He loved to dramatize his vocals...by placing great stress on particular phrases or lines in an attempt to disorientate the listeners.'[36]

John Walters astutely notes Ferry's debt to contemporary avant-garde classical music[37] with his employment of swoops and wide intervallic gaps between notes, often with only passing acquaintanceship with the song's chord structure, as Moore himself points out above. This is best heard, of course, on 'Virginia Plain', in which notes are often notated as 'spoken' which helps Ferry's voice leap chromatically around the melody.

Ferry's lyrics, though, drew almost as much attention as the music. It's perhaps silly to overstress the bleakness and austerity of his imagined words. Pop lyricists have often dealt more in tears than cheers, and in any case the lurch towards cod-poesy of rock lyric writers since the 1960s had created a scene where, given the pre-eminence of a central rock culture preoccupation with the individual against alienating modern/metropolitan capitalist society, the emergence of a Baudelairean/Eliotian take on the world, romanticizing the misunderstood creative spirit, was inevitable. Rock had, out of this world of downers, striven to find a lyrical idiom and, despite the best efforts of Lennon/McCartney, Leonard Cohen, Randy Newman and Bob Dylan, had mostly borrowed other people's.

What, therefore, made Ferry's lyrics stand out from the crowd? Their inconsistency, perhaps, more than anything. The ordinariness of some verses (like those in 'Ladytron') contrasted with the knowing clever-cleverness of others (for instance, the punning 'Bitters End', with its brilliantly timed last line, 'should make the cognoscenti think', closing the whole album, or '2HB', a similarly punning meditation on Humphrey Bogart). This last, written by Ferry 'at the piano with the typewriter balanced on my knees',[38] wasn't, Ferry explained, just a tribute. 'It wasn't that I had a thing about Bogart. It could have been any popular idol of the period, or later – James Dean, or somebody.'[39] 'Chance Meeting', meanwhile, came across as a minimalist précis of the David Lean film *Brief Encounter*.

But what gave Ferry's lyrics their special resonance was less their literary quality than their exquisite relationship to the music and thus to the image of Roxy Music, and of *Roxy Music*. Take the hard vowel sounds falling on almost every emphasis in 'Remake/Remodel', for example. Additionally, the saturnine negativity of much of the lyrical content was delivered in snappily throwaway, poppish strophes. Ferry's lyrics dealt not just with the fantasy and abstract world of much rock lyric writing but with the place of such qualities in a social context. Too many 1970s rock lyrics dealt with the individual's relationship with himself – they are often interior dialogues. Ferry revalorizes the rock narrator as pop commentator, in or out of love, but in social toils wherever he goes, observing as well as living his misfortune. Taut, tough images were delivered with no lack of tautness and toughness but in refined wordplay or imagery, comparable to the lyrics of, say, Jethro Tull's Ian Anderson (who dealt in urban imagery but also in interior abstractions).

Only when Ferry's irony was at its most acidic – as on 'Bitters End' – was the florid rhetoric of rock lyrics allowed to surface, and then only to be sacrificed to the songwriter's wit. The Surrealism, Expressionism and Symbolism permeating lyric sheets in 1972 were smartly satirized. 'At last the crimson chord cascades,' emotes Ferry, as a prelude to lines about 'chocolate gates' and 'pale fountains fizzing forth pink gin', which allows us to see the sheer infantilism of much contemporary rock imagery, much as *National Lampoon* did with their 'Art Rock Suite' lyrical take on Progressive rock in 1975.

SHEER AND CHIC

For all the cogency and tightness of the act on *Roxy Music* – there is throughout an admirable sense of enjoyment and adventure in the playing and writing, and the fact that such a masterpiece of refinement could have come out of a fortnight's work speaks of a great team spirit and intensity of purpose – trouble was brewing. Bassist Simpson, after contributing so much to the album, fell under the influence of Sufism, its mystagogues still busy recruiting among the legions of the lost wandering London in the wake of the 1960s. He became increasingly unreliable and 'very withdrawn, he couldn't communicate with anybody' (Ferry).[40] He left a fortnight before the band were due to play their first 'official' live concert, at the Great Western Festival at Lincoln on 23 May 1972. Pete Sinfield came to the rescue, recommending a friend of his, Rik Kenton, who beat off the challenge of Ferry's old Gas Board band-mate John Porter to take over bass duties.

The swamp that was Lincoln was the band's biggest showcase yet, more prestigious even than the Peel sessions (another of which would soon follow). Kenton was thrown in at the deep end, and his acquaintanceship with Sinfield may have meant that he was already aware of Ferry's fickle attitude towards bass players, but none the less acquitted himself well in the Lincoln rain. Despite footing the bill below such luminaries of lost-hopes as Locomotiv GT and Somme-like conditions, the band won considerable acclaim. He also got to mime to the band's first single, 'Virginia Plain', on *Top of the Pops*.

This single was perhaps the trump card in Roxy Music's impressive hand. An uppercut of a track, brawny and assured bubblegum with brains, it sizzled with energy and was arranged with *Pointilliste* care. While other songs have gone on to become more immediately recognizable as Roxy Music signature tunes, little else quite so succinctly summarizes what the band were, and have always been, about. As the passing years have thrown up so much comment on the song's obvious Pop Art imagery, Ferry's vocal camping and the famous trick ending – a nightmare for DJs – the most surprising thing is the shortness of the song. It clocks in at just two seconds under three minutes, astonishing when one considers the Niagara of detail and contrast that it is.

As Ferry says:

It was a sort of throwaway watercolour...an American dream type of thing. The face of the girl in the painting was based on one of Warhol's Superstars of the time – Baby Jane Holzer – who used to have this amazing huge hairdo. It's about driving down the freeway, passing cigarette ads on vast billboards. And Las Vegas casinos.

Lyrically the song is the best thing I've done, but not the easiest to follow because there are lots of little ideas and bits of ideas that link up for me, but maybe not for anyone else. I used to have a Studebaker...and the first three lines are about our lawyer...[41]

It's hard to top this summary of the song, a collage of popular trash as teeming with detail as Hamilton's *Just What is*

It That Makes... – Havana, roller-coasters, streamlines, hipsters, Acapulco, six-day wonders, cha-cha-chas, midnight-blue casino floors, and the towering pre-eminence of the brand name 'Virginia Plain', which has the power to kill the whole song off, and does, apropos of nothing. The scattershot arbitrariness of Ferry's images also compares to Pop Art discongruities, commenting on the disruptive plurality of images in popular culture that rain uncontrollably upon us. The illusion of consonance in the lyrics – for they are in reality mere nonsense – mirrors the apparent logic of the torrent of sense-data we absorb from postmodern culture.

The B-side, 'The Numberer', was the first track taped by the band which was not written entirely by Ferry. The first version of the song, apparently, contained the bawdy yelling of absurd lyrics, which were later – regrettably – edited out. An expectedly sax-led romp, it consists of a riff garnished with some silly Enoid burbles to frame Manzanera's and Mackay's thoughts on soloing styles in 1960s pop, and after Manzanera's solo points up the piece's harmonic ambiguities, the texture gradually fills with frantic instrumental blowing on one chord, including the whinnying of Ferry's excitable harmonica. It's maybe the most extreme track the band ever recorded, although whether or not it would have satisfactorily fitted into the track listing of the debut album is a moot point. Its omission from *For Your Pleasure*, however, is inexcusable.

In the meantime, the Roxy Music snowball was building. The band returned to the BBC to cut more tracks for *Sounds of the Seventies* and were commissioned to record two numbers on camera for BBC TV's *Old Grey Whistle Test*, the ultimate nationwide platform for progressive and unusual rock music. This would cause its own disquiets, of which more later.

To the surprise and outrage of many in the rock business, the ever-cunning EG Management hustled Roxy Music into the support slot for the leading exponent of theatrical and ironic decadence in rock, David Bowie. In his Ziggy Stardust pomp, Bowie was the toast of rock critics everywhere and was spreading over even the non-musical national press like a virus. After one particularly memorable gig at Croydon's Greyhound came a support slot at London's Finsbury Park Rainbow Theatre. Not content with having engineered their own ladder to stardom instead of climbing up the ones already there, Roxy Music now seemed to be committing another sin in the name of dilettanteism: hanging on to the hem of Ziggy's dresses to scale even greater heights. The press notices, and the audience reactions, however, were as enthusiastic as ever.

What was more, Andy Mackay had the considerable presumption to criticize the headliner, who at the time was the nearest thing to a living god in British rock and roll:

'I can't decide about Bowie. His records are very good, some of his music is very strong, I just think he uses people as a buffer. Although the theatricality is good, it's almost too theatrical. He has good stage presence and it's good for a few numbers, then it goes down. He goes too far on the theatrical side. [Marc] Bolan...is much better because he wants to be a straightforward rock star whereas Bowie wants to be too serious. Possibly more than Bolan he needs an audience who is right with him. I get the feeling that if a few people started booing, everyone would start.'[42]

Mackay, having made his bed, promptly lay on it with the comment, 'He is an excellent saxophone player...a frustrated serious artist.'[43] Time would prove Mackay correct on some points – notably Bowie's usage of people as buffers, and the 'frustrated serious artist' diagnosis is uncommonly prescient. But the relationship between Bowie and Roxy Music remained cordial, if sometimes lukewarm. Christopher Sandford's splendid *Bowie: Loving the Alien*, a book whose detail is sordid and exhaustive enough to expose any jealousy or paranoia on Bowie's part regarding his rivals in Roxy Music, discloses nothing.

The most likely explanation lies in the instincts of Bowie

and Ferry, masters not only of pop expression but of the art of living the pop life; they were both knowing, resourceful and cautious men who recognized the other's strength and found confrontation distasteful, undignified and, most importantly, unprofitable artistically and commercially. Bowie remained the greater draw, but Roxy Music were none the less free to find and cultivate their own public in the pitch Bowie had queered.

While Bowie was king of all he surveyed, Roxy Music were content to be courtiers or pretenders to the peacock throne. They also scored a notable success, prestige-wise, when, astonishingly, they won the support slot for Alice Cooper at Wembley Arena in July 1972. If Bowie was flavour of the month in Britain, Cooper, with his slapstick grab-bag of Artaudian excess – guillotines, chopped-up dolls, fake blood, live beheading of chickens and the omnipresent boa constrictor Yvonne – was the global embodiment of rock excess. Mackay, having cut Bowie down to size, wasted no time: 'I was impressed by the thoroughness of his act, he doesn't try to make it anything but theatrical. Bowie tries to work on the idea that he is really different, but with Alice Cooper...sometimes his act is crude – not musically, but theatrically.'[44]

Mackay knew the way the wind was blowing, and was wise to the image his own band were now pushing; theirs was as much an ironic comment on celebrity in popular culture and its imagistic and sartorial baggage as an act of rock stardom. But he could also enjoy his new-found status. He later told an interviewer:

'It was exciting for all of us, because it was all so new. We were also proving to be a great success. We had hit records, and it didn't matter that we were still losing money like mad, or that we were, in effect, being paid only about £15 or £20 a week...that's all we took then, because we knew we were running up big debts and we didn't want them to get any bigger. Anyway, for a year you can stand all that because of all the energy running through the band. But after two years, when you still can't see the light at the end of the tunnel, and accountants are telling you things could be fairly healthy in nineteen months time, you become aware that you're caught right in the middle of what has become an extremely expensive operation.

And you can't stop, because if you did, you'd be in debt for the rest of your life. And at the same time, much of the original novelty and excitement has been eroded.'[45]

Pop Art fed on fame. Fame would now start feeding on pop's Pop artists.

4: GAY(-ISH) BLADES (1972-3)

NEVER MIND BOB HARRIS, HERE'S ROXY MUSIC

Bryan Ferry relaxed in a bedside chair, casually broached a bottle of champagne and, clad in monogrammed silk pyjamas, celebrated a successful tonsillectomy in his usual super-suave style. Or so the press copy might have gone, after the swift engineering of a publicity opportunity from an otherwise tricky situation. It was late September 1972 and Ferry had been rushed to hospital after losing his voice; EG and Island's publicity men saw no harm in scoring a few publicity points at the same time. They knew what they wanted – Champagne Charlie...topping the pop polls...a sparkling year...getting accustomed to the decadence of the pop world so celebrated in his music – and that is duly what they got.

A more important material benefit of the lay-off was that it allowed Ferry some time to recuperate and reflect upon the previous few months, which had indeed seen him elevated, if not into pop's aristocracy, then at least into its gentry. But that six-month spell had also seen him lapse into deep depression (curtains drawn, a silent TV forever switched on) as he realized exactly what he had taken on and what his band would have to take on in the future.

There was some truth to the hacks' obsequies – after all, it was quite true that times had changed, that private clinics, Moët and monogrammed nightwear hadn't been on the horizon the previous December. Then he had been stuck in supply-teaching, trapped in an environment where the main musical issues discussed among his charges were the respective heaviness of Uriah Heep and Deep Purple and the assumed penile dimensions of Donny Osmond and David Cassidy. Now a degree of the style and luxury to which he had always aspired and had always – if later interviews are to be believed – believed he would attain, were his. Ferry, though, was wise enough to recognize the price payable not only in the amount of work required to maintain such a lifestyle but also the degree of artistic autonomy it cost him. Roxy Music were now the property of the rock business; they were no longer his alone to sculpt and shape. Henceforward their destiny was in the hands of hucksters, A&R men, booking agencies, the shysterly circus of rock production which he had held out so long against joining.

True, it had been fun. There'd been the gigs with Bowie in the summer, when the momentum had been so tangible it could almost be touched; further sessions for the BBC had also been greeted with surprise and delight. There'd been the riot at Liverpool Stadium, when Rory Gallagher fans let their redneck blues bias get the better of them and began chanting 'Poofters! Poofters!' during Roxy Music's support set, only for Eno to sashay across the stage, pouting and goading them to wilder excesses. This wasn't commonplace, however; the band played numerous gigs across the country and won innumerable friends. They played Sheffield University (21 June), the University of East Anglia (24 June), Croydon Greyhound, supporting David Bowie (25 June), Walbrook College (27 June), Lancaster University (29 June) and then Wembley

Arena, supporting Alice Cooper (30 June). The trek had gone on thus: Halifax (1 July), London Wood Green Nightingale (4 July), Leytonstone Red Lion (7 July), Chippenham (8 July), Bristol (9 July), Salisbury (14 July) and then, in another neck-ricking step up the ladder of prestige, the first of the 1972 Crystal Palace Garden Party festivals, appearing third on the bill above Loggins and Messina and below Stone the Crows (29 July). An extra gig followed at Stoke's George Hotel on the last day of July before two more memorable dates, at the Rainbow Theatre with Bowie and slide-guitarist Lloyd Watson on 19 and 20 August.

Ferry had been able to buy a bigger and better apartment, moving out of the Battersea terrace where he lived with Andy Mackay and into Chelsea's Redcliffe Square, a syringe's throw from the rock gutter of the World's End hippie-squats.

How about the chart success of both 'Virginia Plain' and the debut album which had helped finance this upward mobility, the former reaching No. 4 and the latter No. 10? Ferry insisted on cutting singles – preferably non-album tracks of particular distinction – which once again set the band at odds with conventional rock practice (this, remember, was an era in which the two leading UK acts, Emerson, Lake and Palmer and Led Zeppelin, never released singles in this country, regarding it as too commercial). Ferry had no such qualms.

There were the *objets d'art* which suddenly came within his grasp. 'Over the years,' he would later boast to *Melody Maker*, 'I've developed an appreciation of excellence in all things and therefore I have fairly expensive tastes.'[1]

Then there had been the comical reaction of the rock establishment to his success. *Wot larks!...* 'Uppity,' was the rock-biz consensus on Roxy Music, favourable hacks aside. All hype and no talent, a wisp-thin package as opaque as an old négligé; a bunch of posing pop Warhols who'd made it though the backstairs route of weekend hippie gossip and west London artistic élites. Bob Harris solemnly told the nation he didn't want them on the show when they first played *The Old*

Grey Whistle Test (and blew the nation away) on 20 July. It was dangerous to court such enemies, as Roxy Music did, but there was still a thrill, an illicit buzz, about the fact that the slow-witted were buying the whole scam as something intentional. And best of all, Ferry's band still believed in him as they believed in themselves.

Mackay, Eno and Manzanera, galvanized by success, and probably incredulity that they had pushed the envelope this far without failure, urged greater and greater experiment, but Ferry could, at this stage, still counsel caution and be listened to. Manzanera, interviewed in the *NME* in September, had been positively effusive about his boss's qualities.

But Ferry went into decline anyway, and, as Rogan points out, the onset of tonsillitis may have given EG headaches trying to rearrange cancelled gigs on that inaugural UK tour but jolted Ferry into applying perspective to his 'problems'.[2] Those rearranged dates included Weston-super-Mare (29 October), Reading (30 October), Chatham (31 October), Coventry (4 November) and a gig at Manchester's Hardrock Club (9 November). This was to have featured the British début of New York's sleaze-punks the New York Dolls — a twinning with Roxy Music was a choice double-bill if ever there was one — but the untimely heroin-induced death of the Dolls' drummer Billy Murcia led to their hasty withdrawal. The band then followed up with a homecoming gig at Newcastle City Hall (11 November), with Redcar shortly afterwards (17 November), a shared bill with Fleetwood Mac at Leicester University (18 November), a show at the Croydon Greyhound that was so inundated by demand that a second impromptu performance had to be arranged for the same evening, breaking the venue's box-office record (19 November) and gigs at Guildford (20 November), York (22 November) and Lancaster (24 November).

Sure there were flaws, and there'd be more to come. But this was what it had all been for, wasn't it? It might not be stardom by Tyneside's standards in the way the Animals had been stars, but, true to his soul, Ferry had got out and gone upwards further and faster than most of his contemporaries had, or ever would.

AMERICA AND OTHER MISTAKES

Problems aplenty were indeed lurking, not least in the shape of a disastrously misbegotten US tour at the very end of 1972. This was a rare folly on EG and Island's part. If reaction to Roxy Music in the UK had been confused, there was still a native appreciation of a peculiarly camp, eccentric Englishness in the music. That quality was lost entirely on the beer-chugging Bubbas, campus denim-freaks and unsmiling rock purists of the US, the predators to whom an unsuspecting Roxy Music were thrown on that first tour.

Warner Brothers, who had snapped up the band in the States, were largely to blame. Bromides about club reactions being 'amazing' concealed the fact that the band were placed second on the bill to the likes of Jethro Tull and Humble Pie. Prestigious enough, one might imagine, but hardly so when one considers the idea of Ferry crooning 'Ladytron' or 'Bitters End' in intergalactic Teddy Boy regalia to an audience who usually liked nothing better than to holler 'Boogie!' during guitar solos.

A doltish attempt to sell Roxy Music as Britain's answer to Alice Cooper – based, presumably, on no more substantial premise than the fact that they had supported him during the summer – was particularly crass. The greatest material investment Roxy Music had in the presentation of their shows were a fire-eater and a juggler booked to enhance the stage show at Los Angeles' Whisky-a-Go-Go. Ferry was particularly frustrated. Los Angeles and New York club crowds, he conceded, were 'hip and sophisticated', but in the same interview (with Nick Kent in the *NME* in 1974, after another depressing misfire of a US launch) he fumed against the 'mass American audience mentality', 'the dumbest in the world bar none'.[3] Elsewhere he groused that 'US audience are...

incredibly conservative. I think that when they went through all the social changes of the 1960s they seemed to create a new style which was equally as rigid as the one they left.'⁴ On one occasion, when a voice bellowed 'Play some rock 'n' roll!', Ferry retorted drawlingly, 'We *are* rock 'n' roll.'

The US, it seemed, like their sensations as large and loud as possible, and consumable with the least thought, consideration or contemplation. Ferry and his band found out the hard way just how true the rumour of America's native lack of irony was. Fortunately, although Eno was as provocative as ever, the band escaped unscathed. This didn't preclude at least one God-fearing good ol' boy down South winding Eno up, pirouetting round him in a diner yelling, 'Faggot!' Better one hung-up pickup-driver than a hallful of badered Scousers, and by and large reactions in the States were of impatience (*'Rock! Rock!'*) rather than aggressive outrage. But the US was a tragic failure for Roxy Music, the first real career reverse they'd suffered and one which Ferry, with his lifelong mania for all things American, born in the one-and-nines of his home-town cinemas and intensified by his attachment to Amerophiliac Pop Art, found particularly hard to take.

At Miami's Speedway Stadium, things were particularly bad. 'We flew in by helicopter,' says Paul Thompson, 'and there seemed like half a million people down on this racetrack. We got on. No sound check, so it sounded like shit. People started throwing stuff at us.'⁵

Supporting Jethro Tull at New York City's Madison Square Garden should have inspired some optimism, or been read as a possible prelude to greatness, but even this proved a dispiriting lesson in the crudeness and coarseness of the US rock experience in the 1970s, exacerbated of course by the dulled pain of acting as unknown support group to a big name with fanatical followers who generally acted like Beavis and Butthead's dumber older brothers. Ian Hunter, in his *Diary of a Rock and Roll Star*, admirably captures the mood:

A reasonable cheer went up, signifying the crowd didn't know who the hell Roxy Music were. Eno looked like a Spider [from Mars] and Bryan Ferry like a Dracula-type Presley. The first number was a complete mess, and 'Virginia Plain' was ruined by the bass refusing to work until about halfway through the number. Right away you knew that Roxy never had a sound check. By the time the sound was right they were wilting under pressure although I thought they held on extremely well. To my mind doing Madison Square Garden without a sound check is like Marc Bolan fighting Joe Bugner for English heavyweight title. Roxy tried their best, and failed.[6]

Hunter goes on:

... what can you do when they are still putting up lights for the headliner when you are on? What can you do when the sound guy you totally rely on hasn't got a clue what you are about? People are jumping about distracting you from your job, and the headliner's fanatical fans howl abuse, not because they dislike you, but because they are desperate to see their heroes.[7]

Jethro Tull fans, wherever in the world, were (and still are) famously among the most militantly monotheistic of the lot.

Never mind. Britain still loved Roxy Music – or at least the punters did. Unfazed by the indecently late cancellation of the autumn UK dates, they still packed out the venues and unanimously polled them as Best New Act in all four major rock comics, *Record Mirror*, *Disc*, *Melody Maker* and *New Musical Express*. In the meantime, the band returned to the studio in February 1973 to finalize new material for a second album – the refinement of the composition processes having enjoyed welcome extra time granted by Ferry's lay-off.

A second project was the rush release (somewhat against Ferry's and the others' wishes) of another non-album track,

'Pyjamarama', as the next Roxy single (Ferry making a very rare appearance on guitar, the last time he would play guitar on record until the title track of the 1980 Roxy Music album *Flesh + Blood*). This, apart from its musical qualities, was a notable disc in that the B-side, 'The Pride and the Pain', was another outing for a Mackay composition, a further pointer that Ferry's talents were by no means pre-eminent within the ranks of the band. It is, like 'The Numberer', comparable in quality with its A-side, which, given the quality of some of Mackay's later solo work, indicates that his best material was possibly being marginalized. A filmic, slightly Argentinian-flavoured oboe melody is discongruently parroted by Manzanera's guitar; although the piece is rhythmically constant, the textures, both vertically and horizontally, once again start to craze and break down, as on Mackay's 'The Numberer'.

A further line-up change also took place in early 1973, Rik Kenton being ousted by John Porter, who had attempted to fill Simpson's shoes the previous May but had lost out to Kenton's superior technique and the word of Pete Sinfield.

Now Porter had sharpened up his chops and, sporting two of rock's most memorable sideburns – delectably Dickensian wrap-around hedgerow jobs – he joined the band. Sal Madia, however, assumed bass duties for live work, and henceforward Roxy Music eschewed employing bass players as part of the band's permanent core line-up. The dispensability of Roxy Music's bass players, one ex-admirer has quipped, is exemplified by the fact that the bass players in Roxy Music were always the worst or the dullest dressed. Sinfield had left the fold to take up a lucrative position as lyricist and co-producer with his old King Crimson chum Greg Lake in Emerson, Lake and Palmer.

Within the space of a year the band had recorded two substantial albums, two singles, had conducted UK and US tours and had also returned to the BBC on four occasions to consolidate the success of their first *Sounds of the Seventies* session. The first, on 23 June 1972, featuring more début album material, 'Bitters End', '2HB', 'Chance Meeting' and 'Ladytron'. The second followed almost immediately, following ecstatic audience response. On 1 August the band recorded a dynamite version of 'Virginia Plain' and 'If There is Something'. On 9 November 1972 they were ploughing through 'The Bob: Medley', as well as somewhat tentative and dissolute previews of new material, 'For Your Pleasure' and 'The Bogus Man Part II'. The final session of these four (and, as it transpired, the final session that Roxy Music would record for the BBC), taped on 8 March 1973, was possibly the strongest of all, containing bristling versions of cast-iron classics from the new album, a calculated and well-executed piece of pre-emptive puffery for the new disc, 'Editions of You', 'Pyjamarama' and 'In Every Dream Home a Heartache'. All this, however, was to prove a mere trifle compared to the workload Roxy Music undertook thenceforward. Interviewed years later, Ferry remembered with an audible sigh, '1973 was a serious year of work.'[8]

An impressive enough CV by 1990s standards perhaps, but, for reasons best known to various dunderheads in the rock business, not when it came to Roxy Music.

THE BOB HARRIS SYNDROME: HYPE AND ROXY MUSIC

It's hard to grasp today the ethics that pervaded even the more countercultural backwaters of the rock business a quarter of a century ago. Looser maybe were the shackles of artistic control; individual expression may have dominated rock's rhetoric, but rock, for all its hair-down liberation schtick, still nurtured work-ethic Puritanism whose roots were pure showbiz. As Ferry himself put it of late 1960s rock, 'That whole 60s presentation of rock music, and the implied honesty that went with it, was kind of bizarre and was always alien to me.'[9] Ferry referred to an attitude that distantly mirrored the new conservatism of American rock, which deplored any creativity not succeeding on terms comprehensible to that

mythical entity the 'rock community'. Roxy Music's crimes in
the eyes of some in that 'community' were to have succeeded
without paying sufficient dues – for heaven's sake, one of them
couldn't even play a musical instrument! (Paul Thompson's
dutiful toil at the bottom of the rock ladder, and Mackay's
classically honed technique were conveniently ignored.)
Richard Williams summarized it thus: 'They were really hated
because they hadn't been like Hawkwind or Family, slogging
away at the college circuit.'[10] (They had in fact played nearly
thirty club dates by the time that EG had signed them.)

The cherished fiction was that something fondly imagined
to be the folk-soul of rock music existed only in an
enlightened youthscape, in the hearts and minds of the heirs of
the Aquarian illusion. Popular music that did not obviously
derive from this world was treated with suspicion, whether
sharing common inspirational cues or shared conditions of
production. Roxy Music's appearance from nowhere and
apparently affluent financial situation raised hackles, but it was
their imagery that roused most antipathy.

The fact that their theatrical elements were so explicit was
taken, risibly, to be a betrayal of their true origins and an act
of subordination to the corporate manufacture of rock music.
Roxy Music actually went out of their way to assure the world
that they were 'reorganizing the stage act and the costumes to
keep ahead'.[11] Certainly during one TV appearance, the entire
band wore different costumes for the two different songs they
performed. Anyone who tended to their visuals with such
meticulousness surely had something to hide; when the music
was all that mattered, lavish stage visuals were taken to be
unacceptably mainstream detractions from the gnostic truths
of music – which, after all, had long been the most distinctive
public and articulate mouthpiece of countercultural concerns.

Thus the sillier commentators of late 1972 had the wrong-
headed gall to lump Roxy Music with the likes of Gary
Glitter, the Sweet and the Osmonds as mere bubblegum, a
belief which saw sensible cognoscenti from Tony Palmer to

Richard Williams leap to their defence. Such baloney, as was pointed out at the time, blithely ignored the fact that countercultural rock music had been from the start ineradicably associated with visuals, in both the conception of the music and its presentation to the public, a presentation which, in the cases of counterculture heroes like the Who, Emerson, Lake and Palmer and Yes, would soon spiral into pompous and megalomaniacal stage gigantism of the worst sort. But the image of musically empty, style-obsessed dilettantes was a tough one for Roxy Music to dispel, as even two years later Lester Bangs, in tediously familiar fundamentalist accents, would prove:

> Like all glam bands, Roxy Music are more interested in getting their names on the social register and trying on different kinds of clothes than doing anything about real rock and roll. In Roxy Music, you see the triumph of artifice. Because what they are about is that they are not about anything.[12]

In a sense Bangs was right, but only in a very small sense. What Roxy Music were about was presenting the idea of artifice as a meta-message. They did not *depend* on artifice, they merely used it as a tool which *could* have existed independently of the music but was ingeniously indissoluble from it. Roxy Music at least had a lens into rock's falsehoods of image and commerciality, and, having seen enough, decided that the rock experience itself had to be taken with a pinch of salt. Cue Eno appearing on-stage in early 1973 attacking his synthesizer with a giant plastic knife and fork. And Manzanera: 'We're not solemn about our music. We like to give people a good show, dress up and that sort of thing. Have a laugh...'[13]

The final three words were blasphemy enough in avant-garde circles in Britain at the beginning of the 1970s. Never mind that Manzanera added his belief that the band didn't play its best when in a good humour. Such sentiments were treasonable enough to the rockist scheme of things.

But it was perhaps Roxy Music's unashamed celebration of show business and the past that chafed most of all. They had the astuteness to identify rock's unspoken inheritance from the show-business traditions it spurned and highlight rather than conceal them. For Eno:

'What was different about Roxy Music was that we were quite ironic, and this was new at the time...we came out of a context where the accepted mode for pop musicians – and most artists, actually – was to be apparently sincere, committed to one's art and immersed within it. We, on the other hand, wanted to do something that had as much to do with showbiz as with the seriousness with which rock had come to regard itself.'[14]

Eno is probably the most articulate ex-member of Roxy Music when it comes to assessing the band's significance. 'There was a definite Janus feeling abroad at the time,' he muses. 'Looking to the past in a kitsch way, and imagining the future as it might be...but perhaps in an equally kitsch way.'[15] This was what distinguished them from corny retro- satire acts like Sha Na Na or Frank Zappa's Ruben and the Jets project. Those were bands whose acts confirmed the past as something just that – safely past and easy to laugh at, as easy as Monty Python's squawking suburban housewives. The afore-mentioned acts didn't posit awkward questions about the cultural identity of the present or the future. For such bands, the past was to be celebrated only as something defunct, as nostalgic property; for Roxy Music it was something to be celebrated as an integral part of the here and now, and maybe of what was to come. Much of the mystique was again informed by Ferry's undying love of America and its creatures. 'It was all rather curious, I suppose,' he told an interviewer about his childhood, 'to be in Newcastle fantasizing that you were a blond beach idol. I loved the incongruity of it all...and

I think that my own romantic attachment to that kind of glamour offers a clue to the success of Roxy.'[16] Ferry speaks of his 'average' fandom, and compares it to that of Roxy Music's own audiences. 'One of the things I think we've offered... is a fairly glamorous image. One that is manufacturing, or catering to, a kind of dream consciousness in the same way that Hollywood and the whole film industry did twenty years ago.'[17]

Effectively, the whole furore ensured the success of Ferry's attempt to 'design his own career'. It was Andy Warhol who had premiered the idea, and Ferry, like Bowie, subscribed assiduously to it, by 1977 openly telling interviewers, 'I am my own product.'[18]

Well, almost. Ferry has since conceded:

'I will generally try to take the credit for everything, but with Roxy it was very collaborative. Nicholas de Ville's art direction, for example, was hugely important, with its attention to details like the serrated edges of the Fifties-style postcards of us on the first album.'[19]

The Roxy machine (as Antony Price would later, accurately, dub it) had cranked up for the first album, refining image as much as music, crediting not only stylist/designer (Price) but hairdresser (Smile), model (Kari-Ann) and photographer (Karl Stoecker), and was clearly from the start more than adept at the manipulation of how its image was not only produced but also consumed.

One of the main gripes about Roxy Music was their fascination with commerciality, publicity and advertising; the cover of their début album looked like an advertisement for itself. But the Roxy machine's personnel knew George Melly's dictum that 'pop music is like advertising in that they both sell dreams that money can buy'.[20]

Peter York wrote of the era that there was 'a newer and more attractive self-image on offer – the Applied Art media star, in particular the Designer'.[21] Much as pop and rock had engendered a musician boom, the visuals the music demanded spawned a design boom at the end of the 1960s. Average public relations wages were roughly £20 a week in 1973. As Melly puts it, it was still too much of a case of 'the talentless leading the talentless'.[22] Pop music's sense of visual style was considerable, as any browse through a swatch of Hipgnosis album covers will prove, and valuably kicked PR's backside. What Roxy Music did was to professionalize and sharpen the PR discourse of rock and pop in Britain with their expert use of surfaces and imagistic play – while still producing excellent records. In his vast and uneven history of pop, *All You Need is Love*, for example, Tony Palmer patiently upbraids Bangs's fatuous dismissal of the band.

> Ferry's silence, of course [Bangs had beefed about Ferry's 'blandness' at a post-concert lig] could be reckoned preferable to mouthing revolution; musically, it might be a little unfair to dump him with the Osmonds or Gary Glitter. His songs are superior in every way; better constructed, more challenging lyrically, more rewarding harmonically.[23]

Even this, however, was not enough for some, who insisted on meretriciously equating good PR with hype.

Roxy Music's 'reliance on hype' was, in fact, a red herring. They were no more oversold than any other act, and were dwarfed by the promotional indulgences granted to some. For example, in 1970 some £25,000 had been ploughed into the Prog-rock gimmick band Curved Air (sex-pot vocalist in G-string, classical dropouts playing organ and violin, see-through picture disc in polythene LP sleeve). Critics cried hype, but the campus crowd made the band stars anyway. Now the all-hype-and-trousers slurs were being pinned on Roxy Music. Island themselves, Pete Sinfield suggested, put more money into the career of Bob Marley than they ever did into that of Roxy Music.[24] The problem with Roxy Music was that publicity and hype, sullenly owned up to only under duress elsewhere in rock, was celebrated noisily in Roxy Music circles.

Warhol comparisons are helpful here: 'If you want to know all about Andy Warhol,' the bottle-blond social climber once told an interviewer, 'just look at the surface of my paintings and film and me, and there I am. There's nothing behind it.'[25] Robert Hughes, in a critique of Warhol, interprets the story thus:

> Without doubt, there was something strange about so firm an adherence to the surface. It seemed to go against the grain of high art as such. What had become of the belief... that the power and cathartic necessity of art flowed from the unconscious, right through the knotwork of dream, memory and desire into the realized image? No trace of it; the paintings were all superfices, no symbol. Their blankness seemed eerie.[26]

And so, by extension, did Andy.

Roxy Music's game was to offer this line to critics and watch them swallow it; because the catch was that Roxy's music was substantial, a hard, comforting core or kernel at the centre of the imagistic ephemera which was laid on as a blind.

Chief illusionist was Antony Price, who, according to his friend Ferry, made 'wonderful' clothes for the band, the costumes which were taken as the items most indicative of artificiality in the band's discourse. 'He loved dressing us up,' says Ferry warmly of his long-time collaborator, and he still believes that Price's unique instinct for style, and particularly distinctive camp styles, kept Roxy Music one step ahead of the Glam bandwagon; in the eyes of those with the wit to notice, anyway.[27]

For his part, Price counters: 'People also say [adopting camp voice], "Ooh, you styled him." God forbid. Bryan had commercial tastes and knew what he wanted. You can't push things at him.'[28]

Ferry – and his band – would stumble, like Warhol before them, when the obsession with publicity and celebrity stopped being part of an elaborate metaphysical game of imagistic tag, stopped being material for artistic exploitation, and became a concrete part of life itself. This, however, was still some way off.

FOR YOUR PLEASURE

It was probably just as well that the band emerged from AIR Studios, near Oxford Circus, in early spring with an album that confounded even their detractors, an effort which if anything outdid even the two-fingered iconoclasm of their début. For Ferry, proud father of the album, *For Your Pleasure* was 'probably the best album overall', so completely was he 'centred' and 'focused' on it. Every track 'seems to have its place'.[29]

For Your Pleasure, and its companion 45 r.p.m.-only tracks 'Pyjamarama' and 'The Pride and the Pain', are indeed a phenomenal achievement, with knowing world-weariness and darkling self-absorption soaked into every note like absinthe. There is absolute assurance in the way that the whole expressive syntax of the Roxy machine is delivered. This is a band that knows exactly what it wants to say and how to say it.

It could be said that the opening of *For Your Pleasure* would be better served by an introduction which features the first half of the title track. On Roxy Music's retrospective 1990 video, *Total Recall*, it is used thus. The sidling bass-drum taps and hesitant tom-tom rolls menacingly circle Ferry's halting delivery of the lyrics. Such an introduction could perhaps intensify the ambushing impact of the frenzied 'Do the Strand', which, like the first track on its predecessor, careers along at a ferocious pace, with Manzanera's guitar and Mackay's saxophone blazing unrelentingly. This time, however, the music hurtles through a Technicolor tunnel of wordplay. Ferry's pen is still sometimes gauche but is audibly swelling with confidence. 'Louis Seize he prefer...*laissez faire le Strand.*'

'All styles served here,' bellows Ferry – and how. Sequencing 'quadrilles', 'Madison' and 'cheap thrills' is wonderfully audacious, although at times some of the lyrics seem to boast erudition for the sake of it, such as the throwaway name-checking of the Sphinx, Mona Lisa, Lolita, Guernica…

La Goulue and Nijinsky would, to most of the band's listeners, have sounded like a disagreeable French appetizer and a retired racehorse, but Ferry seems intent on getting them in no matter what. The song, incidentally, is a commentary on dance crazes, and how history can be seen as one long taxonomy of them – a dance to the music of time, the lyrics quoting as many dance styles as possible. This magnificent rondo, punctuated by Vesuvian eruptions of Junior Walker-style saxophone from Mackay, is one of the best syntheses of lyrical and musical literacy the band ever constructed.

'Beauty Queen' – which, according to Eno, Ferry wrote practically by himself – sings of the resigned mourning of lost love, adorned by Manzanera's treated guitar, which shines around every line with a continual chordal extemporization. Lyrically, 'swimming pool eyes', 'sea breezes', 'coconut tears', 'swaying palms' are the first unoblique lyrical apostrophes of the Pop Art obsession with the appurtenances of celebrity at the heart of Ferry's work. We soon learn, however, that this beauty queen is a mere dreamer in a provincial town, 'the pride of [her] street'. The instrumental textures are less transparent and certainly less novel than on *Roxy Music*; each instrument seems more fixed in the soundstage, without the sudden furtive appearances in the ear of a flurry of notes or a variation on the melody as with the first album.

There are of course, still great richness and complexity. 'Pyjamarama' is a high-octane case in point. There are some lovely contrasts also on 'Strictly Confidential', a showcase for Mackay's astringent oboe improvisation ushering in an increasingly frenetic texture with Manzanera's florid guitar lines bouncing off the four walls of the soundstage.

On 'Editions of You', Eno's funny-noise solo can't

compensate for the increasing subordination of his tapes in the mix; the enjoyably metallic and abrasive clash of Ferry's electric piano and Manzanera's typically oddball rhythm-guitar lines creates a racket of its own without needing Eno's trickery to distress the surface.

The one exception is 'The Bogus Man', a long (nine minutes-plus) and apparently nonsense piece of *Pointilliste* improvisation in rhythm and texture. As Eno said at the time, the piece was like 'some of the things Can were doing at the time – you know, open-ended, improvisatory, and not just thoroughly rehearsed performances with bits for the band to fiddle around in'.[30]

Apart from Manzanera's choppy one-note ostinato – which lasts throughout the piece – the soundscape is a series of non-synchronous chords and flourishes on saxophone, guitar and keyboards, combining in what is sometimes barely less than cacophony, sometimes a miracle of limpid transparency and beauty, sometimes an afforestation of electronic savagery.

Porter's bass-playing substitutes Simpson's idiosyncratic chromatic walking lines for more reliable and rhythmically tricksy but less distinctive lines, and Thompson's drums seem to be stickier and heavier in tone.

The title track, 'For Your Pleasure', offered some of the band's most adventurous tone-painting thus far – as the instrumental section which mutates with apparent absurdity but impeccable inner logic from the opening chords and melody finally disintegrates, the sacrificial tom-toms, madcap choirs and mellotron chords recall nothing so much as Tangerine Dream's contemporary album *Atem*. Additionally, the title track is a delight, echoing the counterpoints of tone and texture in tracks such as 'Ladytron'. That number's strange accumulation of instrumental voices is also to be found here, infinitely more sophisticated, as the band hypnotically repeat the farewell 'Ta-ra' over a familiar batik of fragmented figures and elaborations from all the players, the effect of glaze-eyed distance and detachment heightened by the austere harmony and producer Chris Thomas's delightfully restrained and controlled use of delay systems. Thomas had worked with the Beatles and, contemporaneously with his first Roxy Music assignment, was mixing *Dark Side of the Moon*.

But this track is also notable for Ferry's increasing boldness with song words, which philosophize without ever assuming excessive ponderousness. He sings that the Roxy Music experience presents itself 'part false, part true'.

This shows just how many layers of irony and meta-messages Ferry was capable of putting over. Just how false – or true – were Roxy Music?

Certainly there seems little irony in the bottom-of-the-barrel blackness of 'Strictly Confidential', where the lyric begins as a regretful letter of parting and ends freefalling into suicidal despair: 'There is no light here/Is there no key?'

'Editions of You' can be read, superficially, as a nod to Warhol's infinitely reproducing star pix – the love object no more than a reproducible experience or image. Better, though, to hear it as a magical piece of booty-shaking rock. Ferry, singing about 'looking through an old picture frame', tees up the graphic-artistic analogy, however, and it seems unfair to disappoint him. No love is unique or special, sings Ferry, just as there is no one authoritative masterpiece or art object in the age of mechanical reproduction ('a pin-up done in shades of blue' does seem to strain the Warhol comparisons a little too much, however). There'll be another shag along in a minute, is basically Ferry's message. This is modern ('in modern times the modern way') and super-urban. The countryside and its joys can't measure up to 'a night with the boys'. Staying cool is the 'main rule', don't overdo the wine and women, and keep your name in the papers by hook or crook. Likewise in 'Do the Strand', Ferry's singing about 'Quaglino's place or Mabel's' presents a man in touch with not only a past decadence but also a decadence of today to be celebrated and enjoyed.

There are lovely archaisms still at work in his writing here, such as the line about billing and cooing in 'Pyjamarama', which is sung with apparently intense seriousness, yet, in 1973, any listener *knows* the phrase is obsolete and Ferry, giving his coyest ever vocal performance, is kidding. The title, apparently meaningless, gains a little logic when one reads the words as the last thoughts before sleep of a lover missing a lover.

Ferry's lyrical satires work better here. In the first album's 'If There is Something', the roses-round-the-door extravagance wasn't counterpointed with sufficient acidity to create the intended *pasticheur* effect, but here the typically romantic cliché of ships passing in the night is handled with brio: 'Soul ships' travel to the stars and pass, although on the way to an unknown, maybe non-existent destination.

Lynn Hanna's later précis of Roxy's musico-lyrical mystique was perhaps the best ever written, and in consulting it we are granted a panoptic view across Ferry's imagination when writing love songs. It certainly applies to *For Your Pleasure*'s love songs, 'Beauty Queen', 'Strictly Confidential' and, by extension, the non-album 'Pyjamarama':

> The precise code of a shared allegiance to romantic adventure, the lost identity in archetype, the blank, unbridgeable distance implied by the inscrutable stare of her sunglasses…in such a space, in the fleeting vacuum that exists at the instant eyes meet, float all of Ferry's fantasies of suspense and anticipation.[31]

But perhaps Ferry's greatest achievement, and arguably his greatest song, is 'In Every Dream Home a Heartache', a song which, perhaps better than any other except 'Virginia Plain', can be used as an idiot's guide to what Roxy Music were all about, a meditation on sex, materialism and the empty fantasies of both. In Michael Bracewell's words, the song is 'the lament of a disconnected millionaire sleep-talking through a wet dream'.[32]

The mass-marketing of 'progressive' gracious living of the kind which so fascinated Pop Art began in 1944 when

Westinghouse took out an advertisement in *McCall's* 'preparing for "living electrically"'. In 1957 Monsanto Inc. opened a 'House of the Future' in Disneyland, 'exposing us to the fortress home's synthetic treasures. The ideal American dwelling went from a quaint clapboard bungalow with a white picket fence to a microcosmic World's Fair of separate rooms and distinct themes.'[33] This equation of progress with luxury, of continual renewal connoting infinite disposability and an eternally reproducing future with an exponentially increasing standard of living presented Pop Art with a continuum of consumption that was an endless source of fascination. Roxy Music, like all good Pop artists, found plenty of inspiration in this phenomenon. Such outgrowths of the superabundance of post-war American prosperity led sociologists like David Reisman to produce pessimistic, neo-Weberian works like *The Lonely Crowd* (1950), which posited an America whose populace had become so atomized and alienated that they had detached themselves from hitherto stable communities to become singular slaves to a media-driven psychosis of 'gracious living' and gadgetry.

Ferry's dream home could well be a thousand Pop collages and canvases – or perhaps it is Hamilton's *Homes of Today*, with the strongman and stripper long dead or moved out. It could be the interior of one of Hockney's Hollywood villas; the inflatable doll could be one of Wesselmann's *Great American Nudes*, synthetically fleshy against the vacant glare of airbrushed interiors: the 'essential comforts' of a ranch-style bungalow are all relentlessly, soullessly material.

The cold half-smile that creases Ferry's face when he sings 'your skin is like vinyl'; the stress that the pool she floats in is 'new' and 'deluxe' and 'delightful'; a 'disposable darling', who cannot be disposed of, so trapped in the gilded cage of consumption has the narrator become; the song he sings is the song of one waking from a nightmare into realization of utter dependency on consumer durables and brand names.

This is the band's achievement too; the shimmering,

polychrome, translucent bubbling of tape and mellotron over which Ferry bemoans his enslavement to a plastic doll is pure genius. There are other neat *coups de théâtre* – such as the telling switch from the dark, phased, delayed electric piano and guitar chords which sinisterly and psychotically introduced 'Beauty Queen' and the relatively friendly soundstage that backdrops the rest of the song and hints at schizophrenic disturbance, at the malevolent lurking of something unspoken in the relationship between the singer and the subject of the song.

ROXY LIVE – WITH ENO

The band's first 'official' UK concert-hall tour tied in with the release of *For Your Pleasure*. The band, still confining themselves to a short set, were given slide-guitarist Lloyd Watson and the band Sharks as support acts – the latter featuring ex-Free bassist Andy Fraser and guitar sessioneer Chris Spedding. The itinerary of the tour was not overly demanding: Nottingham University (15 March), Manchester Hardrock Club (16 March), Bracknell Sports Centre (17 March), Birmingham Town Hall (18 March), Leicester de Montfort Hall (19 March), Plymouth Guildhall (24 March), Torbay Festival Hall (25 March), Stoke Trentham Gardens (27 March), Sheffield City Hall (28 March), Newcastle City Hall (29 March), London Rainbow (31 March and 1 April), Preston Guildhall (4 April), Liverpool Empire (5 April), Glasgow Green's Playhouse (6 April), Edinburgh Odeon (7 April), Leeds Grand Theatre (8 April), Brighton Dome (11 April), Southampton Gaumont (12 April), Bournemouth Winter Gardens (13 April), Bristol Colston Hall (14 April) and Cardiff Capitol (15 April). A European jaunt was next on the agenda, with Ferry introduced to a long-time hero, Salvador Dali, through the offices of his latest escort, *For Your Pleasure* cover-girl Amanda Lear. The Russian-French model, who had once been Dali's mistress, arranged a publicity stunt of admirable tackiness whereby arch-aesthete Ferry would be filmed by TV cameras in discussion with one of his spiritual forebears. Alas, the promised film crew never showed and the afternoon was restricted to forced smiles, tea and a gaggle of paparazzi taking uninspiring stills.

A further cause for concern in the rock industry over the presence of Roxy Music in its midst was their androgynous sexuality. This had roots partly in the judgemental jealousy of the previous autumn's reaction to their ascent to fame. The question was asked with increasing frequency, were Roxy Music really – as the Rory Gallagher faithful had bayed at Liverpool – poofters? Eno was the easiest target, but the whole camp/fashion/art school incense that floated in the band's slipstream aroused suspicion, not just from those who misinterpreted Eno's postures but also from the wilfully ignorant.

Ferry told Gordon Burn that he

'found gays more *simpatico*...a year ahead of everyone else. Being so close to the art world, my friends have nearly always been gay. Most of the people I really know or see at all now are in fashion because they're attractive people, personality-wise, and therefore not incredibly deep.'[34]

Although this led Ferry to lament, 'If I disappeared tomorrow most of them wouldn't notice the difference.'[35] In late 1973, Ferry, in his most explicit interview on the topic, expanded on the gay theme to *Melody Maker*'s Michael Watts: 'Gay people usually have very good taste, and I tend to be fairly camp on stage, anyway. Maybe it's rubbed off on me with lots of my friends being gay.'[36]

Consider this is an era when homosexuality in Britain, if discussed at all, was diminished by parody, one big limp-wrist world of cartoon queenery, hello-sailor T-shirts, Danny La Rue and Larry Grayson, a sitcom world where all queers were antique dealers or haberdashers and were called Nigel or Jeremy and owned cigarette holders and wore cravats. Mindful of that, Watts asked Ferry how he thought Roxy fans related to the band's sexual signals. Ferry replied:

> 'I don't think that there's been any change in sexual habits among teenage rock fans since the New Wave, if you like, of campish characters. I think when boys in the provinces are making up they're making up to attract girls because they think that's what the girls are going to like.'[37]

Ferry could hardly ignore the fact that Eno's Technicolor super-androgyny got him more girls than straight rock rig-out could ever have done, and was no doubt hip to the current belief that girls fancied Bowie because of, rather than in spite of, his dresses. 'If it makes people more adventurous in the way they look then it's probably a good thing,' continued Ferry. Laughing, he added, 'But some of them should really learn how to put on make-up. We see so many garish sights on our travels.'[38] Ferry conjured the image of a 'kid in Hartlepool' running up to his room and 'applying mascara before going out on a Friday night. "Our Derek," he mimicked to Watts, "'you're not going out like that, are you?"'[39]

Ferry was evidently aware that Dereks everywhere were doing exactly that. The previous year Mackay had announced that 'rock music has always been a reaction against accepted standards, that's why there's this gay thing now. A lot of our most solid fans are young boys of fourteen or fifteen who obviously see us as the opposite of what their teachers like.'[40] The danger, the occluded mystery still surrounding homosexuality – indeed, in suburban and provincial England, most sexuality *per se* – was what probably drew youngsters to Roxy Music. There was the whiff of the decadent – which given stories like Eno's sleeping with six girls in one continuous thirty-hour session, and his subsequent homage to golden showers in the title of his début album, *Here Come the Warm Jets*, was hardly surprising. But decadence, in the sexually schizophrenic Britain of the early seventies, was still sufficiently alien and exotic and *unnatural* to warrant at least an elective affinity with homosexuality. Certainly by 1975 Ferry would be gently emphasizing his heterosexuality to inter-viewers; the insinuations, though muted, were continuing. People would still accuse him of using the Roxy Music girls – most of whom became his escorts – as a front for perceived effeminacy.

The gayness issue in Roxy Music came about almost entirely because of the band's artistic language, the images they worked with and the manner in which they worked with them. For Roxy Music were camp, very camp; consider this definition of camp by the art historian Mario Amaya in his discussion of its relevance to Pop Art:

> sports a humorous and constantly changing evaluation of things *passé* or out of style just before they come back into fashion…in the new Super Realism [Pop] the taste of the immediate past, not quite datable and yet not quite out of sight, often comes in for revaluation; Forties pin-up girls, the cars of the Fifties, post-war interior decoration, are all handled as items just out of reach which have not found their place in history.[41]

As a taxonomy of Roxy Music's own obsessions, this could hardly be bettered.

Susan Sontag wrote of camp that it is 'a mode of enjoy-ment…it wants to enjoy'.[42] For Amaya, camp in Pop Art is

> expressed by a love of things being what they are not; by a fascination for the androgynous, particularly in over-exaggerated sexual forms which themselves become parodies; by ambiguity, irony, paradox and inverse humour; and by a feeling for artifice, for surface appeal, for thrilling, timely, sensational stylish anti-conventions.[43]

Christopher Isherwood defined high and low camp in his *The World in the Evening*; low meant Dietrich impersonators, high 'an art of a confident theatricality, not necessarily trivial'.[44] Roxy Music again.

Peter York has summarized, admirably, the 'double-think' aspects of camp: i.e. she's 'bad' meaning she's 'wonderful'.[45] This secretive and slangy gay dialect recalled the pre-Woolfenden days when homosexuality was still criminalized, for it was a shared language for the inducted. It is no surprise that gay men appropriated the slang of another oppressed minority, black men, in establishing a linguistic system for themselves beyond the grasp of a hostile 'straight' society. The later (relative) pre-eminence in London of both the art and the fashion milieux allowed camp language and discourse into the artistic mainstream.

In 1972, camp in Britain was almost synonymous with 'gay'. Indeed in gay British culture, the fallout of Gay Lib in the late 1960s was, according to Peter York, 'a huge turnaround to traditional camp',[46] which, by implication, eased the arrival of the likes of Bowie and Ferry, where the techniques of camp, as outlined above by Amaya, could be used by straights or bis in a self-consciously traditional manner, with lots of mincing and mannerism. As early as the end of 1969, a Bowie gig at the Speakeasy was attracting 'boys in bone-tight velvet pants' and 'hordes of girls with deader than deadpan faces'.[47] As Christopher Sandford has noted, this merely took its place in a rich gay/camp tradition of titillation in show business, a tradition tapped into with varying degrees of success and irony by Liberace, Elton John, even Mick Jagger.[48]

This didn't stop those straights and bis being tarred with the 'poof' brush; even to the counterculture, camp was intrinsically a gay thing. The counterculture took itself, and its projects, far too seriously for any kind of cultural, social or political capriciousness or irony of a camp kind to be accommodated, which effectively excluded gays from much of the counterculture. (Within the counterculture, gays had become the new niggers, the new underclass, to be dealt with by leftists and counterculturalists at will. In other words, as victims in an overall and pre-judged social schema. Avowedly liberal though the counterculture and rock culture may have been (at least in word if not always in deed), gays were not an issue that was relished, and gays knew that if they weren't exactly welcome, they were in the counterculture on sufferance. This may explain their enthusiastic rallying to the Roxy Music banner; camp had for so long driven them to the backwaters of cultural trends past for their idols, but in Roxy Music they found idols who were not only self-consciously 'outside' the conventional postures of pop but also shared their love of camp.

Roxy Music, interestingly, for all their satirical intent and purposely camp posing, never satirized homosexuality. While plenty picked up on the line 'look out, sailor' in 'Editions of You' on *For Your Pleasure*, there are no sideswipes at effeminate behaviour or camp or gay preoccupations, which may have only served to exacerbate hostile innuendo against the band. Its followers – the gays in particular – knew when the band were acting and when they weren't. They themselves could add the postmodern quotation around any activity the band chose to involve themselves in. Roxy Music were all about playing with surfaces, and campness was only one of the surfaces they played with. That they did not parody or belittle it was one reason gays had to be thankful to Ferry and his men.

The issue of gayness would soon be diminished within Roxy Music. By mid-June 1973 one of the main foci of the speculation was, in his own words, running up the King's Road, 'singing and leaping. It was really fantastic – as if I'd left school or something.' Brian Eno, jumping or pushed, left the band.[49]

Ferry's tonsillectomy in 1972 had resulted in a hiatus that forced individual band members into each other's social circle as never before. 'I've still not been introduced to the drummer,' Manzanera had quipped to Iain MacDonald that September and, given the hectic schedule undertaken by Roxy Music (constituent members still disengaging themselves from gainful employment), this unfamiliarity was hardly surprising.[50] Mackay and Eno reacquainted themselves with their mutual love of the experimental, where they quickly found an ally and a friend in the inexhaustibly explorative Manzanera, whose hunger for the esoteric hadn't been extinguished by his bad experiences on the fringe with Quiet Sun. Hitherto individual servants of Ferry's vision, the trio became firm friends and unwittingly established a power base opposite Ferry's within Roxy Music's ranks which would eventually have catastrophic consequences.

This would manifest itself only when instant popularity forced upon the band swift decisions as to imagistic and musical plans. For example, how would the delicate balance of hardcore rock taste and teenybop taste best be catered for in future music, and, for that matter, should it even be considered? Eno, never a good tourer, had rarely made a secret of his belief that Roxy Music were spending too much time on road-work, pandering to mass bubblegum markets instead of capitalizing on their talents with recorded sound and arrangements within the confines of the studio. This, he felt, threatened to corral the band into conformity.

Furthermore, given the sudden consumer rush for the band's product, disquiet was voiced within the ranks over Ferry's share of the subsequent loot. Eno, for his part, conceded that Ferry had earned a greater share than the other members of the band, but quibbled about subsidiary royalties.

Ferry, meanwhile, who had at the start of the year been agonizing about losing control of the band to rock's corporate mechanisms, now agonized about how best to milk those mechanisms. He ruminated on the possibilities of video recordings of the band replacing live performances and (with undeniable prescience) argued the case for video recordings to cement the band's reputation as a commodity fit for TV promotion.

Success, however, was tangible enough for the rest of the band and now it was happening abroad also. A European tour

(September 1972) of Italy, France, Germany, Sweden, Denmark, Belgium and Switzerland had been a sensation. Mackay, in particular, sensed he was touching base when he played there: 'I prefer being in Europe. Some of those old cities have kept a quality that London has lost. The feeling here is that everything is gradually running down. There's a general feeling of depression and decay.'[51] He went on to say that it mattered not a jot to him if Roxy Music made their reputation in Europe as opposed to America.[52] Europe, still then a distant land of package flights or queasy Channel crossings or crackly satellite relays of British football teams getting kicked to bits, was another cipher for exoticism, and EG's speedy plugging of the band's success there helped cement their reputation as connoisseurs of the outlandish. No detail was spared, for example, in telling the world that in Paris – then, for Britons, still equated with the acme of European dissolution and sophistication – the band had stayed in the George V hotel, with its Sun King tapestries, monogrammed bathrobes and inexhaustible cellars of vintage champers and Calvados. The Dali farce was part of the same chapter, but laughable though it might seem, Roxy Music's French sojourn did attract massive public interest. Whether intoxicated on centenarian liqueurs or dallying in designer haberdasheries, Roxy Music had the time of their lives. One TV show was gatecrashed by 2,000 rowdy admirers and a minor cult of imitation was sparked among Parisian Roxyites, much as it had been from the 100 Club onwards in England.

ENO ENO ENO!!! OUT! OUT! OUT!
For all the success that the band had brought to Eno – socially, sexually and financially – the Woodbridge boy was fretting. How populist were Roxy Music going to get? How low a common denominator would they play to? There were rumours of Eno and Ferry quarrelling over the photographs of Amanda Lear for the cover of *For Your Pleasure*, although Eno's reason as given by Rogan ('because Roxy might get

stereotyped as glam rock')[53] seems unconvincing. Eno later told the *Trouser Press*, about the 'star thing', 'The public image of it is one of being terribly flighty and extravagant, but the fact of it is that mentally, you become really stuck.'[54] Such apparently noble purism didn't prevent him from flying into a tizzy when the footage of the band playing 'Virginia Plain' on *Top of the Pops* featured his contribution merely as a shot of a sequinned glove manipulating a synthesizer joystick. 'The only thing you saw was his glove,' remembers Manzanera.[55] Eno was extremely miffed.

Paradoxically, Ferry saw Eno's media *over*exposure as a threat. The very public lack of a leader in Roxy Music disguised Ferry's behind-the-scenes *dirigisme*, but also his own instinctive insecurity, which, paradoxically, barred him from imposing his authority as symbolic 'frontman'. Lazy journalism led to Eno's upfront 'outrageousness' becoming the centre of attention, and Ferry, as bespoke co-ordinator of the band, found himself marginalized. Residual modesty in Ferry had until now constrained him from taking the public mantle of Mr Roxy Music and suddenly he saw Eno having the laurels forced upon him and evidently relishing it. What to do?

Ferry's worry, of course, was theatre versus music, which, by a supreme irony, was Eno's also. Ferry saw theatre as an obfuscation to the classical pop Pop Art music he aspired to; Eno saw theatre as a bourgeois distraction to the potential subversion of artistic preconception in avant-garde music.

Legend has it that Ferry's preoccupation with Eno's public profile was ignited into paranoia by a newspaper article about Eno's alleged plans to record earthworms. That wouldn't sell in Peoria, Ferry griped. Eno was going too far, or seemed to be. Was this a Ferry still besotted with the idea of becoming a part of the great American popular cultural heritage which he so idolized?

There were other issues, not least the fact that Eno had benefited from Roxy Music's arcane stage set-up at Ferry's expense. Eno and Ferry had faced each other across the stage, but audience reaction had so far given Eno more confidence about grandstanding to the crowd. Press responses increasingly emphasized the role of Eno in the stage performance, which Eno later conceded was 'quite unjust',[56] but he also rebuked Ferry for his response, which was one of buttoned-up defensiveness, claiming sole ownership of the entire band concept to whoever would listen (subsequent examination of the press proves that this is either a gross exaggeration on Eno's part or that the journalists involved edited Ferry's statements – unlikely given his public profile at the time). Reviews such as the famous American appreciation of *For Your Pleasure* which credited half the vocal duties to Eno weren't calculated to improve matters in a band which seems, by spring 1973, to have convinced itself – at least between Ferry and Eno – that it would split.

There were signs that management agitation for Ferry to take action and claim stage front for himself had been in action as early as January 1973, when, for one TV appearance, the band lined up across the screen to play, Ferry in the centre, and Eno conspicuously at the back.

By this time, Ferry was already 'having his ear bent by the managers', [57] according to Manzanera. From the beginning, EG had professed doubts about Ferry's potential while continuing to carry his esoteric baggage of sidemen. Ferry was now pressurized to become a 'real' frontman, a 'real' icon, singularly marketable and manipulable.

Now the jettisoning of the most obviously uncommercial sidekick, Eno, seemed to be the first chapter in rewriting Ferry's future to others' demands. 'He was pushed to do it, to come centre stage,' says Manzanera. 'Definitely. By the management and by everyone. The message was, "You've got to have someone, a focus, in the middle, otherwise the band won't be successful." '[58] Ferry, it seems, for all his worldly wisdom in matters of the heart and mind, was all too well understood by his elders and betters.

Producer Chris Thomas remembers that Ferry had 'wanted'

to be frontman. 'And after that, heads down and carry on working', despite palpable disquiet within the ranks.[59]

Ferry told *New Musical Express*, 'I got to the point of saying, "Well, either Roxy doesn't exist any more or else it redefines itself in my terms", more strongly than I'd originally thought. I'd started out very easygoing... diplomatically controlling the whole thing. [But]... I just put my foot down.'[60]

The foot went down most publicly after a concert in York, when Ferry told eagerly outstretched dictaphones that he would never appear again on the same stage as Eno. On a day which had begun with the press singling out Eno as the centre of attention – rumours were flying, that an avant-garde, purely experimental album he'd cut with King Crimson's Robert Fripp was in the can – and had ended with what Ferry thought (mistakenly) was an on-stage walkout by Eno during the Ferry vocal showcase 'Beauty Queen', the tensions which had for so long propelled Roxy Music's creative engine room blew back. Mythology suggests that Eno left the stage to defuse pro-Eno sentiment and deflect catcalls during this song and that Ferry took (mistaken) umbrage at what he thought was an act of arrogance and superiority.

This is almost certainly not the case. The band had already bargained for Eno militancy in the audience with the presence on the bill of his old friends the Portsmouth Sinfonia; Eno's gesture, honourable enough, was used as an excuse to undertake a move long planned but reluctantly carried out. In fact, Eno, aware of the situation and angered by Ferry's refusal to confront him, pre-empted any such moves by convening a band meeting without Ferry and announcing his resignation.

Ferry, in later interviews, owns up to emotional weakness and vacillation in the matter. 'I froze him [Eno] out... I do a very good Garbo freeze-out technique.'[61] Ferry has also gone on the record with the apparently sincere wish that 'in an ideal world, I wish that Brian would have stayed and Eddie [Eddie Jobson, Eno's replacement] had joined.'[62]

In short, Ferry preferred to sacrifice one man for the better good of the five or six that might serve his inspiration better at a later date. Certainly the regular presence of a curly-haired kid called Eddie Jobson lurking backstage around this time, paying particular attention to Eno's performance, suggests that Eno's place in the band had been under review for some time. This wasn't the taxman spying on a rock suspect. This was a new member of the band.

5: UNDERWEAR AND UNDERGROWTH (1973-4)

STRANDED – WAVING NOT DROWNING

One of the most remarkable features of the Eno débâcle was how little it affected Roxy Music's work rate. Despite some objections raised by Mackay and Manzanera at what they regarded as the ousting of their friend and a misguided career move on the band's part – which was translated into banner 'Roxy Split!' headlines in the rock comics – Roxy Music were back in the recording studio by September 1973, just three months after the breach with Eno.

True, Mackay proved harder to convince than Manzanera of the wisdom of Eno's resignation, and for a time resisted the induction of any new member into the band. There was some garbled press speculation about a possible Mackay/Eno single, 'Never a Light Without a Shadow', backed by saxman Mel

Collins and erstwhile King Crimson rhythm section Ian Wallace (drums) and Boz Burrell (bass). If Ferry had hoped that Eno's departure would diminish press interest in him and return it to the band, initial soundings suggested otherwise. Eno talked of forming an ensemble of guitarists, to feature Manzanera, Mike Oldfield and, implausibly, Deep Purple's Ritchie Blackmore. He pondered publicly on another project, Luana and the Lizard Girls, an album's worth of 'hysterical hybrids and musical mutants' which, of course, was in a way largely what Eno ended up nurturing. But the carefully handled circumstances and attendant publicity of Jobson's induction into Roxy Music and the musical possibilities his technique opened up poured cold water on the putative collaboration between Eno and Mackay.

Twenty years later, Manzanera told one reporter: 'There was always a possibility that I could have left when Brian Eno did. I felt very loyal to him.'[1] The guitarist stayed on, however, because 'I hadn't had my fill of being in a pop band. For years that was what I'd wanted to do. When I was sitting on my bed in Caracas, nine years old, listening to the Beatles on the BBC World Service, I just used to think, "Got to get to England, this is so exciting." Roxy fulfilled my dreams of all that very quickly, with the girls and the limos. But after a while I'd think "Actually, I'm a pretty bad pop star", because after about ten minutes I'd get bored with it.'[2]

Brooding discontent – if that is ever what it was – evaded the new music-making, with latest recruit Eddie Jobson seamlessly assimilated into the Roxy Music sound. Jobson was another North-easterner (he was born in Billingham, near Middlesbrough, on 28 April 1955) and at eighteen he was the nearest thing to a child prodigy in British rock. Possessed of breathtaking chops not only on keyboards but also on violin, he had been ideal to replace Darryl Way in the fast-fragmenting gimmick-band Curved Air. Launched amidst a miasma of hype in 1970, they were fast becoming obsolete. The delicate and doe-eyed Jobson, who had mastered synthesizer at the age of sixteen, was none the less hot property in a band going cold, and Ferry knew it. This wasn't just from press reports; Ferry's own sister knew Jobson's sister while studying at Newcastle University and kept Ferry informed of the lad's prowess. After giving Jobson the once-over at a Curved Air gig, Ferry acted.

Jobson was by all accounts well served in Curved Air, but the Roxy Music job had its attractions, although one imagines that Ferry must have perceived Jobson's introduction with equal relish. Jobson was not only a phenomenal musician but an able composer (as his 'Metamorphoses' for Curved Air proves, not to mention a subsequent oeuvre of similarly distinguished if somewhat bloodless Progressive rock-derived pieces).

Furthermore he was an attractive focal point – there was a boyish, porcelain quality about the young Jobson which transcended even his recurrent penchant for the absurd bubble-perms which bedevilled him with Roxy Music. But for reasons of inexperience and natural antipathy, he lacked Eno's instinct for outrage.

He was a visual hook which posed no threat to Ferry's still-gauche frontman role. His technical skills were not so monumental as to alienate Manzanera and Mackay, and he had the right blend of feeling for ensemble discipline and experimental raucousness. In other words, Eno with milk teeth.

Best of all for Ferry was Jobson's relative youth and insecurity, which gave the singer a strong position from which to negotiate. Fissures within Curved Air were threatening Jobson's position. The pornographic dazzle of tits and technique which had carried the band through their early years was fading fast and some musical commerciality was required to shore up the group's future. Uncertain of how to react to that, Jobson gratefully took refuge under Ferry's fatherly wing and Ferry knew he could turn gratitude to loyalty.

It is unjust to read this too cynically. Ferry was an astute man and Jobson, though young, knew what he was taking on. What sweetened the deal for Jobson was that he never became an official member of the band (in spite of all the publicity pictures and handouts and record sleeve notes – where he was always billed with prim exactitude as Edwin Jobson – which suggest otherwise). Therefore, while subject to possible instant dismissal, he could earn reasonable money (incredibly, this excluded record royalties) and bags of high-profile kudos. He could, on a more superficial level, get on *Top of the Pops* and see the world. More appealingly still, his status absolved him of worry over shouldering any of Roxy Music's still-considerable debts. Within months he was on-stage at London's Rainbow Theatre and gigging with the band – acquitting himself admirably, as contemporary footage reveals.

The initial reaction from the press to Eno's split from the band was one of almost ghoulish relish; this, surely, was the end of Roxy Music, a growing legend nipped in the bud to whose untimely demise many flowery columns of what-ifs and if-onlys could be devoted. Little credence was given to Ferry's assurances that the band would go on, although the poaching of Jobson was seen as a statement of serious intent.

A new album was due from the band, the sessions for which backed up on the sessions for Ferry's first solo album, *These Foolish Things*. The recording of that album would come to have far-reaching consequences, not only on the following Roxy Music LP, *Stranded*, but also on the band's subsequent career.

Ferry's sidemen of choice for *These Foolish Things* had left a mark. These were guys 'who I felt were not necessarily better than the Roxy Music players but more professional' (this was, perhaps, a strange sentiment in the light of Jobson's and Thompson's extensive – and Manzanera's occasional – involvement in the recordings).[3] By Ferry's reasoning, *Stranded* should be the result of a leaner, fitter Roxy Music unit at work than hitherto. It's a convincing case, although some commentators have opined that it's a convincing excuse for an altogether less adventurous compositional outlook.

It's easy, taking the albums at face value, to muddle *Stranded* with *For Your Pleasure*. This is not least to do with the overt metropolitanism of the imagery on the former's two stand-out cuts and the lowering night skyline of a city which adorns the cover of *For Your Pleasure*. Further complicating matters, *Stranded* has explicit semantic connections with the earlier album's 'Do the Strand'. There is, however, a discernible musical difference between the two albums, largely concerning texture and composition.

Stranded opens, like its predecessors, with a hard-blowing rocker of a track, although 'Street Life', for all of its many charms, cannot compete with either 'Remake/Remodel' or 'Do the Strand' for sheer momentum and commitment. There's a tang of cynicism about the very opening, too; the advancing wall of white noise seems to suggest, duplicitously, 'Don't worry, it's OK, Brian's gone but nothing's going to change.' Burbling, dissonant squalls of mellotron flute on each chord of the syncopated introduction (which doubles as a middle eight between verses) further enhance the strangeness, but only a few bars of the song suffice to convince even the most neutral listener that radical surgery has occurred at the band's heart.

It's best to return to Allan F. Moore's analysis of the first album to find possible explanations. His comment that Eno's tapes filled the textural centre which enabled the band to 'dispense with rhythm guitars and keyboards, whose normal role in rock is to prevent those central textural holes'[4] is illuminating. The accommodation of Jobson's technique and Ferry's turn in songwriting necessitated changes in Roxy Music's sound as a matter of course. But it also meant that the whole soundstage was radically altered and made congruent and consonant. We have seen how the disruptive and texturally discongruent nature of Eno's tapes lent the overall band *klang* a pleasant sense of flux and unpredictability, adding to the sense of fracture and disturbance. After Jobson's arrival, the instruments begin to sound like ordinary rock instruments in an ordinary rock setting, irrespective of the tightness of the act and the ingenuity with which they were played. None of this can be blamed on Jobson, who did his job with enviable *élan*. None the less, on *Stranded* the band sound as though they are flying in conventional formation, with roles allotted according to rock convention. Gratuitous racket – such as the violin solo Jobson detonates in the middle of 'Street Life' and duly manipulates – doesn't, for all its many merits, compensate for the element of instability that Eno's presence lent to the unfolding of each song. Similarly, the metallic hailstorm of Jobson's keyboards at this point provides a frisson, but it fills the soundstage and everything fits neatly around it.

'My favourite Roxy album,' Brian Eno said in 1977, 'is the third one, which I wasn't on. But it also contained the seeds of their destruction, because it was getting very polished by then and didn't really contain any new ideas.'[5]

'What it lacks for me,' Eno later perspicaciously told another reporter, 'is one of the most important elements of my musical life, which is insanity. I'm interested in things being absurd and there was something really exciting in Roxy at one time. We were juxtaposing things that didn't naturally sit together.'[6]

Eno wisely acknowledges that underestimation of this incarnation of Roxy Music is, none the less, uncharitable. The music on *Stranded* was often deceptively straightforward, but showed that the band could be masters of the simple things as well as the esoteric. The best example of this latter tendency was 'A Song for Europe'.

'A Song for Europe' is, effectively, Roxy Music's most conventional attempt at that stage of their career at writing a pop song. It employs an ABABCB (verse-chorus-verse-chorus-development-chorus) format, with verse/chorus melodic profiles alternating before the interpolation of a solo instrumental closely related to them. It's also the first example on LP of Andy Mackay's songwriting, hitherto restricted to the backwater of single B-sides ('The Pride and the Pain', 'The

Numberer'). Nevertheless, for all the majesty and nobility of his themes, they do owe just a little too much to the melody of the Beatles' 'While My Guitar Gently Weeps' and further normalize and formalize instrumental relationships within the mix.

Furthermore, the 'Europeanness' of the song, and its rather literal musical interpretation, sometimes act as a deadweight on the musical whole. The symphonic starburst of orchestral melodrama in the middle eight, triggered by Thompson's timpani blows and Jobson's Bachian triplets, is a little overwrought. But one does get the impression more of an attempt to emulate Phil Spector's epic pop than Emerson, Lake and Palmer's aspirant gigantism. The song also provides its author, Mackay, with a rare showcase on an album where his instrumental contribution is conspicuously and inexplicably subdued.

The lyrics were Ferry's, and the whole provided one of the album's key moments, an exemplar of what could be achieved by democratic redistribution of responsibilities. Hearing how well Mackay and Ferry could dovetail together helped dispel much of the post-Eno malaise, when it seemed that without the Woodbridge iconoclast further progress was impossible.

'It's a pun, of course,' Ferry told the *NME* of 'A Song for Europe', 'on the Eurovision song contest, one of the more bizarre events in the calendar... Andy came up with the music... it sounded very European to me, so I thought I'd use Latin and French and do it as "A Song for Europe".'[7]

Eric von Lustbader, writing in *Zoo World*, concurred: 'It's a deliberately stylized song, Francophilic [sic], an homage to the heavy heritage of the Continent. It emerges from dark, rain-laden verses to exhilarating choruses.'[8] Comparisons with Germanic cabaret – with Brecht and Weill – are, however, overplayed. There is simply too much classical consonance and predictable homophony, too much smoothness. 'Sea Breezes' from *Roxy Music* has much more Ku'damm authenticity.

Ferry's brooding vibrato, with its Charles Boyer overtones, rarely found a more natural home than on 'A Song for

Europe'. His choice of words, language and dialects is also beautifully and musically appropriate. *Stranded* indeed, in the wake of some unknown tragedy, a broken love affair in territory unfamiliar to the heart as well as the mind, in a city where all doors are now closed. Some have attempted to read into Ferry's persona here an allusion to the 'Lonely Man' of the Strand cigarette television advertisement of the early 1960s, in which a solitary smoker waits in vain for an assignation in a *noir*ish cityscape.

The three stand-out tracks on an album which Ferry at the time tried to pass off as some kind of statement of a musical 'jungle' (the augmented use of percussion might go some way to explaining this curious assertion, but not far) are a triptych of urban pleasure and pain. The most distinctive of the three, even if not the most compositionally memorable, is 'Mother of Pearl'.

'Mother of Pearl' was, at the time, greeted with almost psychotic excitement in the press, and the track most readily lit upon as testimony that Roxy Music *sans* Eno were going to be all right. It is formally unconventional, with two open-ended blowing sections on harmonically ambiguous chords, the first at breakneck speed, the second more laid-back, over which Ferry apparently improvizes his lyrics. The first section double-tracks two simultaneous Ferrys, one strident, the other menacingly seductive, one squalling defiantly, 'No, no, no, noooooooooo!', the other wolfishly smirking 'Yeah!' The textures here, crowded yet flexible and *Pointilliste*, seem to recall earlier numbers, but the majority of 'sounds' are percussive in origin – scrapers, shakers and tambourines – and these fulfil a rhythmic rather than a random function. The hierarchy of instruments in the mix is also conventionally rockist.

In the second section, things improve. Porter's bass, all but inaudible for most of the album thus far but here a little further forward in the mix, bounces between the chords like a rugby ball out of control between the twenty-two-metre lines, while

105

Manzanera's obsessive ostinati and Ferry's throwaway strumming of the piano dodge in and out of the foreground. There's much less organization here and the effect, rather reminiscent of the first two albums, is that the microphones are roaming the studio and briefly highlighting players making their own way around the harmonies. There are fewer chances being taken, however, with everyone staying within the harmonic territories dictated by the song. Everything is very tonal.

The texture of the song gradually decays to the point where Ferry is left singing the refrain a cappella.

Ferry's lyrics for the track are full of fun: wholly blasé, he drawls that time-wasting at parties is his way of life, along with throwaway speculations on life and on throwaway girls.

It would be mawkish if not sung in a vibrato-laden teenybop parody over such a casually deranged vamp. Ferry masterfully describes the internalization of sexual desire, conceiving the love object as a 'mother-of-pearl', 'very Holy Grail'; 'even Zarathustra', emotes his intoxicated brainiac, 'could believe in you'. 'Every goddess a let-down, every idol a bring down...' This lover knows his Nietzsche.

The song is indeed a masterpiece of satire and meta-levels. Is Ferry the lover? Or is he merely assuming the *role* of the lover? 'Canadian Club' and the 'places in the country' – the nods to privilege *could* be him, but he's not letting on, mocking his listeners and critics as much as the beloved in the song.

The rest of the album varies in quality. 'Just Like You', directly inspired by the classic pop material Ferry had been working with on his solo album, is lacklustre and sounds too obviously like an abortive sketch of the later track 'A Really Good Time', without the developmental or textural sophistication. 'Sunset' also has its echoes within the Roxy Music canon, being a windswept and haunting evocation of loneliness that long outstays its welcome, only the interesting falling piano counter-melody appearing from nowhere in the heart of the song being of the remotest interest. 'Serenade' is merely pleasant filler.

'Amazona' also suggested that Ferry's sudden taste for collaboration (possibly occasioned by lack of time – his solo album was in gestation at the same time as *Stranded*) would bear rich fruit. This time he co-wrote with guitarist Manzanera, and the result is, like 'A Song for Europe', first class. It is perhaps a little wanting in individuality, but it is powerful and well constructed. Typically chorusless, the syncopated, jerky, reggae-styled backbeat and choppy rhythm guitar underpin short verses and interpolated variants before crashing into a lengthy middle section which is grandiloquently and imaginatively arranged. Falling guitar figures counterpoint a variant of the verse melody, gradually accumulating upper lines until the whole transmogrifies into an impassioned and speedy guitar solo. The 'false' ending of the song (a brief return to the verse-variant pattern, with Ferry's voice heavily and disorientatingly synthesized through a voicebox) is particularly appealing. Although he is given more conventional lines to play, Manzanera makes the most of them, reproducing the biting and bittersweet tone of earlier albums and adding to it a great and distinct lyrical facility.

'Psalm' might take the prize for the oddest Roxy Music track of all, given that its Christian sentiments seem, as Johnny Rogan points out, to be quite unironic – given the stylistic and syntactical similarities between Ferry's avowals of faith and his language of romantic idealization. A male-voice choir (often drafted in for real during live shows) and cod pipe-organ hint at coarse parody, but Ferry, it would appear, is serious enough here, suggesting a feel and sensitivity for contemporary lyrical and textural method in God rock rarely, if ever, heard elsewhere.

It might also be suggested, however, that Ferry, as usual, was writing about the *idea* of faith rather than about the experience of it. As ever, an abiding sense of ironic distance pervades, implying that the song is about religious belief as an analogue of belief in abstracts of love, beauty and perfection, not to mention a meditation on the absolution sought within the church by many creative artists.

As Ferry has said:

'It's strange how the most degenerate kind of characters can flirt with religion like that. What's always interested me is the gradual process of a lot of poets and the phrases they go through. Like intense love poetry, over twenty years or so it becomes stronger and stronger, and more introspective, until it reaches this amazing religious intensity...John Donne, for instance.'[9]

No matter; the public cult of Roxy Music was as well supported as ever. The press went overboard. Iain MacDonald, no fool, effused in the *New Musical Express* that *Stranded* was 'magnum opus time...a classic, the album Roxy have been aiming at for two years'.[10]

The fans were similarly impressed; *Stranded* was the band's first No. 1 LP in the British charts, and 'Street Life' was a third successive Top Ten single, the band appearing on the five-hundredth edition of *Top of the Pops* to help promote it.

Even in 1981 Ferry could admit that *Stranded* was his favourite Roxy album, possibly owing to its proximity to a definitive point in his own development as a musician – that is, his first solo album. 'People will always see the main reason why it is so different is that Eno left,' he said at the time, 'and that's a reason but it's not the most important one to me.'[11]

The cover and its attendant publicity did the record no harm at all. The Roxy Music cover girl, an object of some fascination since Ferry's well-publicized dalliance with Amanda Lear, was this time more scantily clad than ever. On the cover of *Stranded* she is prone in a posture of either fevered vulnerability or breathless post-ravishment (where does that perspirant glaze come from, the jungle canopy or rumbustious sex?), the ruched red dress torn here and there, the mahogany mane spilled over the pillow of undergrowth.

The objectification of women, always a central theme to

Roxy's thought processes, had begun as a typically ambiguous affair. In 1972, the use of Kari-Ann Moller's body could be read as either cynical 1970s marketing ploy or acute satire on cynical 1950s marketing ploys – a commentary on cheesecake. The fact that Roxy Music girls – in this case, ex-Playmate of the Year Marilyn Cole, wife of Victor Lownes and sometime lover of Hugh Hefner – all ended up sharing Ferry's bed only enhanced the image of the singer as a cold, unfeeling manipulator of femininity. Roxy Music, who had always evoked (but not yet lived) suggestions of the cruelty and impurity lurking as the flipside of luxury and beauty (especially when materially embodied), now seemed to be exponents of just such a blasé exploitation of human bodies and minds.

Tony Palmer, in a vein of exasperated admonishment rather than judgemental condemnation, called Ferry 'the sexist heir in the Seventies to Mick Jagger'. Ferry found this statement more amusing than annoying, in public at least. Palmer, for all his dyspeptic snarling about popular music's love affair with theatricality ('a baubled sewer'[12]) was a supporter of Roxy Music, writing that 'the golden age of rock'n'roll is looked upon with affection. Now it can be seen for what it really was; shoddy, misbegotten and ugly... only Roxy Music seem to have caught the seediness accurately.'[13]

Sexism, of course, was a commonplace in 1970s rock, women's place in the genre being very much as it had been in Stokely Carmichael's view of black liberation – 'horizontal, baby'. Rock was the only area of 1970s popular culture in which nipples could be found – outside the *Sun*, lowbrow British movies and the sex industry, anyway.

Ferry could say without fear of contradiction or even questioning:

'I don't think I'd get on very well with [women's libbers] at all. I'm probably more interested in domination. I don't really know what I think about Women's Lib in general. I do hate all these characters who detest beauty competitions, and [the cover of *Stranded*]...will be dreadful for them. I think it's marvellous, and the girls love it, don't they? They love to show off, and basically you've got to do what you do best, I think...if you aren't very intelligent or intellectual or whatever, but can look fantastic then it's great that you should promote that as much as possible.'[14]

Even Michael Watts, the interviewer, was forced to raise an objecting palm; didn't women resent being considered intrinsically stupid and decorative? 'Some girls don't,' Ferry assured him breezily. 'But I don't believe anybody's a total dummy. I mean, some girls who are unintellectual to talk to can be very interesting to talk to, as interesting as very highbrow people.'[15] (In 1975, he told Caroline Coon, 'If you buy a woman you can control her without commitment. Prostitution has always seemed like quite a sensible thing to me.'[16])

Ferry found no fault in such neolithic attitudes, not least because in 1973 they effectively constituted mainstream sexual discourse, mouthed by poets, peons and publicans alike. *Stranded*'s cover, and Cole's prehensile sensuality, like that of Moller and Lear before her, was the object of far greater admiration than antipathy.

Roxy Music engineered an escapism around themselves, and their artistic syntax, 'particularly in its relation to sex and sexuality, the extravagant decadence which oozed from every measure of the music, kept a lot of people happy. This was arguably mostly thanks to its lascivious titillation of a mal-formed appetite for sexual transgression in a dun-coloured 1970s society still trying to come to terms with the immediate past, let alone the present.

The Roxy Music autumn 1973 tour would trail its gladrags through townscapes of hostility. Strikes in public services were on the rise and power cuts had bedevilled live entertainment in particular for over a year. An entire weekend in late 1972 witnessed gigs blacked out throughout the UK; only bands with the prescience to hire portable generators, such as the Dutch band Focus, escaped the exigencies.

Roxy Music, fortunately, avoided the harshest weeks and did themselves nothing but good while mere mortals brushed their teeth in the dark. In autumn 1973, for example, their eighteen-date tour (while hard travellers, they never did believe in long itineraries of any one territory) attracted massive media interest – mostly due to the gullibility of rock hacks, who had swallowed the band's mythology and were expecting the gig of all gigs. For the record, this tour called at Bath (14 October), Leeds (19 October), Birmingham (21 October), Sheffield (22 October), Bradford (23 October), Liverpool (26 October), Nottingham (27 October), Manchester (28 October), Leicester (30 October), Glasgow (2 November), Edinburgh (3 November), Newcastle (4 November), Bristol (5 November), Bournemouth (6 November), Swansea (8 November), London Rainbow Theatre (10, 11 and 12 November). The set was timed to last precisely seventy-seven minutes per night.

'Surely Roxy Music and room service sandwiches are incompatible concepts. Naïvely, I'd been expecting champagne, banquets, slinky ladies with long, long legs...' complained one reviewer.[17] Roxy Music, of course, had always been about surfaces (a concept that seemed to escape most journalists of the time) and while pricily insisting on the best hotels for the artists, their friends and the road crew, they existed in the same red-eyed inter-gig limbo of chilly rehearsals and irritation as any road-bound band. The Bristol gig was cancelled after a risible dispute with Top Rank, who broke no fewer than five contract clauses in setting up the concert.

Indulgences and star behaviour were, however, rare commodities in the Roxy Music camp. Pete Sinfield remembers, 'The most I ever saw Phil and Andy get up to, for example, wasn't very much. When we had some spare time we'd smoke a little dope, perhaps, and then come back to my flat and play charades. Rock and roll, eh?'[18] In Belgium, one promoter threw up his hands in horror when the band arrived: 'But they look like accountants!'

'It was very civilized on tour,' bassist John Gustafson recalls. 'Andy and Bryan would go off for a meal after a gig. I don't remember too many jolly japes. I remember some of the guys completely blocked my hotel room door with masking tape one night, but that was about the extent of our rock and roll debauchery.'[19]

Celebrity friends were conspicuous by their absence. Gays were noticeable in their attentions, but then so were straights. The hacks gave up. What they did note, however, was that in spite of (or maybe because of) their lack of road experience (they had been touring for only a little over a year), Roxy Music were surprisingly reachable, and fans often overreacted to their generosity. One hotel chain banned them from entering their portals again, not because of anything the band or its entourage had done, but rather because of Roxymaniac unruliness on the premises. Phil Manzanera had cause to understand when he failed to outrun a group of fans in Glasgow and fell into hotel reception with a sprained ankle, which caused him to hobble through the tour on sticks and play at least one gig sitting on a stool.

Island's then marketing director, Phil Cooper, recalls one particularly illuminating incident. In spring 1973 in Leeds, Ferry had asked him to conduct an experiment just before the band boarded the tour bus on their way elsewhere. He asked Cooper to follow him through the town centre on foot, fifteen paces behind, and count how many people showed recognition of the singer of Roxy Music. 'There was twelve people in total who recognized Bryan, which out of 400 or so wasn't all that many,' says Cooper. Later that year, Ferry asked Cooper to repeat the experiment: 'I lost count after the first three seconds.'[20]

There seems little doubt that Roxy Music were, as yet, a giving band – the cancelled Bristol date was replaced by one repeat concert in Bath (16 December) and in Bristol itself (18 December). By now their fans were causing almost as much of a national furore as the band themselves. Bowie boys and girls were yesterday's news, Roxymaniacs were today's. But what Richard Williams had called an 'élite corps...a supporters' club' in late 1971 at the 100 Club was now a swelling battalion. The *NME* began to review the audience rather than the gigs, a process that would reach its acme during the *Country Life* tour a year hence, musing on floppy-fringed boys and 'eager girls wearing...hip-hugging skirts and anything at all made out of fake leopard skin'.[21]

The average Roxy fan, someone calculated, was 'eighteen years old and numbered David Bowie and Lou Reed as secondary, sometimes primary influences'.[22]

For Andy Mackay, 'The audiences certainly did invent a look [sic]...it seemed to come from nowhere, very quickly and spontaneously. I suppose that Amanda Lear had a kind of glam look on the cover of *For Your Pleasure*; but these girls were turning up in mesh veils and Forties shoes.'[23]

Roxy Music, the *NME* would soon be noting, 'were the only band worth dressing up to see'.[24]

ROXY MUSIC LIVE – AFTER ENO

Contemporary live footage of the band actually shows a distinct absence of Roxyites in the audience, which appears to be a largely conventional Progressive rock crowd of beardies and bad-hairs, with the odd dolly bird getting down alongside the tank-topped musos drumming and saxing their imaginary drums and saxes. The column inches devoted to Roxymaniacs were gentle and benignly bewildered in tone, but still sprang from a critical unease at the celebration of artifice and ephemerality. As Rogan points out, 'What was even more alarming was that most of the kids...were far more interested in imitating their heroes' style than creating their own musical scene.'[25]

Live, Roxy Music had become well drilled and polished, yet were as gutsy and invigorating as ever. Individual voices were becoming stronger and clearer also, and not just because of the sudden clarity of textural architecture which Eno's departure brought to the sound. Mackay, who would hitherto have owed just a little too much to free-jazz luminaries like John Coltrane, Ornette Coleman or Rahsaan Roland Kirk (busily torrential and gruffly unyielding of tone), became his own man. By the same token, Manzanera's extemporizing palette is obviously less Hendrix-hued. Most impressively of all, both Manzanera and Mackay had by this stage stopped trying too hard to please. Thompson continued to impress; his fills and paradiddles are never obtrusive but ever more propulsive. There were few drummers at this time capable of decorating a flat 4/4 more tastefully or powerfully.

Visually, the shows were becoming more elaborate, but were still incomparable to the Barnum and Bailey spectaculars perpetrated by big-leaguers like Emerson, Lake and Palmer and Alice Cooper. A Gothic archway stood over the stage, embellished with some palm trees for the *Stranded* tour, when Ferry would appear to a seething barrage of jungle noises.

But perhaps the most striking feast for the eye was Ferry himself, or, more specifically, his stunning new white tuxedo. Its initial import in autumn 1973 was to highlight Ferry (literally) as frontman, to define his role. Attempts to further emphasize his pre-eminence by including selections from his forthcoming solo album, *These Foolish Things*, were sat on by the rest of the band, although excerpts from the album were played over the PA as otherwise incidental music during entrances and exits.

Much as the musical gestation of that album had influenced the music of *Stranded*, so Ferry's associative visual conception of himself as a performer of such classic songs as 'These Foolish Things' influenced his persona as Roxy Music's leader. Ferry, a born role-player, had found a new niche, and would cling to it with unusual fervour.

Certainly his tuxedo became an obsessively worn sartorial constant in a band noted for its quick-change playfulness. In effect, it became Ferry's signature, his trademark; it would both imprint him indelibly upon popular cultural memory and distance him from that culture's most vital and creative currents. Its ability to make him look ridiculous began early, however – for example in Edinburgh, when he insisted on appearing on-stage wearing it above a kilt.

It is without doubt the defining Bryan Ferry image and one of the foremost visual signifiers of rock culture – akin to a heraldic emblem, containing all the suspended memories with which Roxy Music worked in the ether of culture and recall. It is like a Rorschach blot, containing any number of references to privilege, dissolution, isolation that one wants to see, like Rick in his Casablanca bar, the lone sexual voyager, the gigolo and his musical analogue, the balladeer. Ferry, spectral in white, becomes the ghost of crooners past. According to Ferry, 'Antony, like me, liked uniforms very much, [of which] the tuxedo was a sort.' To Ferry and Price it was a livery of sophistication, 'very MOR, very Sinatra-ish'.[26] Price has observed that in its way, the tuxedo enabled Ferry to become to Price what Madonna became to Jean Paul Gautier.[27]

For his part, Price perceived exactly what the tuxedo meant for Ferry himself. 'People began to realize who he was and what he did.' The tuxedo became an insignia, 'like Madonna's cone tits. The white tuxedo was what did it for Bryan. That'll be the image on his gravestone.'[28]

THESE FOOLISH THINGS

It's fair to assume that *These Foolish Things*, then, was an instrumental album in the Roxy Music canon, of which Ferry went so far as to say, 'I consider [it] to be the third Roxy album in a way due to the influence it had on my writing; I made a very conscious attempt to compose conventional but very strong, classy songs.'[29]

To Ferry the idea of recording pop 'standards' seemed logical enough, although an album of 'standards' in the rock climate of 1973 was variously regarded as novel, outlandish or a capital offence of scarcely imaginable sacrilege. Ferry, of course, had a grasp of popular music sensibility broader than most of his contemporaries, and regarded the relationship of contemporary rock music to show business as far more intimate than most people cared to imagine. In Simon Frith's words, the vanguard rock audience of the 1970s may have sneered 'at disco and the mindless pop of teenage culture may have changed their pin-ups for LP sleeves and their dancing shoes for headphones, but their music arrives on the turntable as the result of the same commercial processes'.[30]

Once again *These Foolish Things* brought Ferry into conflict with existing rock ideology. This held not only that the music-maker's individual inspiration was paramount but also that he or she had the sovereign right to be sole 'proper' interpreter of his or her work. Authorship rights bestowed interpretation rights. 'Nobody sings Dylan like Dylan' became the rule, and a freak hit like Joe Cocker's 'With a Little Help from My Friends' the exception to it. The original, the authentic, was always the best, which was a neat ideological way of glossing the realities of rock's relationship with the pop production process. As rock became more obsessed with notions of high art, with producing singular, unique and unreplicable master-pieces (thereby demeaning the commercial techniques of pop), it became important to regard an artist's work as something unique, not a commodity to be touted around and haggled over. As Ferry said, 'Where you once had two clearly defined categories – singers and songwriters – you now have a situation where all the performers have to be songwriters as well and sometimes it doesn't work very well which entails a decline in the art of songwriting.'[31]

As Rogan has perceptively written, the decline in 'standards' in the record marketplace did not just have its origins in the Beatles/Dylan-led auteurist revolution in pop. Rock and roll was also culpable. By positing itself as a commercial force against the established vocal stars of the 1950s, it had to develop its own repertoire, which by definition excluded the music of its consumers' parents. As the record industry fell hopelessly in love with adolescence, standards became restricted to the burgeoning middle-of-the-road market, while rock and pop developed its own hormonally overloaded musical syntax. The music of Bill Haley and Gene Vincent and Carl Perkins had to be seen to be 'happening', to be 'today'. What was the use of their reworking songs like 'Stella by Starlight' or 'Night and Day'?

Ferry's reading of this situation was to appropriate the principle but not the practice of standards singers. He had no intention of releasing a *Ferry on Broadway* or a *Jerome Kern – Ferry Style!* Too obvious, too predictable. His was a nobler aim to apply the principle of standard interpretation to the very pop canon which had given older standards a bad name. The historical perspective was generously long, the homages stretching from the 1940s to the 1970s, but it would have been unwise to expect Ferry, the arch-archivist of pop cultural postures, not to explore the historical formation, in music and image, of the modern pop vocal icon as deeply as possible.

His ambition was, as usual, to get at the kernel of pop-cultural sensibility. One of the main characteristics about the smoother, slicker Roxy Music of *Stranded* was its gestation in the sessions of Ferry's solo album, which had preceded the album recordings. *These Foolish Things* had been recorded with a sizeable slew of sessioneers, and as Ferry has said, '[I] did all these classic songs so I thought I should perfect my song-writing technique. And that was what I was trying to do with *Stranded*.'[32]

He continued, 'I mean, I was there learning all these songs by people I'd always admired like Cole Porter, Smokey Robinson etc. and it made me want to master the art of writing a good melody.' After a beat, he added, 'I'm still trying,'[33] and enthused, 'These people in fact had a far more direct influence on me than the so-called avant-garde.'[34] Ferry's explorations into others' compositions led to some very interesting assessments of his own songwriting method, not least in one long interview with *Melody Maker*'s Michael Watts.

Ferry's relationship to the mechanics of songwriting were laid bare as never before. He admitted to admiring the lyrics of Hal David, and also the words of the Beatles and Dylan, and quite liked Paul Simon. Cole Porter was his favourite of all time. 'You don't find that sort of craftsmanship with rock musicians. I'm not trying to put down the average rock musician but they aren't literary people as a rule.'[35]

Ferry was canny enough to be aware that the great masters of the popular song lyrics used language that had 'layers, double-meanings', and aspired to such transformative creations.[36]

'That's why I try very hard,' he told Watts. 'I scratch away for hours, like an old-style lyricist, because things don't come to me very easily. I find it much easier to write sad things...'[37]

On another occasion Ferry mused:

'I like to interlace not so much humour but wit whenever possible, because it can all seem as though it's getting too heavy. There's something very English about that. There's a certain dry humour that comes out of all that blackness which is very important to me!

'I suppose I play around somewhere between pessimism and optimism. Cyril Connolly said an amazing thing about Scott Fitzgerald's work once: "His style sings of hope, his message is despair."'[38]

Fitzgerald, one of Ferry's favourite authors, conveyed to the singer a content which was 'sad and moving'. The style, on the other hand, '...has a lightness, a charm and delicacy about it. And I've always tried, I suppose, to do that myself.'[39]

Ferry denied that he wrote much outside his lyric impulse: 'I'm not a natural writer in that I don't keep a diary or have to write every day. I wish I did but I'm not disciplined enough.'[40] Upon being asked why a songwriter who took such evident pride in his abilities with words left out lyric sheets, he replied, 'I never put them in because I hate [the lyrics] to be thought of as poetry. I think it's a mistake now, but for the next album I'll probably do a lyric sheet of all the previous albums because I understand now that people just can't pick up the words with the vibrato – I tend to be very "woo woo woo!"'[41]

Ferry's vibrato was, of course, part of the Roxy Music mystique. His vocal mannerisms were, at least as far as *Stranded*, often overemphatic. When one expects a top note from Ferry it often arrives in exaggerated vibrato or in a semi-spoken form. *Sprechgesang*, while being a form which Ferry has – to this writer's knowledge – never referred to in an interview, is key to his vocal stylism, at least in Roxy Music's oeuvre. Even straightforward melodic profiles, such as that in 'Street Life', are mangled this way by this voice, adding appealingly to the foreignness – the *Ferryness* – of the sound of the band as a whole. The voice often attacks the notes from above or below. Even when Ferry is holding a tune, as he can do very well, this effect can be, and often is, mysteriously unsettling. To Michael Watts, Ferry had confessed, 'I like the idea of being a Man of a Thousand Voices but I don't think it works, because there's always a vibrato to the whole thing.'[42]

Ferry was also among the first to flaunt a convention of the form whereby it is assumed that pop singers deliver their words from one heart to another, from the singer's to the listener's, suggesting total involvement and immediacy of expression. Ferry, despite – or possibly because of – the stylization, doesn't. Indeed, parodic and camp had his hiccups and attenuated whoops become that the result sounded not unlike the 'club style' singing adopted as a running gag in the 1990s by British comedian Vic Reeves, a ghastly satire on affected pop sincerity.

To Watts, Ferry said that one of the most interesting aspects of the *These Foolish Things* undertaking was 'to inflict [sic] my style and interpretation'.[43] And what was Ferry's interpretation inflicted on? Sadly, his original plan to record an album full of extraordinary and extravagant cover versions (including a symphonic-scale 'Some Enchanted Evening') foundered on the familiar reef of lack of money and time. However, the compromise, featuring one side of Ferryized songs and another of straightforward, pristine *hommages* rendered as accurately as possible, proved an even more winning proposition.

For all Ferry's avowed indifference towards rock, he did include some songs which, if not 24-carat rock classics, were classic songs premièred by rock singers. These were the Beatles' 'You Won't See Me', Bob Dylan's 'A Hard Rain's a-Gonna Fall' and the Rolling Stones' 'Sympathy for the Devil' (the latter chosen due to Ferry's love of its lyrical dexterity and swagger). 'A Hard Rain's a-Gonna Fall' was, according to Ferry, 'like the Bible', although he would later claim that he disliked 1960s protest songs. 'It's My Party', on the other hand, was warmly apostrophized as 'a kind of tribute to the gay side. I remember I spent a lot of time in gay bars in the past [a comment that caused not a few nostrils to twitch at the time] and it was nice to see these records on their jukeboxes. They were kind of like classics for them.'[44]

The album, heard in hindsight, is an often excellent piece of work and never outstays its welcome, busy with the effort of a man determined to write his place in rock history but never, ever succumbing to the rock star meretriciousness and vanity many had predicted. The album's chief attribute is the cinemascopic variance and felicity of its arrangements, which, while often ambitious, never dazzle the memory of the songs they are supposed to be reworking, and never shade into bombast. This works best with 'Hard Rain' and the splendid rendition of 'It's My Party', but best of all on 'Sympathy for the Devil', a truly stupendous 'Loving You is Sweeter Than Ever' and a surprisingly endearing version of 'Tracks of My Tears'. Surprising largely due to the fact that Ferry's inability to hit high notes does him down in 'A Little Piece of My Heart' early on. It's a natural characteristic which robs him of much soulfulness and may have been what Mike Figgis was referring to concerning Ferry's early days as a vocal frontman. Elsewhere, as on 'A Little Piece of My Heart', arrangements mask Ferry's shortcomings, heavy bass lines and David Skinner's no-nonsense muscularity at the piano giving the song the body Ferry's voice cannot provide. This handicap, however, leads to some of Ferry's most resourceful singing – on 'The Tracks of My Tears' he wrings a performance of genuine vulnerability. The widescreen approach works less well on 'As Sweet As You Are', which merely points up the discongruency of Ferry's vocal to the line he is singing, and on the Beatles' 'You Won't See Me', where the soundstage merely seems cluttered.

When Ferry hit form, though, the album was mesmerizing. 'Don't Worry, Baby', for years the 'lost' Brian Wilson masterpiece, cannot compare with its Beach Boys original, but the bottomless depth of Ferry's soundstage confers an altogether different 'epic' quality upon the song. The effect here is less of symphonic melodrama than of almost ritualistic, public resurrection of a great artefact. There is also magic in detail; it takes only a slight liberty with the vocal counterpoint to 'Sympathy for the Devil' to turn an insistent, *dummkopf* 'woo-woo' into an interesting exercise in writing for vocal ensemble. John Porter's guitar solo on 'Don't Worry, Baby' is ham-handed but occasionally hits harmonic nirvana. The brass arrangements on 'The Tracks of My Tears' are miraculous, as is the deployment of percussion by Paul Thompson (superb throughout) on 'Sympathy for the Devil'. The stand-out piece, however, is Jackie Wilson's 'Loving You is Sweeter Than Ever', where subtle tampering with the rhythmic impulse of verse and chorus and a beautiful arrangement create a true epic which buoys Ferry's voice aloft and allows it to flex what soulful muscles it has. The song is almost worth the price of the album on its own.

The strength of *These Foolish Things* was Ferry's ability to rework songs while leaving their fundamental strengths –

121

usually harmonic, as on 'Don't Worry, Baby' and 'Loving You is Sweeter Than Ever' – quite untouched. Cover versions have rarely been executed with as much knowing craftiness and heartfelt love as on this exceptional album.

Nevertheless, once the exercise was over, Ferry stated his belief that 'it's still more important to write'.[45] Annoyingly for Ferry, though, his thunder was somewhat stolen when David Bowie released his own, radically different album of pop standards, *Pin-Ups* at the same time as *These Foolish Things*. Peeved, Ferry tried to take out an injunction to have the release date of Bowie's LP put back. The end result was that the two albums came out on the same day, 3 November 1973, and were both massive hits.

It probably piqued Ferry that not all were as sympathetic as Watts (who would turn vitriolically on him within two years). *These Foolish Things* was seen by some as unacceptably narcissistic; the very idea of Ferry even aspiring to Dylan's kingly realm seemed risible. Other manifestations of Ferry's perceived vanity were duly noted on the *Stranded* tour – subtle use of the lighting rig to highlight (literally) the tuxedo and totemize Ferry once and for all as leader of the act, not to mention the increasing theatricality and campness of Ferry's demeanour and his carriage on-stage. Was that token cigarette really necessary? That toss of the head? In short, was Bryan Ferry falling in love with the image of stardom, or perhaps stardom itself? What had once been cunning commentary now seemed to be a style lived to the hilt, less pose than praxis.

Comparison with another career-engineer, Warhol, comes into its own here. Of the American, Robert Hughes writes 'Warhol has long seemed to hanker after the immediate visibility and popularity that "real" stars such as Liz Taylor have, and sometimes he is induced to behave as though he really had it.'[46] Warhol, once the mysterious outsider whose personality and art seemed only to reflect celebrity, or satirize it through the endless repetition of Marilyns and Elvises, by 1970 seemed to want to stop playing possum and have fame of his own. Ferry's actions, as Eno faded from the scene, are redolent of this. Hughes on Warhol: 'He has difficulty moving toward that empyrean of absolute popularity where LeRoy Neiman sits, robed in sky-blue polyester. To do that, he must make himself accessible. But to be accessible is to lose magic.'[47]

Ferry, having tasted fame, seems to have pursued it, perhaps as much to know its essence as to enjoy it. He became increasingly engrossed in toying with a tissue of stardom through a repertoire of stolen or borrowed gestures, looks, inflections both visual and aural. He saw pop fame, rightly, to be part of a continuum of admass celebrity, spiralling down the years like a double helix of pop DNA through Valentino, Gable, Bogart, Sinatra, Elvis and the Beatles, and in appearing to allude to this cultic process, seemed to become ever more engrossed in playing, and then living out, the role of star. Warhol may have had no star quality with which to become a star, but Ferry had star quality as deep as Washington's coal seams. Thus he intended to live – publicly at least – as star. But in doing so, he fell into the trap suggested by Hughes – becoming accessible and famous lost him his mystique of sly punster and piss-taker. To one writer he would muse, 'With every song you play a character a bit,' before continuing:

'You take an aspect of yourself and either simplify it or ham it up. To some extent it's like method acting. In an hour and a half show you go through a lot of different moods, one right after the other, and people aren't really like that. You say to yourself, how does this song go? Oh yeah, then you get into a role for it and leave that role when the song ends. You have to be a bit more of a show-off than I am to be an actor. You really have to love yourself, and there are people who really do. I'd rather not be seen than look bad.'[48]

He had, at the age of fifteen, played Malvolio, the bumbling would-be Lothario of Shakespeare's *Twelfth Night*. Michael Bracewell has written that the character's being tricked into wearing extremely outrageous clothes in order to be ridiculed in front of the woman he loves was the exact opposite of Ferry's subsequent career.[49]

That is maybe debatable, given Ferry's romantic record through the 1970s (picaresque yes, traumatic at times, but hardly Malvolian). Ferry received a good notice in the *Sunderland Echo* for his performance, with a photograph that 'was like a quick flash of fame. I loved dressing up as someone else; it was much easier than going on-stage as yourself.'[50]

Caroline Coon, author of one of the finest-ever pieces on Ferry, wrote of his stage presence in 1975, 'His despair, dragged across the stage, could so easily become cheap melodrama. But it never does. A fraction more hamming emphasis and that wry smile would turn into the smirk of a thwarted werewolf.'[51] On visiting Ferry, she noted the preponderance of star pix on Ferry's walls – 'Monroe, Elvis, Kay Kendall'[52] – and in doing so she hinted at the double-edged sword that celebrity was for Ferry. 'He's something of a masochist, living on the knife-edge of an identity crisis.' Coon is disappointingly coy as to what it might be.[53]

She asked Ferry if he took refuge – specifically after *These Foolish Things* – in other people's songs. 'That's right,' assented Ferry, 'singing other people's songs takes a burden off me, and I learn an awful lot from doing them.' He explained his understanding of this process by using the analogy of an author taking time out to review others' works. On stage costumes, Ferry told Coon, 'I needed the disguises much more when I first started than I do now. On *Top of the Pops* last week I was wearing a suit I'd worn for days.'[54]

Coon asked, reasonably, whether the dressing up didn't betray dissatisfaction with his own personality. 'I'm always dissatisfied with everything,' replied Ferry evasively. 'On the other hand, it would sound terribly conceited to say that I was quite happy as I am.' Finally, he concluded 'I've never really wanted to be anyone else, even in my lowest moments…' None the less, Ferry added that one of his heroes was 'Howard

Hughes...I'd like to be a completely unknown figure like that, but it wouldn't work. I have to make myself available a bit.' Ferry also evinced a desire, within the same 1975 article, to be Stephen Ward...there's something to be said for the courtesan'.[55] Ferry as detached observer of the blood rituals of love and death once again.

It is maybe an exaggeration when Rogan points out that there is a recurrent motif in Ferry's lyrics of an unease with real human emotions[56] – Ferry as narrator is almost always alone, declaiming on a love gone or expected – but the detachment, the observer's or diarist's distance, is there. It is one of Ferry's strengths – as we have seen, he short-circuited the whole tediously self-confessional conventions of the rock vocalist by standing apart from what he was singing, or seeming to sing.

In one review, Allan Jones stresses the degree to which Ferry exploits the figure of the romanticized European decadent artist. Central to the development of artistic modernism, that figure – at least in unmediated, *echt* form – is none the less one unfamiliar to rock and roll. For Jones, though, it crystallizes in Ferry's artistic persona around the time of *Stranded*: 'the classic European notion of the doomed romantic celebrating the inevitability of his isolation and forever frustrated in his search for an ideal'.[57]

One American critic wrote in 1975 of Ferry, 'Like Baudelaire's dandy, he lives his entire life in front of a mirror.'[58] This is a somewhat shallow and obvious portrait of Ferry but it does revive the Europeanness of his apparent themes and thought processes.

The 'decadent' figure as identified with Ferry was a late-nineteenth-century phenomenon, the creature of what William Gaunt has termed 'the aesthetic adventure'. A refined and fragrant individual, he made a lifestyle out of the maxim 'art for art's sake'. Personified (with some degree of irony) by Wilde, immortalized and mythologized in Joris Karl Huysmans' classic novel of the dissolution and dissipation of an aesthete, *à rebours* (1884), the decadent became the first modern embodiment of self-absorption, vanity and corruption. Lining up Ferry with such a figure was too easy a chance to miss, but it is neither a groundless nor a worthless comparison. Of course, the pose of *l'art pour l'art* was central to the rock project – particularly that of Progressive rock – in the 1970s, but Ferry, as ever was keeping one step ahead. He was not *being* an aesthetician, he was *acting* being an aesthetician. For his part, Ferry countered, 'The whole decadence thing really came about through people who knew of little, silly things like the...wearing of make-up on-stage. Nobody else was doing it, I suppose.'[59]

There were other, better reasons for the Baudelaire comparisons. In *The Painter of Modern Life* (1859), the Frenchman writes, 'By "modernity" I mean the ephemeral, the contingent, the half of art whose other half is eternal and immutable.'[60] This 'painter', in Baudelaire's eyes, uses urban modernity as his *atelier*, with its 'fashions...morals... emotions...the passing moment and all the suggestions of eternity it contains'.[61] This disturbingly accurate analogue of Ferry the songwriter is doubly disturbing when one reads of those who people the world Baudelaire describes. The essay personifies Baudelaire's archetypal dandy, the painter and illustrator Constantin Guys, whom he praises for depicting modern life, in Marshall Berman's words, as 'a great fashion show, a system of dazzling appearances, brilliant façades, glittering triumphs of decoration and design'.[62]

As early as 1845 Baudelaire had complained that contemporary art paid too little heed to the 'modern' and to 'the new'. 'The true painter we're looking for,' he suggested, 'will be one who can snatch from the life of today its epic quality...next year let's hope that the true seekers may grant us the extraordinary delights of celebrating the advent of the *new!*'[63]

Ferry awkwardly evaded such issues, perhaps out of a lack of confidence in discussing their relation to his own creative mechanisms. On the issue of decadence and Europeanness he refused to be drawn: 'I suppose some of the themes I write songs about have a certain amount of sophistication to them and true decadence, whatever that is, springs from a kind of dilettante sophistication, certainly from a kind of high-income lifestyle. I never really use the word [decadence].'[64] He was wrong there, as any examination of nineteenth-century decadence and the milieu that the word in its modern form derives from shows. Many of the artistic types who made decadence fashionable in the previous century were practically destitute – Ernest Dowson (1867–1900), the Symbolist poet and aesthetic martyr being perhaps the most famous British example. (It is true, however, that decadence also had overtones of personal wealth. The aspirations of decadents usually concerned luxuriant debauchery and leisured contemplation of a distinctly imperial kind. Des Esseintes, the hero of *à rebours*, is a thoroughgoing exquisite, and is based on a real decadent, Robert de Montesquiou, who carried a gilt tortoise with him every day.) Decadence's overall elective affinity, however, was with excessive self-obsession, which, after continual reminders both expressed and otherwise that Roxy Music was 'his band' – and a solo album to boot – Ferry seemed now to personify.

Vanity, to Ferry, wasn't a vice because

'it all depends on how you use it. It can destroy people. I'm only vain in the sense that I'm unsure of myself. I'd love to be the sort of person who never looks in the mirror because they're always confident that they look great. I generally feel that I look terrible which is why I don't like cameras or being photographed.'[65]

A valiant case. But in 1974, rock discourse, as it was then constituted, could hardly have allowed these words to present the endlessly photographed Ferry as anything but a stereotype of lofty acquisitiveness. Rock hacks affected to despise conspicuous wealth, their reports dwelt voyeuristically on how he had swapped his Renault for a BMW and then for a Daimler, haunted the chauffeured and chandeliered precincts of Mayfair and Belgravia and whooped it up at Annabel's and Tramps. When asked later how he would define glamour, Ferry replied, a trifle self-consciously; 'Questions like that are inhibiting because one sees such marvellous definitions of things like style and glamour in *W* magazine – "style is a white carnation on your dinner table". I suppose I'd define glamour as the best of its kind.'[66] Or some such platitude. He was, publicly, a fan of Bonnard but also, more interestingly, of Wyndham Lewis who, by 1982, was 'the favourite of the people I collect'.[67]

The years 1973–4 witnessed a sea change in attitudes towards Ferry. Britain was too harsh a place to accommodate wealthy aestheticism, particularly Ferry's brand. Even the gay community felt the chill, with the high camp of the post-gay lib years flip-flopping to embrace the sweaty clasp of reactionary gay chic, with biker leathers and the hard-hat and hairshirt look of construction workers. Inflation peaked at 27 per cent. The oil crisis decimated industry. And 73.4 per cent of school leavers were unemployed by the dawn of 1974. Such conspicuous hardships within the formerly sunny prospects of rock's fanbase provoked a backlashing bout of breast-beating in the rock press at any signs of excessive consumption. Music criticism became social criticism, and found newer, bluer-collar ways to enjoy itself with pub rock, with hard rock, with the music of the terraces, of the chippie, of the disco, of the football special and, eventually, with Punk.

Ill-considered and wrong-headed much of these sentiments may have been, but that didn't diminish the fire levelled at the likes of Ferry. In truth his increasingly lordly attitude did him few favours. There were some eyebrows raised at apparent intellectual snobbery. His public repudiation of 'very simple people…average Joes' like 'Gary Glitter and Alvin Stardust' met with revulsion in the industry. Ferry, apparently, saw them 'trapped in images they have created for themselves'.[68] He loathed, Caroline Coon wrote, 'people who have stopped taking risks to achieve the impossible [and unspecified] dream', the unintentional irony of which last clause was lost on nobody.[69] His misgivings about and slight reserve from the world in which he moved – 'I'm not part of any café society,'[70] he protested at one point – was read as just another shameless piece of *flaneurism*, a facile nod towards Baudelaire's dictum to nineteenth-century artists, *épouser la foule* or 'embrace the masses'. Ferry just sounded ungrateful for his fame.

Not that Ferry needed to worry unduly in the first months of 1974. Following on from several more whistle-stop tours of the continent, he and his indefatigable publicist Simon Puxley flew to America for a lightning publicity blitz to prepare the ground for a renewed Roxy Music assault on the US later in the spring.

Warner Brothers, whose incompetence had been so culpable for the failure of the 1972 tour, had since dropped the band. Sadly, their successors, Atlantic, were little more accommodating. Despite having broken Led Zeppelin and (against the odds) Yes in the heartland of America, they blandly informed Ferry and Puxley that the music was 'too eclectic' if they wanted Roxy Music to succeed in the US. This was a fact that both men had found out painfully for themselves eighteen months previously, but they bravely carried on with a three-day, five-city whirlwind of canvassing the press and, more importantly, radio stations. This took in Boston, Chicago, Philadelphia and Cleveland.

Since the rock and LP revolution in the late 1960s, US independent radio had fragmented into a small cellular structure of musical ghettos, mostly catering to the hard rock or MOR markets, and, increasingly, to an anaemic hybrid of the two named AOR (Adult Oriented Rock). Acts whose music fitted none of these formats were lost to America like keys down a well. Ferry was particularly pained to see that even his solo material, which was relatively more listener-friendly, wasn't wanted either. What had seemed so clever twelve months before – a literate but easily comprehensible attempt to rework the popular tradition – still baffled stateside tastes. Ferry, the rock stations cried, was patently no rocker; MOR stations found him an upstart. Not even his even mellower new material, scheduled for LP release in the summer, won friends.

'People wanted me to go to America for this album, to work with one of the big-time American producers and to make an "American" album,' he admitted later, but to no avail.[71] The Roxy Music tour went ahead, but apart from consolidating small bridgeheads they'd made among New York's avant-garde loft set and a few gains in Detroit and Cleveland, the band seemed no nearer to acceptance in the US.

Ferry found once again that his adoration of the American Dream was scarcely reciprocated. There were pleasant diversions when the cultic and fanatical nature of his feeble support visibly shone through: for instance, in Detroit a kid called Ferry from Canada during a radio interview and told him that he took pictures of the singer to the barber's and asked for a 'Bryan Ferry'. 'I was very flattered,' said the singer.[72]

About the most memorable thing Ferry did in the US that summer was to conceive and execute one of his most striking imagistic coups. He flew the *Vogue* photographer Eric Boman out to shoot the cover of his forthcoming album, *Another Time, Another Place*, in Los Angeles, and doing so created the ultimate expression of the Roxy Music statement. On this sleeve, a languorously tuxedoed Ferry is gloweringly at large in the lavish La La Land of Beverly Hills. There he stands, fag at ease in his hand, before the limousine effulgence of shimmering and sleazy blues and greens, the pool and the aromatic lawns where the super-rich flit like wraiths in the monied haze of a Hockney print or a Helmut Newton photograph. Among their number, incidentally, is Manolo Blahnik.

It is undoubtedly eye-catching, but didn't convince everyone. 'It misses,' wrote Caroline Coon, 'that listless, aristocratic *Last Year in Marienbad* touch by a mile. José by the Pool Last Summer in Benidorm is more like it.'[73]

The American feel Ferry sought hardly makes itself known on *Another Time, Another Place.* His vocals are more to the fore, and the musicians more conventionally arrayed around him – compare the reconfiguration of Roxy Music after Eno's departure – but the album is hardly a concession to US tastes, save its somewhat lacklustre textural laziness. The fact that it was recorded in London, at Basing Street, Ramport and Island Studios (kicking off an evergreen relationship with the engineer/producer Rhett Davies), might have had something to do with this lack of stateside vibes.

Ferry enthused to one reporter about the influences of Pop Art gods Tom Wesselmann and Richard Lindner on the album. Wesselmann's (not entirely healthy) influence on Ferry will be discussed later, but as Ferry says, Lindner was 'very "In Crowd"'. I think that track conjures up a kind of image rather like his pictures – that kind of neo-Berlin kind of thing. It's the kind of thing one feels one can offer with a European intelligence.'[74]

Ferry is right about the song, at least – beginning innocently as a bracing singalong paean to black street hipness in the early 1960s, Ferry's *sprechgesang* completely subverts the imagistic suggestions of its lyrics and conjures wholly new cityscapes with them, but that may be due to the voguish use of bubblegum-styled fuzz guitars in lieu of brass battalions as background. Beyond that, Ferry's Pop Art heritage served him hardly at all – save for the use of 'spin-a-disc' as a verb on the title track.

The richness of *These Foolish Things* was replaced by a workaday rock frugality (drums, bass, keys, guitar, all present and correct), although some nice details remained, as with the sharing-out of the vocal lines ('Gotta Have Fun!') on 'The In Crowd'; John Wetton's remarkably fun fiddling; Ferry's delicate piano figurations around the chords of 'Smoke Gets in Your Eyes'; Chris Pyne's excellent and jaw-dropping trombone solo on 'Fingerpoppin'' the raunchier older sister of 'Let's Stick Together'; Davy O'List's 'In Crowd' solo, a plaintive (yet unconvincing) reminder to Roxy Music of what they'd missed; the restless, unannounced movement into new and darker harmonic language of '(What a) Wonderful World' and 'Help Me Make It Through the Night'; the hard-bitten deep brass accompaniment to 'Walk a Mile in My Shoes' and the incongruous pairing of bluegrass picking guitar and trombone on the otherwise hideously overextended 'You Are My Sunshine' (the song's maudlin atmosphere was, presumably, intended as an ironic joke, but all jokes wear thin after five or so minutes).

Ferry, however, was clearly intent on getting down to the nuts and bolts of what made a pop song popular. He often retains the architecture of the songs he treats – intro, verse, chorus – and applies less of his own instrumental and vocal colour. String and brass arrangements are all too often ubiquitous, all too often just too 1974. The guitar solo from the otherwise show-stoppingly sensitive rendition of 'Funny How Time Slips Away' is too white, too florid, lacking the acerbic Steve Cropper economy the song demands.

However, Ferry, who finally indulges himself by including his long title track at the very end of the LP (it's a well-crafted, slightly overblown potted summary of Roxy Music cast-offs), is on peak vocal form. His louche, Leslie Phillips-inflected smarm into the opening lines of 'Funny How Time Slips Away' is the work of a vocalist fully cognizant of a well-developed mastery of his art.

The album did little to dispel an image of Ferry as increasingly self-referential and self-serving. Whether Ferry cared or not is debatable; his actions in that summer of 1974 to promote both the album and the singles taken from it (thankfully two of the stronger tracks, 'Smoke Gets in Your Eyes' and 'The In Crowd') displayed either a total disregard for accepted rock and pop practice or were meant purely to annoy a media who, he imagined, had turned on him.

For a start, he appeared on BBC's *Twiggy* show in July, duetting on 'What a Wonderful World', which, if not sufficiently mortifying to Roxy diehards, was sung in cartoon school uniform across a 'classroom' set. Within a week he was appearing on ITV with Cilla Black, this time giving the blue-rinses a rendition of 'These Foolish Things'.

Whether Ferry intended this *kitschfest* or had simply risen above critical mores is uncertain. Indifference to press opinion seemed, to most people, highly unlikely. But by the time Roxy Music returned to the British stage in autumn 1974 Ferry was dangerously near laughing-stock status in some quarters. Editors would not excise verbal *faux-pas* from his interviews ('I see everything *visually,' Melody Maker*)[75] and missed few opportunities for fun and games with Ferry's image. The *NME*, perplexed at Ferry's increasing sensitivity about reaction to his public persona, would not, as a point of editorial policy, refer to him by his real name in any headlines or straplines. He was forever Byron Ferrari, Brain Fury, Biriani Ferreti; whatever weapon came to hand was deployed.

Ferry once said, 'An entertainer cares more about the audience than the work he's doing and the reverse is true of an artist' – a theory which he expounded in 1982 but had always held, and one which cut little ice with critics in 1974.[76]

COUNTRY LIFE

By September the patience of Ferry's critics was wearing visibly thin, and the ridicule that greeted Ferry's return to Roxy Music with a UK tour was probably as much prompted by his perceived conceit as an objective judgement on what he was wearing when he first emerged on-stage.

Antony Price's newest creation for Ferry was, to put it mildly, refined. It was a loose-fitting passion-on-the-pampas quasi-gaucho ensemble, a bad dream of a Valentino cast-off, complete with hat on a silk chinstrap. The main talking point was whether the trousers or the shirt attracted the more derision. The insouciance of both led Nick Kent to comment,

'It really is the art of the gaucho taken several degrees beyond camp.'[77] The tuxedo had been as striking, but had been such a perfect complement to the Ferry discourse that comment had been restricted to unanimously admiring acknowledgement of a stroke of genius and an awareness of the meta-messages his imagistic manipulation was sending out. This time, however, dirtier adjectives and metaphors surged forth. Ferry attempted to rebut the criticisms with his usual keywords, 'romantic', 'swashbuckling', 'Valentino', 'Hollywood', but this was a record most critics wanted changed. A palpably amazed Kent, previously the most loyal of stalwart supporters, continued:

> 'You couldn't imagine him whipping and larruping the steers clean across the brazos in those velveteen pantaloons, and anyway... Paul Revere and the Raiders, Sam the Sham and the Pharaohs, Dave Dee, Dozy, Beaky, Mick and Tich have all made complete klutzes of themselves trooping around like extras from *Blood And Sand* at one time in their careers and they're all ugly varmints anyway so they only did it for larfs.'[78]

He summarized Ferry, with acidic accuracy, as 'the George Lazenby of the Argentinian corned-beef market'.[79]

Ferry went on the offensive. 'The gaucho thing was blowsy, romantic, it fitted the image,' he blustered.[80] Price had come up with it for him some six months previously, he said, which merely made onlookers wonder if it had taken Ferry six months to summon up courage to wear it. It was a look that was 'got' only by 'connoisseurs', he bridled.[81]

No matter; suddenly it was open season on those connoisseurs and all of Ferry's collaborators. From amused analysis the previous year, the hacks opened up on the Roxymaniacs as the band returned to the British stage in autumn 1974. Roy Carr, in the *NME*, wrote of 'flat-chested *femmes fatales* and their frail skinny-hipped chaperons, heavy-booted waterfront B-girls with scarlet slashes for mouths and pug-nosed palookas for protectors, sixth-formers fresh from raiding their grandma's wardrobe and fresh-faced fops in white ties and tails'.[82]

Charles Shaar Murray, in the same issue, was unrelentingly savage throughout his very Bangsian piece of crudely reductionist whingeing. 'Everyone looks like apprentice hairdressers,' another writer carped.[83] Even the other members of the band didn't escape the spray of bile; Manzanera's stage costume, the NME wrote, turned him into 'Victor Mature playing Antonio des Mortes'.[84]

In the furore Price's other première, of a militaristic insignia, breeches and boots set, was relatively overlooked. In the years before Rock Against Racism shook the music world into confronting its own dangerous experiments with irony and Nazism, there seemed little harm in this – it was less ridiculous than the gaucho-drag look, even if, in the words of one writer, it made Ferry look like a 'Spanish traffic warden'.[85]

Neither was much said about the (somewhat clever) use of an 'RM' emblem being sewn on the arm of Ferry's shirt or emblazoned in gold on a massive curtain behind the new stage set. The use of a gold eagle with a thirty-foot wingspan which climaxed the set by swooping over the heads of the audience across the hall was ignored. Comparisons with Bowie, whose increasingly psychotic obsession with the inter-war amorality of post-Wilhelmine decadence and its relationship to the expression of authoritarian identity, were obvious, although not taken up (Ferry later accused Bowie, playfully, of 'stealing' from him. This wasn't strictly true, and Bowie, earlier the following year and with apparent sincerity, told the press that Roxy Music were 'the only band worth seeing').[86]

As regards political overtones concerning the uniform chic, Ferry's penchant for playful irony probably got him off the hook. In the mid-1970s Bowie's very public living-out of his Nietzschean philosophy of the beauty of cruelty and authority and Ferry's history of artifice and ultra-ironic subversion, meant that few people could take Roxy Music's militaristic images as serious expressions of an abstract idea. Moreover they didn't, unlike Bowie, give Fascist salutes on returning to London railway stations. They had a residual sense of humour. Additionally, as has been pointed out, Ferry's uniform is one of considerable subtlety – add a monocle and he becomes a Third Reich Gauleiter, add mirror shades and he becomes a US motorcycle-cop.

To Ferry's credit, he counterattacked by informing the world (specifically, the *NME*'s Max Bell) that the gaucho costume had been a direct reaction against the tuxedo, which he 'could have worn until it died the death, but I always wanted to change the image'.[87] He had been conscious of the effect it had been having on his profile, even if he hadn't cared much what the rock comics thought.

Sadly, it was too late to expunge the memory of the white tuxedo, the afterimage of which hung forever around Ferry's shoulders and burned itself like a dazzle-spot on to the public's retinas. Ferry had, it seems, genuinely wanted to reinvent himself, but now not only was it too late to do so but he also courted a complete loss of dignity in the attempt.

The best counterblast of all was the *Country Life* LP, which followed the tour, somewhat overdue, in November 1974. Despite rumours that EG boss Mark Fenwick had had to stand over Ferry at his desk all night watching him write material for the new LP (another legend suggests that Fenwick forced Ferry to buy a new house so expensive that the mortgage repayments meant Ferry had to deliver on time to keep up with them), the new material was greeted with surprise by a wrong-footed press.

Ferry promoted the album warily, and wasn't above utterances of genuine fatuity, such as explaining that the reason the album sleeve wasn't a gatefold was 'our gesture for ecology'[88] (this from a man who, on the *Stranded* tour, had packed a stage with fresh palm trees night after night).

More people read the cover of *Country Life* as dirty-minded than green-minded. Little space need be given over here to describing the now-infamous picture of Evaline and Konstanze – respectively, the girlfriend and cousin of the guitarist Michael Karoli, of German band Can – caught in the flashlight amidst the Portuguese palm fronds. Suffice to say that the position of the former's middle fingers and the latter's hands were enough to ensure that in the USA the album had to be sold under green polythene, in Canada with a rather fetching shot of the vegetation around the girls and in Germany – most effectively – with a close-up of Evaline's face.

Ferry and Price had met the two girls in a bar in the Algarve in Portugal. Ferry was on a working holiday, sketching lyrics for the new album and throwing ideas around about the likely cover artwork.

Price recalled:

'These two Valkyries walked in. That's the only way to describe them. Konstanze and Evaline...I remember we went on boat rides, sailing through these sea caves, and Konstanze, the one on the right, with her massive shoulders, was sitting in the front of the boat, she just looked like a figurehead on this boat...I was stoned off my tits! She was an incredible creature.

For the shot, we lined them up against this hedge...in complete darkness. I was assisting – what was I doing? Well, there wasn't much going on in the clothes department. I was holding an OMO box which we used to get the focus on the cameras right in the dark.'[89]

Ferry's intention with *Country Life* as a visual concept had been to gently lambast the propriety of the English magazine of the same name. Here were two girls in the countryside, yet hardly the hale-faced Henriettas, jodhpured Jemimas or swishly tailored English roses of that magazine's debby pages – these girls were obviously foreign, practically naked, with Cruella de Vil eyeshadow and bloody fingernails. But Roxy Music being Roxy Music, darker and subtler affinities were also hinted at. There were counterpoints of backstairs nookie, clandestine blue-blood gang-bangs, weekends of alfresco hanky-panky, costly call girls, the exercising of high-income licence and licentiousness. The band hinted publicly at a suggested impression of a latter-day Profumo scandal with dark nameless girls in the undergrowth, paparazzi discoveries, men in masks. Roxy Music were intensifying the sexuality of their concept like the slow arousal of an aristocrat's tackle.

Musically, however, the album shows a distinct cooling in the band's energy levels, although the whole hangs together well around some moments of exquisite inspiration and reckless energy, and benefits from sensitive pacing. The sound has been clarified slightly, with Gustafson's bass less treacly than on *Stranded*; his lines are more gymnastic, more lyrical, adventurous around upper registers, as were the lamented Simpson's on the first album.

The album can best be approached as two collections, one of up-tempo and one of slower numbers. This dichotomy is in itself enough to suggest a greater accommodation of the more commercial dictates of pop production. But there is much to enjoy in both fast and slow numbers. The opener, 'The Thrill of It All', is another high-voltage overture. Despite the suspicion of rather cheesy string-sweetening beneath the jagged and metallic surface, with simultaneous rilling runs of darting instrumental solo work, it has enough acidity and discord to match the best of the past. Its white soul refrain owes much to Ferry's two solo albums, a consonant singalong which is almost bubblegum in its conception. Mackay's grating, hurting sax mutters away in the contrasting middle sections.

For all its levity and energy, the song is a dark affair. As Allan Jones writes, '"The Thrill of It All" evokes Pynchon's SS *Anubis* and its band of time-locked celebrants wandering a wrecked Europe in *Gravity's Rainbow*,'[90] a ship of fools, or maybe, to use a cinematic analogy, the cast of the MGM movie *Between Two Worlds* (1944), where the dead of the Second

World War sail to the afterlife on a ghostly ocean liner.

'All I Want is You' is a little too contrived and hybridized to work as well as its irresistible melody and bootboy bassline suggest it should. It sounds like a revised early draft of 'Editions of You' and the galloping tom-tom rhythms and screech-owl guitar cacophony in the middle eight are a little too redolent of 'Ladytron'. The song, however, remains one of Roxy Music's best attempts to date at chorus and verse structures.

Country Life is without doubt Manzanera's album. His choice of timbre is always impeccable, never excessively granitic or unyielding, and with always a few delicious, piercingly pure notes among the tumbling gravel of the rest. He is in prime form on 'Casanova', laying down imperious lines at will, paying only lip service to the chords and thoroughly muddying an otherwise ordinary song with playing that is simultaneously both tuneful and sensitive though timbrally storm-laden and, at times, downright filthy to hear. 'I was always a terrible session player,' is Manzanera's précis of his own style. 'I could never learn a solo and I stuck that "not quite right" approach on to Roxy.'[91]

The fade-in of 'Out of the Blue' almost treads on the departing tails of 'All I Want is You', heightening the clever musical suggestion that this is in fact the reintroduction of a piece left aside from hitherto. The key is edgy (not unrelated to that of 'In Every Dream Home a Heartache') and the grim automatism of the instrumental textures is that of the glinting metal of death machines. The notion of connectivity is enhanced by the similarity of the melody to 'All I Want is You', which diminishes the song's identity. Similarly, Gustafson's bravura solo bass passages and the frantic instrumental ensembles are often forced, sounding too like rock's contemporary fad of attempting to emulate the jazz-rock fusion of Return to Forever and the Mahavishnu Orchestra. Jobson's violin solo, with Mackay's oboe in pursuit, is melodramatic and not a little exciting, but there's a sense that, among the sound and fury, the band are trying a little too hard.

These are familiar effects, but executed with too much super-charged panache – the band were still aware of whispers that Eno's departure had robbed them of spontaneity, danger and discord and, on 'Out of the Blue', seem to be going all out to try and sound off-the-wall to counter such slander.

'Prairie Rose', the closer, is the last of the up-tempo numbers and sees a worryingly predictable groove develop. It's workaday, though nimble and rambunctious enough to avoid the adjective 'plodding'. Mackay's saxophone provides enough vitality, and there is something of the old *Pointilliste* Roxy Music chaos in the instrumental backdrop to Manzanera's solo. This, incidentally, is another raging and shirtless affair which rounds off his best contribution yet to the band's oeuvre and obviously whetted many appetites for the guitarist's solo album, which was by now reputed to be in the works. In retrospect, though, the song loses a little for having overt similarities, especially in the melodic line, to the much more ferocious 'Whirlwind' from 1975's *Siren* (see below).

The slower affairs often provide the more interesting music and the more opaque and thoughtful arrangements, which here far outstrip in purity of tone and imagination those of *Stranded*.

'Three and Nine', more mid-tempo than slowie, based on a disused Mackay melody titled 'Roman Blue Eyes', is a nightmarishly askew take on teenbeat angst, highly chromatic and with some of the strangest progressions and resolutions the band had yet used. Jobson's keyboards, though filling predictable areas of the soundstage, are baldly and unsettlingly plaintive. Mackay's saxophone is emotionally harrowing; Ferry's harmonica-playing sounds thoroughly surreal, so incongruous does it seem to the ear.

'Bitter-Sweet' is, like 'Sea Breezes', a calculated homage to Brecht and Weill. This time the tricks are performed with greater discipline in terms of melody, arrangement and lyrics. Piano, mellotron strings and deep percussion dominate the early measures, but there is an overwhelming sense of fastidiousness and through composition, a sense that everything has been exquisitely prearranged as it might have been for the Berliner Ensemble, an effect which Manzanera's manic attack on the lower strings half-way through the second chorus does little to dispel. None the less, it's an impressive track, although the homage is taken a little far when Ferry growls his way through a Germanicized rendition of the chorus. Mackay's short oboe cadenza over Jobson's mellotron, played a little distance from the mike, is sublime.

'A Really Good Time' is more vintage Roxy Music, characterized by finesse of arrangement and off-centre textures and rhythms. It's introduced by sickly, out-of-tune string figures and Mackay's mournful, out-of-sorts saxophone; it's jolted into a rhythmically complex, beautifully arranged Ferry paean to yet another elusive beauty. Jobson's electronics, particularly the glittering synthesizer arpeggios he spins and which descend over the music like fireworks just contrary to the beat, add a nice ambiguity and unpredictability to the beat and the rhythmic emphases.

One pleasant track which never made it on to the album was Paul Thompson's compositional debut, the cutely titled 'Your Application's Failed'. Little more than fluff, it is still well-made fluff. It consists of little more than a phrase which one can imagine Thompson might have whistled in the studio at some stage and it is prettily decked out by the band to greater and lesser degrees of seriousness. It could almost be a birthday present for the drummer, but real effort has gone into the arrangement, more interesting than many on *Country Life*, and Manzanera is in magisterial form in the higher registers.

Among the reviewers, the individual performances – particularly Mazanera's – were praised. Even Paul Thompson – now semi-satirically dubbed 'The Great Paul Thompson' upon every mention of his name in the *NME* – transcended the grudging acknowledgements usually handed to drummers and garnered plaudits by the score. Some praise was exceptional; Manzanera was, for the *NME*, 'our most creative guitarist'.[92]

The album as a whole was received with now-familiar glee: 'I can't seem to remember a display of instrumental kineticism executed in a recording studio with such inspired finesse this year'(*NME*).[93] *Melody Maker*, with a rare flash of insight, summarized *Country Life* succinctly as 'an intense and occasionally savage documentary on contemporary decadence and moral corruption'.[94] Writing with hindsight, Allan Jones suggested a vaguely historical context for the album ('Europe in the 1930s, lingering between affluence, despair and, finally, carnage'),[95] which, while somewhat distant from Ferry's stated aim of satirizing the English establishment view of leisure, is a really rather good analogy.

Some comparisons were misguided, but Bryan Ferry and Ray Davies is a tempting juxtaposition, especially with Davies having issued his epic satires *Preservation (Acts 1 and 2)* in 1973 and 1974, for it enables us to see better what made Ferry different, un-rockist, singular.

Davies's inspiration clearly flowed from the standpoint of disaffected Everyman – even in his comical and exaggerated assumption of roles distinct from that class milieu – and deals in a dramatis personae immediately recognizable to anyone occupying a certain stratum in the British class system. Ferry, on the other hand, concentrates on the sybarite, the jadedly aesthetic, the acquisitive, writing more about individual character traits and their relation to social situations than the actions of characters in a preordained dramatic schema. Luxury, consumption, sexual exhaustion, shameless expense – these were, as we have already seen, not traditional rock topics, or even the stuff of popular cultural discourse, at least not in any critiqueing or satirical sense.

Response to the ructions over the cover and also to the favourable reviews was predictable enough; truckloads of copies of *Country Life* were sold, although, disappointingly, the album failed to make No. 1 and thus emulate its predecessor. Indeed, despite attaining the No. 3 position, the album had disappeared from the charts within ten weeks. While sales were healthy enough, this was still the sign of a predominantly cult band having its wares snapped up in a trice by dedicated core followers. 'All I Want is You', by comparison, laboured up the singles chart to No. 12, stalled and fell. This was not good news. It was the first Roxy Music single not to achieve Top Ten status.

The *NME*, for all their goading bile, relented a little by paying Ferry the considerable tribute of calling him 'the most important songwriter of the 70s' but the damage had been done.[96] Ferry, however, had been genuinely hurt and affronted by the carping of the summer and early autumn, and withdrew into a sulk. Henceforward his relations with journalists – always measured – would be marked by caution and outright reserve. To compare his interviews with Nick Kent in the *New Musical Express* of 19 January 1974 and with Max Bell on 21 December is illuminating indeed. 'I'm the most sensitive person in the world,' sniffed Ferry in December, 'so I've had to develop a hard shell.'[97]

In one particularly impassioned and rather silly outburst, he claimed, 'I am the prime target in British rock at the moment.'[98] Interestingly, the next few years saw Ferry interviewed almost exclusively by female reporters, notably Lisa Robinson and Caroline Coon, as if editors imagined this might induce him to open up a little.

6: THE TIMES OF THEIR LIVES – ROXY MUSIC AND THE 1970S

'DIM THE LIGHTS, YOU CAN GUESS THE REST'

It's maybe one of the most memorable non-musical introductions to any single – the footsteps approaching casually across the gravel, there's the squeeze of the door-handle, the growling catch of the cylinders at the turning of the ignition key and the receding slipstream of a high-performance engine. A high-pitched electric guitar squeals out, a saxophone clears its throat and a five-note bass pulse begins. A roll of timbales, and it's Roxy Music's 'Love is the Drug'.

Its release in 1975 was indisputably the high point of the first half of Roxy Music's career and remains not only one of their four signature pieces (the others being 'Virginia Plain', 'Dance Away' and John Lennon's 'Jealous Guy') but perhaps the song that best fixed Roxy Music in the popular cultural subconscious. Yet within six months the band had effectively broken up – despite mollifying reassurances from band members and Ferry in particular, it was assumed that the split was permanent. How could this happen?

Roxy Music had always been a temperamental entity. Friends of the band and the odd journalist have commented on the relative maturity of the core members – corroborating Ferry's comments that 'with Roxy Music there was never a major row that I can remember, never a night when people stormed out shouting that they would never work with each other again'.[1] Pete Sinfield's story of Mackay, Manzanera and the games of charades, and indeed the whole heritage of Roxy Music and its constituent members' entrances into the business by non-traditional routes, suggest a prudent avoidance of conventional rock behaviour, not to mention a considerable degree of emotional maturity. Peccadilloes, and Ferry's patronage of the avant-garde and the fringes of London's smart set aside, Roxy Music were, it would appear, an unusually easygoing and urbane bunch of people who lived little of the world their stage characters could be imagined to inhabit (if anything, this served only to concentrate their aura still more magically). The degree of collaboration on solo recordings says a great deal in support of this argument.

Manzanera's 1975 *Diamond Head* set featured Jobson, Mackay, Thompson, Eno, Dave Skinner and John Wetton – totalling six extant, former or future Roxy members or guests. Mackay's 1974 set *In Search of Eddie Riff*, for its part, employed John Porter, John Gustafson, Jobson, Thompson and Manzanera (Mackay would also use the latter two for his 1978 set, *Resolving Contradictions*). Mackay, Manzanera, Thompson and Wetton turned up on Eno's first two albums, and Ferry, routinely portrayed as the chilly and disdainful *generalissimo* feared by his men, used almost every Roxy Music member, full-time or otherwise, on his solo albums (except, intriguingly, for Mackay). A full list of these collaborations, which border at times on the nepotistic, can be found in the Discography, but even the examples featured here speak of a strong bond between like-minded musicians, artistically and frequently personally founded.

All the same, it may be conjectured that for all their matey mutuality, these very solo outings hastened the 1976 Roxy Music break-up (or 'devolution' as it was tweely termed at the time). If so, this would have been only too 'rock and roll' for the time – maybe the most conventional rock and roll thing the band had yet done.

They may have asked questions of the 'auteurist' nature of rock creation, and posed an interesting critique of rock praxis as naturally 'self-expressive', but Roxy Music's musicians were explorative and inquisitive to a degree that demanded that they express their own musical motivations as and when the opportunities arose. Manzanera, for example, riding the crest of the band's success, found he was able to pick up the phone and choose sidemen – any sidemen – when recording *Diamond Head*. Temptation indeed.

The nature of Roxy Music, and the musicians within it, demanded that the constituent members work outside the band unit. That unit was nominally propelled by the internal combustion of conflicting musical pressures within it, and it was only natural to expect other outlets for that emotional energy to be found.

This was one rock and roll cliché, then, that Roxy Music found impossible to avoid – solo albums, thought to be safety valves of creativity, actually forcing apart the band that they had been calculated to invigorate.

Manzanera's solo ventures almost caused him a full-scale breakdown, less for particular technical or personal difficulty than for the investment of sheer obsessive workaholism they demanded. The first to hit the shops was *Diamond Head* in March 1975 (a highly accomplished and extremely underrated album of instrumentals and quirky songs; the second was a timely and generous revival of Manzanera's old band Quiet Sun. Manzanera's success, and his continued friendship with his old partners in failure, Charles Hayward and Bill McCormick, led to suggestions that increased wealth and prestige accruing to Manzanera might enable an album to be recorded. Manzanera had called his friends into the *Diamond Head* sessions and such were the results that an immediate decision was taken to try to immortalize some of their one-time repertoire on tape during the hiatus prior to a renewed Roxy Music assault on America in April.

SIRENS ON THE SEASHORE

Manzanera's workload that spring might almost be interpreted as a bravura piece of nose-thumbing in Ferry's direction, to prove that it wasn't only bandleaders who could work themselves into an early grave. Apart from recording two albums and playing (alongside Andy Mackay) on Eno's second solo album, *Another Green World*, Manzanera had to assume lead guitar duties for Roxy Music in the US, Japan, Australia and New Zealand. He coped – just – but the longer-term implications were clear: could such energies be stilled for long, and what would that mean to the continued survival of the band?

Japan, in the event, bewitched Ferry. The whole trip had been a calculated risk, in the van of several other UK acts (such as Deep Purple) who had ventured into the untried Japanese market and tapped an omnivorous appetite for Western pop product. With record distribution still at a primitive stage in Japan, Roxy Music contented themselves with winning friends on a concert tour, and duly did so. Ferry's gaucho and stormtrooper vestments went down better abroad than at home, and, as on the UK tour the previous autumn, the band were accompanied by two rather ordinary female backing singers, dressed by Antony Price in uniforms that could best be described as 'Third Reich stewardess'.

Among the friends they won was Kazuhiko Katoh, leader of

Japan's top rock attraction, the Sadistic Mika Band, who would go on to support Roxy Music on their autumn 1975 tour of the UK. Ferry's love of the place seemed genuine enough, coincident with the sudden chic of Yamamoto and Kenzo menswear in the West; he would return and pay his respects (and Kabuki himself up idiotically for the cameras) two years later.

The US had the band again picking an itinerary which minimized mileage or stagework, and emphasized promotional aspects. The optimism of yore had been replaced by cautious consolidation, notably in the swelling cult cells across the heartland, such as those in Detroit and Cleveland, where even a chorus of screams could now be looked forward to when traversing the airport. Ironically, after all the foot-slogging, Roxy Music's first breakthrough on a coast-to-coast basis in America was simply the release of one single, 'Love is the Drug', later that year.

Ferry's dreams of America, it seemed, were finally losing their nightmarish edges. His exposure to Beverly Hills' manicured and oxygenated perfection the previous year had left its mark. He was making friends in the States on both coasts; most importantly he had made much more than a friend in the Texan model Jerry Hall. An eighteen-year-old of considerable wealth, sophistication and beauty, Ferry had spotted her on the cover of a 1974 issue of *Vogue*.

Having embarked on affairs with the previous three Roxy Music cover girls, Kari-Ann Moller, Amanda Lear and Marilyn Cole, there was a kind of inexorable logic about Hall's pencilling-in as the next Roxy Music cover girl. She rapidly established herself as the most stable and long-lived of Ferry's relationships with his muses; an attentive press dutifully recorded innumerable and distastefully public mutual declarations of love – both genuine and invented – until Hall's sudden departure into the arms of Mick Jagger three years later.

The provocative appearance in lollipop-pink chiffon of Kari-Ann Moller, insinuating her way through an excellent promotional video for Ferry's summer 1975 hit, the sultry and sulphurous 'You Go to My Head', turned a few heads, but Ferry was as much preoccupied with Hall as many had ever seen him, and such was his attachment that most of the words expended on the video commented on its unusual assurance and professionalism.

It's a shibboleth that Queen's 'Bohemian Rhapsody', later that year, finally established the rock promotional videotape as a viable field of creativity, but this is to overlook the work of others throughout the 1970s, of whom Ferry and Price were two. 'You Go to My Head', for all its cornball playing to Ferry's detractors with its shiny surface of white sands and turquoise surf and colonial cool (Ferry brooding on a white sofa while Moller glides silently around him, Ferry floating in the Caribbean shallows), was a fine piece of video promotion. The exquisite composition of each frame and some neat grace notes (the still from Moller's *Roxy Music* cover sessions above the fireplace, for example) show just how accomplished Ferry had become at this sort of thing.

The cover concept for Hall, though, was another story, and a lengthy one at that. It was to take its inspiration from the working title for the band's new album, *Siren*. After some brainstorming, Ferry settled on an idea and transported himself, Hall, Price and a team of stylists and photographers to the coast of Anglesey in North Wales. It was an operation of epic proportions, the moment that the 'Roxy machine', in Price's words, 'reached its zenith'.[2] Hall was rendered outlandishly as a piece of cruel cheesecake *beauté-maudite* as much like something from a Moreau canvas as a fashion shoot. She became a stylized siren, with fins, elongated nails, golden eyeshadow and various piscine appurtenances. Price, who with Ferry had selected an appropriate location for the shoot on Anglesey, takes up the story:

'The week I'd gone before it was an incredibly rough sea with massive boiling waves and everything was green so we decided the shot would be all green. When we came back the next week the whole scene was blue...still as anything, the sea had dropped thirty feet...I said to Bryan, it's going to be blue, we'll have to go with blue. Luckily I'd got some tins of blue car paint with me and had to respray the whole costume blue. We had the sun directly overhead, 100 degrees, the hottest day of the year. Everything was melting. We had the glue from the costume welded into her fanny hairs, the nails were coming off. When we finished, we immersed her in this bath of make-up removing liquid, couldn't get it off her...we had to run around with her stark naked wrapped in a towel. We ran for the train at Holyhead, opened the door, shoved her on, jumped on ourselves and the train left.

'All the way back to London we had her hanging out of the carriage window taking pictures. I thought, oh my God, in a minute she'll catch her hair on a mulberry bush or something and her head will be gone.'[3]

The result was perhaps the most famous of all of the Roxy covers, probably more for the identity of the model than for the quality of the composition, which, while striking and sensual – the camera clearly adores Hall – lacks the audacity of earlier efforts and leans towards more mainstream Robert Carlos Clarke mannerism than the centrefold satires of earlier albums. It none the less pays tribute to Price's assistants in that such a fine piece of cover art resulted from such anarchic conditions.

Manzanera's *Diamond Head* collection had, in the meantime, scrambled into the charts at No. 40, where it perched precariously for a week before dropping out again. This first indication of the commercial potential of subsidiary Roxy Music members was to be an augury of the future, but in the meantime the band concentrated on the recording of the new album, undertaken on familiar ground at AIR Studios with the redoubtable Chris Thomas at the controls of the production console.

There seems little doubt now that for all of the celebrated luminescence of 'Love is the Drug', for all its tightness and soulfulness, it has an air of sheeny immaculacy which spreads over the rest of *Siren* like golden syrup. Pretty, at first, but ultimately suffocating and disappointingly uniform in its sweetness of texture. How much Ferry's long-avowed desire to crack America (an ongoing preoccupation of his management also) influenced the more sedate and cautious Roxy Music of *Siren* is unclear; Ferry has never let on either way.

'Love is the Drug' is without doubt the most unself-conscious attempt at making a contemporary hit record to contemporary specifications to date in the band's repertoire. With unironic *hommage* paid to 1960s r'n'b, the arrangement is precise and sparely deployed, with Jobson's muttering Hammond organ, Mackay's hep embellishments, Manzanera's needling, unrelenting rhythm attack. The song's masterstroke is, however, to use these devices in a less than soulful key; the atmosphere is uniformly grim and depressive, ditto the sex sung about in the song. The arrangement is for taut and rollicking energy, the harmonic language and melody anything but. The clanging, dissonant chord which closes the song adds to the lowering malaise – intriguingly but perhaps tellingly, DJs usually faded the song out long before it occurred. Ferry couldn't quite plump for populism outright even in a song as straightforward as this. Unfortunately, he continued trying the populist seam for the majority of the rest of the album, and it suffers accordingly.

Manzanera later fretted that by this time the band were treading water, but perhaps what's most frustrating about *Siren* is that they expend so much effort in doing so. That endeavour could, given time and a more felicitous working relationship easily have produced another *For Your Pleasure* or *Country Life*. Roxy Music are, to any discerning pair of ears, obviously on top of their game, empathically blending voices; the compelling, primeval polychromatism which introduces 'Sentimental Fool' shows Jobson and Manzanera, in particular, dovetailing superbly. The sheer willpower involved in making simpler music, however, seems to vastly outweigh the effort that went into creating such gems as 'Mother of Pearl' and 'If There is Something', effort which seems almost negligible. Roxy Music are trying very hard here to be something they were not. To those listening to later albums, such as *Manifesto* and *Avalon*, their credibility as chart musicians seems more secure; here, it does not, and the music suffers, succeeding in being neither loftily sophisticated nor Top Ten fodder.

The strain shows particularly on 'Sentimental Fool', which cannot decide whether or not it wants to be pop pastiche and thus criminally wastes the superbly silvery haze of fuzz guitar and synthesizer which rings the curtain up on the piece, with Jobson's impressionistic Fender Rhodes notes glinting evilly in the murk. The rest of the track, however, is rather like hand-me-down 10cc, complete with false ending. 'Could It Happen to Me' doesn't even have the redeeming quality of that parody-or-pastiche ambiguity. The soundstage, very Ferry-heavy, is thoroughly workaday here; this could, literally, be any Top Ten band, with only Mackay's fatly chirruping saxophone and Manzanera's bristly guitar lines to emblematize Roxy Music identity within the song.

'Whirlwind' does at least boast real sinew and muscle, although the band hasn't quite washed the melody of 'Prairie Rose' out of its hair. The musicians here are obviously *enjoying* themselves, a quality notable by its absence on most of the other tracks, although the feeling of recycled goods is a difficult one to dispel. Few critics missed the almost identical similarity of the bass line of 'She Sells' to that of Led Zeppelin's epic 'Trampled Underfoot'. It might have been less culpable had the track not featured on the album Zeppelin had released some six months before, *Physical Graffiti*.

A good way to critique *Siren*, given its simplification of vertical and linear development in the band's compositions, is to examine the role played by each musician within the soundstage.

Paul Thompson's room for spectacular fills and liberties with the 4/4 beat seem unduly restricted, and he is too often reduced to the role of mere metronome; only on the thoroughly bland 'Just Another High' do his characteristically meaty snare-drum shots reach the front of an often dreary mix.

Mackay reasserts himself richly on this album. There isn't the incandescent exhibitionism of the first two albums, but enough rhythmic impulse and creamy-toned playing (such as on 'Both Ends Burning') to keep his fans from revolting.

Jobson's violin work, too, is rationed; his duties now seem merely to be upholstering the texture, his ability to carve his own individual instrumental identity within the sound severely cut back. The delayed alarm calls which plummet out of nowhere across the stereo image and kick-off 'Both Ends Burning', not to mention his smothering string-synthesizer chords throughout the same song, betray both sides of his role in the band.

Manzanera, meanwhile, is a relative spectator for most of the time. His rhythm guitar work – never before much noticed, because never much needed – is a revelation of precision and punchiness, but his solo work, once so randomly ranged across the music, is now safely corralled in its allotted solo spots. *Siren*, and most specifically the contribution of Phil Manzanera, was when Eno's talk of 'spaces for members of the band to fiddle around in' became a reality. For a player coming off two dazzling showcases of his art, Quiet Sun's *Mainstream* and his own *Diamond Head* LP, not to mention with the praise for his contribution to *Country Life* still ringing in his ears, this must have been hard to take.

It's perhaps unfortunate and maybe unintentional that Ferry, the architect of the simpler approach, had a field day. While the album is not a vocal or lyrical *tour de force*, his shaping of phrases was becoming more and more assured. The deranged squawks and vibro-massaged whoops may have been absent, but Ferry, after two solo albums to practise on, tailored his style well to his own material, crucially sacrificing none of his individuality. Aware of the music's consonance, he could apply tweaks and tricks where he pleased, as with the sarcastic sneering at an ex-lover's travails on 'Just Another High', which contains traces of Ferry's *sprechgesang* glory.

Having forgiven Ferry for his perceived excesses the previous summer and gone gaga over *Country Life*, no such indulgences were shown to *Siren*, which was felt to be the statement of a band resting on its laurels. After a promising reception for 'Love is the Drug', *Siren* barely picked up a single good review, hardly a propitious send-off for yet another tour. In the interim, however, another sideman had jumped ship, John Wetton having been lured away by a wallet-fattening offer from Uriah Heep, currently in one of their periodic convulsions of personnel changes following the departure of the ill-fated Gary Thain. John Gustafson, the bassist who had accompanied Roxy Music on *Stranded*, *Country Life* and now *Siren* in the studio, was asked to tour in Wetton's place, with the odd date being given over to Rick Wills. Gustafson was a veteran of the Liverpudlian Beat Boom, and had served with the Big Three before knuckling down to a life of sessioneering which brought him considerable cachet and not a little cash in the 1970s. When *Siren* was entering the charts in November 1975, Gustafson was already there as a sideman on the album *Voyage of the Acolyte* by Genesis guitarist Steve Hackett (a classic of straight-laced, pastoral Progressive rock), witness enough to his popularity and versatility.

The autumn 1975 tour, gaining momentum with the sales of 'Love is the Drug', was a resounding success; clearly nobody was reading the reviews. The stage costumes were a little altered from 1974, the backing vocalists now divested of their Swastika-Air uniforms and, under the less than imaginative rubric of the Sirens, wearing brutally adherent skin-tight, split-seam pink and red. Much as this flattered their physiques, it did little to distract critics from their vocal contributions, which many thought were still undercooked. *Melody Maker* made do with two words: 'dopey chicks'. British dates included Liverpool Empire (3 October), Leeds University (4 October), Stoke Trentham Gardens (7 October), Glasgow Apollo (8, 9 and 10 October), Newcastle City Hall (12 and 13 October), Manchester Belle Vue (14 and 15 October), London Wembley Arena (16 and 17 October), Cardiff Capital Theatre (20 and 21 October), Stafford Bingley Hall (23 and 24 October).

Fortunately for the fans and posterity, recordings drawn from the tour, as with the previous two, had been earmarked for the issue of a live recording of the band. The ever-industrious Manzanera sat down with some sixty hours of tape to sift the available cuts, the results of which would be heard on *Viva! Roxy Music*, issued in the wake of a sudden but scarcely unexpected split in the band's ranks the following summer.

None the less, Roxy Music stood, in 1976, as one of the most potent cultural symbols of Britain in the 1970s. Part of their popularity – or at least their mystique – resided in the fact that with the retirement to Berlin of their only chief rival, David Bowie, they embodied many aspects of their time otherwise occluded in popular culture: metropolitan experience, sex, fashion, hipness, none of which was dealt with in any depth in contemporary rock discourse. There were still two years to elapse before Punk booted them into the cultural foreground, but for the time being Roxy Music still personified a particularly adult form of emotional and sexual musical expression which has since concretized their identity in cultural history – and made their reputations and fortunes. Just what was Roxy Music's relation to popular culture that caused this image of them as troubadours of untold decadence to be impressed so deeply upon us? Three contemporary phenomena which both shaped and were shaped by them can provide us with some pointers.

THE IDEA OF HIP IN THE 1970S, LONDON CHIC AND ROXY MUSIC

As Robert Hughes writes of Warhol's New York City, so the same can be said of post-Beatles London:

The Sixties...reshuffled and stacked the social deck: press and television, in their pervasiveness, constructed a kind of parallel universe in which the hierarchical orders of...society – vestiges, it was thought, but strong ones, based on inherited wealth – were replaced by the new tyranny of the 'interesting'. Its rule had to do with the rapid shift of style and image, with the assumption that all civilized life was discontinuous and worth only a short attention span: better to be Baby Jane Holzer than the Duchesse de Guermantes.[4]

Through such machinations did pop, camp and fashion, and the luckier practitioners of each, find fame thrust upon them.

While many have tried to explain the formation of London's underground and counterculture in the 1960s, fewer have tried to formulate theories for the extraordinary marriage of popular and aristocratic tastes in the capital which would forge such lasting links between pop, fashion and the media, links which Roxy Music would use to create an image for themselves, and later as a means of survival and visibility. George Melly's incomparable *Revolt into Style* is one such attempt at explanation.

Melly postulates no one theory, but for the purposes of this book a strand can be traced through his work as instrumental in the creation of the London which produced Roxy Music and sustained the band as the major troubadours of its hang-ups and preoccupations throughout the 1970s: the coincidental alignment of fashion, art and music and their concomitant social circles.

Melly draws the strands together at the beginning of the 1960s, with London startled by the arrival of the discotheque. 'From the Midi, post-Bardot and Sagan,' says Melly, 'came the discotheque, musical extensions of coffee bars.'[5] There had already been twisting at Madame Cordet's Saddle Room, where rag-trade hoi polloi were mixing with gentry from the early 1960s onwards. Discos, wrote Melly, were essentially classless places at a time when snobs were still trying to ingratiate themselves 'by using the word "yeah" where it wasn't really necessary'.[6]

Artists (Blake, Hockney) and photographers (Bailey) became hip first, pop stars (the Beatles, Jagger) later. For Melly, Stones producer Andrew Loog Oldham had been the key to pop music opening society's doors: 'Through his own glamour, [he] raised the producer into a position equal, not only to the pop musicians he was recording, but to the whole swinging route; photographers, rag-trade designers, fashion models, film actors, the lot.'[7] Thus was produced a world which liked to imagine, and preen itself on account of, its own classlessness, where a penguin-suited Jeremy Thorpe could be (famously) photographed scrutinizing the fretboard of a Gibson Flying V guitar under the patient supervision of Jimi Hendrix.

London's bright young things couldn't resist ('This pop thing is just so mad'). Pop and rock, and their consumption, became a lifestyle accessory for the rich and young, whether it was the rugby club seeing Emerson, Lake and Palmer at the Queen Elizabeth Hall ('My mind's really blown, man, it's just so blown'), or, for the ladies, the liberating aroma of rough trade, being shagged backstage at the Royal Albert Hall by some anonymous bass-playing sweathog. Whatever, the young money was suddenly on hearts and flowers and bells and beads, and selves were being expressed like there was no tomorrow – from Stratton Street's Petit Café to the Loose Run; in restaurants like Searcy's, Santa Croce and Ma Cuisine; in chic design emporia like Casa Pupo; at Apple, at Biba's; in the Dress Circle in Harrods, everything was allowed to hang out as far and as loudly and as conspicuously as possible. This was the era of Ritz magazine, of Right Nigels and Mayfair Mercenaries, the era where the first people with money began to get something substantial and lasting out of the 1960s laissez-faire diktat. They could afford a better class of the sex and drugs and rock and roll that middle-class interest in the counterculture liberated from the counterculture itself. Anyone who even mentioned the words 'fashion' or 'photography', with their bohemian resonances, had a 50 per cent better chance of scoring at a party in London than someone who didn't. 'You only had to pretend you were in the rag-trade or a musician or say something like, "*Oh shit*, forgot my camera" and you'd have an heiress on your arm,' remembers one survivor.[8]

These were the circles in which Roxy Music, or more precisely Bryan Ferry, moved, although Eno, with his thirst for experience, made his own reconnaissance of London's avant-garde fashion set.

Two of the major catalysts in this social shift on the rag-trade side were Mary Quant and her husband, Alexander Plunkett Greene, who, like Ferry, were former art students, having attended Goldsmith's College together in the 1950s. Quant's flair 'for what people would accept next – combined with Plunkett Greene's aristocratic dandyism – produced a new alloy of talent and outrage,' wrote Melly of her contribution towards London's class-blurring Pop look and Pop life.[9] Quant, for Melly, was 'the one true pop manifestation in the years between rock and roll and the Beatles'. That conviction in her own instinct for popular expectation (a faultless gauging of the zeitgeist), combined with single-minded imagistic stubbornness, provides a fashion analogue with Ferry's designing of music and its image.

Fashion being the draw it was in contemporary London, it is unsurprising that camp, that other Roxy Music staple, would be such a life-force. Melly writes of the ascendancy of fashion in 'polite' London society at the end of the 1960s:

> The classless (or to be more accurate class-aphrodisiac) accept-ance of pre-war homosexual circles, their belief in the self-sufficiency of the chic, the 'amusing', the new, the love of glitter and danger, the belief in hard work at the service of sensation, these are now acceptable within a heterosexual context.[10]

This unexpected parade of (very Roxyesque) qualities previously thought exclusively homosexual fitted neatly with the libertarian nature of the pop revolution in London, to which doing one's own thing, or being seen to do or imagining one was doing one's own thing, was a prerequisite.

The popular 1960s concept of 'kinky' had helped, that first snickering mass acceptance of any concept of remotely deviant sexuality. 'Kinky,' wrote George Melly, 'was at some stage during the 1960s a word used to describe almost everything except perhaps Brussels sprouts.'[11] In the mid-1960s it suddenly 'seemed important to make sure that everyone understood the kinky joke'.[12] Androgyny and exaggeration burst out all over, particularly at the extremes, and prompted iconoclastic young designers like Andrew 'Alternative Miss World' Logan, Vivienne Westwood and Zandra Rhodes, who took on Quant's mantle of pushing the boundaries of what the fashion-conscious would accept and pay money for. They got away with it too – and an entire subculture, or rather a hybrid of *demi-monde* subcultures rode the spirit of devil-may-care amorality. Good taste was there for the taking, and Roxy Music played on the tranny in the background.

Ferry, having turned this world into song, threw himself into it. At Logan's Thames-side warehouse residence, he attended the avant-garde designer's inaugural Alternative Miss World in January 1975, in the company of Molly Parkin, 'who,' Peter York notes, 'got thrown in the pool'.[13] Parkin was perhaps unwittingly the most vivid embodiment of the anything-goes highlife of London – she could be a character in a Roxy Music song. She took a London which was still very much besotted with anything fringe, cultish, 'liberated' or, better, 'street', a Warholesque voyeurism of degradation, squalor and unformed 'creativity'. Her career there betrays the contemporary values of the place. Another provincial art student, she'd scaled the fashion world less by talent than good fortune and erotic flair, starting at *Harpers and Queen*, graduating to *Nova* magazine ('by pure luck' she notes in her autobiography), being 'in at the start of Biba'.[14] She married the Surrealist painter Patrick Hughes in 1970, opened a costly bistro – Red Brick – in the King's Road and had been photographed by Karl Stoecker, onetime Roxy Music house-photographer. She criticized 'poverty thinking' and 'could tell at a glance the cost of what anyone had on'. 'I couldn't remember whose bed I'd just left,' begins one line of her autobiography.[15]

Her progress seemed to embody every popular cliché about fashion and the metropolis, the it's-who-you-know nepotism, the success in spite of talent, the hollowness, the spiritual void, the crypto-Tory obsession with wealth and glamour. How else was a just-moderately talented writer given the chance, and the advance cash, to write a string of books of the kind that Parkin gratefully produced (epics of middle-class softcore, *A Bite of the Apple*, *Full Up*, *Breast Stroke*, *Cock-a-Hoop*, *Up and Coming*, to be anthologized in books with even more hilarious titles, such as *Molly Parkin's Purple Passages*). Her look-at-me shockwork was archetypal. The world in which she brazenly advertised her participation – or her instrumentality – was a world newly sexualized by the 1960s and of a non-bourgeois moral code, licentious and lascivious, urbanely decadent and luxuriating in corruption. 'Beauty Queen' from *For Your Pleasure* could have been written for, or about, her.

But Parkin cannot be judged for whipping up a zeitgeist that she merely surfed. Worse things by far were done in the sphere of art, fashion and pop in London in the 1970s, a world where everyday morality was an optional extra, and whose chief eulogists would be David Bowie and Roxy Music. Quant's pubic hairs, barbered into a cute heartshape, and the fame of transsexual model Tula, once Barry Cossey and latterly a brave litigant for transsexual equality, showed that anything went now. Bowie and Bryan Ferry, fortunately for us all, were there, diving in, looking on, taking notes, and waiting.

DAVID BOWIE AND ROXY MUSIC

Ferry was seen backstage frequently at Bowie gigs, according to Christopher Sandford's wonderfully erudite biography of the Thin White Duke, *Bowie: Loving the Alien*.

As we have seen already, Roxy Music and Bowie diplomatically kept their distance throughout the 1970s. There was too much at stake for their paths to cross or converge, although had it ever come down to a contest for hearts and minds in the popularity stakes, Roxy Music wouldn't have stood a chance, and they knew it. If nothing else, this was due to the considerable head-start Bowie's career had enjoyed. Bowie was already a major star when *Roxy Music* was hitting the shelves. While Roxy Music were still playing pubs, David and Angie stepped from limousines into flash-bulb frenzies at royal film premières. In 1974, *Diamond Dogs* turned Bowie into a superstar in the US, while Roxy Music were still struggling to break out from their bridgeheads in Detroit and Cleveland.

Bowie and Roxy Music are still lumped pejoratively together under the faded bunting of the glam-rock rubric, yet almost never compared and contrasted, a throwback to the calculated efficiency of their (probably unconscious) strategies of mutual distancing in the 1970s.

Ferry's grumbles at Bowie's choice of release date for *Pin-Ups* and his tetchy dispatch of a telegram noting his displeasure to Bowie's French studio betray just how important it was for Bowie and Ferry to stay out of each other's way. The comparisons were just too many.

Bowie greedily sought out and courted gay approbation before Ferry found it landing in his lap. Bisexual from his adolescence, Bowie moved easily and lubriciously within gay circles, counting Lindsay Kemp among his earliest conquests. 'Oh You Pretty Thing' screamed the *Melody Maker* about Bowie, prior to the release of *Ziggy Stardust and the Spiders from Mars*. Ferry found queerness intriguing but no more.

Popular understanding of gayness in 1972 can pretty much be gauged by the unthinking (and unfeeling) application of umbrella categories to Ferry and Bowie as practitioners of something loosely imagined to be gay rock. Some malicious tongues went so far as to say that Kari-Ann Moller, on the cover of *Roxy Music*, was in fact Ferry in drag.

According to Antony Price:

'Bryan was more of the school of "less is more…" Bowie had his make-up artist who went completely berserk with him. Bryan is just a voyeur of that kind of thing.

'Bowie's camp was definitely the real thing. Bryan's camp was for him and the band, but Bowie's camp was definitely himself, he was pushing himself. As a film actor, like Bowie became, you have to go out there and stand up there and convince that camera and that audience of who or what you are.'[16]

In the same interview, Price went on to say, vehemently, that 'wild horses wouldn't get Bryan in drag'.[17]

Similarly, Bowie's coprophiliac obsessions with the danker recesses of Warholian depravity dealt actively in a world of perversion and inversion, a world that only interested Ferry as a *flaneuriste* observer.

Price's interesting assessment of the two acts also begs other comparisons, specifically between Ferry's and Bowie's differing attitudes towards stardom and identity, but this is to diminish any comparison between the important material and public postures of their parallel careers, which again help us understand each artist.

Bowie, for Sandford, 'brought into rock and roll not only a native habit of introspection but also a quality that survived and flourished in the relative isolation of English suburbia in the 1950s – self-control'. This was to 'distract attention from his extreme inhibition on stage'.[18] For Pete Sinfield, Ferry was 'just about the most awkward mover there ever was on stage… he had a few moves which he developed in his own quirky way later on' but he was also 'a control freak'.[19]

The tendency of this attitude to spill into the making of rock visuals matched Bowie's almost detail for detail. Bowie designed his own covers, using blue-chip photographers and designers such as Alan Motz and Justin de Villeneuve. To realize

Bowie's tour proposals in 1974, for example, 'the designer Jules Fisher was hired to create a set midway between *Diamond Dogs*' nightmare of urban decay and the stark, robotic world of *Metropolis*'.[20] Bowie suggested as props 'tanks, turbines, cages...girders...Albert Speer'.[21]

That also usefully illustrates detail differences in Bowie's and Ferry's respective imagistic thought processes. For Bowie, individual crack-up and fragmentation was microcosmal of pre-millennial fractures in society. For Ferry, dislocation of and damage to self came in spite of, not because of, the world's ills. Society's logic, far from consuming the individual in its own apocalypse, ensured his perennial pain by the very immutability of its human dynamics of love and loss.

The Orwellian nature of the world about which Bowie sings, best summarized in the stentorian blank walls which hem in the entire worldview of *Diamond Dogs* (where even the love songs spoke of their heroes' 'hysterical detachment' from feeling), compares better with 801's *Listen Now!!* than with any Roxy Music track. The science-fiction cues were closer calls. Roxy Music's take on outer space and future shock was marginally the more original, being such an obvious subversion of the optimistic astronautical Futurism of the space-age man currently in vogue, and which Bowie only made over with eyeliner, a bit of glitter, costume jewellery and a pantomime cockade, as opposed to Roxy Music's fastidious re-creation of a past age's imaginings of things to come.

There were also vast disparities in material circumstances which differentiated the artistic outlooks of the two acts. In 1972 in the USA, for example, Bowie was greeted warmly by Truman Capote and inspired Warhol's tolerant interest; Alan Bates and Anthony Perkins turned up to his début gig in New York (touts prospered at the then astronomical sum of $50 a ticket), while Roxy Music were trounced in Miami. (Bowie too, however, got the bird from aggrieved Hoosiers in the Midwest and for years denied ever having played the American heartland.)

Bowie/Ferry methodologies compared well too, particularly in Roxy Music's and Bowie's early years. Lindsay Kemp, an early Bowie mentor and paragon of avant-garde dance and camp culture in London, said, 'You simply go and see everything, and you nick the good ideas. Then you do it better, simply by using Scotch tape, sawdust and a little imagination'.[22] Rather how Bryan Ferry might have outlined his *modus operandi*.

Like Ferry, Bowie pioneered promotional video – as for 'John, I'm Only Dancing' (1972). Like Ferry, Bowie was an inveterate worker, sometimes subjecting himself to forty-eight-hour work jags.

Roxy Music's inspirations often trespassed on Bowie's, and vice versa. Imagistically, at least, the cinema provides both acts with a ceaseless fund of ideas. Bowie's 'Life on Mars' ladles on the filmic images – the heroine 'hooked to the silver screen', watching a film which is a 'bore' and that she's seen 'ten times or more'. Other visuals chimed too – Bowie's red plastic boots in his early *Ziggy* phase were replicated in various hues among Roxy Music personnel, as any scrutiny of early publicity stills will attest.

As Allan F. Moore has observed, the lack of journalistic attempts to ascertain a *musical* language for glam rock is annoying when the evidence suggests that there is one. The unanimously shared glam obsession for pop sensibility and atavistic nostalgia should be enough to alert even the least literate rock hack. Both Bowie and Roxy Music were classic adoptions of musical policies which interacted with their visual conception and often posed pertinent and thoughtful questions about 'artifice' in both musical and imagistic planes while doing so.

Sandford has written of the centrality of Bowie's stage dynamic with his guitarist Mick Ronson to his development as a superstar. Bowie, like Todd Rundgren, was much more obviously a musical parodist, or at least an imitator. While he was a masterful magpie of styles, his musical integration of them was not as instinctive or as assured as Roxy Music's; hence his reliance on rabble-rousing riffs, such as the one he blithely thieved from Bo Diddley for 'Jean Genie'. Bowie was a rocker, first and foremost. For Roxy Music, rock and blues convention were merely parts of the machine, not the machine itself. With Bowie, the stylist input often came from sidemen – notably Mike Garson's jazz flavourings, ranging from piquant to blatant; listen to his fabulous 'stride'-style playing on 'Time' from *Aladdin Sane*.

This plainly rockist outlook of Bowie's is an unusual certainty in his otherwise capricious art and artistic identity; and it is here that we come to the final and most ambiguous feature of the Roxy Music/Bowie matrix. For Sandford, one of Bowie's strengths is that his music 'allow[s]...a personal involvement with his songs that wasn't possible with Gary Glitter'.[23] In other words, a human being breathes beneath the tinfoil. But who, precisely? A question doubly pertinent when Bowie gloried so much in asking it, of himself and of his public.

For Sandford, Bowie is like Peter Sellers: 'a cipher; an innovative changeling; a blue screen; and, as he put it himself, a Xerox machine, somehow able to wander between images and come up with a composite no one else would have thought of'.[24]

Of his own image, Bowie has said that he is/was a 'natural ham'.[25] He 'acts' songs rather than sings them. He and Ferry (see Chapter 5) did not, of course, patent pop theatricality. Their ham was well-seasoned ham; Ferry's early adulation of Johnny Ray and Bowie's own childhood taught them that they were merely followers of a tradition, a tradition to be respected but also enhanced. The difference with Bowie and Ferry was that so much of their acts was allusion and illusion – as opposed to the supposed sincerity of Ray and his crooning ilk – in Bowie's (Warholesque) words, his pop star act became the 'policy of the self-invented man'.[26] This was more or less Ferry's own point of departure.

The degree to which the two men lived their own lies is

illuminating. Ferry glided in and out of high society like a
tuxedoed ghost; Bowie, however, became, or aspired to
become, the Queen Bitch of his own fervid imagination.
Neither man, having discovered the masques of London's
bohemian and fashion *demi-monde*, could have failed to
understand the camp undertones of switching and concealing
identities, and the effects it had on the self. For hip sociologists,
the 'meta-message' of the Bowie boys was 'escape'. 'Disguise
and dandyism,' suggests Dick Hebdige in *Subculture*, 'confused
Bowie's transcendence of gender.'[27] Bowie once told an
interviewer of his wish to 'end gender' and dressing likewise.
What he did not discuss were the psychological imbalances
such emotional play might trigger. Bowie's manager, Tony de
Fries, by all accounts got RCA to proclaim that Bowie *was*
Ziggy. 'David fell for it,' Mick Ronson told Sandford.[28]

Antony Price differentiates Ferry from these aspects of
Bowie's psyche, and insightfully provides a reason why Bowie
became the racist hermit of Berlin and Ferry the distracted but
obviously sane sybarite of Los Angeles. 'Bryan can't lie on
camera, Bowie can,'[29] he told an interviewer, the implication
being one of selves; Ferry had to maintain a hold on his, but
Bowie didn't care what happened to his as long as it was neon-
writ.

Not that, given Bowie's treatment of sex and his obsession
with its place in society, his personality was likely to be
anything but public property, a civic entity of provocation
which begged different interpretation and reactions. His own
sexuality was multi-faceted; always ambivalent and tending
towards dominance, it had been powerfully shaken by a play
entitled *Pork* which opened briefly in London in 1971. This
was a classic piece of pornographic, neo-libertarian 1970s
garbage beneath whose bleated pretences to opening minds
lurked a sad and vague attempt to imagine what it might be
like to be Andy Warhol. What action there was consisted
largely of one long screw, showcasing kinky violence and
explicit excretion. Mr and Mrs Bowie alike told an actor how

they were 'sexually turned on by the performance; its plot and, significantly, its "look"'.[30] It perfectly embodied the victory of the shallow, the hedonistic and insensate slurry that the 1960s had left as its legacy, the London that Andrew Logan, Derek Jarman and Roxy Music so cynically and grimly used as artistic *matériel*.

It prefigured Bowie's imperial treatment of amorality and cruelty (and its psychosexual application in interbellum Berlin) and informed his predictions of social breakdown in 1976, not to mention his deranged flirtation with Fascism, which was still a cool word at the time (the Sensational Alex Harvey Band and assorted groupies plastered themselves over *Melody Maker* at an armband-sporting 'Nazi party' that same infamous year).

But where anything had to go to remain trendy, anything went and often did, including violence. By the mid-1970s, torture-chamber hipness had come to gay London, with the fist-fucking parlours the Anvil and The Mineshaft. Fashion had terrorist chic, Mao caps and jackets. Peter York ingeniously drew pornography and fetishism's fleeting vogue into alignment with paramilitary style, with 'mercenary crops, IRA berets and balaclavas'.[31] With an admixture of concern and glee, York writes that 'teenage style groupings lost their innocence in the 1970s'. The Cockettes, hairy gay hippies in Frank N. Furter costumes, were at large (*The Rocky Horror Show*, with its camply shrieking laughter at sado-masochism, was a hit on stage and screen – another triumph for sex as assault and battery). The only taboo left was death.

Yet Bowie was not alone in the anaesthetizing of sexual sensitivities in the 1970s. Roxy Music too could not help but reflect and endorse what was happening to sexuality and its relationship to art, fashion and society.

ROXY MUSIC, COVER GIRLS AND SEX IN THE 1970s

Perhaps the best account of bohemian and upper-class sexuality in London in the 1970s is Martin Amis's *Success* (1978), a novel

167

narrated alternately by the council-estate adoptee/low-grade clerical scruffbag Terence Service and his foster-brother, the aristocratic, bisexual, decadent Gregory Riding. Few if any books better illustrate the unfeeling hedonism and capricious brutality of London's beautiful people in the 1970s.

Gregory, a handsome, muscular, pert-buttocked, silver-spoon wraith in a world where values are those of money, fleeting stimuli, ennui and aesthetic detachment, is a young man who patronizes hip bistros, costly clubs and the lawns and dining rooms of the rich, not to mention cocaine-fuelled Kensington orgies hosted by the ancient gigolo Torka. He revels in his stratospheric snobbery, boasting of his numberless endowments, not least his savage and athletic brilliance as a lover, which only sharpens his appetite for the humiliation of the undersexed, underpaid Terry. Of his lifestyle, Gregory is given to such throwaway litanies as:

'We always go to the grandest restaurants. We're always in those plush, undersea cocktail bars (we can't bear pubs). We always love spending lots of money. We rage on late into the night and always end up doing mad things. Often I'm musty in the morning; I feel fragile until I have my Buck's Fizz before lunch. It's not a hangover, of course; I don't have hangovers; only yobs have hangovers.'[32]

Of his leisurely but diary-filling sexual exploits, he muses:

'Nothing sordid ever happens at Torka's. His glossy apartment is without the sickly tang of some decadent venues I've glanced in on, the tang of rough trade and sado-masochism, the tang of concealed cameras and one-way mirrors, the tang of crime. No: it's all very luxurious, immensely civilized and definitively good fun.'[33]

And afterwards: 'We cackle at the clowns in the review sections and talk of Proust, Cavafy and Antonio Machado –

before streaking off in our cars to Thor's and its slow, slow Sunday luncheon.'[34]

Amanda Lear, on the cover of *For Your Pleasure,* could herself be headed for Torka's. Marilyn Cole's dalliance with London *Playboy* brought her into contact with the orgying classes. Any account of London's bohemian *demi-monde* in the 1970s cannot but plough through puddles of narcotics and jissom. Gregory's old-monied snobbery aspires to the bestial and throwaway vacuity of new-monied snobbery, of the classless and violent weirdos who eventually take over his prized place as centre of attention at the orgy, but fails, and he finds himself an outsider as the old privileges of old class structure are replaced by the new indulgences of new aristocrats. These decadent *parvenus* are comparative lowlife, the creatures and sometimes the creators of popular culture, the aristocrats of what Robert Hughes calls 'the tyranny of the interesting', those who through the new social matrices of chance and luck have made the loudest and strangest and most colourful noise for the longest duration – photographers, rock stars, footballers, models or simply the professional posers their tinselled circuit attracted.

'The yobs are winning,' complains Gregory, and in the end they do. The message of *Success* is a bleak one – finally, even the downtrodden Terry ends up, although triumphant, a sexual sadist like his now degraded and emotionally broken foster-brother. That such sexuality – violent, psychopathic – could and did find widespread cultural currency was largely due to the same 1960s resexualization of London that accompanied the shakedown of class, fashion and pop. In this sexual natural selection, the strongest, dirtiest and toughest sexual behaviour won through as chic.

Hardcore movies gatecrashed mainstream cinema in the 1970s in the shape of the Marilyn Chambers movies *Deep Throat* and *Behind the Green Door. The Devil in Miss Jones,* starring Georgina Spelvin, was another example. 'Judges were beating their gavels in disgust,' wrote Derek Fell gleefully in

Crawdaddy magazine. 'A smut storm was spreading across the country. Weird sex publications were travelling through the mail in record numbers...lewd liberals were flocking to celebrated trials in defence of necrophilia on film and critics were praising the X-rated flicks as "profound" and "important".'[35]

I include this overview as a means of contextualizing the sexual aspect of Roxy Music in their prime, as both sex objects and commentators on sex, as well as a cultural commodity that took their cues from the worlds of fashion, sex and media.

Ferry was a major sex object. 'I was totally in love with all of them,' Mackay's wife later told Michael Bracewell. 'And then I got to marry one of them.'[36] For her part, Brian Eno's assistant told the same writer, 'I was crazy about Bryan Ferry, and now I've got Brian Eno for a brother-in-law.'[37] Taking a partner to a Roxy Music gig was a difficult undertaking. If a man's girlfriend didn't fall for Ferry or any of the other members of the band (Mackay always got an enormous amount of mail, in addition to Ferry and Eno), then his boyfriend might. Conversely, a girl's girlfriend might be smitten, or a girl's boyfriend. Better by far to go alone.

But Ferry wasn't a conventional show-business sex object, and none of the sex in the Roxy Music constellation was conventional show-business sex, whether real or abstract. Ferry wasn't Robert Redford – not mature enough – or Paul Newman. He wasn't Jimmy Page or Robert Plant – not obviously *young* enough. And people who wore tuxedos, whether they meant it or not, were outside commonplace sexual equations in the 1970s – if they had sex at all, it would be in a porn film or in a Helmut Newton photograph. Maybe, but it's preferable to see Ferry as an artist who realized just what sex meant to rock and roll, and to popular culture, and the selling and buying of same. He intended to add his own contribution to the history of rock and sexuality by playing with sexual notions as easily as he'd played with imagistic, musical and sartorial ones.

Rock sexuality was, until the mid-1970s, taken for granted. The duality was of rock sex – demonstrative, aggressive, disposable, masculine, super-phallic, a white-boy appropriation of soul sexuality – and pop sex – conversely chaste, meaningful, emotionally charged, exemplified by soul-mate snogging rather than bed-mate bonking.

Roxy Music's take on sex was clearly neither. Ferry sang of one-night stands ('Love is the Drug'), yet his lyrical thrust was often to do with the travails of true love. If he had a common theme, it was an adult one, largely unexplored by rock musicians, of sexual/emotional obsession and dependency, its effects on the narrator and on the beloved, and the tensions between them. The phenomenon of love was his territory, such as the notion that the love of being in love is the equal of the love for a beloved. Roxy Music's output often accrued a frisson due to its very allusiveness, much as the Hays Code had forced screen sexuality into erotic allusion. The open-ended harmonic patterns of the band's music and the unfamiliar instrumental textures helped lend an air of uncertainty and foreboding to the records which further confused the actual sexual issues involved in Ferry's narratives.

The most explicit sexuality in the Roxy Music product was always the 'Roxy cover girl' as she became known. This was to be a feature of the band's output which died after the onset of Punk, the only really memorable effect of which had been on the social aspects of rock – most notably the relationship of rock to sexuality. A latent feminist tendency evolved in rock criticism and within the ranks of rock musicians themselves, and one of their prime targets was the use of femininity as a marketing tool. Meriting little more at first than bluster and guffaws, a review of rock sexuality was given momentum by rock's own development of disturbing tendencies towards not just routinely exploiting female sexuality but also degrading it. While the post-Punk *NME* quietly jettisoned its most notorious feature, the liberal garnishing of gig listings with soft-porn photographs, the rest of the business continued to milk the female body as a cash-cow. Record sleeves featured anything from straightforward centrefold nudity to more alarming items (négligéd coeds menaced by psychotics, submissive trollops on chain-link leashes, fawn-like innocents cowed by symbolic phalluses). Promotional imagery was, if anything, worse, with all number of instrument firms paying nymphets to suck off erect and shiny guitars or basses in the name of hardware (sic) sales. This was material which couldn't be dismissed with a nonchalant pair of imagined postmodern quotation marks or a 'bit of fun' rejoinder.

It's maybe unfair to blame Bryan Ferry for all this, but that is what many did. According to Johnny Rogan in *Style with Substance*:

> His deliberately sexist stance had worsened over successive albums in which female sexuality was a means of exploiting the more gullible consumer. This, in itself, was despicable enough, but even more alarming was the effect that such sexploitation was to have on the rest of the record company art world.[38]

He then, somewhat inconsistently, continues:

> Although Bryan Ferry can hardly be held accountable for the sexist nature of modern advertising, there can be no doubt that the Roxy Music sleeves of the early 70s promoted a form of loathsome exploitation which still permeates the darker and more repulsive areas of the rock industry.[39]

First, female flesh – twelve-year-old female flesh, no less – had already set that ball rolling in 1970 with Blind Faith's use of Ginger Baker's daughter to sell albums. Second, as already emphasized, cheescake covers were nothing new – some 1960s jazz sleeves are, for their time, extraordinarily pornographic, as much from the pages of contemporary softcore titles like

Ferry addressing the Roxy youth, onstage c.1974

Phil Manzanera, 1972

Eno: the ear of the non-musician, 1972

The band taking tea with Salvador Dali (third from left), Paris,

Eno, in Paris with For Your Pleasure Cover-girl Amanda Lear,

Andy Mackay, 1972

Paul Thompson, 1972

Ruler of all he surveys, Bryan Ferry, 1972

Topper as 1970s rock sleeve art took its cue from the likes of *Knave*. Roxy Music may have pushed the bandwagon, but they did not build it, and their approach to record sleeve art and the pin-up tradition, while sexist in nature, merits at least some investigation, for it, as with many other features of the band, poses some interesting questions.

The most basic arguments of the pornography debate need not be entered into here, but they provoke others of considerable relevance. Is the exploitation of female flesh intentional? If it is meant ironically, does this diminish the exploitation?

There seems little doubt that the first Roxy Music cover, despite Ferry's claim that 'pretty girls have been used to sell everything...why not rock music?', was a joke. It was not so much the perceived availability of showgirls, cocktail waitresses, soubrettes and starlets that Roxy Music were dealing with as the idea of that availability, and they had Kari-Ann in a parody of availability ('*Hey, big boy!*') to prove it. This poked fun at the language of the portrayal, as well as providing a meta-message as to the band's imagistic preoccupations. 'Ferry,' said York in the October 1976 issue of *Harpers and Queen*, 'should hang in the Tate, with David Bowie, the most important *pasticheur* in Britain today.'[40]

Ferry was obviously not using contemporary sexual imagery to sell the high 1970s device of the phallic symbol is missing; the pink rose in Moller's left hand looks too sad to be thus representative. Similarly, Moller's nightdress is noticeably old-fashioned. It is a comment on the cheesecake tradition, but a necessarily subtle one. To use a Petty or a Varga girl, for example, would have been too blatantly retro (Petty and Varga girls featured from 1933 and 1940 to the 1950s in *Esquire*, were elegantly stylized, anatomically improbable society innocents, flirting in person or on a white telephone, often blonde and *always* barely dressed). For all Ferry's claim that he and Price wanted to mimic a Busby Berkeley look, however, Moller is more *Playboy circa* its 1953 inauguration, or, better, an emulation of a screen idol from the fuselage of a wartime USAF bomber. Her posture – knees drawn up to conceal the inner thighs but with voracious come-on in the bared teeth, is very early 1950s. Her ultra-tacky *addenda*, the pink rose and the gold disc, are added talismans of 1950s attitudes in men's magazines, where urban sybaritism, success and sophistication were so feverishly idolized (Mammon is as much in the details of pornography as God is in the details of Pre-Raphaelitism).

Amanda Lear on the cover of *For Your Pleasure* is, on the other hand, more fetishistically dressed even than in most contemporary mainstream pornography, leathers and rubbers shining like the wet pavement of the waterfront night she moves within. It is Ferry's and Price's most allusive sleeve art; like *Roxy Music*, it suggests exclusivity and costliness. Ferry, as ogling chauffeur, is a blunter cipher of same; Lear's cheetah connotes carnivorousness and cruelty, as does Lear herself, intimating unknown pleasures of domination and submission – hence the leash – and, more obscurely, the licence and lawlessness of sexual experiment mirroring the licence and lawlessness of the city. This is *Cabaret* chic done droll. It recalls, inevitably, almost the entire oeuvre of Allen Jones, from the liquorice-stick heels upwards. But also it has links in contemporary photography with Robert Carlos Clarke's *Les Poissonnières* and *Wet Girl*.

Stranded, of course, we have already dealt with; here, and in its successor, *Country Life*, contemporary pornographic themes are hinted at. In each the element of the exotic is emphasized. The vegetation surrounding Cole is sickly and overripe, wallowing in its own splurged primary colour, likewise the hedges from which Evaline and Konstanze emerge. The auto-erotic element – present in Konstanze's breast-kneading as well as Evaline's mimed masturbation – is subtly downplayed by the withering detachment in the two models' facial expressions. The sublime and/or transcendent nature of sexual experience is reduced to sex as accessory of a world where the only transcendence is measured in material luxury, where all the licences of morality have been rubber-stamped and clandestinely cleared.

Thus Ferry consorts with Helmut Newton and Robert Carlos Clarke, with the acme of 1970s sexual art and the representation of decadent consumption. Of the many photographers who came to prominence in the 1960s Newton and Carlos Clarke perhaps more than any others made an international living out of glamorizing its often seedy sexuality. They bulldozed the earth mothers and hippie chicks, the *Shaft* studs and rock stars and instead equated sexuality not with spiritual enlightenment, decathlete virility or authenticity of experience but with a decadent faith in wealth and luxuriant circumstances; sex, through the eyes of Newton (described by one sycophant in 1976 as 'the grand couturier of fashion photography'[41]) or Clarke, was, in its most idealized form, the creature of a supernal world of suffocating *confort luxe*, a refined Shangri-La with strictly limited membership, a stylized two-dimensional rendition of the entire 1970s angle on sex.

The locations for their photographs were either glossy urban interiors or tropical hideaways. Newton's models were clad (if at all) in clothes conspicuously classical or avant-garde (or sometimes hybrids of both). Veils, pillbox hats, boas, plumages, feathers, sailor suits, tranny 1930s drag – all very hip in the right circles in the mid-1970s, as we have seen – featured widely. 'In the Berlin of the Thirties, where I grew up,' writes Newton, 'there was an air of mystery, like the kind you find in the stories of Schnitzler...they're sensual and erotic, although there are no actual scenes of making love, just an atmosphere of heavy Austro-German sensuality.'[42] Ferry could have attached these words above the sheet-music score of 'Bitter Sweet' and nobody would have batted an eyelid.

Newton's women were ravished on the back seats of limousines; they were folded in four by grim moneymen in ties and tails; they impishly cocked champagne glasses through windows at Parisian nightscapes or (as in Newton's famous

Piscine III) stretched catlike and volcanically bronzed by sapphire swimming pools, those ageless Pop Art signifiers of the Good Life. Newton's work deified money, not just in the obvious and lavish expense invested in each photograph, but in the accoutrements thereof, each a codified homage to 'a world where money buys a particular *brand* [my italics] of exotic liberation, where the exquisite packaging of sexual objects and erotic ideas conveys a kind of absolution on dreams...'[43] This later smiles approvingly on the fact that Newton has a 'talent' to take photographs of shocking and misogynistic images and be embarrassingly well-paid for them. Newton has made capital out of a world where scandal and dislocation are sources of erotic pleasure. Ferry's casual allusion to the Profumo affair in the conception of the *Country Life* cover fits neatly into this Newtonian matrix. Similarly, the dehumanized demeanour of Roxy Music girls – cold, physically powerful, stripped of tenderness (Price: 'I wanted buxom, powerful women'[44]) – can be compared to Newton's models. Nobody smiles in Newton, or in Carlos Clarke; nobody smiles on Roxy Music album covers either, apart from Hall, and her 1975 siren's smile is a parody of a smile, with red mouth hiding razor teeth.

This is not to argue that Ferry, through this use of ironic distance and play with contemporary images of sex, excused himself entirely from rock's drooling exploitation of women in the 1970s. But the visual imagery established by himself, de Ville and Price does raise some issues about the difference between pin-ups and art. Pin-ups are traditionally regarded as intentionally exploitative, predicated entirely on the inspiration of sexual activity and the accretion of money; in art the turn-on is incidental. In Roxy Music record covers, neither intention can be said to be predominant. Rather it is the *idea* of the admass erotic that is being used as well as the image of a woman to sell records.

Tom Wesselmann's *Great American Nudes*, a Pop Art epic still in progress in the 1970s, can also be brought to bear on this discussion. As the only true Pop Art nudes, and certainly the best known, they establish tensions between the ideally rendered nude female body and a number of different contexts, including collaged representations of consumer objects of desire. Many Pop artists have used commercial renderings of the female nude as material, but few have engaged in such an intimate and long-lasting exploration as Wesselmann's as to how the erotic actuality of the female body is located in a world of commercial exploitation and media signs that is the late twentieth century. Much of Wesselmann's work has concentrated on the relationship between the idea of female nudity and its sensual plasticity and the real, commercial environment, as the backgrounds to his nudes have changed.

But these paintings, rather like Ferry's record covers, open up new issues about reality and art and commerce. To regard such paintings as mere meta-narratives, however brilliantly executed, dodges the question of reality – it may make us question the relationship between erotic and commercial realities, but offers no answers about how such relationships are misused. These paintings often risk entering the twilight zones in which the ideas of women being used, whether as clothes-horses or simply as empty receptacles of desire and sperm, become actuality. Even if one believes that art should remain merely a silent observer of society, Pop Art's cavalier usage of exploitation is unsettling. Does its neutrality on the issues of exploitation mean it is endorsing it? Exploitation and the packaging of dreams are abstract material, but they are also material realities lived and consumed and endured. That Roxy Music, through their lyrics and imagery, could deal with such topics – and that Ferry could live some of the dreams he packaged – was an altogether new discourse for rock and roll.

Another case for the defence of Roxy Music's sexuality, however – perhaps a clinching one – is what it meant when compared to sexuality in the British mass media in the 1970s. Roxy Music was a transcendent expression of eros as luminous and distinctive as an orchid in a cabbage patch.

Sex in popular culture meant, for the most part, irremediably trollopy pornography of both hard- and softcore varieties or kiss-and-tell fabrications garnished with bikini shots. Sex in Britain's cultural life was still somewhat coyly marginalized as sensationalist ghetto. *Oh! Calcutta!* and Paul Raymond's *Festivals of Erotica* on the London stage were in effect the exceptions that proved the rule in a country which still treated sex as a dirty little secret. The inability of mainstream show business and media to cope with the enormous economic and social impact of the 1960s meant that a desperate resort to sex would always be tried whenever youthful attention was required by the entertainment industry. It was assumed by those who controlled the distribution of image that young people had been driven sex-mad by the 1960s, and no opportunity to bring pictures or shock-horror accounts of alfresco hippie copulation to the breakfast tables of Britain in tabloid form was spurned. Which serves now to remind us that in the 1970s, incredibly, the proto-girlie mags of the 1930s, *Titbits* and its putative heirs, the appalling *Weekly News*, *Reveille* and *Weekend*, lived on, with all manner of naughties splashed between the nipples, mostly in the vein of what bored Fleet Street subeditors called 'nude vicar had Corn Flakes box on head' stories.

Sex was still unremittingly equated with unallowable indulgence; porn was linked more explicitly with glamour than ever it had been. It had always been linked, as we have seen, with a certain lifestyle – normally urban – of indulgence and decadence. Even in the 1970s a swimming pool would always feature one way or another in stills or film footage. *Deep Throat* and *Emmanuelle*, the decade's quintessential masturbatory film smashes, both fetishizing exotica and super-wealth in varying forms and to varying degrees, as though the supertax-bracket settings were as much intended to arouse the viewer as was the sex on show. Sex in any other context was unthinkable, save for the squalid screwfests of the *Confessions* and *What's Up?* series of movies, of which more later. Jacqueline Susann, Jackie Collins and Harold Robbins, the decade's best-selling novelists, were no less culpable; *The Pirate*, *The Lonely Lady*, *The Bitch*, *The Stud*, *Once is Not Enough* – all made money and exotica preconditions for good sex, as though orgasm were not the logical outcome of foreplay but the result of an accumulation of wealth, helipads and penthouse suites. Common sex was cheap and comical, privileged sex expensive and indecently good; a contrast of Watney's Red Barrel with vintage Armagnac. Omnipresent advertisements for Lamb's Navy Rum, featuring buxom skin-divers on tropical beaches, were everywhere in Britain, much as were the palpitating blondes which peered down on us from the fronts of buses to sell Robbins's doorstep potboilers. Sex was always associated with 'abroad', with 'Europe'. Dutch, Finnish, French, Danish, Italian, Spanish and, of course, most famously, Swedish girls were perennially knicker-dropping orgasm addicts.

In Britain, because sex was used so shamelessly as a commercial device, the manner of its imagizing was often singularly unappealing. The British film industry, dying on its knees in the 1970s, was a case in point. The *Carry On* movies went from smut heaven to smut hell, and as if that wasn't enough, in the name of letting something spurious and unnamed all hang out, there were the aforementioned *Confessions* movies, which dominated popular culture's view of sexuality in Britain.

Perhaps the worst and certainly the least sexy sex films ever released into the cinematic mainstream, their remit was to try and make comedy out of sex life in Britain in the 1970s. But in doing so they managed to be formidably unerotic. Fantasy was diminished by farce and stereotype, sex was a giggle, not a narcotic or epicurean pleasure. It was a furtive, dog-eared world of gropes in huts, allotments, car boots, suburban bedrooms. The sexuality was about as much 'now' as *Police Gazette*. 'Star' Robin Askwith's buttocks, white as two hard-boiled eggs, bouncing up and down on top of a dolly bird in pulled-aside chainstore briefs lying on an old mattress was as good as it got. Picture, if you dare, the premise: the hairnetted matriarch-in-law serving fish fingers on Formica tables, the subfusc furniture, the strange omnipresence of leading characters called Sid; more often than not, 'Sid' doubled as another fixture, the permanently on strike and sex-mad slob on the second-hand sofa with the fags and a copy of *Sporting Life*. Or, of course, sprawling open at page three, the *Sun*.

There was something horribly provincial, compromised and self-disgusted about it all. The tabloid press had, like their cousins the pornographers, got drunk with courage on the 1960s and began to feature sex more explicitly on their pages, much as the split-beaver pose began to spread over the shiny pages of men's magazines throughout the 1970s.

By comparison, Roxy Music were Renaissance men of refinement, restoring to sexuality its mystique, sensuality, tactile luxuriance and multi-dimensional character. Roxy Music covers, for example, could be consumed as sex objects and satires thereon. This never was, and never could have been, the province of *Rustler* magazine, Mary Millington or Robin Askwith. For that, Roxy Music should be hailed as sexual sophisticates in the wilderness.

PASTICHE AND PARODY – ROXY MUSIC AND THEIR PEERS

The concept of irony was a new one to rock in the 1970s, yet as the countercultural experiments of the previous decade degenerated into self-indulgence or politicized ghettos, the new decade was found to be short of a signature sound. Intriguingly, though, many of the most distinctive acts of the early part of the 1970s scored by their very refusal to accept rock creativity as a Beatlish teleology, always sod-busting its way forward into virgin territory, but as a historical whole with treasures to be found in the past as well as the future. Progressive rockers made many fine albums by subordinating the r'n'b roots of rock, but others did so by seeking to make the past a part of what was to come, and also by looking laterally at related fields of music such as soul and funk, which mainstream rock distanced itself from. Bowie and Roxy Music were among the pioneers of this postmodern approach, but others in the game included America's Todd Rundgren, Sparks and Steely Dan, while Great Britain offered 10cc, Steve Harley/Cockney Rebel and Sailor.

Rundgren and Steely Dan were, like Roxy Music and David Bowie, responsible for releasing a key rock album in 1972. Dan's album, like Roxy Music's, was all the more astounding for being a début LP. Its peculiar charm (not unlike that of Todd Rundgren's astounding double-set *Something/Anything*) was probably its clandestine suggestions of Beatledom. Two years after the Fab Four's split, rock still craved a replacement; anyone whose music seemed to echo the as-yet-unacknowledged hybridity of Beatles music – and the seamlessness of that hybridity – struck a chord often too deep for cognoscenti, at least in rock, to isolate. All they could do was praise the music.

The gift of the Beatles – and, to a lesser extent, the Beach Boys – was to assimilate, on a very deep level and without prejudice, innumerable popular song traditions and wring from them something new yet of matchless pedigree. They were filters for mass musical information and distilled something wholly fresh. Rundgren and Steely Dan's Walter Becker and Donald Fagen operated similarly; whereas pop, for most rockers, was seen as the ultimate dead end, for these performers it was merely the beginning. Intimate knowledge of tension and release, of timing and of the emotional codes of pop composition, is plain in the output of both Rundgren and Steely Dan; also of Latin and soul grooves, anathema to rock mainstreamers but not to these mavericks.

The words 'parody' and 'pastiche' were indiscriminately sown throughout all discussion of the music made by these acts. This was often without true cognizance of the words' actual meanings; a cardinal error, for such meanings are vital to understanding the genre. The assumption that (for example, Rundgren's or Steely Dan's) retro treatments must in some ways be ironic (parody) underlay much of the criticism. After all, no rocker could really take Latin seriously any more, surely? Or Motown? But in truth Rundgren, Fagen/Becker and Sparks' Ron and Russell Mael were not parodists but expert *pasticheurs*, affectionate synthesizers of sources. Apart from making some wonderful music, the craft and easy facility with which the materials were handled begged questions as to the degree and kind of pop's pastiching and parody. Meanings in pop, and the use of pop music in both creative composition and creative listening, thus began to blur.

Bowie and Ferry were masters of this craft. Even when, as on 'Bitters End', satire is apparent, one is never too sure how broad a satire upon doo-wop Ferry intends, so deeply woven in the fabric of his creativity is a respect for the form.

Also germane to the discussion is the music of 10cc, a Manchester band whose status as onetime saviours of British rock and roll is now unjustly forgotten. Their 1974 and 1975 albums (*Sheet Music* and *The Original Soundtrack*) were unanimously, and rightly, hailed as works of mercurial genius; the rewiring of the pop reflex and the treatment of pop's emotional syntax are unquestionably breathtaking. But that often came in tandem with a self-consciously arch parodic take on pop cliché that was a little too blatant for its own good – 'Donna' and 'Rubber Bullets', the band's first two singles, are the best-known examples; but fun was being mercilessly poked at all manner of stylistic quirks right up until the band's demise in the late 1970s. There is a coarsely supercilious atmosphere at times, despite the unimpeachable songwriting qualities on display. 10cc made sure you heard those postmodern quotation marks being drawn, and sometimes the listener can hear them being riveted into the very heart of the music – a riff there, a vocal swoop there. Frightfully clever, but not a little heartless. With Ferry and Bowie one could never be sure whether they were there or not. The nostalgia was just too well integrated.

Predictably, there were also acts who were openly plagiaristic of Roxy Music, the silliest being Sailor, who in

1977 were described, generously, as 'a kind of European cousin twice removed of Roxy Music'.[45] Little attempt was made to disguise the debt; 'A Glass of Champagne', the band's first hit in the UK, unashamedly ripped off high-life Roxy Music imagery and Georg Kajanus, who claimed 'Russo-Nordic' (shorthand for half-Finnish) origins, minced unappealingly in *Slaughter on Tenth Avenue* matelot togs while affecting a hiccupy vibrato. Sailor were, contemporary accounts state, fond of 'shanty-brunch rhythms' (whatever they might have been – the articles are uninformative). They were, in short, what Roxy Music *might* have looked and sounded like with one third of the talent and with clothes acquired from Mr Byrite instead of from Antony Price. They made much of an 'atmosphere of the red-light quarter' in interviews.[46] 'We want,' they claimed, 'to revisit lost Light Entertainment.'[47] They got lost on the way and were, mercifully, never heard of again.

A more credible challenger was Steve Harley and Cockney Rebel, who sounded like the title of a paperback by Richard Allen but were, thankfully, an incomparably more literate entity. Harley, briefly, was the toast of the rock comics, making larger-than-life, over-the-top claims for his band and his art, filling the void of provocation vacated by Ferry and Bowie. For example, they played, much-heralded, at Biba's in October 1974 with mime artists supporting, and much being made of Harley 'limp-wristing' around the stage.[48]

Harley's inescapable spiels of self-indulgence dominated 1974; but whereas Bowie's and Ferry's calculated teasing of public opinion helped establish them in rock mythology, Harley's ended up exempting him from it. Novelty succeeds only by being new, something the ex-journalist couldn't seem to grasp, and the portfolio of second-hand postures – androgyny, camp, irony – that Harley flourished in rock's face was greeted with gasp one year but a yawn the next. Sadly, it undermined history's estimation of his music, which was often of a high quality. Far more musically straightforward than that of Bowie or Roxy Music at their best, it was none the less the work of an imaginative songwriter wholly in control of his art and with a nicely instinctive way of making it fit his chameleon personality.

VIVA! ROXY MUSIC

Ferry's press-induced huff had, if anything, worsened by 1976 and contact between him and the British press dwindled to almost nothing, caused partly by mutual mistrust and partly by the peripatetic existence of Roxy Music around the globe.

According to Ferry:

'When I read criticisms of my work, I feel rather scornful of it, because it will only point out something I know already. I rarely find critics perceptive. They usually see things which are totally ridiculous, which shows that they have no real feeling, or aren't terribly…articulate. In fact, a lot of the people who write about me don't have a clue as far as I'm concerned. And I can't be bothered with people who don't have any emotional depth or intelligence'.[49]

Ferry's temper could hardly have been improved by the fate of 'Love is the Drug'. He is a pop singer refreshingly free of rock-snob airs when it comes to singles – he *wants* his singles to be teenybop sensations and tells everyone so – but his thoughts of a first British No. 1 were dashed on this occasion. Not for the last time, a Roxy Music single was kept off the top of the British charts by a single sales phenomenon. 'Love is the Drug' enjoyed almost blanket airplay on BBC Radio 1, but was rudely elbowed aside in mid-November by the juggernaut of Queen's 'Bohemian Rhapsody', a song that would occupy the top slot for the next nine weeks, after which a chastened Roxy Music would already be planning their follow-up single release, 'Both Ends Burning' (it flopped, badly).

The band wasted little time regretting what might have been, packing in two more US visits in December 1975 and March 1976. Tensions, however, were obstinately refusing to disappear. This was nothing tempestuous – other situations had arisen for the constituent members of the band and on this occasion, they chose to put them before the good of the group. Nobody was particularly culpable. Manzanera suggests, 'We were sick of the sight of each other';[50] Ferry, for his part, maintains, 'We needed a rest from each other.'[51]

Manzanera had already begun pooling ideas for a new solo album, going into Basing Street Studios in London (which had already admirably served the purposes of the Brian Eno albums he'd played on) and recording tracks for an album which would eventually see the light of day two years hence as 801's *Listen Now!!* Mackay had even bigger fish to fry in the shape of an ITV television programme he'd been commissioned to score the previous year. Jobson was being headhunted by Frank Zappa.

Press foreboding was repulsed with a robust piece of flim-flam from Mackay himself: 'Roxy Music, as a group, has a life of its own,' he assured the hacks (they should have known something was awry – Ferry was usually the man for such duties). 'The group has an identity which has grown stronger and is nourished by the fact that we are able to pursue separate projects. We don't see very much of each other when we're not recording or touring as Roxy,' he went on – a statement of the obvious to mollify publicists. 'But when we get together in the studio to record for a Roxy Music album, it is surprising and fresh and exciting, because the identity of Roxy Music takes over and asserts itself. The history and the style of Roxy which we as a group created.'[52]

On 26 June 1976, shortly after this statement was issued, it was made official that for the foreseeable future Roxy Music wouldn't be asserting any kind of identity at all. They were breaking up, or, in the phrase chosen at the time, embarking on a 'devolution', allowing members to go off and release creative energies.

Ferry glosses this corporate newsspeak neatly: 'Everyone would go off and sulk about the break-up.'[53]

Ferry blamed 'wives and lovers and money and publishers and managers and lawyers'[54] for the break-up, not to mention the preponderance of solo interests that were now motivating the Roxy Music personnel.

The capital irony was, of course, the reaction the live album received. While missing out on the passionate endorsements of the first two LPs, *Viva! Roxy Music* was very well received indeed.

It's a shame that the album does not specify the dates upon which its eight tracks were recorded; the sleeve note just says between November 1973 and October 1975. There are some ill-fitting delusions of grandeur burdening several tracks which fits with contemporary accounts of the 1975 tour, whereas others have an effortlessly energetic dedication to maximizing their musical qualities. Given the martial nature of the 'RM' image and totalitarian chic after 1974, there are elements of this album which reflect Ferry's admiration for Nazi visuals but unfortunately do little to help the music. One shouldn't overplay the notion, however, that the Roxy Music live experience after Ferry's assumption of his military uniform was in any way wanting. The version of 'Out of the Blue' from *Country Life* which opens the album is startling, almost aerobically stimulating stuff, Manzanera's guitar as sharp and motoric as a chainsaw; Jobson's solo, melodramatic enough in the studio, raises the roof, smartly interpolating melodic elements. The menacing first theme, however, lumbers somewhat, prefacing worse to come. The album often lacks snap and brio, even 'Pyjamarama' dragging its heels and coming across as somewhat bleary-eyed. The soundstage is big and beefy, but closely miked enough to impart *jouissance* and tension. 'The Bogus Man' starts off slowly enough to suggest the band are showing a very slow learner guitarist how to play the song. The climax of 'In Every Dream Home a Heartache', a classic piece of rock release, only detonates a mighty plod, as imposing as Godzilla but unfortunately just as subtle. 'In Every Dream Home a Heartache' is ruined by the surreally incongruous melodrama of timpani flourishes and guitar riffs in the middle of Ferry's possessed narrative, whose initial impact came from the fact that it was so static and so featureless. Its very sparseness was evocative of the moral exhaustion of its satiated and self-disgusted protagonist.

The band sound suitably wired, however. 'The Bogus Man' may lack a little vim, but none of its clangour; at times, this sounds as brutal a funk exercise as anything Cabaret Voltaire might have been playing at the same time. For all the supertanker clumsiness of the pulse which clay-foots the end of 'Heartache', the racket from Manzanera's guitar is awe-inspiring. The elaborate opening out of 'If There is Something' to accommodate solos from Jobson, Mackay and Manzanera is mercifully disciplined; Mackay gets to play a solo on what might be a prototype of the synthesized wind instrument, the lyricon (the sleeve notes are silent). Otherwise the maelstrom of the mix obscures him somewhat unfairly; on the encore, 'Do the Strand', he is uncharacteristically out of sorts, missing an early entry and otherwise grumpily muted. Manzanera, on a roll in the studio, contributes mightily; his guitar blazes like solar flares in 'Chance Meeting'. This serves merely as a taster for 'Both Ends Burning', whose slinky sexiness is undermined by a flat-four fundamentalism and also by the jaw-dropping horror of the Sirens, whose backing vocals would be acceptable if they could a) hit a note and b) not sound vile. One is almost tempted to imagine that their dissonant shrieking is Eno's revenge, a latter-day sonic disruption planted by the band's old colleague. Ambulance sirens would have added more. The album, however, avoids empty spectacle, save for the climax to 'Chance Meeting', whose widescreen vocal harmonies, mellotron, synthesizer and bass pedals lend a big-sky grandeur worthy of Genesis. It's evidence of a band full of life.

Thus did it seem an all the more oddly poignant way to bow out; the irony of the title, loosely interpretable as 'Long live Roxy Music', seemed a final ironic postscript to the most ironic of bands.

7: GLOBAL COOLING – FERRY'S SOLO YEARS (1976 – 8)

LET'S NOT STICK TOGETHER

To recap, one of Roxy Music's major trump cards was the apparent adultness of nearly everything they said or touched. It wasn't necessarily heavy squareness; it was a means of expressing the emotional and sexual condition of adulthood in terms adolescents could relate to. This adultness extended to the way they conducted themselves professionally.

Roxy Music had always been a band containing many frictions. The basis of the band's inspiration had been difference – between, in Mackay's words, his own 'classical influence', Manzanera's 'slightly West Coast American style' and Ferry's 'strange kind of Fifties and Sixties pop influence'.[1] Disputes within Roxy Music were thus personally awkward but creatively fruitful. And personal differences were, as a rule, sorted out maturely. Furthermore, each member of this febrile band had exterior interests, the most intriguing of which were Mackay's.

In 1975, Mackay had been approached by Verity Lambert, Thames TV's head of drama, as a creative consultant for a projected drama series centred around a hopeful rock band. Written by Howard Schuman, the programme, *Rock Follies*, was a smart-alecky and watchable if occasionally strained account of three women, Anna (Charlotte Cornwell), Dee (Julie Covington) and 'Q' (Rula Lenska), fronting their own rock band, the Little Ladies. The resultant depiction of the business in which the Little Ladies found themselves was, expectably, a sour-pussy shriek against corruption, sloth and shiftlessness. Six hour-long shows, produced by Andrew Brown, were made and appeared between 24 February and 30 March 1976. Schuman also collaborated with Mackay on the eighteen songs which featured in the first series, twelve of which were set aside for inclusion on a compilation disc drawn from the series.

Public reaction was startling: the series was a major smash hit, Covington was inundated with offers, Mackay was fêted for his score and the resultant 'soundtrack' went to No. 1 in the album charts, an achievement (as Ferry must have enviously noted) that only *Stranded* of Roxy Music's own output had equalled. Acclaim within the television industry, voiced by critics, professionals and executives alike, was equally good.

With the bouquets came brickbats, though, because within rock itself the series was derided. In the rock comics especially, *Rock Follies* became a byword for garbage, so grotesquely and cartoonily unrepresentative of the rock business that it was almost camp. Rockism, still protective of its 1960s illusions and desperate to deny its hand-in-glove relationship with show-business, mistrusted television, and rock cognoscenti railed with increasing vigour against the attempts of show business to appropriate rock music to lend ubiquitous 'nowness', first to the music and now to TV. Show business and TV, it was claimed, didn't 'get' rock. And Mackay, though richly rewarded by praise from television's cognoscenti and critical fraternity, and a slew of enquiries concerning new commissions, was left fuming by the response of his musical peers. In 1979 he raged to *Record Mirror's* Rosalind Russell:

> 'It was one of the most original TV programmes of the last ten years. It was made in opposition to what the TV companies wanted. It was seen here as a commercial programme which it conspicuously was not. In the three years since *Rock Follies* there has been nothing else as exciting…you got an hour of hard creative television.'[2]

Mackay hastened to point out, 'It related rock business to show business which most rock and roll musicians find offensive, but I think it's true, it is related. People in the rock business tend to be insular.'[3] They often were, but it didn't automatically follow that their judgements had no validity. For instance, much of the criticism of the way the rock experience was portrayed for those who created it was spot-on. The girls' career exists in a kind of rock limbo, a tinker toy environment created by Schuman, cued not by the experience of those who had lived, produced or consumed the rock milieu but by the prejudices of those who hadn't. 'Caricature' was the most used word in rock's critical response to the series.

None the less, it would be unfair to deny that all three actresses performed splendidly and possessed singing skills shading from good (Lenska) to superb (Covington). The latter's astonishing impact made her one of the faces of 1976, and had her No. 1 rendition of 'Don't Cry for Me, Argentina', from Tim Rice and Andrew Lloyd-Webber's *Evita*, won her the show's lead in 1978 she would surely still be one of the country's most luminous performers. Certainly she maintained her momentum, and Mackay's, in 1977, by starring in a second run of the show, *Rock Follies 77*, which, while not equalling the success of its parent programme (the novelty had gone), was a ratings winner; the inevitable album was a disappointing failure, though, not even reaching the bottom end of the charts. A single, 'OK?', released in May of that year did scrape into the Top Ten, albeit with expectably minimal airplay from a miffed BBC, and Mackay had become a rich man, the first Roxy Music member apart from Ferry to accumulate notable music-derived wealth.

Mackay's enthusiasm for the *Rock Follies* project and Schuman's jaundiced view of the industry he earned a living from could have owed something to Mackay's apparent sense of political and social injustice and distaste for exploitation, which first manifested itself during interviews for his first album, *In Search of Eddie Riff*. Given the chance to emerge from behind Ferry's tuxedoed form, he proved volubly opinionated on a range of subjects, not least the need for revolution in society and the fact that the Baader-Meinhof gang were really pretty cool guys and gals.

In 1978, substantially enriched by the proceeds of *Rock Follies*, Mackay took a sabbatical from music and went to see the likely alternatives for himself, spending months in the People's Republic of China, the musical results of which would manifest themselves on *Resolving Contradictions* (1978). Both this and *Eddie Riff* will be examined in depth below.

Mackay's unprompted agitprop and grouchy view of the music industry as expressed in *Rock Follies* might have seemed incongruous coming from a Roxy Music member in 1976, but such sentiments at least evidenced an ear to the ground for contemporary social and cultural developments.

THE CASE OF PUNK

Not that one needed an ear to the ground to detect the approach of an out-of-control steamroller called Punk rock which was about to collide with the British music industry and the subsequent welter of flob, primitive musical Situationism and expletives the impact would create.

On paper, Roxy Music and Punk rock would appear

fundamentally antithetical. Ferry's affected Clark Gable moustache, his resplendent occupation of colour supplement and glossy pop-mag pin-up pages, and his ostentatious consumption and unrepentant loucheness appeared as positively pantomime enactments of the complacently bourgeois malaise that Punk claimed had befallen rock and entertainment in general. Ferry, for instance, would gladly tell eager reporters of a 7,000 mile round trip he had made from Japan to the Raffles Hotel in Singapore and back, a 'detour' whimsically undertaken during a hiatus in his first solo world tour. Johnny Rogan, in *Style with Substance*, neatly characterizes Ferry as an aspirant 'rock and roll Somerset Maugham'.[4]

'It was all frightfully polite and proper there, the way the English are meant to be,'[5] he was reported as saying, but as this featured in a breathtakingly tasteless piece of pre-*Hello!* money-voyeurism in the magazine *OK*, written by a young Rick Sky, it may be a fictional quote. The same piece features Ferry, still globe-trotting, deep-sea fishing in the Pacific and hauling in a giant barracuda. What hardly helped Ferry in the eyes of his detractors was that, as a son of the working classes, he had so conspicuously betrayed – or so it appeared – his roots.

But even before the Jubilee summer, it was clear that Roxy Music, while they wouldn't be spared censure, would avoid the genuine and instinctive dislike engendered in the young by other bands. There was too much common inspirational ground between Roxy Music and the Punk vanguard, who, after all, had grown out of a similar art school milieu to Ferry and had nourished related ideas about the links between fashion and identity and the disposability of artistic endeavour.

Ferry, for his part, while sceptical of Punk, intriguingly refused to condemn the trend as 'anti-musical' in the van of many of his peers. 'I liked the energy of Punk – and the hair – but not much of the music,' he remembered later.[6] None the less he could and did tell *Miss London* magazine that 'a lot of it seems very manipulated and I find *most* [my italics] of it quite dreadful.'[7] Ferry was hardly the man to talk about manipulation, but when one considers his lifestyle in 1977 and the cavalier way in which he spoke of it, it is obvious he didn't much care who thought what about him:

'I'm not ashamed of the way I behaved, or of anything I've ever done. But some people have always resented me. They resent the fact that I'm successful. They resent the fact that I wear nice suits. They resent the fact that I can afford them... it's a pathetic kind of jealousy really.'[8]

This neo-Thatcherite homily on the politics of envy was delivered in 1978 and is Ferry in uncharacteristically mean-spirited form. It was the perfect example of his rare errors in unwittingly playing his press-allotted caricature. Even *The NME Encyclopedia of Rock* (1977), perhaps the best-written and most authoritative volume of its kind ever published in Britain, in its entry on Ferry wrote, 'It's hard to reconcile the humourless, image-obsessive mid-70s Ferry with the vintage Roxy visionary.'[9] One of the best observations of Ferry at the time was Julie Burchill's, 'The only thing one can imagine him getting mad about is a crease in his cravat.'[10]

Ferry became easy copy, the pop star who never smiled. In a post-gig stupor of exhaustion after an Albert Hall warm-up gig for his forthcoming world tour, he realized he couldn't win – even when he attempted, as on this occasion, to be self-effacing, it was interpreted as chilly hauteur. But if he didn't frankly seem to give a damn, he had good reason. The enforced retirement of Roxy Music freed him to concentrate on establishing himself in his favourite territories, Europe and America, where Punk meant little and would remain an irrelevance for years. Europe had already been wooed; it had now merely to be conquered. As for America, first with Jerry and then with the surprising fruitfulness of the 1975 visits with Roxy Music, it had started smiling on him and he intended to capitalize.

Internal wrangles at EG and the decision of Ferry's management to hand over tape leases to Polydor, who took on a
substantial part of EG's business, suggest that Ferry was wasting
no time in getting where he wanted to go. American appetites
had been tantalized with the bizarre *Let's Stick Together* album,
released by Atlantic in 1976 in the immediate wake of the Roxy
Music split. A US-only release, its existence was predicated on
little more than commercial anxiety. 'In America,' explained
Ferry sourly, 'you're not allowed – because it's all high-pressure
business thinking there – to release fun things like EPs.'[11]

The *Extended Play* EP, a pointless if affectionate exercise in
nostalgia (the trend at the time had been for ponderous 'maxi-
singles') which showcased four excellent *hommages*, was a
substantial hit for Ferry in Britain during the autumn of 1976.
The airplay track was a furiously excitable supercharging of
the Everly Brothers' 'The Price of Love', all foot-stomping
drums, pounding piano and banshee backing vocals, and while
the other numbers (Gallagher and Lyle's plaintive 'Heart on
my Sleeve', Betty Wright's 'Shame Shame Shame' and the
Beatles 'It's Only Love') may not have had the same startling
purpose and punch, they enchanted none the less. Atlantic,
however, with the pusillanimous vacillation that marked their
relationship – indeed, the whole of the American music
industry's relationship – with Ferry and Roxy Music, balked at
putting the EP on the market and instead bundled it up with
'Let's Stick Together' along with a surreal batch of B-sides,
alternate takes and new arrangements of old numbers.

Atlantic can be castigated for their cowardice, but it did at
least produce an intriguing accident of birth which, while
musically uninspiring, is a must-have document of the band's
history for Roxy Music fanatics, and it was presumably that
hard core that clamoured so loudly for import copies that in
1976 Island decided to release the album officially in the UK.
David O'List, resurrected by a forgiving Ferry for the *Another
Time, Another Place* sessions, reappears on 'Chance Meeting',
and among the sessionmen appearing at various phases of the

record are guitarist Chris Spedding from Roxy Music's 1973 support act Sharks, bassist Rick Wills (who had handled bass duties at a couple of 1975 concerts for Roxy Music) and percussionist Morris Pert. Also in attendance are bassist Alan Spenner and saxman Chris Mercer from the *These Foolish Things* days, all of Roxy Music save Mackay, and a young guitarist named Neil Hubbard, who would later become a regular back-up guitarist on late Roxy Music sessions for *Flesh + Blood* and *Avalon*.

No one is given the chance to use the album as a calling card for their instrumental skills; hardly a superfluous note is played on what is a cogent, urgent piece of work which could stand proudly as a fresh item in the Ferry canon rather than the grab-bag it is. The Roxy Music covers are of chief interest for their reflection on the originals; the results are indecisive, but entertaining. 'Remake-Remodel' is the most radical statement, daringly turned into an unshaven, back-to-basics piece of contemporary US funk, with the (uniformly excellent) chorus squalling out the 'CPL 593H' line while Wetton and Thompson work wonders within the basic 4/4 pulse of the melody. Prefiguring Ferry's later *Taxi* work, only the chords and melody remain, with Jobson's bad-tempered violin, Ferry's B-movie spooky-organ and Spedding's sharp guitar prowling around the remains. The rest of the reworkings are less audacious, and smack of 'if only'. 'Casanova' sports a very early drumbox, and the economy of the bass/piano/ drums and broken guitar chords (Mel Collins proving an excellent surrogate of Mackay) gives the song room to breathe. Ferry's lyrics – such as the magical line, 'Casanova, is that your name or do you live there?' – enjoy deserved prominence. On 'Sea Breezes', the soundstage is fuller, the lines more authoritative and confident, with more of a will to elaborate. Even Thompson is lighter and subtler on '2HB'. The piano lines on the latter are more assured, the figure underlying the chorus genuinely delightful. The chiming Fender Rhodes piano lends a Hollywood sparkle. Jobson takes command on

'Chance Meeting': while the halting, jarring simplicity of the original stimulates, the slight enriching of the chords and the uncompromisingly metallic wall of noise which bring the track screaming to a halt are worthy of inclusion on the first album; hearing this, the neutral listener could venture the opinion that Eno might as well never have existed.

The remainder consists of highly accomplished if somewhat lightweight cover versions, save for the jackhammer intensity of 'The Price of Love'. Shattering the icy image of dilettanteism, Ferry loads the album with bluesy bravado. It's a nice, and unexpected, two-fingers to his detractors. His own harp playing merits applause, and Spedding's shit-kicking guitar tone on 'Shame Shame Shame' might have been dredged from the stews of the deepest South. Wetton and Thompson are as strong and sinewy as a hawser, the muscled centre of volatile music.

'You Go to My Head' and Gallagher and Lyle's 'Heart on My Sleeve' are maybe the exceptions; the former is anaesthetized by string and brass arrangements that the most hardened producer of formula soul might have turned down. The track's intended sumptuousness is as tacky and tawdry as mass-produced tiramisu. Fortunately, the harmonic sophistication which depth-charges unexpected key changes in the former and subtly diminishes the syrup in the latter saves the day. 'Sleeve' maintains its lyricism, but through the tenderness and stinging sweetness of the arrangement, which are altogether less effete than the original. Lennon/McCartney's 'It's Only Love' is an uncomplicated Roxyfication, albeit lacking the edge of Manzanera's guitar.

What followed, though – what was *intended* – was a record of far greater thematic coherence: all Ferry's self-penned work. This was an obvious attempt at relaunching the man's solo career.

In Your Mind (February 1977) was a palpable change of tack. Ferry appeared on the cover, moustacheless but oddly incognito in shades, wearing an enforcer's frown in harsh white light, and dressed only in a casual white T-shirt. The typeface was a smudged, blown-up manual typewriter font, in brash colours. It's tempting to read this truculent minimalism as a concession to Punk, but as sharp an imagistic operator as Ferry might have been, the visual and typographical syntax of Punk hadn't been around long enough for him to want to try and pastiche it. It's debatable that he could have been bothered to do so in any case; America and the patrons of tawdry dance floors in high-income discotheques were those who Ferry wished to seduce.

The album backfired horribly. Reviewers on both sides of the Atlantic dismissed it out of hand. Disco was still anathema to the majority of critics and musicians alike, and even those who had always credited Ferry with the capacity of staying several steps ahead of what his detractors and friends were saying and thinking saw *In Your Mind* and disco as a manhole waiting to open under him. It did, however, spawn a British hit in 'This is Tomorrow' (a belated and sidelong nominative tribute to his Pop Art spiritual parentage, Hamilton, Paolozzi et al.) and won Ferry his first airplay in the US, thereby fulfilling some of its intended function.

Apart from Ferry's typical melodic flair, *In Your Mind* is a disappointing affair, and makes one wonder (as Rogan does, explicitly) what Brian Eno might have done with it. At around the same time as Ferry had been huffing and puffing in the US, trying to adapt his music to the unyielding form and straitjacketing forms of disco composition and production, Eno had been in Berlin with David Bowie and had set about radically reinventing them. Eno had shown vague interest in Ferry's idea of a disco-oriented album, and as the conveyor-belt anonymity of Ferry's arrangements seep in one cannot help but think of Bowie's *Low*, the invigorating panoply of suggestions and ideas by which Eno helped turn it into a defining document, melodic, danceable and thoroughly new. *Low*, some mischievous critics went so far as to suggest when discussing 1977 Ferry, invoked the vertical and linear invention of early Roxy Music, in terms of the reassemblage of sounds and textures within the arrangement and the easy invention of the melodic lines. It manages to outshine Ferry's album even when considered as a commercial proposition. One critic wrote with uncommon perspicacity that Bowie was 'creating musical Alphaville with *Low*. It's supremely possible that when it [*Low*] is finally completed, Ferry will be appearing on the opening night at its equivalent of the Talk of the Town.'[12]

The ground that *In Your Mind* made for Ferry in the US came in spite of rather than due to the efforts of Ferry's record company, which, true to form, dragged its feet over *In Your Mind*. Not that the album begged special attention; it suffers from comparison with its two immediate predecessors, and the somewhat indeterminate cover statement decorates a sheath for undecided aspirations and dreams. This is an artist learning how to work his compass. The sound of *In Your Mind* is indeed too prototypical, too redolent of the admass show-biz fodder Ferry had hitherto made his fortune satirizing. None of the tracks sounds confident, as though Ferry is unwilling to commit his own notes and words to non-Roxy Music players (previously his albums had been stuffed with the ideas of others, after all). His lyrics are frisky and knowing: 'All Night Operator', a stab at classic telephone-love soul, views its protagonist as 'a final connection; a bridge before the fall'. Choruses are tried, successfully, on the worthwhile 'Rock of Ages'. There is, however, too much emasculation; Ferry sounds uncommonly subdued (a shame – his mannerisms are expertly handled, evidenced by the exquisite flash of sharks' teeth in the smilingly seductive line 'let's share a silk caress' in 'Love Me Madly Again'). The instrumental textures are lacklustre and unimaginative, and the solos drearily common, Mel Collins's solo on 'All Night Operator' being a play-by-numbers case in point. The boxy, undernourished production makes an undifferentiated mess of the production, the treble–heavy mix benefiting only the excellent Paul Thompson.

Compositionally, there seems little direction, although no one number could remotely be described as a failure. 'One

Kiss' hints at Beatle aspirations, a real-time narrative of the end of an affair, with everything in the present tense. 'Love Me Madly Again' has its cake but fails to eat it, trying to wedge in three melodic ideas into a less than epic frame; unfortunately, Ferry's melody means that the track might as well be titled 'This is Tomorrow Again'.

It's unfair to judge *In Your Mind* too harshly; Ferry's stylistic vacillation is forgivable. In 1977 he was regarded as too much of a stylistic and formal polymath to have any public problems over concretizing his variant inspirations into a coherent whole.

In Your Mind being nothing like a coherent whole meant that it failed critical litmus tests everywhere. The fact that the beauties reside in the detail sums the album up: the hesitant, broken phrases and chromatic shimmer of guitar which underpin the sultry, enigmatic flugelhorn entry to 'Rock of Ages' were among Ferry's most enchanting inspirations to date and would later inform many of the interpolations of musical reverie that made themselves felt on later albums, notably *Taxi* (1993). The statement of the pentatonic melody that introduces 'Tokyo Joe' is a delight, but sadly the song never makes much of that profile's potential, despite the assured brilliance of the lyrical inspiration. The title track's hoary romanticism – all that guff about 'the frozen chimes of winter' and 'the silver-studded mountain' (which should really have been left to the troglodytic likes of Ritchie Blackmore's Rainbow) – could only have been ironically meant in the wake of 'Bitters End', although the interminable trudge of both rhythm and melody is just a little too ELO for comfort. Ferry, truly, seemed checkmated, stuck at the crossroads, an ideas man lacking worthwhile applications.

Time made Ferry more realistic as to the merits of *In Your Mind*: in a radio interview in 1994 he described it dismissively as 'my least successful album by a long chalk. It all sounds very square to me...I didn't have a producer, and that was one of the reasons.' He suggests that Chris Thomas, the producer used and trusted by Roxy Music for four albums, would have done a more methodical job.[13]

The live experience was premièred in the UK just after Christmas 1976 with a string of gigs at the Royal Albert Hall. The papers were reasoned and respectful, although *Melody Maker* commented on 'less colour' among the audience – who also seemed to be considerably older than at most Roxy Music gigs – 'They might have been welcoming a speaker at a sales conference,' wrote Allan Jones of the good-natured restraint of Ferry's initial welcome on-stage.[14]

Ferry must, in retrospect, have been glad to see the back of England when he set off on his global jaunt with a sizeable entourage (featuring Roxy Music colleagues Thompson and Manzanera). Exacting though the schedule was, he was still determined not to overtax himself or his employees, as the diversion to Singapore already mentioned testifies.

The Australian leg of the tour was more demanding. This was the tightest part of the trip and some performances commenced at midnight by order of an ill-planned and overfilled schedule. None the less, the extra effort would have been lent extra motivation by the firm residency at No. 1 in the Australian charts of Ferry's *In Your Mind* album and some ecstatic cover stories in the local rock comics. The proceedings, while richly rewarding, were not problem-free: Ferry's three backing singers simultaneously contracted hysterical flight phobia (it was suggested), but fortunately the size of his ensemble managed to cover for their absence when the tour reached the US, although at the cost of some degree of sensuality in the performances.

Ferry was mortified on arrival in the States to find *In Your Mind* very much on Atlantic's back-burner and the new single, 'Tokyo Joe', in which he had invested considerable effort and faith, nowhere to be found on any radio station. He seethed:

'When they released my last single everyone thought it would be a big hit. I thought it would as well. But I never even heard it played once on the radio. I thought the album would do well over here because Americans like things very *punchy* and it was the punchiest thing I've done.'[15]

He would claim, in self-justifying if pointless broadsides against the continuing refusal of American radio stations to entertain the idea of playing his music:

'I do very emotional music, but in America they like to have their emotion smoothed down, with all the edges taken off…except your black American can get into emotional music. It knocks me out when I see black people in the audience, but very few of them know my music.'[16]

For someone who had learned his craft through near-religious observation of black performers and who proudly wore his love of soul like a scouting badge, this last must have been especially galling for Ferry. His uncritical overestimation of his own work aside, it is hard not to sympathize with his plight. He had been at the head of an expensive and complicated operation shipping a considerable stage show around the world – Ferry ever the control freak – and had knuckled down for three weeks on the road in a country with serious misgivings about his music, only to be confronted with record company apathy of the highest order. Atlantic had even suggested to Ferry that he write off the rest of the tour. Seeing his American hexes return to haunt him, Ferry scorned this escape clause and struggled on with the three-week tour to the bitter end in the summer of 1977.

Finally, on the verge of nervous and physical collapse, he shuffled off the tour coil and returned to the American environment which had recently shown him most hospitality – Los Angeles, where it was forever Another Time, Another Place.

BY THE POOLSIDE: FERRY, JERRY, PERRY

In Los Angeles, Ferry found himself, as his critics had predicted, slowly assuming the lifestyle of what in those days was still termed 'the jet set' – and not caring a whit. Jerry Hall, in spite of the uniformly admiring attention paid to her by an increasingly tabloid and tittle-tattling British press, was homesick, and her recent engagement to Ferry made a move to Bel Air appear logical. Ferry, in Rick Sky's article – less a homage to the singer himself as a slavering paean to his lifestyle accessories – seemed to have had his head turned by the place. His opinions on the Californian lifestyle, irrespective of the degree of editorial interference, make unappetizing reading:

> 'Most [Californians] love success and I'm finding a lot of their influence is rubbing off on me... I love the enthusiasm of people over here and the way that all business gets done over lunch or over cocktails! They've got such style! At the same time everything gets done so professionally and so quickly! It's unbelievable.'[17]

Ferry here sounds like the prototype for another Martin Amis creation, the proto-Thatcherite lover of the American way with materialism, John Self, in *Money* (1984), where all Stateside businessmen 'talk about money in that sharky American style, as if money were the only gauge of anything, the only measure. They're pretty relaxing company, I find.'[18] Self is a monster of greed who constantly fantasizes about 'winging out' to California to have an entire 'body transplant'. There was no apparent desire to return to England now, and Roxy Music were dismissed out of hand: 'There would be no point in our working together again as a band... Roxy Music just ran its course.'[19] These were words which Ferry would soon have cause to reflect upon.

Ferry had, in effect, achieved his unvoiced aim of 'making it'. He could now scan the Hollywood Hills and move in the stratosphere of indulgence and material luxury he had first dreamed of, then painted, then sung about, where the beautiful people were, spectral among their gilded trellises, the leisured class finally reachable, touchable.

At the time it seemed like not only a dream move but a sensible one. Hall had her pals from the pages of the glossies and the film lots; Ferry could regroup and relaunch his career among friends and far from carping envy. Ferry sold up in London, his Kensington house being bought by the comedian John Cleese, and moved himself, bag and baggage, to the West Coast of the USA. Not that that dampened the ardour of the British supermarket media, for whom Ferry and Jerry had become an ideal item, a reliable fall-back on slow days for news or gossip. Few details were spared in the outlining of the gluttonous luxury of their new home, a Spanish-style villa in Bel Air that once been the property of the actress Leslie Caron. It could have been the villa hosting the party at which Eric Boman's famous *Another Time, Another Place* cover was shot: arboreally manicured, the consonant sheen of pool and patio, of prickly pear and palm trees, white walls paying mute tribute to the wealth that resided within.

Hindsight, however, suggests that the whole move was merely acting out. Ferry, for all his faith in fame and consumption, was motivated as much by an obsessive fascination with the meaning of those two concepts as much as a healthy craving for their material reality, and the final furlong of the move into actually being rich and famous, out of the role of the man who would parody precisely that condition, proved problematic. For all the charges of selling out, he could not, unlike Warhol, become entirely that which he had made his money by satirizing – that is, a star at ease with a star's lifestyle. Warhol became a celebrity with ease, 'going after publicity with the single-mindedness of a feeding bluefish',[20] but Ferry did not. It was all very well to be initiated into the world of the privileged, to see if the alienation, emptiness and satiated self-disgust that pervaded his view of fame was a reality. When those qualities began to invade his own life, Ferry found himself trapped. 'I'm not pretending I didn't enjoy [LA],' Ferry hastily assured *Melody Maker*'s Allan

Jones. 'I'm not that much of a hypocrite.'[21]

He found out the reality of his imprisonment soon enough. California's national product, vacuity, has been catalogued and mocked in enough films, books and plays to warrant only a passing mention here. Anyone with a desire to see what Ferry was living twenty-four a hours day is directed to Woody Allen's *Annie Hall*, in which the heroine is seduced away from Allen's Alvy Singer by a Californian high life of libertarian lip-service, moral corruption and emotional void (filmed, interestingly, the year before Ferry's move there).

California was a state where automobile bumper stickers said things like 'Bucky Fuller Says Everything's Going to be All Right', a souk of pseudo-science, a wasteland of alternative therapies, enough cocaine to fill Madison Square Gardens, relentlessly overvalued trash and the universal adoption of casually zonked optimism. California's other growth industry was human perfectability. If happiness couldn't be bought, it could be acquired through Gestalt, aikido, TM, primal scream therapy, Zen and, above all, Werner Erhard's triumph of crypto-Nietzschean, auto-suggestive flim-flam, Est. Ferry's attitude to the worship of Mammon, and his fascination with the ways the human body and mind could be indulged, were duplicated here, but, disastrously, without the irony he so loved. He had always been 'terribly intrigued' by the glamour of Los Angeles, he later admitted, but found it a honeytrap.[22] He even briefly befriended one of the prescribers of Californian brain-death, Dr Timothy Leary, whom he met through a friend, the writer Henry Edwards, who was in Los Angeles to work simultaneously on a biography of Leary and the script of the bloated cinematic dramatization of *Sgt Pepper*.

The stifling weight of money and exclusivity in Bel Air swiftly told on Ferry. Here society was purged of all warmth, all intimacy beyond the air-conditioned eyrie, the garden hedges and gatehouses guaranteeing seclusion and/or the party and business lunch. This necessitated a lack of human contact which even Ferry, who once told Caroline Coon that he preferred 'a little of a lot of people' to 'a lot of a few people',[23] quickly found oppressive. Stories exist of him taking his own laundry to an automat and watching it spin while dressed in white tennis shorts, simply to escape the oxygenated spaces of the house and discover some human existence that wasn't hunched in a car or 'doing lunch' elsewhere. Thoughts began to turn inexorably homeward, although Hall appeared thrilled by the return to the States and energetically integrated herself into LA's colonies of the seriously loaded. Some form of compromise appeared to be the answer: 'Jerry's learned to cook the English way,' Ferry explained to Rick Sky, 'so we have roasts as often as possible.'[24] The very idea of Hall sweating at the stove, while the mutely obeisant Latino staff look on, is comic indeed.

To distract himself from an atmosphere which, novelty gone, he found increasingly oppressive, Ferry decided to gear up and do his job – by working on music. Communications were reopened with the recalcitrant Atlantic Records and a new album discussed. A compromise was reached, with Ferry agreeing to employ an Anglo-American band, featuring bassist Alan Spenner, fast becoming a Ferry staple and the first bass-player since his old Newcastle alumnus and friend Graham Simpson with whom he had established a lasting rapport.

The most significant American member of the band was Waddy Wachtel, one of the most famous of all of the architects of the West Coast FM success story, a guitarist wreathed with the muso cachet of his innumerable sessions of FM-friendly instrumental prowess which had propelled Linda Ronstadt and Jackson Browne to success.

This came as a direct result of Atlantic continuing to nudge him towards Americanized music, a process which included their none-too-subtle setting up of some informal meetings with Richard Perry, who fortuitously shared Ferry's love of tennis, and over a few sets in Bel Air the two men exchanged ideas as well as aces. It wasn't for Ferry. He wanted his music to sound like Bryan Ferry, not a corporation.

It quickly became apparent that Ferry, as one of rock's more original thinkers, wouldn't be easy to negotiate with. American rock, by 1977, had atrophied to a degree that, outside of the New York Downtown/Punk scene and isolated awkward-squadders like Steely Dan and Todd Rundgren, it had become besotted with furnishing FM radio with sellable music to punctuate the ads. Producers like Perry and the West Coast studio imperium of sessionmen and singers were applying a lacquer of timbral and melodic uniformity to everything that moved. While Ferry continued to write and play straightforward pop songs, they were, palpably, his own individual work. Ferry's years in the business had implanted a deep-seated and idiosyncratic *modus operandi* which extended to all aspects of creativity, composition, harmony, production and mixing, which was anathema to a top-line producer and a top-line US label such as Atlantic.

Clearly, this wasn't going to be easy for Atlantic or for Ferry. But soon enough, in November 1977, Ferry had more than an album to think about when, apropos of nothing, Pop Art and its pop culture clichés got their own back on him with a hammerblow of pure comicbook corniness: his girl went off with a man he had called his friend.

AFTER JERRY

If Hall's autobiography is to be believed, she loved Ferry, if only briefly. Her account of the relationship has its beginning the night after the chaotic shoot for the cover of *Siren* in 1975, and not before. For a while the relationship worked like a dream, but as she interestingly observes, there were unexpected clashes of character. She suggests that innate paradoxes of uptight reserve and passionate expressivity were inherent in both Texan and English characters. Hall was not always receptive to Ferry's brooding songwriters' reveries – in which, she claims, he would flex his ears *à la* Stan Laurel. Ferry was often recolted by Hall's good ol' gal exhibitionism, not least her penchant for public leg-wrestling matches. Far from encouraging her to join him on-stage to perform 'Let's Stick Together', Ferry (Hall maintains) forbade her from so doing after standing mortified on-stage at an Atlantic Records invitation gig at New York's Bottom Line club, looking on as the song ended and the audience broke into chants for her to return to the stage-front.

Ferry could, she added, also be domestically demanding, criticizing her easygoing ways. He chided her for being unable to keep a clean house even with a maid when his mother 'was able to manage all on her own'.[25] When spending Christmas in 1976 with Hall's family in Texas, Ferry could barely conceal his distaste when a cockroach crawled across the wall of a dining room, or, in Hall's words, at his prospective mother-in-law's cooking.[26]

For all that, Ferry emerges as a considerate and cultured, if not always a concerned lover. The Mick Jagger situation, however, was clearly afoot long before the Montreux split. Hall had been falling in love with him for a little over a year, and at one stage Ferry, once the Rolling Stone's friend, refused to go out with him again in Hall's company, so obvious was Jagger's flirting and ogling. Ferry's stock summary of the end of his relationship with Hall is that it was an 'adult education course',[27] a rather wittily poignant comment from a man whose facility with the language of lost love is usually reserved for musical utterances.

According to Simon Puxley, this relationship was a 'prison ship' for Ferry, and one headed for the rocks. Although a long-time friend, Puxley has gone on record as saying that disaster had been inevitable in the relationship. He affirmed that even Ferry soon realized that the best thing that happened in it was when 'she ran off with Mick. Everyone was very upset at the time, but...'[28]

It's easy to castigate Ferry for his intolerance of the press whose attentions made him famous when their attentions became unwanted, but reportage of the Jerry affair, even for those well informed about the break-up, was insensitively slipshod in the extreme. Not always malicious or malevolent, perhaps, but simply sloppy to a degree that an unhappy Ferry must have found intensely demoralizing. If the prurient speculation as to the exact circumstances of the separation weren't enough, the way in which the mess intruded into all subsequent coverage of his life and work for the next two years must have chafed intolerably. For the record, the circumstances were extremely awkward, with the ironic squalor granted only to splits among the social élite; Ferry and his ensemble had set up to record in Montreux in November 1977; two members of the entourage stumbled upon an item in a Nigel Dempster *Daily Express* column about Hall's departure to Jagger and broke it to Ferry, who, on making enquiries, was consternated to find it was all true. Hall owned up and told Ferry she would come to Europe and try to patch things up, thought about it, then changed her mind.

One particularly and enduringly idiotic piece of misinformation surrounded *The Bride Stripped Bare*, his new LP, which was recorded simultaneously with the end of the affair, and was and has since been described almost invariably as a cathartic bawl of wounded and indignant despair at the end of things with Hall. It was, in fact, nothing of the sort. While probably the bleakest of Ferry's entire album output, its emotional tenor goes deeper than the immediate trauma of Hall's departure and, in any case, all the tracks bar one ('When She Walks in the Room') were written *before* that departure.

It is axiomatic that Ferry was – and, indeed, still is – a sex symbol of the first magnitude. In the preceding chapter we examined the sexuality that Roxy Music stood for; in the 1970s more interest was lavished on Ferry's own sex life. As we have seen, he was hardly a conventional sex symbol and it may be that his *difference* was the decisive factor in this, his very absence of 1970s airs.

Ferry's ownership of a car and distinctive stylist pose had done well for him back home on Tyneside. No doubt that the nonchalant hipster relaxing against the blue hull of the

Studebaker in 1967 would have had next to no trouble impressing the opposite sex, despite his own oft-claimed shyness (a quality verified by friends). Furthermore, Ferry was – and is, by all accounts – civil and civilized, charming and disarming. He speaks thoughtfully, Geordie cadences elocuted to a minimum, but apparent enough to be endearing. There is an element of the *soigné* unusual in the circles in which Ferry moved; in a London teeming with screwed-up and liberated selves of graphic raucousness, Ferry was, by comparison, a companion of some elegance and restraint.

This didn't stop his fame causing him to run headlong into some damaging relationships which, given the content of many of his songs, unfurl through the years like a depressingly self-fulfilling prophecy. The fact that many of these dalliances were with Roxy Music cover girls led many to reason that Ferry was an inveterate Casanova and did more than perhaps anything else to set in stone the popular assumption that Ferry quickly began to live the mythologies which so fired his creativity.

Amanda Lear was the first of the cover girls to enter into a liaison with Ferry, followed by Marilyn Cole, later in 1973, after the sessions for the *Stranded* cover. The subsequent affair – while Cole was still married to her then husband, Victor Lownes (chief of the Playboy organization's London office), was recounted in gruesome detail in a London tabloid in 1980. So editorially airbrushed is this narrative (into what, for the uninvolved, must have read as a hilarious high-tabloid classical style) that individual details seem almost unimportant. Cole, with a forensic attention to minutiae amplified to the acme of prurience by some *Daily Mirror* subeditor, blethers about how 'different' Ferry was from her usual partners (Hugh Hefner himself had numbered among her lovers and was partial to lubricating her entire body with baby oil), discovering 'after far too long…just how beautiful a young man's body can be'.[29]

Ferry, having had to weather that storm, read more of his

exploits in the press the following year when Kari-Ann Moller gave her own inventory of personal carnality to the *Sunday Mirror*. 'I resent it,' Ferry told a reporter of his residency in the gossip columns. 'I say, "Go to hell."' Ferry might have resented it; Moller and Cole, presumably, didn't.[30]

Moller had followed Cole into Ferry's affections. Mutual attraction had been established during her *Roxy Music* cover stint, and, according to her, when she later appeared on a Mott the Hoople album sleeve, Ferry called her and demanded that she appear on no more album sleeves; this possessiveness would later find an outlet in a physical desire which Moller evidently shared. The affair – Moller's marriage was already in disrepair – took place in 1974, when the 'neat, clean and rather straight' Ferry she'd first met in 1972 had become a debonair catch of thoroughbred proportions.[31]

Rogan, in *Style with Substance*, is often harshly judgemental in his examination of Ferry's love life. Why, he demands, 'if personality and integrity are the prime attractions for Ferry... has he had the unfortunate judgement to involve himself with women who have relentlessly and thoughtlessly exposed his most intimate secrets to the gutter press?'[32] Presumably because Ferry's libido did not possess the powers of psychic perception Rogan expected of it, or make allowances for the excesses of tabloid editorial politics and chequebook journalism. Ferry, fair game for the gossipmongers, was hardly likely to blow his own cover, and, given his track record, the law of averages suggests that a fat enough cheque will bring the requisite dirty linen out of some spurned lover's closet instead, as indeed it did. On the other hand Amanda Lear (for the most part) and Susan McLean, two other notable Ferry girlfriends, remained silent; even Jerry Hall, by and large, kept her counsel.

On this, Rogan himself remains silent. His reasoning actually reinforces rather than debunks the Ferry myth, fore-grounding Ferry as forever the predator, his lovers as palpitating putty in his hands. Even the notion that Ferry might have been the game rather than the hunter never enters the equation – although, to be fair, he does acknowledge that 'sex-seeking young models whose only desire was to measure his performance in bed' actually existed within the Roxy Music orbit.[33]

Rogan reads, and diagnoses, Ferry's involvement with women over six pages of impromptu psychoanalysis based on self-righteousness, tabloid nudge-nudgery and the facilely Freudian interpretation of a few song lyrics. Ferry, he concludes solemnly, is a man obsessed with making self-destructive 'madonnas' or 'mothers of pearl' out of women, confining them to a romantic ideal, subconsciously choosing those he knows will destroy it and him.

Ferry's meeting of and subsequent marriage to his present wife, Lucy, a little while after these words were written – the only really poor lines in Rogan's otherwise admirable and fair-minded work – render them faintly (but suitably) ridiculous.

Rogan at least follows sensible leads. Ferry is without doubt a brazen romantic. In 1982 he told the *NME*:

'I think romantic love has been constructive because it often goes hand in hand with unrequited love, and the best art seems to come out of those emotions, that sense of longing produces great art because it's almost as though you're creating something to replace what isn't there. In a sense you're making a surrogate love object.

'I think,' he continued with a rare flash of public coarseness, 'it helps if you're a bit fucked up in the head.'[34]

He could also be drawn on another of Rogan's themes, the ideal. Answering the question, 'Is there an element of unattainability in glamour?' he replied, 'When a thing is well presented it sometimes seems unattainable. There is something glamorous about something you want and can't have.'[35]

But unattainability meant something different for Ferry than for average mortals. Sexually, Ferry could have had any girl he wanted at a heavy-lidded glance; romantic fulfilment tended, at first, to evade him, although to say this is down to over-idealization on Ferry's part is a hasty and rash conclusion. Certainly the durability of his present marriage suggests that perhaps idealism of one sort does not preclude the arrival of an ideal of quite another sort.

The popular image of Ferry and his women wasn't helped by the singer's own *faux-pas* on the subject in the press. As well as the magisterially sexist outbursts quoted in Chapter 4, he did himself no favours by claiming plaintively that he pursued good-looking girls because he found them mentally 'stimulating', 'as interesting to talk to as highbrow people'.[36] This would be faintly believable if it had not been so often repeated, as Ferry did publicly in various permutations throughout the late 1970s.

Around this time, public interest was heightened when novelist Edna O'Brien, upon whose arm Ferry was snapped turning up at a London theatre, seemed to be wafting into Ferry's eyeline, but this, it quickly transpired, was mere friendship. Rumours flew that Caroline Coon, for Peter York 'the most socially clued' of all rock writers,[37] and the voluble daughter of a Wiltshire landowner, was a Ferry consort.

Such morbid and insatiable interest in Ferry, the irrepressible and inexhaustible DJed Don Juan, served only to emphasize even more the painful gulf between Ferry's success as a bandleader and his inability to make a convincing case for himself as an artistically or economically dependable solo performer. The majority of the column inches devoted to him concerned Ferry and Jerry stories, in which his role in the story was reduced to escort. Atlantic had behaved badly over *In Your Mind* and 'Tokyo Joe' had been a fiasco, mostly due to their backsliding. The world tour had almost cost Ferry his shirt. Now even musical interest in England and Europe began to wane. Quite apart from Hall's high-tailing it away with Mick Jagger, Los Angeles had become darkened with disappointment.

Hall had been intimating a possible return to England not

long before the split and Ferry had been speedily revising his gilded opinions of Californian mores, railing to those who'd listen about the commercial psychosis that reduced everything to monetary values. Reflecting on the LA interlude some years later, he mused:

'You can go a bit weird if you start running around with strange movie-type people. I got into one of those slip-streams when I was there, where I saw the same people every night but in different locations. I wrote *The Bride Stripped Bare* while I was there and that's a very gloomy album.'[38]

To Allan Jones, Ferry was unequivocal. 'The whole movie business stinks,' he roared.[39] For all the frivolity and tinsel of his success, Ferry remained an inveterate worker. To one interviewer in 1978 he declared firmly that work was 'the only thing worth doing'. He hadn't 'got much to offer except work' and he 'got bored when he wasn't working'.[40] To another interviewer later the same year he confessed that in Los Angeles he had become

'very solitary, very involved with myself and my work...the parties have to stop sometime...people think that because I attend premières and mix with celebrities I do nothing else. But I'm the son of a Newcastle miner. I'm the working-class lad who feels guilty if he's not working.'[41]

This sounds disingenuous until one examines Ferry's résumé of his career during the 1970s. His recording career didn't start until 1972 and by 1978 he had recorded ten albums (ten and a half if one considers the rehashes on *Let's Stick Together*). Professional and personal acquaintances readily concede that Ferry, in the 1970s, was a workaholic.

For that tenth album, the solo *The Bride Stripped Bare,* Ferry found himself back in Europe, financial reasons having prevented any recording taking place in American studios. The studio he settled on was Mountain Studios at Montreux, extremely fashionable in 1977 – Emerson, Lake and Palmer and Yes had recorded there in the previous twelve months, and the place's enviable technical armoury made it one of rock's most sought-after creative locations. Montreux itself, especially in winter, was not such a draw, a spa resort deserted by its clientele of absentee aristocracy, the Montreux Palace Hotel an echoing hulk of hibernating *grand confort* in which Ferry installed himself.

The setting was incongruous and hardly conducive to indulging rockist whims. Greg Lake had spoken for the yahoo tendency that same year when he said of Montreux, 'It's so boring. Nothing ever happens. You get sod-all inspiration'[42] (this in the middle of Europe's mightiest mountain range and on the shore of one of its most picturesque lakes). But Montreux at any time of year had one big advantage: the favourable position of Switzerland in the global matrices of income taxation also ensured Mountain Studios' success, especially when tax rates on pop stars in England assumed punitive proportions.

Ferry's band, though admirable musicians, were evidently of Lake's boorish persuasion, and to ensure that the sessions passed in a lively enough fashion, they made their own entertainment (things had started promisingly when bassist Spenner had to be carted off the plane in Geneva in a wheelchair, having drunk himself unconscious). Ferry spent plenty of time deflecting the questions of journalists eager for angles on the Jerry–Ferry situation.

The surreal atmosphere also meant, according to Ferry, that 'a lot of passion went into the music...a lot of anger, angst'.[43] The studio sessions were 'very remote, very lonely, very crazed'.[44] One imagines that the anger and angst could well have been the musicians' reaction to being stranded in midwinter in a dead lakeside town in the most expensive country in Europe in which to get pissed and/or stoned, one imagines. Ferry was, however, more than pleased with his charges: 'It looked great on paper and they were all big-hearted players, very soulful. But they were half-English, half-American...they didn't understand each other.'[45]

This 'very emotional music', with 'guys almost crying into their instruments',[46] wasn't enough, however, to dispel Ferry's lingering sense of malaise. After selecting a raft of tracks from the enormous amount of material taped in Montreux, his shaky confidence took a further battering when, uncharacteristically, he began to question his own material and even, one suspects, his own judgement. He immediately re-recorded some numbers which had been left out of his intial selection and gratefully flew out to New York in the late winter of 1977–8, stopping off to grant some brief interviews in London.

Ferry's latter-day evaluation of *In Your Mind* as his least successful album begs the question as to his current feelings about *The Bride Stripped Bare*. The later album shows thematic advance – Ferry is more secure with his own writing abilities for a strange outfit – but the new confidence and coherence are undermined by the depressing pre-eminence of West Coast studio musicians dictating the pace and even the shape of some of the songs. There's the slightest sense of desperation about this album, that the rootless disorientation of *In Your Mind* has become a man drowning, not waving.'

The whole starts appealingly enough. Ferry was effusive about 'Sign of the Times', the album's opener, and its long, repeated, unresolved melody, delivered with withering sarcasm and cynicism, is promising indeed. Its sardonic, chatty guitar attack shows that Ferry undestood the implications of the new wave for music, even if he felt that he didn't have to pay empty lip service to it. But from here on in it's largely downhill; the newly established hegemony of the guitar in the band sound is dominated by Wachtel's all-purpose fusion of contemporaneously sellable American styles from blues to country. It stinks up 'Can't Let Go' (also burdened with fashionable AOR road-song imagery of headlights and wipers and 'riding the storm'). His electric twelve-string vandalism of the Irish traditional 'Carrickfergus', particularly when heard over Herbie Flowers' exquisite contrabass accompaniment, should be a capital offence; Ferry should have informed him firmly at the outset that this was *not* a Linda Ronstadt, Poco or Dr Hook album. Elsewhere, in spite of Ferry's best efforts – his vocals are as dependable as ever – Americanisms lie heavy on the album, albeit not quite as heavily as they otherwise might have done. The banal soft-rock male backing chorus on 'When She Walks in the Room' is pure Kokomo, utterly unsuited to an agreeably original Ferry meditation on lost or imminently lost love. Even soul standards, so gamely handled by Ferry on early solo albums, lose something here. 'Hold On (I'm Coming)' could be any LA bar band, and 'Same Old Blues' is a really pretty shameful attempt at courting Bob Seger's AOR constituency. The insistent reliance on guitar textures – which, this being 1978, have been percolated through white musicians' studio techniques from black soul styles – also help destroy an otherwise promising 'That's How Strong My Love is', whose climaxes have explosives built into them but here simply lack a cutting edge. Moments of real Ferry inspiration – the jagged, uncompromising melodic lines of 'When She Walks in the Room' and 'This Island Earth' – are diminished by otherwise superfluous details of convention and ordinariness. It makes the bald, unadorned 'Take Me to the River', with its ruminative, zonked bass line and obsessive rhythm guitar, all the more incongruously abrasive, almost the equal of Talking Heads' own version of the song on the album *More Songs About Buildings and Food*, released July 1978.

Ferry's subsequent observation that the album was 'a real eye-opener which changed my whole way of working after that...like concentrating on the spaces between notes' is surprising.[47] The textures do, however, point forward to *Manifesto* and *Flesh + Blood* and, particularly, *Avalon*. 'When She Walks in the Room' has premonitory suggestions of 'More Than This' and Rick Marotta's expert work on hi-hats and rimshots suggests a rethinking of percussive impulse behind Ferry's music which would later lead to the exclusion of Paul Thompson from Roxy Music.

One interviewer asked him whether *The Bride Stripped Bare* was his 'riskiest' record. Ferry, with some nerve, responded:

'In a sense it was. It was done...when the Punk explosion happened and I was aware that if I made a record like my first records from six years before, which were sort of rough-edged, it would have been just right for the time. But instead I endeavoured to make an album that was smooth on the surface, but jagged underneath – on its emotional side. So yes, that was a risky thing to do.'[48]

But this didn't much matter. Apart from a sensational review of the single 'Sign of the Times' in the *NME* in the summer, critical knives were duly sharpened and plunged in yet again. Ferry was close to despair.

NEW YORK CITY: FERRY IN ROXYTOWN, SIX YEARS TOO LATE

New York had, however, offered some solace. The drawn-out saga of *The Bride Stripped Bare*, which had begun while Ferry was still an item with Hall, came to an end at the skilled hands of New York studio engineers who remixed the tracks to the singer's satisfaction. A chapter had closed and Ferry appeared to be relishing his new domicile, with his name once again romantically attached to a famous face, Ryan O'Neal's ex-girlfriend Barbara Allen. Even in 1982, Ferry could tell interviewers that New York was the 'only city I really enjoy being in...because it's very easy to become anonymous there'.[49]

New York was, after all, one of the shining cities of his youth, the Big Pop Art Apple, alchemizer of modern consumer culture into artistic statements. Ferry's energies began to return, although how satisfactory New York seemed is questionable. Allen was, many noted, a beauty of vaguely similar physiognomy to Hall; in a sense the torpid vacancy of the social scene he'd fled from in Los Angeles was replaced by another batch of over-wealthy smilers and posers, with the saving grace that this time they were unashamedly megaphonic vulgarians who flaunted rather than attempted to spiritually justify their instinctive appetite for consumption. New York was, after all, home to Studio 54, the consummation of disco's camp obsession with glitz and dissolution where dance-floor space was allotted by wealth and gossip column inches won. New York was also the nexus of the then allied cynosures of avant-garde art, commerce and sexual decadence where Andy Warhol still prowled with his Polaroid camera, snapping the celebs for his preposterous gossip-rag *Interview*. The Mudd Club was open and doing roaring business; Quentin Crisp was an Englishman at large, a Noël Coward with talent and f-words.

Ferry had first met Warhol at a party in early 1975 ('I just turned around and there he was.[50]) While there are no public records of the two having met during Ferry's 1978 New York sojourn, to suppose that they did not is implausible. Likewise, Brian Eno, who had just moved to a Lower East Side loft himself and was working with fave Downtown raves Talking Heads, must have crossed Ferry's path at some stage (Eno was another character who could be caught motionless with rapt fascination in the glare of oncoming paparazzi). Details are annoyingly scant – what one can be sure of is that Ferry, for all the posturing stupidity rampant in New York at the time, enjoyed himself more than he had in Los Angeles. Here in New York, there mingled among the mighty enough 'cultural space-debris' (as Robert Hughes has described the hangers-on of the Downtown scene)[51] to make the place interesting and reawaken in any right-minded observer questions about the nature of celebrity and the transience of pleasure and wealth, the sheer indefatigable metropolitan glamour of danger and risk.

It is true to say that the Studio 54's regulars were hardly likely to plummet to the gutter; Studio 54 was a Babylon of unearned fame, a temple to the proprietary grandeur of celebrity. It was, in short, the natural place for the two most creative spirits behind the soul of Roxy Music to fetch up. Robert Hughes again, talking of Warhol's court-photographer role to the discofied chosen:

> All *Exposures* [Warhol's shabby portfolio of celebrity Polaroid mugshots] was about [was] a photograph album of film stars, rock idols, politicians' wives, cocottes, catamites and assorted bits of International White Trash baring their teeth to the socially emulgent glare of the flash bulb. I am flashed, therefore I am. It is also the sole subject of Warhol's house organ, *Interview*...
>
> With the opening of Studio 54... the magazine found... its spiritual home. It then became a kind of marionette theatre in print: exactly the same figures, month after month, would cavort in its tiny proscenium, do a few turns, suck or snort something and tittup off again – Bianca [Jagger], Margaret Trudeau, Marisa [Berenson], Halston and the rest...[52]

The 1970s having soured at the centre, the only thing left to do for those who could afford to do it, was to party hard, fast and long. Discos became the new court balls, the new salons, where nothing mattered, nobody cared, save for the admiring attentions of others, and the next night on the floor.

This, as dignified by the few brave intellectuals – such as American cultural critic Richard Dyer – willing to dignify a ritual which to the majority of youth was an expression of terminal vapidity (hence the popularity of 'Disco Sucks' button badges and bumper stickers), brought mainstream leisure into line, for the first time in many years, with gay and camp leisure. The love of the trashy and the fake-glamorous in disco chic, the devotion to fleeting sensation and to metropolitan, nugatory *divertissement,* mirrored that of gay and camp 'scene' lifestyles. Once again, these lifestyles were, of course, anathema to modernist, idealist and most countercultural philosophy, where absolutes and infinites *mattered,* where the weight of the world could not and should not be dispelled by one night's dancing. The fact that disco never entertained such aims for a second, and York's 'camp double-think' of irony and allusion replaced human honesty and truth-to-feeling – not to mention the inevitable marriage of disco and fashion, another world where surface and disposability were all that mattered – further maddened disco's foes. It also ensured that disco was the natural home of Roxy Music aesthetics in the late 1970s. The discontinuous urban existence where data was a series of imagistic flash-cards had been richly mined and made sexy by Warhol during the 1960s, and his valorization of the low and superficial was one of the currents of thought that legitimized disco first as a cool place to hang out and later, disastrously, as a site of postmodernist resistance.

This was largely due to the fact that the modernist discourse of rock, based on the bourgeois notion of working nobly towards reward, was irrelevant to both disco and fashion, infuriating modernists and delighting postmodernists. Fashion and disco were celebrations of the caprice of the postmodern city, where fame could come unearned and money, sex and indulgence were free for those initiated to the metropolitan code of occluded connections, a social phenomenon redolent of the exclusivity of the gay lifestyle.

Thus it was not only urban postmodernist theoreticians who were delighted by disco; the gender games and elusiveness, codification and occlusion of gay and bisexual identity in a society that still effectively excluded them posed questions about the fragmentation of identity that chimed neatly with pre-eminent themes and thought processes within the avant-garde, which, in New York, had long been suckers for anything explicitly faggoty or deviant. Superficiality became *de rigueur.* Molly Parkin, Ferry's old mucker from

London's *demi-monde*, was a favourite in New York at the end of the 1970s. Other refugees from the brief Punk vogue in London, when bleached faces and bondage were fleetingly smart-casual, included Little Nell, Jordan and others.

Where nothing mattered, there was a vacuum, and if colour or sexual orientation didn't matter, neither did any morality – another winner for New York loft set, their liberal palates for so long consuming the city's promise of libertarianism, cruelty and decadence. Clubbing, the selective tasting the salt-lick of inner-city depravity to a good beat, thus became a popular pastime even for twenty-something movers and shakers on the alternative Village Voice side of town, like Cynthia Heimel, Vitas Gerulaitis and Patti Smith; Prog-rockers addled by hep minimalist cant and seeking artistic regeneration – Eno, Fripp – also fell for the bright lights and the beat.

In short, with its kinetic collage of slumming rich kids, queens, aesthetes and the dumb consumption of the middle class, New York discos in 1978 effectively provided a personnel for Roxy Music songs six years after the event.

The fact that Ferry, too, didn't hang around in New York is testimony to a man who still, despite the encounters with the state of the super-rich, remained an outsider. His attempt at becoming a disco star, or even a parody of one, had failed. Disco accrued most-favoured status in the record industry mainly because of its eschewal of the kind of working practices Ferry employed – he, like most white rock performers, insisted on studio time and space in which to 'compose', not to mention indulgences regarding live performances, which were infinitely more expensive than producing conveyor-belt disco singles. Ferry had presented to him a social niche but not a musical one.

This status was depressingly confirmed by a continual plunge on the Ferry progress graph. Ferry's uncertainty over the content and quality of the tapes led to repeated tamperings and delays, which put back the release of *The Bride Stripped Bare* for six months, a move greeted with disdain as the prissy perfectionism of a spoilt and diminished idol.

'Sign of the Times', a fine single and one in which Ferry invested considerable emotional capital, was none the less an ignominious flop, liked by some, loathed by others. The scale of Ferry's frustration and near-paranoid hatred of the press can be gauged by his reaction to a *Melody Maker* review of the single which told the world that Ferry had 'nothing to say to humanity'.[53] In an interview with Allan Jones, Ferry seemed to be in trouble. Despite appearing in good spirits, few lines the man speaks carry hints of a future. He complains of the audience on his live tour in 1977 'slipping away',[54] doubts sprout everywhere, in his own work and in his perception of others. He launched a broadside on a young *MM* hack, Chris Brazier, for his 'Sign of the Times' review; a livid Ferry said, 'You can't get away with saying that I have nothing to say to humanity, man. That's just too heavy a thing to say about anyone.'[55] For a man who, admirably, had steered clear of the trad jazz syntactical affectations which still so littered rockspeak (and who never mentioned 'cats' or talked about 'my lady') using words like 'heavy' was strong stuff. He could also be read spouting such bleak lines as 'maybe the album's doomed. I don't think it is; even though I'm aware that these last singles have done worse than anything else I've ever done. I'm especially disappointed that there's been so little artistic response.'[56] He may have been referring to the most ignominious débâcle yet, the next single from *The Bride Stripped Bare*, the rather lovely 'Carrickfergus', which did not even chart in the UK. This was the first Roxy Music-related single so disgraced. Humiliation piled on humiliation. A projected UK solo tour was cancelled after poor ticket sales. Ferry, to judge by the tone of these interviews, was a rudderless ship.

But a lifeboat was at hand. Even before the 'Sign of the Times' had so dismally gone belly-up, Ferry had activated his ejector seat. The Roxy Music 'machinery' had been discreetly reassembled. Manzanera and Mackay were contacted and were standing ready.

8: HAIRDRESSER'S DELIGHT (1979–81)

RE-ENTRANCE WITH DRUMBOX: 'DANCE AWAY' AND *MANIFESTO*

'The reasons that guys gravitate into and out of groups,' Bryan Ferry has gone on record as saying, 'it's quite often to do with the details of their domestic arrangements. Guys get married, they leave a group. Guys divorce, they get back into a group.'[1]

How pertinent this statement was to the reconstitution of Roxy Music is unclear. Nobody denies, surprisingly, the possibility that Ferry's revival of the band was linked directly to his loss of Hall, although such a rationale seems altogether too dependent on tabloid logic to bother us further.

Other suggestions that Ferry's solo career had not come up to the expectations of himself and his employers seem nearer the mark. While Ferry strenuously denied this, one comment to a journalist in 1978 suggests that the option was one which never left his mind and, in effect, the band could have been convened at almost any time:

> 'I had the idea for *Manifesto* for simply ages. That's always
> happened with every album we've made. I always have the
> title down first. I saw it as the perfect statement of intent if
> you like – a very strong word which conjured up cross-
> references with the Futurists...not that I'd be so immodest
> as to align myself with them.'[2]

Manifesto was, Manzanera said, the 're-establishment of a
better working relationship'.[3] But did anyone really imagine
that any of the members would suggest otherwise? Nobody
was going to say 'I needed the money, man.' The result was
urbanely bromidic; the band had, like all reunited combos,
'grown up a bit more', etc. Had they asked Jobson to rejoin,
asked one impertinent hack. 'No!' replied Manzanera. 'He's
probably rather pissed off.' There was 'no point' recalling him
and the subject dropped.[4]

Jobson's non-inclusion raises speculative questions which
make a passable parlour game but little more. How would he
have adapted? He had in the Roxy Music hiatus become a
major instrumental star in his own right. Following virtuoso
displays with Zappa on *Zoot Allures* and the live album *Zappa
in New York,* he had, however, begun to flounder in the
moneypit of the Prog-rock supergroup UK. Founded in 1977
with ex-Roxy Music/King Crimson bassist John Wetton and
ex-Crimson drummer Bill Bruford (Jobson had played briefly
on Crimson's *USA* album in 1975, and Crimson had been EG
stablemates of Roxy Music), the line-up was completed by
guitarist Allan Holdsworth. Critically reviled, the band
struggled on through three albums which are much revered by
Prog-rock purists but often run on empty as to instrumental
virtuosity. Having thus been given his head in the cod-classical
bombast stakes by EG, a recall to Roxy Music's ranks seemed
unlikely, if not unworkable. When UK threw in the towel in
1980, Jobson took time out to record his own album, *Zinc/The*

Green Album (1983), which at least reveals a tantalizing penchant for finger-popping hooks which might after all have served him well with the re-formed Roxy Music.

The new incarnation of Roxy Music posed for the cameras on the occasion of the 'official' public relaunch in the third week of November 1978 (the announcement had been made in August and the body of the forthcoming comeback album, *Manifesto*, was already in the can).

The selection for the ever problematic bass position raised a few quizzical eyebrows. Ferry, on the recommendation of his bass-playing friend Herbie Flowers, had been to check out Gary Tibbs, late of the Vibrators, one of Britain's more boneheaded Punk bands. As had been the case with the teenaged Jobson, Ferry saw in Tibbs a musician who fitted the bill. He moved in for him. Tibbs must certainly have enjoyed puncturing a few preconceptions by his performance in the band; those who saw the barnet of straw with the blunt-scissors cut and expected an illiterate Punk thrummer were confounded. Tibbs's playing on subsequent Roxy Music recordings and in live gigs offered some of the most sensitive bass playing the band had enjoyed, and he compared well with the high-roller sessionmen who would henceforward increasingly fill out the band sound in the studio.

There were some rather more obvious nods to the passage of time and trends. Skinny ties and casual Italian jackets with the modest sheen of money and groomed locks (Tibbs aside) were the order of the day, the studied urban cool of a hip solicitor which high fashion had distilled from the uncompromisingly metropolitan chic of Punk. Mackay looked even more formal, not unlike a trainee TV evangelist.

The comeback, then, had been planned and executed with customary style and fastidiousness; now it only remained to hear the music. How had that been revamped?

By and large, bands which fundamentally didn't 'get' Punk never stood a chance of being a part of it, and the harder they strove for hipness the harder they fell. Haircuts out of *Battlestar Galactica*, slapdash and half-hearted two-tone geometries on album sleeves and ham-handed lyrical potshots at urban alienation and computer takeover were thought to be enough to maintain relevance and interest (among the sadder examples being Genesis' *Abacab*, Renaissance's *Camera Camera* and Camel's *Single Factor* fiascos, not to mention the sins of a multitude of continental European bands). Roxy Music's unfashionable concentration (for the 1970s) on experience derived from an essentially metropolitan existence for their visual and musical language offered them an advantage in so far as they handled the new vocabularies of rock expression with at least a degree of familiarity.

Initial soundings were, however, unpromising. A re-release of the band's wonderful 'Do the Strand' in November 1978, backed with the equally whip-cracking 'Editions of You' (bagged in a fine sleeve pastiching Warhol's pastiche of Mondrian's 1930s dance-step diagram paintings), flopped entirely. It was the first Roxy Music single not to chart in the UK. Little better followed when the first offering of the new line-up, 'Trash' (this time backed with the flaccid 'Trash 2', a mimsy cop-out of a take on the original) stiffed also. 'Trash' reached only No. 40, still the lowest chart placing in Britain for any of the band's UK single releases. Press reaction was unanimously derisive. Real doubt began to creep in. Manzanera, with considerable understatement, said, 'At first it looked like it wasn't going to work. The first single came out and it didn't do fantastically well. Then "Dance Away" came out and it was a big hit and it kind of saved our bacon. And we were off.'[5]

'Dance Away' followed the release of *Manifesto* in mid-March 1979 and, while the band were still picking, brows furrowed, over the press judgements of the album in dismay, the miracle duly occurred and the single caught fire. It was kept off the top only by two of the mightiest sellers of the era, Gloria Gaynor's 'Never Can Say Goodbye' and then Art Garfunkel's 'Bright Eyes'. None the less, 'Dance Away' sold in cartloads, staying in the charts for fourteen weeks, a Roxy Music record.

In 1973, discussing *These Foolish Things*, Ferry could say honestly, 'I haven't written any standards', but by 1979's 'Dance Away' he had done just that, a piece of music that became as much an archetype of musical environment as anything that Brian Eno was currently designing. The soft finger-clicking of the drum-machine introduction is almost as richly evocative of the band as the approaching footsteps and receding car that prefigure 'Love is the Drug'. Originally slated for Ferry's *In Your Mind*, held over until *The Bride Stripped Bare* and then rejected again, it proved a third-time-lucky smash for Ferry. Its emulsified, calorific richness of tone and timbre owes much to its reworking in a New York studio, the presence of pianist Richard Tee and drummers Rick Marotta (lately of *The Bride Stripped Bare*) and Steve Ferrone helping no end.

It also did wonders for the album. Initial critical response had been disappointing, although not as cruel as that directed at 'Trash'. *Manifesto* was recorded at what was now the Roxy Music circle's studio of choice, Basing Street in London, but also at Ridge Farm in Surrey (Roxy Music had already begun to move themselves into London's rock hinterland of home studios and multi-bedroom haciendas among the pine ridges and copses of Surrey Downs). The sessions were attended by engineers Rhett Davies (who had previously worked with Ferry and on Eno's *Before and After Science* and *Another Green World* albums) and Jimmy Douglas. Latterly Ferry took some of the tapes to New York's Atlantic Studio, as he had done with *The Bride Stripped Bare*, and applied finishing touches which work better in some places than others – on 'Dance Away', for example. An 'American' feel was the aim, specifically for the second side (Ferry had originally wanted to allot an 'east side' and 'west side' to the LP, to highlight European and American influences on the band's writing and playing). The album reached No. 7 in Britain's charts, and stayed in those charts for thirty-four weeks, practically until the very end of 1979. Critical opinion was benign, if sometimes perplexed. 'It ain't half tepid, mum' sniggered the *NME*, but Max Bell, despite fretting that 'the profundity barometer' was 'not moving', had affection stay his hand. 'An assured dip into friendly territory – an entertaining, pleasant album,' he wrote in a magazine then sold on its hacks come-outside-then provocation of its hapless readership. Bell considered that the album as a whole added up to 'a lot of that mentioned style but somehow missing the content of true surprise'.[6] Old stoutheart Richard Williams voted with his feet for the album in a robust *Melody Maker* defence: 'Certainly it pulls some punches,' he wrote, 'but reservations aside, this may be the first such return bout ever attempted with any degree of genuine success. A technical knock-out against the odds.'[7]

Ferry's assessment of the album, and of its hit single, 'Dance Away', in particular as 'hairdresser's music' raised a few eyebrows among the faithful and would have surely aroused his own ire had the comment appeared in the review columns of any of the rock comics. Yet it is an honest enough appraisal of the music, which, given the changed musical context into which it was launched, was relatively a considerably more effete offering than Roxy Music diehards might have expected. Its textures and musical interplay owed much to the production techniques of disco. This was, of course, par for the course in 1979, but what enhanced the Roxy Music take on the sea change in rock was Ferry's instinctive compositional feel for soul, which both enhanced the disco 'feel' and lent the music a faintly superior edge; having stolen disco's clothes, the songwriting abilities from all on show displayed them to rarely seen effect.

The opening cut of *Manifesto* is the title track and it is a gauntlet-throwing challenge; a title track which invites attack, an overweening statement of the band's new direction. It mouths a litany of possibly ironic personal belief lifted by Ferry from a poem by the US Pop artist Claes Oldenburg which purports to a world view but implies little other than that Oldenburg should stick to graphic art. The song is built on a rising sequence of chords whose conclusions always confound the listener's expectations of the resolution. Longer-breathed instrumental phrases abound, especially in the keyboard department, where an orchestral backdrop to the song is now the order of the day. Taken overall, the whole is just too ponderous, desite the use of backwards-running tapes and the treated mellotron voices at the conclusion, although it compares respectably with the poppy Eno of *Here Come the Warm Jets* or *Another Green World*. In Richard Williams's words in *Melody Maker*, Ferry's entrance is 'a moment of pure theatre, custom-built for the arena and the spotlight'[8] – not necessarily healthy implications, despite the tautness and apparent self-belief inherent in the swaggering self-confidence of the track. Things deteriorate, however, with 'Trash', a misconceived pastiche of New York new wave sensibilities, the nasal whine of its garage-band organ and piping sax being too smart-arse an attempt at Punk pastiche; the song's protagonist, you feel, just *has* to be 'only seventeen', flitting through an older man's view of a youth culture he stands apart from. This, for *NME*'s Max Bell, is 'where the punkettes walk'.[9] The closure, half-way through a melody, is a gesture at the disruptive techniques the band once mastered, although Manzanera's yah-boo riffing and nursery-school one-note ostinato in the first chorus are appealing. 'Angel Eyes', later disco-remixed, is infinitely more engaging in its original r'n'b form. Tellingly, the version hidden here on the album is perhaps the earthiest and most interesting music the sessions threw up; saxophone and guitar lines are promisingly non-synchronous, and heavily enough adrenalized to suggest delights, but the chord sequences are still obstinately non-threatening, a characteristic which dominated the album. The open-ended harmonic sequences of the first albums are preserved, but with less audacity.

The bass-drums-vocal centrality of 'Stronger Through the Years' hints at soundscapes to come; the jangly guitar runs which flit in and out of the soundstage like exotic animals in a Rousseau jungle, with enticingly strange fruit provided by Dave Skinner's choice of decorative piano notes. 'Ain't That

So' merely presents a case for Paul Thompson's increasing plaints about the uniform funkiness of the new material, for aside from the superfluous beading of percussion upon the song's exterior, it is pure ballast. 'Dance Away', on the other hand, in all its several forms, dazzlingly puts Ferry's case for revisionism, a lithe and loose-limbed smooch of old preoccupations and modern challenges in the tradition of the best Roxy Music tracks. Its combination of balladic regret and hesitant, multi-stranded instrumental funk was as irresistible and perfect a coupling as 'Virginia Plain' had been a marriage of the subtlest elements of crooning technique and melodic profile with the freshest characteristics of glam-rock energy. Planned as a track on *In Your Mind*, Ferry's 1977 solo album, the track finally emerged with the splendour of a new-hatched butterfly. The introduction alone, with its chance collision of icy guitar chords, piano figurations and drumbox, is an acme of cool and confidence. The flash-card rapidity of instrumental texture behind Ferry's splendid vocal – shuddering guitar, bombastic bass, melodramatic Fender Rhodes – is comparable with the best of *For Your Pleasure*. The confidence in the arrangement is absent from Ferry's persona. (He sings it as a professional pop star; he acts it, still, impeccably, as a lover whose belief in the show-biz/soul staple of the tearful clown is over – he can't smile through his tears any more. He's just too tired.) Manzanera's hesitant extemporization in the third verse is among the subtlest in the band's entire repertoire. The whole is a stunning example of instrumental choreography, a perfect deployment of the vital emotional graces of the ideal pop song – the sax riff, the guitar run – all done in miniature, without the rumbustious chaos of the original Roxy Music, but losing little of the panache and chutzpah.

Best of all, this proved to be the album that unlocked America. While success was limited (*Manifesto* went Top Thirty, but no further), the considerable enthusiasm with which April and May dates arranged across the US were met was a refreshing change and augured well for the future, in spite of some critical reservations centring on the abandonment of old material for very substantial airings of new material from the album. This was useful fuel for a promising run in the European charts. After the dramatic success of 'Dance Away' came 'Angel Eyes', an expert and audacious venture into disco rhythm and texture which scored mightily despite the simultaneous presence on the chart (in Britain at least) of Abba's own 'Angel Eyes' song. Fortunately for Ferry and Co., this latter was one of the Swedes' feebler efforts and neither song, despite aiming at similar consumer territory, impeded the other's progress.

Ironically, the year had kicked off on the home patch of the Scandinavian phenomenon. The *Manifesto* tour had begun in Stockholm in January, with the band appearing on a TV special benefit for UNICEF, organized and hosted by Abba. Provincial Sweden followed, then Germany, Holland, France, the US and Japan, and with an unusually elaborate and some-what ugly and over-fussy stage set which mixed Gothic and sci-fi influences (Pugin designs the Home of Tomorrow) the world suddenly became the band's oyster again. Ferry this time sported a comfortable blood-red leather jacket, while Mackay was belligerent in Mao ensemble, Man at Tiananmen Square. The set was longer than of old (two hours instead of seventy-seven minutes). Mackay and Manzanera shone even more brightly than before, and Thompson, despite initial difficulties in adapting to the lighter, funkier touch required by much of the new material, busily came into his own, proving again how much can be achieved by undemonstrative drummers in contributing to a unique musical euphony such as Roxy Music's.

The band came home to an assuredly rapturous British reception, playing Leicester (2 May), Birmingham (3 and 4 May), Manchester (6 and 7 May), Glasgow (8 and 9 May), Newcastle (10 and 11 May), Liverpool (12 May), Bristol Hippodrome (13 May), Southampton (14 May) and London's Hammersmith Odeon (16, 17 and 18 May). Even the press, who had been keeping their powder dry in readiness to riddle

Ferry, grudgingly agreed that the band had handled the transition well and indeed had made a creditable fist of self-criticism and revision. They also appeared on a ninety-minute special broadcast on the prestigious ITV arts slot *The South Bank Show*, which featured the band playing live in London.

As eager as ever not to stretch themselves too thinly, the band promptly withdrew from the public eye a mere six months after their re-entry. This time, Ferry assured the public, there would be no 'devolution', splits, warfare or retirement of any kind. As if by way of confirmation, the band appeared on the *Kenny Everett Video Show*'s Christmas special at the end of the year, churning their way through Wilson Pickett's 'In the Midnight Hour', an event greeted with enough enthusiasm within the circles of the band and their acolytes to see it pencilled in for their next LP.

One of the chief anomalies of *Manifesto* and possibly one of the strongest indications in the whole comeback panoply was the absence of a Roxy Music cover girl. True, *Viva! Roxy Music* had featured Ferry megaphonically serenading one of the Sirens on stage, but all the studio LPs to date had featured what had come to be viewed as one of the band's trademarks, and fulfilled an ancillary function by helping fill gossip columns as to how the young lady in question was fitting into Ferry's social life.

The *Manifesto* cover, however, is as powerful and individual an image as anything else that Antony Price had achieved thus far. Mannequins from his King's Road shop, Plaza, dressed in his own creations are subtly lit in a *Pointilliste* dazzle of strobe lighting which tumbles over the scene like a sleet of gold-leaf, the figures motionless as though transfixed in the centre of a dance floor in the restaurant at the end of the universe. Almost none is smiling, and none of their gazes addresses the viewer. The effect is simultaneously opulent and spare, striking and unsettling by turns.

There had been no little interest shown in just who the cover might be. Price remembers:

'The Roxy girl, being the Roxy Girl, was really something. The word went round the model agencies like a flame through petrol. They were queueing up to do it. Bryan and I would sit and draw these things [the cover designs]. Then we'd decide who to get and there'd be castings. Like that scene in *The Producers*! For the *Flesh + Blood* cover all the major dragons wanted the part, and it went to three little girls, complete novices…little Olympian nymphs. The spears weren't got hold of until the night before, thank God in the right colour…'[10]

It should be noted, of course, that the Roxy cover girls for *Flesh + Blood* differed from their precursors in so far as there was more than one of them, they weren't in any way recognizable and were noticeably desexualized. No translucent underwear or exposed thigh here.

Manifesto remains a classy cover, but one which suggests that the covers of yore had been examples of misogynist titillation outweighing artistic intent. Price and Ferry did just as good a job with the relatively allusive sensuality on show here as with Evelyn and Konnie's nakedness and Marilyn Cole's sheeny cleavage.

HAIL AND FAREWELLS

Ferry, meanwhile, made a somewhat belated acting début in a Swiss–French TV serial, *Petit Déjeuner Compris* (*Breakfast Included*). A continental cousin of *Crossroads* set in a *pension*, it's hard to tell who was kidding whom when Ferry turned up in the show as a loosely veiled parody of himself. Continental television is not noted for its sense of irony, and continental soaps even less so. It's probable that Ferry did the job for a laugh, or maybe even a dare, for acting had held only fitful appeal. Acting less to type than to stereotype, he here seduced the hotel's lady boss with a misunderstood–artist patter, even throwing in yarns about a poor coalfield childhood. One rather surreal touch (again, it's uncertain whether or not this was meant as a self-referential joke) was that the relationship was ended with the reuniting of *patronne* and *patron* at...a Roxy Music concert. In the meantime, Ferry had to run the gauntlet of renewed press intrusion when Marilyn Cole's scuzzy account of their amorous encounters was splashed gruesomely across the pages of the *Daily Mirror* in a style less broad-brush than rollered.

One person who might have read this with less than avid interest was Paul Thompson, who in the early months of 1980 finally parted company with the band. Ferry's stated reason for dropping Thompson was 'inflexibility'.[11] This seems a little rich when one considers Thompson's fine contributions not only to *Manifesto* but also the subsequent tour. And the rhythmic impulse of the new album, *Flesh + Blood*, hardly required a master of drop-beat and polyrhythm and there is precious little flexibility required when metric variation is so minimized. Thompson, after all, was nothing if not a brilliant timekeeper. But what is telling is the choice of replacements, Andy Newmark, Allan Schwartzberg and Simon Phillips (an old buddy of Manzanera from the *801* sessions). All three are awesome technicians, but excel also at restraint and the illusion that there is really no drummer playing on the record at all – that is, masters of easy funk comprehensibility. Thompson, in short, could not – at least to Ferry's ears – sublimate enough of his individuality to contribute. Chris Bohn, in the *NME*, asked Ferry if he had actually requested Thompson to absent himself from the *Flesh + Blood* sessions. 'Well, yeah,' said a 'ruffled' Ferry. 'His interest died a long time ago,' was the explanation.[12]

Ferry's comparison of Thompson to Andy Newmark that same year in an *NME* interview was ill-informed and also insensitive; Ferry harped on Newmark's 'professionalism'. His contrasting of Thompson as an 'inspired amateur' was unusually crass and musically unjustifiable for reasons that should be apparent to anyone.[13]

That said, Ferry did invite Thompson to play drums for the

band on the forthcoming live dates in 1980. 'Thompson's a great live player,' he stressed.[14] But this can also be read as a tacit admission that while nobody could play Thompson's lines like Thompson, just about anyone could play the new stuff, and it made sense to hire the best anyones around. And given that the new live performances would be occupied in large part by new material, why not hire his old friend to play the music in the studio as well as on-stage? Ferry never let on. Unfortunately, the luckless Thompson broke a thumb while indulging one of his hobbies – fast motorcycles – on the eve of the tour. Newmark stepped in, and Thompson's career with Roxy Music effectively ended there and then.

Tour manager Chris Adamson commented, 'You couldn't fault Andy's drumming but it never sounded the same. We nicknamed Paul "Blooter Blatter" because that's how he played, *blooter-ta-blatter-ta-blooter-ta-blatter-ta*. Andy was looser, more jazz-oriented.'[15]

The increasing concentration of creative duties around Ferry led to a commensurate concentration of instrumental contribution from Mackay and Manzanera, and the direction of the music itself required fewer individual timbres from supporting musicians. While Roxy Music's bass men had always been, in effect, sidemen/guests, keyboards and synthesizers had played a central enough – though sometimes wildly variable – role in their textures and in the conception of the music for them to need a reliable player around. Jobson may not have been an 'official' full-time member of the band but his attachment to them was of considerable importance.

Close examination of the construction of titles on *Manifesto* reveals that, both horizontally and vertically, keyboards and keyboard colorations are not sufficiently varied or integral enough to the arrangement of the overall sound to warrant a 'name' player. The nominal replacement for Jobson, David Skinner, was a respected and hard-working musician, but the qualities Ferry exploited on first his own solo albums and later on *Manifesto* make it obvious that what was required was merely a top-line professional to make sure that the simple things were done as well as possible and to remain, in effect, as anonymous as possible. (Manzanera and Mackay, in particular, were developing extracurricular interests. In December 1980 the two cropped up as the Players, playing an ornate 'Christmas' single released on the American Rykodisc independent label, and informed sources name them as the brains behind a spoof Christmas single, the Dumbells' 'Giddyup'/'A Christmas Dream'. In April 1981 Mackay would enter the publishing world with his first book, *Electronic Music*, an excellent and erudite work put together during various pauses in Roxy Music activity.)

The touring in 1980 began, as before, in Europe on 28 June, the very day that *Flesh + Blood* went to No. 1 in the UK. Unfortunately for the band, ill-health struck again, with Ferry the victim this time. After a concert on 14 July at Port Barcares, in the south of France, Ferry collapsed and, following the diagnosis of a serious kidney infection, was airlifted back to Britain for convalescence, threatening to wipe out the rest of the eight-week tour. Ferry battled back to fitness in an impressive nine days, resuming the tour at Brighton Conference Centre on 23 July. The tour's centrepiece, a short run at a sold-out Wembley Arena from 2 August, survived but other dates were rearranged with admirable speed for the following winter, by which time Roxy Music would have a wholly new pinnacle to their live act.

Supporting them (and getting justifiably rave reviews) were the Passions, an ethereal post-Punk band with whose singer, Barbara Gogan, and drummer, Clive Timperley, Ferry would kick around a few ideas and record some demos in the hiatus between the July dates and the rearranged winter schedule.

FLESH + BLOOD

Recorded at the start of the year at Basing Street and Gallery Studios (Phil Manzanera's Chertsey home) with Rhett Davies assuming production duties alongside band members, *Flesh + Blood* evidenced two clear tendencies: the increasingly nuclear character of the band's line-up as Manzanera, Mackay and Ferry, with attendant sidemen; and the enduring fascination with Americanizing the sound, with mixdown taking place at New York's Power Station by Bob Clearmountain and added US input from drummers Andy Newmark and Allan Schwartzberg, as well as erstwhile Carlos Santana sidekick Neil Jason playing bass. Tibbs held on to his place, but only as one of a pool of players; he doubled on bass with Jason and the now most favoured Alan Spenner. Even Manzanera's territory was not sacrosanct, Neil Hubbard playing a few lines here and then after impressing Ferry on the sessions for *The Bride Stripped Bare*. Ferry himself played some guitar on this album – on a Gibson Flying V nicknamed Vidor – contributing to the title track.

Newmark was one of the percussion world's MVPs, his talents fought and bartered over in the lucrative meatmarket of American sessionwork. Still young, he had played with an enormous number of artists, including Dan Fogelberg, Carole King, George Harrison, Rickie Lee Jones and, perhaps most notably, Bowie on his groundbreaking white-funk showcase *Young Americans* (1975). Newmark, then, specialized in loose funk-blues patterns. Ferry oozed enthusiasm, telling one reporter, 'Sometimes he's in the dressing room practising for two hours before a gig.'[16]

The enforced absence through industrial action of the IPC titles *Melody Maker* and *New Musical Express* during the late spring and early summer of 1980 diminished the role of both publicity departments and rock-comic hacks in the promotion of *Flesh + Blood*. That said, its contents, when first unveiled, were probably created with different sensibilities in mind to those of post-Punk campus kids who inked their fingers weekly on the rock broadsheets. The frothing self-abnegation in the album's shadow undertaken by the *Sunday Times*'s Derek Jewell, apostle of pop conservatism, who by 1980 read rock consonance as holy scripture, was enough to suggest that this was, if anything, an even more effete affair than *Manifesto*, one for a hard day after first-job work; one for planning a marriage to; one for being sensible to.

Paul Morley's journalistic gorge rose with predictable verbosity and routinely juvenile philosophic hypertrophy in the *NME*: Roxy Music had 'reduced themselves or extended themselves to selling bittersweet fantasies and seductive happy endings, making music where the nostalgic tendencies are impossibly correct,' he wrote.[17] As per his colleague Ian Penman, Morley's obsession with assuming the character and style of a French post-structuralist fatuously fugs up otherwise pertinent observations about the commercial implications of pop sincerity and emotional syntax in a logjam of textual obfuscation and misplaced allusion. Put simply, had Ferry been ten years younger, and on an independent label, he would have been a prophet; instead, time and place made him a pharisee. Music, inevitably, had nothing to do with it. The absurd reaction of the *NME* to new popsters Depeche Mode and ABC a year hence would prove that. Other reviewers were (comprehensibly) kinder but no less baffled as to exactly how deeply this new-found commercialism ran in Roxy Music's, and by implication Ferry's, musical juices.

Good points survive beneath the blanket of Morley's bombast. Emotion is now commodified in Roxy Music's musical syntax without the benefit of *l'ironie d'antan*; the construction of the ballads now sounds too personalized, the reconstructions of entire songs ('In the Midnight Hour') or styles (the Everlys with 'Over You') too calculated, too cynically Roxified, to be simply the clever double-edged swords, the backhanded compliments to the pop tradition of hitherto. These statements are here, first and foremost, to shift units. They say, with subdued elocution, *No bullshit. Let's go to work.* DJ Richard Skinner was later quoted as saying that Ferry, rather than composing, 'purveys a mood',[18] a sentiment that the singer showed little dissent from. It's an interesting observation and one that bears some study when listening to *Manifesto* and *Flesh + Blood*.

Conventional wisdom has it – not inaccurately – that *Manifesto* and *Flesh + Blood* completed Roxy Music's migration from rock to middle of the road, which, for some of the more obtuse critics, had begun as early as *Stranded*. There can be little dispute, however, that they are very much less interesting and novel than their precursors, and concern themselves with making quite different statements about, and with, music than, say, *For Your Pleasure*. Then the emphasis was on using the pop song and its emotional reflexology as a palette with which to create new emotional responses in listeners, using extant musical structures – verse/chorus, call/response, walking bass lines, specific styles of instrumental soloing – to create emotional responses while maintaining the form and identity of the old ones. By the time that *Flesh + Blood* is wheeled out of the hangar, however, the pop song is the end, rather than the means, of the compositional effort. It is a form to be endlessly explored, with minimal disruption to its structures, an endless process of refinement. It can offer the possibility of some excellent essays in the form, but can also just as easily offer some pretty unstimulating music.

This, of course, isn't to bury *Flesh + Blood*. The exquisite ballad 'Oh Yeah' is, in fact, classic Roxy Music stylism, a piece of almost innate commercial nous, the most consummate understanding in the entire orbit of Roxy Music's extant recordings of AOR requirements while maintaining individual melodic flair and textural integrity. Ferry's usual open-ended harmonic patterns here are firmly closed. This isn't necessarily a track that anyone else could have written, but that *someone else* could have written, a crucial denuding of Ferry/Roxy Music exclusivity. The choice of downbeats for the song lends it a kind of limp, a hobble, the shade of a long-held dream run aground, a vulnerability. Above all, it is a tender song, Ferry sounding as if he is looking after the heart of his lost beloved as well as his own, a strangely charitable sound. The sheer panache with which the whole is executed, however, and the familiar discontinuities in the soundstage – principally from Manzanera – carry the day. This is still Roxy Music.

This increasing reliance on texture above and beyond compositional idiosyncrasy (Ferry's voice was so unique as to evade comparative analysis) was hammered home by the immensely influential 'Same Old Scene'. What would once have been a charging rocker was now a hybrid of that erstwhile rock energy with dishevelled funk suavity which just managed to keep its dignity long enough to become another minor classic. The drumbox, the guitar chords with delay that rattle like a pinball settling, the alternating choppy staccato and legato chords played by the keyboards twinning with similarly delayed guitar and vaguely funky, tinnily percussive bass guitar became a part of pop's bloodstream and was imprinted upon every new popster's eardrum almost immediately, most notably in the case of Duran Duran, who first built a début single ('Planet Earth') and then a career upon this one brief moment of Roxy Music studio harmonization. The techniques, of course, can be traced back to US disco, notably those cultivated by the brains behind Chic, Bernard Edwards and Nile Rodgers, but the *élan* with which Roxy Music married them to rock rhythms and melodic impulses – with Manzanera's tautly muscled attack giving extra energy – presented post-Punk chart pretenders with a critic and fan-friendly *klang* which would ultimately supersede its channellers.

The other single most salient characteristic of *Flesh + Blood* is its employment of the strophic forms of pop, the short-syllabled form friendliest to formulaic popular music. It is present even in the better songs ('Oh Yeah'). Compare the strophes, if you will, of 'Same Old Scene', 'My Only Love' and 'No Strange Delight'; the words, syllables and emphases of all three are distressingly interchangeable.

The lack of involvement audible among the sidemen hamstrings the album; the sheer radiance of the textures in an otherwise amusing Everly Brothers pastiche, 'Over You', is almost surreally misplaced (a 1960s organ against Manzanera's very up-to-date guitar arpeggios – he would do it so much better on his own 1982 album *Primitive Guitars*). Ferry's uncharacteristic double-tracking of his own vocals here and there is another sign of indecision and a willingness to trust everything to the narcotic capabilities of electronics. One thanks the powers that be for preserving the most unbuttoned of Ferry's vibrato straining irresistibly through the mix here and there. Mackay, significantly, is nowhere, save perhaps on 'My Only Love'. The drumwork, apart from on 'Oh Yeah', is lackadaisical; the underlying structures of the melodies, profiles growing more familiar and comfortable, lack the instinctive knowledge that the explosive impulse of a Paul Thompson can take them wherever.

None the less, the album was greeted as a masterpiece of refinement.

The military precision and arrangement of the textures on *Manifesto* gathered pace on *Flesh + Blood*. The overall effect is orchestral in the classical sense of the word in the way that legato keyboard and guitar lines support chorus and verse vocal lines, best exemplified in the (admittedly superb) ballad 'Oh Yeah', which does an admirable job following up a so-so version of 'In the Midnight Hour', with which they had originally so wowed British TV viewers. The song, perhaps the most sophisticated and adult melody line that the band ever attempted, and twinned with an effective chorus, remains one of the finest songs, perhaps their only truly memorable exercise in the classic verse–chorus format.

Certainly the album is besieged with the kind of obsessive fidelity to the classic pop song that hitherto had been reserved solely for Ferry's solo work. 'In the Midnight Hour' and the Byrds' 'Eight Miles High' imply a revived preoccupation with song form of a type that continued to plague Ferry. This evidenced itself in *Flesh + Blood* tracks such as 'Over You', which attempted to be both a 1960s recall (Hammond organ) and 1980s (Manzanera's raised quills). The problem, with this as with many other tracks that also aspired to classic proportions, was the sheer lustre that classic pop-song arrangement lacked. The brio of the originals couldn't be replicated, but the anaemic versions Roxy Music served up didn't even work as revisionism, especially when viewed in the hindsight that encompasses both Ferry's *These Foolish Things* and *Taxi* albums; double-tracking Ferry's vocals hardly helped dispel the notion that this was nothing but a superior piece of nostalgia with none of the warmth or affection inherent in earlier Roxy Music or Ferry solo work. Ferry's vibrato seems just too cowed by the production; the bass lines are fatly overblown, as though suffering gastroenteritis, a problem building since *Siren*; the other sidemen seem uninvolved, less even than on Ferry's own solo albums. The length of lines, the shape of the strophes, with which Ferry builds the verses, are just too similar to those of 'Same Old Scene' and 'My Only Love'. Where, might one ask, has Mackay's oboe gone to? 'I think we were a bit too "Euro Soul" for the Americans,' says Thompson of the latter-day failures. 'Bryan thought we would sell more records there if we used American musicians, like Rick Marotta. And I don't think that works.'[19]

The album's most influential track, if hardly its zenith, was 'Same Old Scene', whose qualities were put in relief by, as in so much Pop Art, its detail. The drumbox, the delay-treated guitar chords and alternating 'choppy' staccato and chord keyboard arrangements duplicated on guitar and Chic-style Nile Rodgers bass line helped map the dismally duplicative terrain of new pop. These would be textural standards which, set by Roxy Music, eventually represented an acme which the band themselves would end up emulating.

Flesh + Blood concluded and concretized the slow evolution from the many-coloured, hyper-variant soundstage of the original albums to a more leisurely, relaxed deployment of instruments over the structure of songs. Hitherto, the wide and unusual spread of notes over short periods in a conventional melody – 'Remake-Remodel', for example – with unusual notes emphasized in chords to diversify the sound of the arrangement, or the root of a chord emphasized first on one instrument and then on another, made Roxy Music a vital force. This characteristic declined in influence later; almost anyone could have written or, more pertinently, arranged and played some of the material on *Manifesto* or *Flesh + Blood*. Only the class of the act and the way that the melodies are moulded to match Ferry's own whimsical phrasing makes Roxy Music still intrinsically interesting. Nobody else could sing the material like that, and that was its redeeming feature, its badge of individuality, its singularizer. Derek Jewell, in the *Sunday Times* wrote, in one of the fields in which he had at least some expertise, that on *Flesh + Blood*, Ferry's vocal style had 'newly matured' and was 'totally original'.[20]

Accusations of Roxy Music's 'commercialization' were problematic. A band that had made their name on the subtle satire of commercial show-business postures made their own apparent adoption of such postures harder to call. But none the less, the sunnily unassuming inoffensiveness of much of *Flesh + Blood* seemed pretty conclusively to affirm that Roxy Music were becoming an overtly commercial band. The shift towards verse-chorus structures, subtle and accomplished as it was, had seen to that. Roxy Music, once a band chasing hit status by musically and imagistically parodying hit status through the years, now chased hit status without any sense of irony at all, or so it seemed.

Commercial success was 'fairly important' for Ferry. 'It goes in phases where I don't care too much and then I want something and find I can't afford it. I think, gee, I should be selling more records.'[21] Alas, for all the commercial thrust of the band's — specifically Ferry's — writing and despite cleaning up in England (No. 1 album and two very widely airplayed Top Ten singles), America was proving obstinate once again.

Ferry:

'I thought that "Oh Yeah" would do it in America. We probably did a lot of things wrong. Mainly, the music didn't fit into the radio format. It wasn't heavy enough to make it on the rock stations. Except college radio, things like that, where it was just quirky English music.'[22]

In other words, little or nothing had changed.

NEW DECADE, NEW ROLE, NEW ROMANTICS:
ROXY MUSIC, PUNK AND FUTURISM

The Gogan/Timperley project bore no fruit, despite Ferry taking the tapes to his beloved New York studios for some stardust-sprinkling that never materialized. The music hung around for some time, and consisted of a number of fragments and outtakes. There was some speculation that this might be the next Roxy Music-related project but it came to naught, and Gogan and Timperley were, unfortunately, left hanging in mid-air. While hardly Ferry's intention, some have since read this as a betrayal.

Sadly, the highly talented Gogan and Timperley faded somewhat from view, having been tipped for big things during their stint as Roxy Music's support act. Their most successful single, 'I'm in Love with a German Film Star' went from an independent track favoured by John Peel to campus cult status and the outskirts of the charts – with its Berliner imagery, prickly guitar and mellifluous sense of foreboding, it was compared by some to early Roxy Music. Their otherwise ethereal image, however, would be widely diminished by tales of general dissolution which undermined their rightful claims to nationwide success. This was not only inaccurate but demeaning to a band with a highly developed sense of identity, and enough class to warrant their inclusion in this biography.

Roxy Music, with Ferry fully fit, were rehearsing for their rearranged string of UK dates with some European roadwork in late 1980 – specifically, the long-running Rockpalast indoor festival for German TV in Dortmund, when news filtered through of the fatal shooting of John Lennon in New York City. Andy Newmark, who had played on Lennon's final

Double Fantasy sessions in New York that very year, strongly supported Ferry's suggestion to his musicians that the band pay tribute to the dead singer. Ferry's own affections for Lennon, while not always musically apparent, had been real enough.

The reaction to Lennon's death throughout the world was remarkable enough; in popular culture, it generated passionate interest, and in rock music itself the mourning hinted at times at mass hysteria. Ferry probably did himself no favours but spoke honestly and for many others when he stood firmly against the grain of accepted Lennon eulogies by telling one interviewer, 'I always think of Lennon as a "Jealous Guy" rather than a politician. He was very human and made mistakes, which was what I liked about him.'[23]

Bearing this in mind, and the fact that 'Jealous Guy' was one of Ferry's favourite songs – he'd been 'planning to do it for four or five years'[24] and, he had astutely noted, one of the great hits Lennon never had which had lain unloved because unknown and unknown because unloved, this was his choice for the Roxy Music tribute.

In Dortmund the fans rose to the song, giving the band a standing ovation for just this one four-minute track, and in the general hubbub which followed Lennon's shooting, the band were deluged with requests for a recording of it to be made.

Many have questioned the band's – and, by direct implication, Ferry's – motive for releasing 'Jealous Guy' as a single. Certainly the bewildering intensity of rock culture's reaction to Lennon's end conferred guaranteed-platinum status on almost any product with the slightest material or nominative connection to the ex-Beatle. There were, then, the inevitable cries of 'cash-in' when the single was released (among other things, despite having been recorded months after the album, it helped extend *Flesh + Blood*'s chart run to an incredible sixty weeks). But it must be remembered that the release date of 'Jealous Guy' was 13 February 1981, two months after the shooting, by which time the wave of grief and embittered nostalgia seemed to have just crested.

Roxy Music were to regenerate the entire process of mourning the dead Beatle but such details are rendered irrelevant by the sincerity of the recording, Ferry's stunning vocal performance and the sheer brilliance of his choice of material.

'Jealous Guy' was just what Ferry said it was, hidden treasure, and in recording it Roxy Music ensured their third, and possibly most readily identifiable, signature tune. Ironically for Ferry, that tune was someone else's, but what of it? The band scored their first-ever No. 1 single in the UK after nearly a decade of trying. As Rogan writes in *Style with Substance*, it is noteworthy that this single's massive commercial success did not tempt the band to ice the cake by recording a follow-up album. It also vindicated Ferry's long and hitless years of recording other people's material. Finally the *hommage* hit paydirt. Ferry, so often portrayed as glacially calculating in his quest for fame, spurned this most golden opportunity and, as Rogan says, he is to be congratulated for that.[25]

Antony Price has called Ferry the 'Prince Charles of the music business', saying 'He could have had his name on a glamour product years and years ago. But Bryan is obsessed with his music.'[26] Ferry admitted to some sentimentality about Roxy Music as late as 1980, when he told the *NME*, 'Most of my best work has been done under that banner. Because it's the work I feel most passionate about I spend hours and hours sweating over it – millions more manhours than anyone else in the band.'[27] By way of a postscript, he added, 'So I never feel that the others are hard done-by at all.'[28]

That might not have been calculated to win Bryan Ferry too many friends in music in the aftermath of Punk, but it wasn't Ferry's lordly attitude that mattered – it was his pose.

We have already seen what Punk meant to Ferry, and the band, in its heyday. A few years later, tempers having cooled, Ferry could afford to be a little more magnanimous – and so could many of his Punk tormentors. 'I always had great faith in myself and felt that I wouldn't be discarded by a discerning audience,'[29] insisted Ferry in 1978 with perhaps just a bit too much relish. 'I remember talking to John Lydon and he was totally dismissive of Roxy Music for being too bourgeois. But Sid Vicious was positively gracious to me,' recalls a somewhat nonplussed Andy Mackay.[30] Siouxsie and the Banshees met at a Roxy Music concert at Wembley Arena on the *Siren* tour. James Truman of *Melody Maker* recorded one moment of awestruck tribute in 1980 when he noted Ferry being accosted backstage at *Top of the Pops* for autographs by members of the Undertones.[31]

There were other and more complex affinities. Price's shop, Plaza, was situated at the end of the King's Road. While it may have been wanting of the hip appeal and easy shock value of Seditionaries (Vivienne Westwood and Malcolm McLaren) or Sex (McLaren on his own), it none the less proved a magnet for those at the precious end of London's 1970s art school esoterics and was one of the lodestones of the New Romantic movement in the capital (Plaza it was who supplied the clothes for the dummies on the cover of *Manifesto*).[32]

The contiguity of Punk and Roxy Music might seem incongruous, but becomes clearer when both parties are closely analysed. The incongruity arises largely from ongoing misinterpretation of much of the Punk project, and certainly that which came after it. Punk was not, as is popularly imagined, simply about safety pins, saliva and shitty guitar playing. As many writers and academics have perceived, its preoccupations were as much imagistic as musical, as much to do with sexuality, identity and leisure as bondage, bumflaps, hairdye and kicking in the heads of teddy boys.

Briefly, Punk's art school vanguard, led by Malcolm McLaren and Vivienne Westwood, offered a commentary on youth style and subculture by using a visual language in which mass communication and consumerism were targets to be simultaneously celebrated and abominated. This owed as much to Josef Beuys as to Andy Warhol – the relegation of either communally or individually derived transcendence, the displacement of artistic endeavour from the singular object to the mass commodity. 'All that's left to celebrate is the market,' reported the academics Simon Frith and Howard Horne with some distaste, 'everyone can be famous for fifteen minutes because everyone is a potential commercial object.' Feebly he concluded, 'This needn't have a Reaganite concluson', clearly ignoring the ludicrous sums that pop ephemera would fetch in New York's auction houses of the 1980s.[33] Pop, Warhol and Beuys have enriched your life, the line went, because their placing of ephemera in galleries has made everyday life an art experience. Even Punk craved something a bit less boring. The objects chosen by Punks as iconic signifiers – safety pins, ripped T-shirts, cheap tartan trousers – were faintly original. For Dick Hebdige, these things were objects manufactured simply to be discarded, both as useful objects and as signs. Punk style was *bricolage* of postmodernity and discontinuity; in Vivienne Westwood's formulation, 'If the cap doesn't fit, wear it.'[34] For Punks, as for Roxy Music, appearances and surfaces meant as much as content; they were malleable qualities to be exploited at will, and the surface qualities of both dress and musical expression were the keys to novelty of expression. This was the same artistic syntax with which Ferry had approached the culture of the late 1960s.

Ferry had vehemently expressed his incomprehension at the apparent 'sincerity' of 1960s-derived rock and had quite disdained hippiedom, preferring to investigate the liberating qualities of the metropolitan and the superficial. More incidentally, the band's avowed Pop Art loyalties also found resonances in Punk, for Punk's Situationist, anyone-can-do-art aesthetics found Pop Art's sublimation of high/low cultural categories and elevation of everyday clutter extremely sympathetic.

Much the same could be said for the first wave of Punk-derived rock stars, who were overtly in Roxy Music's debt – what were loosely (and risibly) termed the New Romantics. A kind of subcultural hybrid whose extraordinary media visibility at the dawn of the 1980s in the UK has never been adequately explained then or since, the New Romantics were mutant outgrowths of the interface between Punk, art schools and fashion who exploited an imagistic void at the heart of popular culture and benefited no end from music press coverage that ranged from the sympathetic to the sycophantic. Rarely, if ever, were these acts of lasting musical interest, but they contributed something to the history of pop production and consumption in Britain, largely due to their adherence to a path blazed by David Bowie and Roxy Music.

The overriding New Romantic preoccupations were style and surface, which made them a grotesque adjunct to the postmodern theory running riot in the pages of the rock comics following the cues of the Punk vanguard. As Frith and Horne point out, the Warhol/Beuys-informed Punk project to make an artistic statement of the environment of admass and of (post-) modernity made personal fashion, made the person, made personal consumption and its visual adjunct, an artistic statement. This was rewriting the 'Romantic gesture of refusal in the terms of mass fashion'.[35] Posing became performance art, the poser a ready-made art object.

When interpreted and utilized by the (relatively) more skilful and literate of their kind – Haircut 100, ABC – this use of image and music brought forth unimaginable hyperbole, especially in the pages of the *NME*. The subculture spawned its own magazines, *The Face* and *I-D*, and art school and rag-trade creativity ran headlong into the meretricious embrace of the generation of the Punk posers swilling around the upper-income reaches of London's bohemia. Style, consumption and superficiality were once again OK – not just morally acceptable but hip too. Talent was an option, usually not taken out. In *Art into Pop*, Frith and Horne emphasize that 'New Romanticism meant a new pop slogan – everyone, as a consumer, was equal'.[36] Facile poppycock, of course, as they rightly affirm; personal economy apart, the celebration of consumption was no different to advertising. Furthermore, the individual style as opposed to a group identity that New Romanticism stressed was hardly new – the most casual reading of any Roxy Music gig reportage proves that.

The result was to resurrect Roxyite iconography into a surreal cosmos of the borrowed and half-forgotten; London looked like the sleeve art of *Manifesto*, a coke-raddled, pimpled farrago of Helmut Newton, Berlin, Surrealism and camp. The 1920s and 1930s became stylistic avatars; anything which connoted an interpolation of surface and irony between direct experience and artistic expression, from Kurt Weill and *Neue Sachlichkeit* to Marinetti and Futurism, was deemed valid. Kitsch was suddenly the very protein of youth 'innovation'. In effect, the entire era in youth culture replicated the cleansing period of *Neue Sachlichkeit* or objectivity in 1920s Germany scourging the land of self-consciously subjective Wagnerism. For Hindemith and Brecht read Joy Division and Peter York, for Nietzsche and Mahler read Richard Neville and Led Zeppelin. No surprise, then, that the foppish heroes of ITV's *Brideshead Revisited* were the most celebrated faces on British TV in the early 1980s.

There were more than visual affinities between Roxy Music and New Romantics. *Manifesto*, especially in its use of keyboards, bass and drums, actually prefigured a lot of New Romantic textures, Duran Duran's most of all. For example, affectation of voice became a prerequisite in early-1980s pop music. It marked immunity from the legacy of the hippies, which Punks had urged us not to trust. It implied distance, irony, commentary. Even the more talented of the newcomers, the failsafe note-hitters, the Martin Frys and Tony Hadleys, fitted because of their affectations. Billy MacKenzie and Julian Cope of the less obviously musical (or parodic) tendency had listened to Ferry records and learned.

Upon being asked in 1982 by the *NME* (which, incidentally, remained largely uncommitted to the inspiration of many of its new heroes) whether or not he was aware of the interest his music and image had generated, Ferry was disarmingly modest: 'No, that's one thing I don't find too interesting. I listen to the radio when I drive, especially if I've got a record out, I'll listen to see what it sounds like on the radio and how it compares to the other records being played.'[37] None the less, he was not entirely indifferent, as he revealed when pressed about contemporary developments in pop:

'I...don't feel that it's my place to criticize other people's work. And, there's always something cute about something even if it's lightweight. Soft Cell, for instance, look really weird. In all the gay bars you've ever been in you see guys like that with really bad make-up, and I think that's kind of interesting. It's...very English; a very provincial version of Berlin decadence.'[38]

The amateurish or, precisely, 'provincial' qualities Ferry refers to here were among the most endearing aspects of Roxy Music. They were, at their best, always a specifically *English* band; their sideways look at American pop could never have been conceived or delivered without this gift of self-conscious distancing. By the beginning of 1982, however, those qualities would have been all but forgotten. And when they were, it was clear that Roxy Music, having lost their main source of uniqueness, had only a limited shelf life.

9: ENO: BALD MAN SEEKS MUSICIANS, VIEW TO SOMETHING DIFFERENT

Writing about Brian Eno's musical career subsequent to his spell in Roxy Music is not only a hazardous undertaking, it is one of dauntless scale and even, possibly, pedantry. There already exists the excellent *Brian Eno: His Music and the Vertical Colour of Sound* by Eric Tamm (1989), a scholarly examination of the evolution of Eno's music and methodology whose musicological zeal, at first forbidding, is tempered and redeemed by a warm affection for the subject which allows the humanity of the composer – and the author – to shine through.

Additionally, the aesthetics of Eno's major contribution to music in the 1980s – Ambient – are discussed to the nth degree in Joseph Lanza's superb *Elevator Music* (1995) which, although it treats Eno cursorily, is indispensable on the roots of music-as-environment that Eno found such a stimulating idea.

None the less, given Eno's contribution to Roxy Music, to completely ignore him – especially as this book also deals with the music made individually by Andy Mackay and Phil Manzanera – seems absurd. It does, however, make the nature of such an overview all the more awkward an issue when dealt with in the context of a book about Roxy Music. Integrating the narrative of Eno's career and musical development into that of a band that he just happened to once be part of is a herculean task. The initial thought is 'Why bother?' – and as Eno himself might say, it was a long time ago and of little relevance to his subsequent work. But as I hope to point out, the contrasts and comparisons between Eno and Roxy Music can enlighten us further upon both, and add to the ongoing debate about the nature of the heritage of the art school and its effects upon musical creativity in this country. To this end, preferring completeness, I have included Eno's subsequent career in this book. I might add for the sake of the uninitiated that Eno's music is often of a compelling quality that should be better known, and if this book is a means of propagating it, and further clarifying the issues regarding Roxy Music's own creative processes, then so much the better.

Given also that apart from Tamm's book and Eno's and Russell Mills's own rather didactically toned (despite himself) retrospective *More Dark Than Shark*, few critical accounts of Eno's career exist in English at present. Furthermore, such material as exists is often of a less than critical nature, its arguments somewhat dazzled by preconceived wonder at Eno's method and formidable loquacity.

Eno's cachet has always resided in his ability to play and talk a good avant-garde game; his status in British music, even when within the ranks of Roxy Music, has always been of a kind of curiosity, a mascot, a talisman. In Eric Tamm's memorable phrase, he has often impressed people as a kind of 'cerebral hermaphrodite'.[1]

His early success was based on highly talented music-making and the ability to charm the socks off reporters who, encountering such polysyllabic volubility from another musician, might have dismissed it as a verbiage. But his ability to apply avant-garde theory to recognizable rock-related situations emulates, at least in part, his idol John Cage's ingenious gift for laterally thought-out twists in the conception of how music is composed, played and heard. Also, his enthusiastic espousal of 'non-musical' status has ensured at least something of an audience in a country – England – which so famously deplores grandiloquence and technical display in any of the arts.

Eno's best riposte to those who accuse him of valorizing the unskilled came in a *Guardian* interview in 1998:

'There are two ways of being an artist. One is to really explore one furrow, and a lot of artists that I really like best, actually, do that. Randy Newman, Joni Mitchell, Samuel Beckett...[this attitude] comes from that kind of thinking, of saying, "This is my language, and I'll get better and better at speaking it." But I'm not that type of artist: I'm really thrilled by suggesting other ways of talking, other languages one could speak, and then letting other people make use of them.'[2]

ENO THE ROCKER

Eno read Cage's book *Silence* in the late 1960s and became fascinated with the concepts of chance operations in music. Cage's own 'anti-musical' and 'non-musicianly' approach had immense influence on the young Eno, but just as great an impact was made by the minimalist music of Terry Riley and Steve Reich, whose employment of chance and systemic thought and structure in their compositions bowled him over. He found Riley's *In C* (1964) and Reich's *It's Gonna Rain*

(1967) particularly beguiling. Both use mathematical repetition and delay to create distinct and subtly overlapping lines of music which in turn enable the audience to listen 'creatively' and recognize new musical structures from the endless permutations of sound patterns randomly arising as a result, finding out what's between the notes, what the spaces create for themselves and what the mind's ear fills those spaces with. Both pieces, definitively mapping out minimalism, were subtle endorsements of an axiom Eno would come to valorize: 'Repetition is a form of change.' They were, in effect, highly elegant and ingenious experiments in 'the psychology of musical perception'.[3] Of the Reich piece, Eno has since said, '*It's Gonna Rain* was the most influential piece of music I've ever heard, as it showed me how variety can be generated by very, very simple systems.'[4] Elsewhere, he has been more specific: 'The use of hidden structural devices in music appealed to me. Even when all the cards were on the table and everyone hears what is gradually happening in a musical process, there are still enough mysteries to satisfy all.'[5]

The elements of music arising from the chance and hazard elements of overlapping and interactive systems was what most appealed, for it suggested that the very simplest music, created in the simplest manner without any great technical expertise, could have intellectual as well as emotional value.

The concepts of systems and random events informed Eno's first project outside Roxy Music, a collaboration with King Crimson guitarist Robert Fripp entitled (*No Pussyfooting*), which was released by a sceptical Island Records with the reluctant say-so of an even more sceptical EG Management in autumn 1973. Fripp had first met Eno during sessions for the Matching Mole LP *Little Red Record* in 1972, and, impressed with the Roxy Music man's articulacy and originality, became a firm friend. One day that autumn at Eno's invitation, he turned up on the latter's doorstep with his guitar and the two began making music, albeit in a highly impromptu and unusual manner. According to Tamm:

Eno had worked out a way of producing music by using two tape recorders set up so that when a single sound was played, it was heard several seconds later at a slightly lower volume level, then again several seconds later at a slightly lower volume level, and so on. The length of time between an event and its repetition depended on the speed of the tape and the distance between the two tape recorders.[6]

This enabled a looped signal to repeat and decay indefinitely, new sounds could be layered on extant ones without erasing them, and the passage of time would slowly induce gradual distortion of the repeating loops, with commensurate and infinitely subtle variations of tone colour. Fripp's task was to play (or choose not to play) guitar lines over the loops. At Eno's home the pair recorded a long piece entitled 'The Heavenly Music Corporation', which would later provide one side of the (*No Pussyfooting*) album; side two, 'Swastika Girls', was recorded a year later, after Eno's departure from Roxy Music, at Command Studios in London.

The collaboration produced two albums of variable quality. The first, its title inspired by a Fripp maxim, sold respectably on novelty value alone and convinced Island/EG to offer the partnership a second album deal. This effort, *Evening Star*, followed in 1975. Most of the music is pleasantly narcotic, slightly epigonic minimalism, inspired by Fripp's assured and idiosyncratic playing. There is also historical interest with the slow development – particularly by side one of *Evening Star* – of the Ambient musical genre which Eno would do so much to create in the early part of the 1980s. Contrary to preconceptions, the only truly aggressive piece of dissonant, obviously avant-garde music is 'An Index of Metals' from *Evening Star*, an experiment rarely found again in Eno's work. Nonplussed by their album success, Fripp and Eno hastily organized a tour, trying to extend the Frippian dictum of 'first takes only' to the live setting, maximizing the elements of chance and hazard. A half-hour set was agreed on but the début gig saw a ten-minute fiasco, with the formerly flamboyant Eno reduced, like his partner, to a shadow in the dark, while the audience stumbled around trying to get a fix on the films being projected behind the pair.

It might be imagined that Eno's highly individual outlook would demand as great a degree of individual control over his music as possible; but given his lack of conventional musical ability, collaboration was, to a greater or lesser extent, thrust upon him. Also, his years at art school had impressed on him the potential of the collaborative environment, and, as he saw it, the input of human spontaneity was a prerequisite for the activation of the systems he felt he needed to create music.

To this end, his first 'real' solo album, *Here Come the Warm Jets* (February 1974), featured no fewer than seventeen session musicians. A financially burdened Eno, reeling from the weight of unpaid Roxy Music debts, of which he was co-creditor, sought the cheapest studio he could find in September 1973 and set to work, with Andy Mackay playing keyboards and 'saxophone septet', Paul Thompson diligently drumming and Phil Manzanera on guitar – in other words, all of Roxy Music save for Ferry.

Criticism of *Here Come the Warm Jets* beyond the most superficial level is, as with all of Eno's albums, superfluous in the face of Tamm's systematic musicological analysis. Suffice to say that *Here Come the Warm Jets* is a delightful and often eccentrically whimsical combination of the weird and the approachable, often within the same song, sometimes within the same chord. Also, Eno's twee terminology for musical instruments begins on *Here Come the Warm Jets*. Tamm writes that Eno's vocal style is directly modelled on that of Bryan Ferry, and in places it's a view that is hard to dispute, the only question being whether this was meant satirically or not (although as this would constitute a satire of a satire, its value must be questionable). The tinkling piano and 'aaaah' vocal open vowels of 'Cindy Tells Me': compare and contrast with Roxy Music's own view of 1950s mood-music.

'I don't think,' Eno would later say, 'that [*Warm Jets*] deserved the good reviews it got. There was a sort of mystique about it which protected it — it made you think that if you didn't like something about it, it was your fault and not mine.'[7] The notices were hardly raves, but none the less satisfactory — although this may have had something to do with the indulgent attitudes towards Eno already fermenting in the rock press. True, there were some who derided him as a dilettante, but the man obviously had talent, and the guts to overcome a self-proclaimed musical handicap. Moreover, the result of this protean struggle was music that was ballsy and, more significantly, different enough from that of the increasingly reviled Ferry that he must have seemed a good critical horse to back in the rock stakes.

Eno, for all the plaudits, was poor, wretchedly so, living in Augean conditions, surrounded by cockroaches, without heating in a cold winter and neglecting his health and diet. In desperation for money and prospects, he first cut a single, 'Seven Deadly Finns', which sank without trace, and then unthinkably teamed up with a bar band, the Winkies, and attempted to revisit his outfront role with Roxy Music. Johnny Rogan, in *Style with Substance*, cleverly reads this as a 'backward step to Roxy Music...a rock star fantasy...[the] same fantasy that had inspired Bryan Ferry'.[8]

The Winkies were a band local to Eno's part of west London and were led by a highly able singer–guitarist named Phil Rainbow. Other members included Phil Desmarais (drums), Brian Turrington (bass) and Guy Humphreys (guitar, vocals). Eno suggested to the quartet that they become his backing band. Given Eno's reputation, the rest fell in, but after five dates of an over-hastily arranged tour and a session for John Peel at the BBC,★ Eno's right lung collapsed and he was rushed into hospital.

★Broadcast on 5 March 1974 and featuring 'Paw Paw Negro Blowtorch', 'Baby's on Fire', 'Totalled' and 'Fever'.

He later described the project as the only 'abortive' one of his career, but refused to blame anyone but himself. Of the band he said, 'I must give them all credit because they were very, very good. It was my fault for not thinking straight about it. I don't like touring and I don't feel any inclinations to be the leader of a group. It's just not my role. I was the singer, the focal point.'[9] To another reporter, he said of the immediate aftermath of the Winkies episode, 'I decided that I didn't want to be a star – the sort of figure that Bryan became, I knew that becoming that would only inhibit what I really wanted to do.'[10]

Turrington became a friend and collaborator on later albums – in addition, through this connection, he would record with Phil Manzanera, John Cale, Sean Tyla and Robert Calvert – but Eno, in the meantime, had scraped enough contacts and cash together to try his luck promoting himself in the USA, and in spring 1974 he followed in Ferry's and Puxley's footsteps to court American public opinion.

He conducted forty-eight interviews in New York City alone, but, as Rogan observes, 'sometimes entertaining but more usually boring the pants off a populace who had yet to come to terms with Roxy Music, let alone Eno'.[11] Reaction was, predictably, even more lukewarm than that which so disheartened Ferry. Eno desultorily recorded some demo tapes for the fledgeling proto-New Wave band Television and met and became friends with John Cale, his onetime hero from the Velvet Underground and now a solo artist.

Cale, much to Eno's amazement and surprise, offered to collaborate with him, inviting Eno to guest on some forthcoming recordings which would see the light of day later in 1974 and in 1975 as the albums *Slow Dazzle* and *Helen of Troy*. This enthused Eno no end:

'You get in there, you set yourself up and the tape's suddenly rolling. You're playing and you don't know what the number is, you don't know what's going to happen. You finish, he says "Great" and that's it, that's your take, finished, done. Because, and this is something I've picked up, if you catch someone on their first time through they do some very odd things, before they start getting to know and polishing it up. You get this kind of liveliness in it which is a mixture in a sense of danger and excitement.'[12]

Eno's flair for networking and facilitating began to reappear. He helped set up and also appeared on the bill of the infamous 1 June 1974 gig at the Rainbow, Finsbury Park, a brute of a set featuring Cale, Nico, Kevin Ayers and himself which was later released as an LP on Island Records. Eno deplored the 'supergroup' hype that immediately detonated around the project upon its announcement in public. It was, he would later say, 'a depressing experience'.[13] As it concerned, in Eno's words, 'a lot of people who are professionally committed to discovering novelty, this was seized upon and blown up beyond its real significance'.[14] The gig had been, he complained, 'underprepared...there's a real bogey among rock musicians about talking about music – they seem to think that if you discuss it, the magic dies or something. Generally speaking, people weren't willing to surrender their positions for the greater good.'[15]

Something else that Eno brought back from America in 1974 was an ingenious concept for a second solo album. Strolling the streets in San Francisco's Chinatown, he had chanced upon some postcards depicting a Maoist 'heroic' ballet, *Taking Tiger Mountain (By Strategy)*. The idea provoked a strange fascination in him, rationalized later as a resonance upon his love of systematic thought and action. The 'Tiger Mountain' concept, he said, felt archaic, 'strategy' felt 'modern' (it should be pointed out here that the etymology of the word 'strategy' in fact dates back to the ancient Greek *strategia*, or 'generalship'). 'Strategy interests me because it deals with the interaction of systems, which is what my interest in music is really, and not so much the interaction of sounds,' Eno told reporters.[16]

Subsequent events in the USA formalized yet further the methodology of the next album's genesis. Staying with a girlfriend, Randi, in New York, Eno took some mescaline and in his subsequent delusion-soaked sleep heard, clearly and memorably, snatches of nonsense lyrics which he committed to paper immediately upon waking.

This method of random assemblage, he felt, could apply also to the process of putting words to music, and on returning to London he co-opted Phil Manzanera into the experiment. A process of putting together innumerable scraps of tape, musical doodles and afterthoughts was undertaken to see how, given the impulsive nature of Eno's lyrical inspirations, they might best fit into songs. Manzanera would tell him what key they were in and suggest convenient connections. Backing tracks were compiled, Manzanera would play them in basic form and Eno would sing the first thing that came into his head.

Eno's intention was not pure ecstatic creative flow, however, but automatic writing: 'Presenting as art the unprocessed contents of consciousness and of the unconscious was not enough, there was a distinction to be made between the vision and the form in which it was presented, and the working out of the form was as important as the vision itself.'[17]

'I didn't have a message,' Eno later confessed to an interviewer, 'so I had a problem with the function of lyrics. All my favourite songs had lyrics which I didn't quite understand.'[18] Eno, in that instance, quoted the suggestive and allusive but ultimately borderline-nonsense lyrics of the Velvet Underground's 'What Goes On'.

Of his method, Eno said:

'I begin by just shouting to a backing track, gradually building up a system of syllable rhythm, then getting the kind of phonetics that I want and gradually begin...It works from sound to words and from words to meaning, so it works quite the other way round from the way people normally think lyrics are written, I think.'[19]

For Eno, however, lyrics were becoming an increasingly untenable proposition. They burdened the music, he said, with extra-musical 'intentions', which implied associations not necessarily in the musical expression itself. He had to 'trick' himself into writing lyrics, he said. John Cage once spoke of the 'problems' he had with music that 'attempts to control me'. For Eno, 'Some music comes so laden with intention you can't hear it for the intention.'[20]

This, he explained, was what accounted for the absence of anything resembling a traditional love song, or indeed a song speaking of anything but companionship, throughout his entire rock output of 1974–8. 'Love songs,' he has said, 'make a number of statements, which I'm very wary of doing.'[21] Which goes neatly to prove the wrong-headedness of some particularly idiotic Ray Davies comparisons which were made with 'Cindy Tells Me' from *Here Come the Warm Jets* – although as Ray Davies comparisons were made with any songwriter who even alluded to lower-middle-class actuality in the 1970s, it can safely be consigned to history. Besides, Eno never had much of a head – or a brief – for rhyme; as horrors like pairing 'teeth sir' and 'ether' testify.

Others have interpreted Eno's somewhat Baroque approach to the song form, especially when put into context with his intellectualism, as a frigid, very English evasion of emotional explicitness. In a 1979 conversation with Lester Bangs, Eno attempted to explain his attitudes, returning to the theme of the 'love song':

'I'm not interested in it. I mean, I'm not interested in writing about it. It's certainly not something that I would ever use music to discuss, at least not in clear terms like that... You see, the problem is that people, particularly people who write, assume that the meaning of a song is vested in the lyrics. To me, that has never been the case. There are very few songs that I can think of where I even remember the words, actually, let alone think that those are the centre of the meaning. For me, music in itself carries a whole set of messages which are very, very rich and complex, and the words either serve to exclude certain ones of those, or point up certain others that aren't really in there, or aren't worth saying or something.'[22]

Returning to *Taking Tiger Mountain (By Strategy)*, Eno would on this occasion use nine musicians, in addition to his old mates the Portsmouth Sinfonia as 'string section'. Among the guests were Andy Mackay and Phil Collins, Phil Manzanera acting as a major musical collaborator.

Eno began to find his feet, and a reputation as a solo artist. All was nearly brought to nought, however, one cold night in January 1975, when, returning from a late session with Phil Manzanera at Basing Street, Eno was struck by a taxi and nearly killed. 'You stupid cunt, you brought this on yourself,' was Eno's formulation of the incident.[23] 'I knew absolutely that I was responsible for it. It was not an accident at all,' he later concluded.[24]

Always a believer in the power of creative thought and the generative autonomy of human activity, this does seem a little extreme even from Eno, although he told the same interviewer (the *NME*'s Iain MacDonald) of morbid and macabre thoughts of his own mortality that had been plaguing him for days prior to the 'accident'. Eno's convalescence would, however, prove a creative godsend; this was to be the genesis of his legendary and ground-breaking Ambient music projects, and in turn would lead to enough intellectual activity to fuel him for many years to come.

More immediately, however, he set up his own record label with help from EG, Obscure Records, partly in response to the revelation of an 'environmental' music which would, necessarily, require non-mainstream outlets and, secondarily, as a useful means of distributing avant-garde music at affordable prices to experimental but doubtful listeners – 'cheap to make'.[25]

We will return to Eno's use of Obscure for his own recordings – specifically, Discreet Music, the first of his experiments in Ambient or environmental music – but it is also worth noting that the majority of releases on the short-lived Obscure label were of music written or performed by Eno's acquaintances. A detailed list can be found in Tamm's excellent discographical notes, but for the record they feature work by Gavin Bryars (*The Sinking of the Titanic*, OBS1, 1975), Michael Nyman (*Decay Music*, OBS6, 1976), The Penguin Café Orchestra (*Music from the Penguin Café*, OBS7, 1977), Cage, playing his own works in collaboration with Jan Steele (OBS5, 1975).

Fully recovered and fighting fit, Eno set bout his third album, the superb *Another Green World*, widely held to be his best, and by now interpolating Ambient-style synthesizer drifts in between the increasingly off-the-wall and mercurial Progressive rock pieces. This time Eno used another pool of sessioneers, including Robert Fripp, Phil Collins, Fairport Convention drummer Dave Mattacks, Brand X bassist Percy Jones, John Cale, Paul Rudolph and electric pianist Rod Melvin from Kilburn and the High Roads.

Eno's stated intention was to bring these diverse musicians together for the sake of it and see what resulted. He encouraged them to play in as awkward and uninstinctive a manner as possible. In Rogan's words, this was 'not a glorification of amateurism, but an attempt to turn inhibition to advantage through spontaneity.[26] In the studio, Eno worked by a series of verbal suggestions and visual image and body language to analogize the sound he wanted his musicians to produce. 'It's a very good way of talking to musicians, particularly bass players, because they tend to be into the swirling hips.'[27]

Another Green World was the first album on which Eno is credited as the sole composer of all the pieces. A stickler for the most precise statement of textural intention, Eno mixed and produced twenty-two different versions of *Another Green World* before selecting one he deemed fit for release. By this time, he was an in-demand session man, adviser and general mascot to the Progressive rock industry, and he brought varying degrees of influence to bear on numerous albums of the time, all of which are listed in the discography at the back of this book.

He began travelling more extensively, spending large amounts of time in Germany and the US. In the summer of 1975 he jammed on-stage in Hamburg with Dieter Moebius and Hans-Joachim Roedelius of the semi-legendary German electronic group Cluster, whose work he had known of and admired for some time. It would lead to productive friendships and refinement of Eno's gestating ideas about environmental music.

Eno's return to full-time work also led him into a productive endeavour outside music that would assist him in music, the writing of the controversial *Oblique Strategies*. This was a set of oracle cards modelled on the I Ching, or *Book of Changes*, an ancient Chinese Taoist text. He had turned to aphorisms to overcome blocks during classes at art school, 'to give him a new perspective on working when he got bogged down in specific details, was unable to maintain a large perspective on what he was doing, and was thereby losing sense of his creative options'.[28] While with Roxy Music, Eno cultivated the habit of writing his aphorisms down and randomly distributing them around the recording studio. He had then met the painter Peter Schmidt, who, he found, did likewise, writing self-conceived and creatively lubricating maxims in a little notebook. EG, by now trusting their instincts with Eno, published the fruits of the inevitable collaboration, 113 aphorisms on cards the size and feel of playing cards, which sold well and went through two more print runs in 1978 and 1979. Purchasers bought a handsome black card-board box with gold-embossed lettering and the following set of instructions.

These cards evolved from our separate observations of the principles underlying what we were doing. Sometimes they were recognized in retrospect (intellect catching up with intuition), sometimes they were identified as they were happening, sometimes they were formulated.

They can be used as a pack (a set of possibilities being continuously reviewed in the mind) or by drawing a single card from the shuffled pack when a dilemma occurs in a working situation. In this case the card is trusted even if its appropriateness is quite unclear. They are not final, as new ideas will present themselves, and others will become self-evident.[29]

Oblique Strategies (subtitled *Over One Hundred Worthwhile Dilemmas*) was 'an attempt to make a set that was slightly more specific, tailored to a more particular situation than the I Ching, which is tailored to cosmic situations.'[30] It encouraged the substitution of goal-oriented thinking with lateral thought, which Eno much admired. The aphorisms are occasionally twee ('consider the most uncompromising details'), sometimes meaningless, sometimes shrewd ('honour thy errors for their hidden intentions'). Sets of the cards are now hard to find.

Oblique Strategies was of most use to Eno in the short-term during his work with David Bowie. Ironically, his obsession with systems had effectively systematized him into a corner. His thoughts were no longer producing the random flashes of inspiration and brilliance that had taken him thus far, and Bowie's unexpected phone call from his self-imposed exile of bunkered, blinkered paranoia in Berlin, summoning Eno to assist him on his forthcoming album, *Low*, at least had the benefit of being an intriguing and possibly stimulating diversion.

The work, however, was anything but. It was an arduous task, comprising gruelling all-night sessions closeted with a man in the advanced stages of psychosis. Eno learned to live off breakfast cereal, Bowie swallowed raw eggs; Fripp called in, summoned by the Thin White Duke to add guitar, as he would do more extensively on that autumn's follow-up, *"Heroes"*.

The nature and importance of Eno's presence in Bowie's studio (and subconscious) have been hotly debated. Certainly it seems unlikely that the peculiar timbres of these two albums would have been so strikingly unique were it not for him. *Oblique Strategies* cards were used extensively, for work on 'Sense of Doubt' in particular. Eno must have impressed Bowie, for Fripp and Eno count for much more on *"Heroes"*. There was a piecemeal, haphazard approach to *"Heroes"* that was more assemblage, than composition. 'Moss Garden', for example, was for Eno a 'very sloppy sort of technique – like, I was just playing around with this chord sequence on the Yamaha synthesizer and I said, "Give us a shot when you think it's long enough"...and David looked at the clock and said, "Yeah, that'll probably do," and we stopped.'[31] Which is exactly where the piece ends. Everything on the album – except 'Sons of the Silent Age', which was written beforehand – evolved in the studio. Also, all tracks were recorded as a first take – reminiscent of Fripp and Eno's recording process together. Second takes were executed but found wanting. 'Art Decade'(*"Heroes"*) was largely Eno's work, a meandering tune for piano (four hands) that Bowie left unregarded, until one day during the leader's absence Eno rescued the piece: 'I...dug that out to see if I could do anything with it. I put all those instruments on top of what we had, and then he liked it and realized there was hope for it, and he worked on top of that adding more instruments.'[32]

Successful though the sessions were, they were suffixed by a nervous breakdown which drove Eno to the brink. He was still stymied in his search for a final form of *Science*. In the end, he decided to issue it irrespective of reaction – 'I had to burst the balloon' and 'didn't care' if people 'don't like it'.[33] He took a cut in royalties to enable him to market the album with four prints of watercolours by Peter Schmidt, his *Oblique Strategies* collaborator.

Before and After Science: Fourteen Pictures finally emerged in early 1978. Manzanera was back in the fold, as were Cluster's

Moebius and Roedelius, ex-Free bassist Andy Fraser (here playing drums), Can drummer Jaki Liebezeit, guitarist Fred Frith and Dadaist pioneer Kurt Schwitters adding some incomprehensible vocals. Collins, Melvin, Jones, Fripp, Mattacks and Turrington resumed. A non-album track, 'RAF', was also recorded around the same time, featuring Eno's long-time friend Judy Nylon and Patti Paladin of New York new-wavers Snatch. This backed a single, 'King's Lead Hat' (an anagram of Talking Heads) and caused a minor stir at the time for its apparently ambiguous attitude to the German terrorist group the Red Army Faction. One especially perceptive reviewer wrote that *Before and After Science* was 'the record that Pink Floyd could make if they set their collective mind to it'.[34]

He had been contributing pieces for films, including Derek Jarman's *Sebastiane* (1976) and *Jubilee* (1978). Writing for film, however, was too 'restrictive', and Eno turned his attention to writing background music for films which did not yet exist.[35] The result was *Music for Films*, a highly entertaining hotch-potch of old and new material, released in late 1978 of which 'Inland Sea', 'Quartz' and 'Final Sunset' were taken from *Sebastiane*, 'Slow Water' was used in *Jubilee*. 'Sparrowfall' was borrowed from music Eno had written for an Alan Drury play staged at the Hampstead Theatre in 1976.

ENO THE ANTI-ROCKER

By the dawn of the 1980s, Eno had effectively finished with playing rock music and appeared reluctant to involve himself too deeply in the genre. In 1980 he castigated rock musicians for an unwillingness to 'dabble and play', and for being too 'goal-oriented'.[36] The irony of this comment issuing from a man whose indecision over the final form of an album had driven him to nervous collapse was not raised.

'Any music worth anything is born in clumsiness and chaos,' Eno said.[37] He also attacked perceptions of musicians, both by the public and by musicians themselves. He debunked the myth of the 'musician or artist as an impulsive, drug-taking romantic. I don't reject that view, I know some artists like that and they do good work as well. But there's another kind of artist who thinks about what they're doing and talks about what they're doing and wants to articulate it and doesn't believe as some do that talking about it reduces its mystique or deflates the work.'[38]

He also began launching crabbed salvos against Progressive rock, 'the well-known and gladly departed orchestral rock tradition', as he put it.[39] He pinned the blame on 'the early 70s, when recording had just gone from four to twenty-four tracks in a very few years. Rock became grandiose and muddy, like a bad cook who puts every single spice and herb on the shelf in the soup. I started thinking in reductive terms.'[40] This conveniently overlooks what even his biographer Tamm terms a 'saturated acoustic space'[41] on the first four albums, especially notable in what he calls Eno's 'assaultive rock' songs, such as 'Baby's on Fire' from *Here Come the Warm Jets*. Eno would no doubt rejoin, reasonably enough, that this texture was intrinsically less organized and regimented than the quasi-symphonic precision of Progressive/classical rockers.

At times Eno's opinions have seemed fashionably iconoclastic for the hell of it, most usually when they concern conventions of Western art music, particularly the symphony orchestra (something that has been a too easy Aunt Sally for liberal musical thinkers for too long). This has won him many admirers, but while he is entitled to these opinions, they are often underpinned by less than faultless logic, as Tamm points out. Eno has stated the old rock/pop shibboleth − albeit with more elegance than most of its semi-literate subscribers − that complicated, difficult music is less 'flexible', and necessarily cramps emotional and imaginative possibilities. Why it should be necessary to do anything with it in the first place is a question never addressed. Ditto the interpretative possibilities inherent in skilled performances − from the licence applied to orchestral works by conductors to more extreme examples, the keyboard improvisations possible, and at times prescribed, in the music of countless composers from Scarlatti to Messiaen.

Eno's views on composition can infuriate. His dislike of what he imagines to be the rigorously disciplined, teleologic writing of much art music springs from his own 'empirical' style, developed in the early 1970s: 'Each thing you add modifies the whole set of things that went before and you suddenly find yourself at a place that you couldn't possibly have conceived of, a place that's strange and curious to you.'[42]

By way of illustration, Eno quoted an instance of working with Robert Fripp. He mentioned some harmonies and a melodic line he had thought of, but didn't know how to answer Fripp's question as to what harmonies they were until he played them. On finishing, he turned to Fripp, who said, 'That's very interesting. Because nobody would have arrived at that harmony by writing it out. There's a wrong chord in it.'[43] This echoes one of his *Oblique Strategies* – 'Honour thy errors for their hidden intentions'. In 1981 – presumably after a brainstorm – he attempted to convince the public that this was a 'new art form' which should be known by a 'different name' to ordinary music.

Even the admiring Tamm dismisses this for the piffle it is. As the latter asserts, some of history's most ostentatiously symphonic composers – Mahler, Bruckner, Rimsky-Korsakov – worked empirically, using the entire symphony orchestra as a sounding-board for ideas and revision. 'It is entirely possible that, having had no experience with musical notation himself,' writes Tamm, '[Eno] underestimates the degree to which a traditional composer can hear his music in his head as he writes it out.'[44]

There may be a hint of English asceticism and native distrust of the sublime and transcendent in Eno's ambivalent attitude to art music, or music deriving from it. This is not un-reasonable, and his preferred approach – music as introspective search – has given us a trove of beauties. He patently dislikes overt Romanticism and, as we have seen in his treatment of the lyrical domain, overt representation, feeling that there is too much extra-musical intent in the genesis of the piece. This might seem curious when one thinks of his extraordinarily poetic gift for titling his pieces: for example, 'The Fat Lady of Limbourg' (*Tiger Mountain*), 'In Dark Trees' (*Another Green World*), 'Energy Fools the Magician' (*Before and After Science*), 'Dunwich Beach, Autumn 1960' and 'Lantern Marsh' (*Ambient 4 – On Land*).

He is more of an absolute musician, and his development of Ambient music as necessarily undemonstrative background music – *Gebrauchsmusik* in all save the name – works in, at best, a suggestive framework. The sound textures he uses as his basic musical material might conceivably, according to Tamm, suggest a geographical location or a childhood scene; there is representation, but it's mostly at the primary level, and literalism is simply not part of Eno's agenda. They make the listener reflect on his or her own feelings rather than any feelings of the composer, which can be read in Eno's statements as fundamentally intrusive.

This mirrors the Japanese artistic technique of *ma*, intentionally leading the viewer or listener to a state of emptiness and relaxation, and lies at the core of the music Eno would make after his Progressive rock LPs. Emptiness and relaxation were the stuff of the convalescence Eno had to undergo following his contretemps with the taxi, and it was in a semi-drugged, half-wakeful state that Eno listened to an album of virtuoso harp music that his friend Judy Nylon had thoughtfully lent him to soothe him. Eno had busted stereo equipment and a busted body which hindered him from easily adjusting the controls, but the result was little short of revelatory; the music passed in and out of audibility, and in and out of consciousness. Eno immediately hit on the idea of music that could be ignored, that could be listened to as passively as his more complicated music had to be listened to actively.

His thoughts were directed once again to the music of his spiritual masters, Cage, Reich and Riley, in which the minimal was stressed, and especially to Cage's dictum that the entire environment could be classed as a musical event, that music did not have to reside solely in the 'art object' of a composition. Summarizing Satie, who had composed 'furniture music' in 1890s Paris for the salons of the arch-aesthete Péladan which could be attended to or otherwise as per choice, Cage wrote:

> We must bring about a music which is like furniture – a music, that is, which will be part of the noises of the environment, will take them into consideration. I think of it as melodious, softening the noises of the knives and forks, not dominating, not imposing itself. It would fill up those heavy silences which sometimes fall between friends dining together.[45]

Eno in any case identified strongly with the systematic bent in Satie's compositional *modus operandi*: 'He was a systems composer, you know, planning chord changes by numeric techniques. In the midst of extraordinary chromatic experimentalism, with everyone doing bizarre things, he just wrote these lovely little pieces of music.'[46]

Satie's credentials as a 'non-musician' were impressive also. He was self-taught, and technically unschooled. 'It is clear,' according to Cage, that 'no musical idea presided at the creation of works like Satie's *Trois Morceaux en forme de poire* or *En Habit de cheval.*'[47] If pushed, one could also compare Eno's and Satie's penchants for strange but ornate titles.

The results of Eno's epiphany were first heard on his 1976 LP on Obscure Records/EG, aptly entitled *Discreet Music*, complete with erudite sleeve notes explaining the music's conception and execution and function. It was followed in 1980 with the consecration of a wholly new series of recordings, this time bearing Eno's own rubric for his conception, 'Ambient music'. The first LP was titled *Music for*

Airports. 'The stuff that is presently played at airports changes your consciousness in quite the wrong way. It has this kind of nervous tingly quality to it. And it is not relaxing at all, which just makes the whole operation seem terribly cheap, and unreassuring somehow.'[48] Sympathetic souls were drafted in to add their own interpretation of the Ambient phenomenon, including trumpeter Jon Hassell, keyboard player Harold Budd and zither/hammer-dulcimer player Laraaji. Robert Fripp planned an entire cycle of Ambient albums, *Music for Sports*, *Music for Palaces*, *Music for Kitchens*, none of which, somewhat ignominiously, has ever materialized.

Eno, however, was in his element, once again attracting the avid attention of rock cognoscenti and dispensing wisdom on his revolutionary breakthrough. Initial reaction was cautiously favourable, if a little sceptical. 'Active listening', that which Eno sought to discourage with his new idea, would take some shifting.

The initial Ambient efforts are much of a fairly pleasurable muchness. The latter-day preponderance of Ambient electronic drift effects now renders the music somewhat ubiquitous, although the vocalese of *Airports* and the 'mental chess games' of the cross-stitched melodic fragments in '2/1' from *Music for Airports* stand out. The question begged by the latter, however, is just how such involving musical interplay is meant to discourage the active involvement of the human ear.

Eno moved to New York for a spell from 1978 and, predictably, found a particularly warm welcome in a city besotted by art as whoopee-cushion, the art of the disorienting and disoriented in art. He had enjoyed his sojourn in the city in 1974 and his work with John Cale put him within the orbit of the Velvet Underground and their successors. He had worked with Television a little, but now on his return found from tiny acorns a thriving new-wave scene full-grown. Eno saw that these musicians proceeded

'from a "what would happen if" orientation. The English Punk thing is a "feel" situation: "This is our identity, and the music emanates from that." I've always been of the former persuasion. But there's a difference between me and the New York bands. They carry the experiment to the extreme; I carry it to the point where it stops sounding interesting, and then pull back a little bit. What they do is a rarified kind of research; it generates a vocabulary that people like me can use.'[49]

He made his first forays into video art in New York, undertaken in his Manhattan loft in 1978 when he hired a rudimentary video camera, turned it on its side on his window ledge and filmed the changing hues of the sky (the comparisons with Warhol's exercises in filmic ennui such as *Empire State*, twenty-four notorious hours of the skyscraper recorded on celluloid, are almost too obvious). He lectured at a 'New Music, New York' festival at the Kitchen in 1979, informing the audience that 'experimental music involved too much intellect and not enough sensuality, that creating charisma is a useful and even necessary thing'.[50]

By and large, however, Eno adored the place, and it adored him. The chemistry was similar to that which made Roxy Music unlikely icons of Punk. Eno's aggressively marketed 'non-musician' status was only part of it. The Downtown scene – Laurie Anderson, Glenn Branca, Philip Glass – flourished in the scorched earth left by the 1960s, by Pop, Cage, Warhol and the Factory, talented and talentless running amok in tandem, the almost *de rigueur* defiance of high/low art boundaries, the elevation of the workaday to the degree that anyone could and should 'do' art – notions that had, of course, always sustained Eno himself (and Ferry, for that matter – he once told an interviewer that Pop Art was a 'smooth, painless activity' for someone who 'couldn't draw very well').[51]

One of the more articulate and original members of the musical fringe of this community was David Byrne and his band Talking Heads, whose use of the media representations of stardom as creative tools vaguely recalled early Roxy Music.

His solo album, *My Life in the Bush of Ghosts*, was very much a combination of the Ray Conniff textures and the sensuous energy of Afro-American music, intensely and devilishly spiced by Eno's random feedback from McLuhan's global village. The intrusions come from all over the world, making the whole a fiendishly clever and compelling listen. It sounds positively routine now but was courageous in 1981; Eno's bravado still couldn't be faulted, even if his musical expertise could. The album, conceived at the birth of sampling, ran into legal trouble; one right-wing radio evangelist, Elizabeth Coulman, insisted that the album's sample of her couldn't be used (even for $1,000,000) and the prepared pressing was duly and meekly scrapped. Then, after the album's issue, the World Council of Muslims demanded that the pressings currently available be scrapped, for they featured the religious insult of having recorded Algerian Muslims singing verses from the Koran, a sacrilegious audio analogue of a graven image, of making an idol of Muhammad. Again, Eno and Byrne complied.

'WHAT DOES HE DO AGAIN?' ENO THE PRE-MILLENNIAL CELEBRITY

Eno, for Tamm, is 'among the few prominent musicians from a rock background who has taken rock to its stylistic limits, gone beyond them, and stayed beyond'.[52] This is one of the best précis of Eno's contribution to music that the author knows of. Furthermore, Tamm takes the musicologist Philip Tagg's 'axiomatic triangle', used for classifying art, commercial and folk musics, and cleverly shows that Eno doesn't fit anywhere within it.

Eno remains obstinately eclectic. He retains an admiration for the fustiest of English musical conventions: for example, the hymn-like sonorities and melodic profiles on 'Some of Them are Old' and the guarded admiration which Eno has expressed for English Church music, particularly hymn composition, is echoed very strongly in the compositions of his underrated musician brother Roger. Yet similarly, and paradoxically, he likes the harmonic randomness of much folk music. Eno's catholic tastes are sometimes explicit to an almost wincingly precious degree; he told one interviewer in 1986 that a gospel record he had just heard 'changed my life.'[53]

But that catholicity, no doubt fuelled by the laterality of Eno's thought, led him into other areas where the fecundity of that thought and his natural loquaciousness won him enough friends to have careers fan out before him. For instance, Eno's reputation in the art world matched his growing prestige within music. In 1986 the highbrow glossy *Artforum International* ran an Eno special, with a full-length interview and, featured on its cover, a colour photograph of *Living Room*, one of the composer's 'video sculptures' whose shaded rectangles and pastel geometries were vaguely redolent of Mondrian. The magazine also contained a pull-out flexi-disc of a new piece, 'Glint (East of Woodbridge)'. The BBC TV arts flagship programme *Arena* produced a special show in his honour in 1984, featuring the paintings of Russell Mills. The title track of *Another Green World* had for some time been used as the programme's theme music. Eno's first 'real' compilation disc, *More Dark Than Shark* (1986), was as much a showcase of Mills's paintings as a recorded document of Eno's work.

Eno's chief role in the 1980s, however, was initially still as imaginary soundtracker to the chattering classes. The Californian appetite for blissfully bulk-erasing the critical consciousness had by this time extended into the sphere of music, which brought an unwilling world New Age music, a phoney excuse to incorporate uncommercial, passive-listening fringe musics into a phalanx of lifestyle accessories for the emotionally palsied. In short, the heritage of passive-listening music, brilliantly summarized in Lanza's *Elevator Music*, was, with truly contemporary Reaganomic vigour, being branded. Eno's Ambient project, originally conceived as a healing mechanism itself in the wake of his 1975 mishap (*Discreet Music*), was being cited as a chief witness in the launch of a new, corporate-generated musical genre of narcotic homophony.

It is superflous to try and précis the arguments of Lanza's book and how his defence of Muzak and its antecedents related to the growth of New Age; suffice to say that the legacy of Satie was being homogenized in 'restful, reflective soundscapes' by failed guitarists and ivory-tinklers from Osaka to Oshkosh. As Eno himself succinctly put it, New Age lacked the twin shadows of 'evil and doubt'[54] which undeniably stalk his own soundscapes and, from Hildegard of Bingen onwards, lend Western music its peculiar emotional appeal. It is true, as Lanza points out, that

> Despite Eno's strident anti-Muzak stance, this project [*Music for Airports*] differed from garden-variety canned music only in degree. It interwove lackadaisical piano phrases with an unearthly choir; and Eno borrowed a technique that Jackie Gleason had perfected...by structuring entire pieces around such sensual utterances as 'oooh' and 'aaah'.[55]

Similarly, a project of Eno's from 1983 lent international credibility to the fledgeling US genre of 'space music'. *Apollo*, an album Eno cut with Daniel Lanois and his brother Roger for a commission by the American film-maker Al Reinert, was the big-name endorsement nerdy US synthesists had long been waiting for to equate the vastness of space with aural comfort and cheap beauty, instead of the kind of harsh loneliness and terror evoked by the likes of Subotnick's *Silver Apples of the Moon*.

Eno's rationale for the album was that Apollo astronauts heard Muzak while floating through space, and as such *Apollo* is a kind of postmodern tribute to them and to what Eno presumably imagined to be the aesthetic properties of their voyages, the earthbound banalities of Muzak on the one hand, the limitless grandeur of space on the other.

Despite his unavoidable and unwelcome sanctification as

New Age's musical mentor, Eno's dedication to environmental music continued to serve him well throughout the 1980s, cross-fertilizing with his climbing fine art reputation to enable him to muscle in successfully on the installation market, plumbing Ambient sounds into artspaces as part of a *Gesamtkunstwerk* to stimulate the eyes and the ears, blurring the boundaries between aural and visual art experience.

One, an 'audio sanctuary', was recently installed at the Toyota Amlux Auto Salon, a fourteen-storey temple to automotive engineering, in Tokyo. Multimedia sculptures have been commissioned from him by institutions in Venice, Milan, New York and Los Angeles. Elsewhere Eno's triumphal Ambient progress was not quite unhindered. In a postscript to the 1980 La Guardia experiment of piping *Music for Airports* into the spaces of a real airport, in 1982 Pittsburgh's Three Rivers Arts Festival piped the same music into Pittsburgh's international airport for ten hours each day from noon. Customers complained to airport personnel that it made them 'uneasy' and demanded that the former Muzak be restored to the loudspeakers.[56]

Eno continued to produce in a similar vein, however. *Thursday Afternoon* (1986) and *Neroli* (1992, used to soothe mothers in the pains of childbirth) were 'the purest expressions of what I thought Ambient should be,' said Eno to *Mojo* magazine. 'Endless, relatively unchanging moods.'

Later in the 1980s Eno found his métier, which continues to propel his life forwards and upwards today: production.

Eno's initial forays behind the production desk came with Roxy Music, but by 1973 he was striking out on his own, producing the Portsmouth Sinfonia's album *Portsmouth Sinfonia Plays the Popular Classics*, a task he would return to for the benefit of its successor, *Hallelujah* (1974). His involvement in the sonic creation of many of the more difficult works on his own Obscure label, the intensely rigorous refining process of his own albums, notably *Another Green World*, and most definitively the centrality of the architecture of sound to his own artistic thought processes ensured that Eno would be a star of the mixing console from day one. He ventured on to the fringes of the new wave in England to produce Ultravox's début album in 1977, and did likewise in America with Devo's *Are We Not Men?* the following year. Production duties on the Ambient series, in collaboration with their musical creators such as Laraaji and Harold Budd, were inevitable, although his work on the Hi-Life of Edikanfo's *The Pace Setters* came as something of a surprise. Musician Jon Hassell would benefit particularly from Eno's expertise; four of his albums bore Eno's co-production credit.

It was his work on U2's breakthrough album, *The Unforgettable Fire* (1984), which transformed Eno from 'cerebral hermaphrodite' to hallowed and failsafe fixer. For the time being, however, Eno had other things on his mind; the setting up and maintenance of his own record label, Opal, for one, which occupied much time in the early and mid-1980s. His brother-in-law would oversee the later establishment of All Saints, a specialist label for uncommercial but often charmingly tonal and picturesque music that fitted neither avant-garde nor New Age pigeonholes. Stable of Eno's brother Roger as well as (among others) Bill Nelson and Kate St John, the label quickly became widely renowned for the luminous and unusual brilliance and lyricism of its roster's inspirations.

Eno went on producing, landing lucrative and lauded sessions for U2 (*The Joshua Tree* in 1987, *Rattle and Hum* in 1989, *Achtung Baby* in 1991 and *Zooropa* in 1992 – apparently, he advised the band with self-tried wisdom, and had them conceive music as 'soundtracks for imaginary movies'.[57] This he interspersed with joyously diverse plunges into the recesses of popular music's gazetteer, producing a live album for Japan's Yellow Music Orchestra, trekking to Africa to work with Geoffrey Oryema on his *Exile* (1990) and working with Jane Siberry on her *When I Was a Boy* album for WEA (1993).

By this time his U2 work had finally broken him as a major production name; shortly, he was working with characterless campus popsters James (*Laid* and *Wah Wah*), David Bowie (*Outside*) and Laurie Anderson (*Bright Red*). He also won himself a notable reputation as a remixer, applying his touch to EMF's 'Unbelievable', Depeche Mode's 'I Feel You' and 'In Your Room', INXS's 'I'm Only Looking', Suede's 'Introducing the Band' and Massive Attack's 'Protection'.

Eno has none the less continued to record his own work, and in 1991 was involved in an unseemly dispute with Warner Brothers as to the American release of his work. *My Squelchy Life*, his first album in a while, and slated for September release, was unaccountably put back to the following February. A piqued Eno withdrew it; the tracks 'Under', 'Over' and 'Some Words' were later featured on a box set.

Compilations trickled out; TV and film commissions trickled down, most prestigiously for BBC TV's *Mr Wroe's Virgins* in 1993, which reunited him creatively with his brother Roger. Derek Jarman's penultimate major project, the BBC commission *Glitterbug*, summoned the director's old comrade Eno to soundtracking duties.

Recorded albums showed Eno at his most inventive for some time. *Spinner*, his 1993 collaboration with ex-Public Image Limited bassist Jah Wobble, had the gifted instrumentalist reworking themes from Eno's soundtrack to Derek Jarman's BBC-commissioned *Glitterbug*. *Passengers* (1995), an extremely bizarre and critically overlooked all-star effort, relatively starved of publicity at the time, featured Luciano Pavarotti, Holi, Howie B. and Eno's principal paymasters U2 in a strange sample-led hybrid of stylized songs and impressions either recorded or messed with in Eno's studio in Kilburn, London. This record, explained Eno, was U2's attempt to get away from 'song-led' forms and into more impressionistic music; strange, as their contribution is the most leaden-footedly chartbound fodder on the record.

Eno's own material continued to impress. *The Shutov Assembly* (1993) was an attempt to warp the thoughts of orchestral musicians, with Eno's home-brewed material interpreted by trained classicists ('So, if this sound goes "dnnngeeeee", you might need to have a damped tubular bell and a violin player working together to make that one sound.'[58]) *Neroli* (1992) was a modal exercise; a 'single piece developed from Eno's experiment with a synthesizer customised 'to observe... only the harmonies which fit into the mode you intended to play in, so each note was a sort of baby recapitulation of the whole piece'.[59] Eno played a short melody into a primitive sequencer, and contrived the right-hand part to loop at normal tempo while looping (separately) the other at incrementally lower tempi ('It starts out in its individual form, as I played it, then the parts slip apart, like tectonic plates.'[60]) It works, albeit with emotional means disturbingly similar to those on *Music for Airports*.

The Drop (1997) is, at press time, Eno's latest. An attempted rethink of sequencer usage in popular music, it's a courageous failure. Sequencers, Eno told *Mojo*, were fine for beats, grooves, cycles, but not for inventing melodies.[61] Unfortunately, on this occasion, neither is Eno himself.

True to form Eno's value, however, still resides less in the field of individual and autonomous musical creation in the sense of an existence as a 'musician' or 'composer' and more as a kind of inexhaustible motive (and motivating) power source, a synaptic entity within the late-twentieth-century's musical body politic. For Michael Bracewell, who conducted a lengthy interview with Eno for the *Guardian* on the occasion of the artist's fiftieth birthday in 1998, he is 'a pixel-manipulated cultural tourist; the liquid engineering in the manufacture of contemporary music'.[62] In Eno's own words, he is 'a conceptualist, an enabler and a creative catalyst'.[63] He lectures; he writes; he organizes. He is a supranational citizen of an increasingly borderless musical world.

One witness suggests that Brian Eno today is much happier than his old adversary and friend Bryan Ferry,[64] and it is true that the world has been kind to him. His ability to act as a lightning-conductor for the creativity of others, added to his own dauntless exploratory nature and the priceless gift of being socially in the right place at the right time has paid handsome dividends. He has become an honorary editor at Faber and Faber, the London publishing house, producers of both his own musings and Eric Tamm's unofficial biography; he is now professor of Multi-Media Installation at the Royal College of Art; he is a published diarist; he lectures wherever and whenever he can, delivering the Turner Prize's commissioned one-minute speech in 1995, the year Damien Hirst won (ironically, he used it to implore the fine arts to become similarly accountable to public processes as science and dispel its inbred narcissism.[65]) In music, he ripples with the shiny musculature of high prestige; his name is sought for both hip and radical cachet. His involvement with catalysing musical expositions, from the Música Visual Festival in Lanzarote, to the directorship of one of the pavilions at Expo 2000 in Hanover, Germany, is seemingly endless. This latter, beamed Eno to Bracewell, was a 'huge space, expecting up to 153 million visitors'.[66]

'His reputation as a conceptual thinker,' gushes Bracewell, 'in the age of the New Pop Establishment, has reached to the official showcases of European government.'[67] To this end, he also eagerly plugs a conversation Eno had with (then Prime Minister-in-Waiting) Tony Blair at the House of Commons on 'the future of communications'.[68] 'I ended up having a discussion with him, which was rather one-sided on my part, about whether it was productive to invoke concepts of good and evil in thinking about legal structures in society.'[69]

There's no doubting the infectious energy, and no criticism is implied, of the essentially good-hearted nature of Eno's zany brainiac hyperactivity, but suspicions remain. The future seems to grin as boundlessly and bountifully in Eno's world as the Cheshire Cat smirk of Tony Blair irradiates the future of Britain. But what sometimes grates is the almost evangelical faith in human capability and the benevolence of technology and mass communications. Eno's optimism foretells a shiny world of leisure and popular culture; he has mooted compulsory Media Studies for children 'so that they know how to recognize the mutation of information within the process of mediation'.[70] It sounds horribly familiar; it is the happy-clappy refrain of the scary new liberalism, where everyone will be 'set free' by cybernetics, but where corporations, exploitation, manipulation of message and multinational capital suddenly, and conveniently, never seem to get into the equation. Unnervingly, Bracewell concludes his *Guardian* piece by wondering aloud if Eno 'has predicted the social climate of the new millennium'.[71]

On the other hand, is Eno, as Bracewell provocatively suggests, a man who integrates 'pure aesthetics and social conscience', linking him to 'the humanism of Josef Beuys, returning the basis of European art to a morally questioning but spiritually centred sense of collective witness'.[72] The jury's out as yet, but one Eno feature that is permanently and pleasantly definitive is that he won't allow the questions about him, or his work, ever to stop.

10:M & M, OR THE ROXY SOLOS

MANZANERA AND MACKAY: AFTER-SCHOOL ACTIVITIES

It was Mackay who first followed Ferry into the marketplace with a solo album. Ferry's *These Foolish Things* had been out for some seven months before Mackay's *In Search of Eddie Riff* hit the racks. Since Eno's ousting, Mackay was undoubtedly the band's most photogenic face after Ferry and his saxophone playing perhaps the most distinct component of the band's sound. That is not to denigrate Jobson or Manzanera; but their playing was almost always very much in a contemporary vein, whereas Mackay's stylistic palette was altogether less specific. One minute he was Junior Walker, the next Stan Getz. A Mackay solo album made commercial sense, and it's no surprise that the man himself smoulders on the cover with an almost David Cassidy–like lustre.

Eddie Riff is rarely more than pure padding, its musical insubstantiality exceeded only by its guilty knowledge of its own conceit. The album is structured interestingly, with five standards framing four Mackay originals. The cover versions are lacklustre; the much-vaunted reworking of Wagner's 'Ride of the Valkyries' from *Die Walküre* which opens the record was probably not meant as anything more than an updating of the sillier reaches of novelty 1950s instrumental pop, little better than the Cougars' Tchaikovsky gloss, 'Saturday Night at the Duckpond'. The crassly emphatic contrast of the two motivic sections of the piece is particularly reminiscent of that sad period in rock history.

'End of the World' is a little bit too 10cc in its literality, a straight delivery of the pop song and its stylistic universe as all of a package, the only condition being the substitution of the voice with tenor saxophone. So perfunctory, so workaday is Mackay's laboured rendition of 'What Becomes of the Broken Hearted' that the listener is tempted to suggest that the broken-hearted probably end up reduced to listening (or recording) piffle like this. 'A Four Legged Friend', even if meant satirically, is enough to convince even the partisan that Mackay *really* shouldn't have cut this album. Schubert's 'An die Musik' is quite tastefully done, although its succession to the above gives it the feel of a pearl after swine. Manzanera's nice bluesy guitar counterpoints to the melody, and the enchanting simplicity and timelessness of Schubert's melodic shape even suggest for a few moments that the piece could have been written for a pop audience in 1974 and not for a Mitteleuropean bourgeois one in 1824.

Mackay's originals are disappointing, especially given the maturity and colour of his compositions on his next album. 'The Hour Before Dawn's harmony is obviously classically influenced, and the unreconstructed sax-organ textural combination and rigorous strophic structure are most diverting. The title track is meandering and pointless, while the cod fugue of 'Past, Present & Future' and aspiration towards Renaissance dance forms and rhythms are meretricious. The metamorphosis into the second theme, with its slow accumulation of a more modern texture, is ingenious, and Manzanera's querulous and black-hearted guitar solo adds a much needed note of real emotion to the proceedings.

True, one can rarely predict the harmonic progressions of Mackay's music, but when these qualities are applied to material as frankly ordinary as 'Walking the Whippet', a Shadows-with-a-sax piece of nonsense with 1974 adumbrations of bubblegum rhythms and hep fuzz-guitar, the listener really shouldn't care less. 'Summer Sun' was, presumably, an attempt at a hit single which might have been more convincing had Mackay been able to sing. The single that was eventually released in August 1974 was 'Wild Weekend', a long-time Roxy Music stage interlude and imagined crowd-pleaser. Backed by 'Walking the Whippet', it was a dismal failure.

The emptiness of *Eddie Riff* is made all the more inexplicable when one hears Mackay's much less fanfared successor, *Resolving Contradictions* (1978). The death of chairman Mao and the fearful cataclysm of a massive earthquake in 1976 had reintroduced Communist China to Western liberal consciousness, and musicians quickly sought to explore the contemporary musical potential of a country newly accessible to Westerners.

Mackay, replete with the profits of *Rock Follies*, had visited China on sabbatical in the spring of 1978 and his typically articulate account thereof features in the album's sleeve notes upon its CD reissue:

I... was very impressed. The natural beauty and splendid buildings, the huge numbers of curious but affable people, the food. And then the drab uniformity, the discipline, the palpable oppression and terror? Well, no, I can't really claim to have picked up on the last one. Was I charmed or was I conned?

Since the late 60s Mao's bizarre, original and dangerous cultural revolution had made China, always remote and fascinating to Westerners, even more secretive and mysterious. Only a little more than a year before, the 'great helmsman's increasingly shaky hand had finally slipped off the tiller [and] we were able to visit as 'foreign friends' what seemed a different world.

...the music, like the culture, was a mixture of the ancient and subtle, and the grandiose and vulgar. The contrasts with my world were exhilarating and irresistible. Hence the album was never really about China, but about myself and that curious flat period of the late 70s,[1]

Honourably, Mackay, for all his apparent Sinophilia, acknowledges the Tiananmen Square massacre of 1989 as having subsequently coloured his views.

The album, recorded at what was now the Roxy Music home patch of Basing Street studio between May and July 1978, was swiftly forced to share shelf space with an album by the Greek keyboard virtuoso Vangelis entitled *China*; issued in early 1979, it too purported to be a musical impression of the East.

Both albums have moments of laughable naïvety but also of immense beauty; when one considers the improvement in Mackay's music since *Eddie Riff*, his album must be considered the more successful of the two. Supported by Manzanera and Thompson and a host of musicians familiar to him from the *Rock Follies* sessions (guitarist/arranger Ray Russell, drummer Peter van Hooke, keyboardist Chris Parren), as well as fellow wind player Tim Wheater, noted bass sessioneer Mo Foster and others, the results were at times of breathtaking quality.

The first side of the album is comprised of a more or less continuous stream of music, broken into several discrete compositions; the initial theme, 'Iron Blossom', which is subtly varied and reworked throughout the first side, is as beautiful as anything on the Vangelis LP. Compositonally, the first side is ill-disciplined and fills its spaces with little care and attention, but the textures are so limpid and subtly coloured that they deflect all criticism. The background, in particular, is an eldorado of occluded detail, the percussion and counterpointing of percussive figures particularly delightful. The fanfared second motif – 'Trumpets in the Mountains' – is beautifully built, and a smart satire on socialist-realist composition. The deranged triplet-based march which kick-starts the side, 'Off to Work', another fine piece of backhanded musical complimenting, and in the midst of it all the funkiness of Mackay's sax, brawny and brazen in its most soulful tone, is little short of surreal. The meditative violin variation of the opening theme over the 4/4 r'n'b-disco beat which follows, 'Unreal City', is maybe a little too knowing. Throughout, the chordal language is magnificent, and Mackay is on top form when soloing between them.

The second side is a collection of songs, seldom great but always likeable. 'Skill and Sweat' has an annoying but fiendishly adherent main theme, widescreen and wider by the minute. The faintly Bilkish intonation of 'The Ortolan Bunting's bluesy theme is counterpointed by a blossom-storm of falling pentatonic figures on flutes and whistles, a true dream of a track. 'The Inexorable Sequence' is in fact a progression of intriguing chords; floodlit by Manzanera's blazing solo, there are fewer vamps which use more ingenious chord progressions than this. Recalling the album's first side, 'A Song of Friendship's succulent melody, a crossover of chromaticism and pentatonicism, is led through a clever passacaglia, complete with more lovely flute and whistle arabesques.

It's often a wholly aimless album, but one whose explicit display of literacy is never undermined by vulgar showboating. There are exceptions: the bloated final track and its heavy-footed conclusion is strangely reminiscent of the upbeat climactic moments of such Eastern Bloc Progressive rock acts as the Soviet Union's Eduard Artemiev★, Czechoslovakia's Modry Efekt or Hungary's Fermata. Whether this was another subtle snook cocked at Communist ceremonial music or not is unclear; there are too many beauties on the album to make

---

★Specifically, the albums *Ode to the Bearer of Good News* (Melodiya, 1982) and *Warmth of Earth* (Melodiya, 1986).

it worth arguing about. The closing track of this final medley is a beautiful and oddly incongruous Lester Young-phrased solo, 'Gold and Cream', over wistful Fender Rhodes chords. (For the record, fans of Progressive and symphonic rock will also draw many comparisons between Mackay's leadership on this record ard that of another saxophonist, Tom Barlage, of the Dutch band Solution.)

Its qualities are amplified by the context in which it was recorded. Progressive rock musicians, beguiled by studio wonders and increasingly excluded from the live circuit in the wake of Punk and with the advance of age, were recording ornate concept albums all over the place. Led by the likes of Andrew Lloyd-Webber's *Variations*, staffed by jazz-rock stalwarts Colosseum II, increasingly effete efforts from the likes of Sky, Jack Lancaster and Francis Monkman were cropping up all over the place. Ironically, when the British film industry was on its deathbed, British musicians were touting themselves around as potential film composers. Few fulfilled the ambition as brilliantly as Mackay. But for that matter, few could touch his Roxy Music colleague Phil Manzanera.

UNIMPEACHABLE GUITAR

Manzanera's compositional credentials were good. 'Hula-Kula', a Roxy Music B-side, had been a bit of fun, but one that was well crafted. 'Amazona' was one of the band's most outstanding tracks. His work as soloist and textural illustrator and facilitator on *Country Life* had been dazzling. It was only right, the rock community agreed, that the man the *NME* had called 'our most creative guitarist' finally be given his head.

Manzanera's *Diamond Head* sports one of rock's more distinctive covers, if nothing else because of the image's fame independent of music. It is an unadorned reproduction of a famous publicity still used in the 1950s by the Union Pacific railroad which shows one of their beautifully designed streamline diesel locomotive units hauling the City of Los Angeles express through Echo Canyon, Utah. Its nod to Roxy

Music's own preoccupation with faded American iconographies of bourgeois progress and comfort is just sufficient to identify Manzanera as an inhabitant of their universe; beyond that, it is a bold and individually distinct imagistic step surreal enough to work.

In the sleeve notes of a later album,* Manzanera listed his early influences: Satie, Miles Davis, Rodrigo, Varèse and *musique concrète*. The shameless eclecticism of Roxy Music seemed to promise multicoloured fireworks on *Diamond Head*, and Manzanera delivered, with a schizophrenic combination of classical and blues voicings and Latin and jazz instrumental techniques. On the opener, 'Frontera', for example, a conventional Prog-rock intro develops into a leisurely and charming pop song vamp, with Eno and Robert Wyatt singing in Spanish. 'East of Echo' is a taster for the Quiet Sun album that would follow *Diamond Head*, with McCormick and Haywood to the fore. Fuzz bass and bagpipes battle incongruously at one stage, and although the jazz-funk strut is slightly archetypal, there are interesting similarities between the bass line of the song and that of the Roxy Music number 'Mother of Pearl'. Both 'East of Echo' and 'Alma' boast long, snaking melody lines which rumble on endlessly over ambiguous chords; this is pure Prog rock, and splendidly executed. For all his avowed desire to have his guitar sound like the organ of Soft Machine's Mike Ratledge, Manzanera, however, can't quite accommodate Prog's obsequy to the Western classical tradition, as the blues voicings of his solos and vocals ('Alma') prove.

There's a rather charming sense of nostalgia which lingers around the music, as though this is the album that the young Manzanera had always wanted to produce and had maybe dreamed of in his pre-Roxy Music days in 1970–71. 'Alma' and 'Frontera' are laden with post-psychedelic guitar and organ sounds, and the soundstage is fuzzed to within an inch of its life. Manzanera's guitar sound, after having assumed many

---

Primitive Guitars, 1982.

experimental guises in Roxy Music's name, expectably becomes a signature; saturated and effects-laden, whining and howling, flitting from channel to channel, yet undertaken with exquisite harmonic sensibility.

Diamond Head also contains rare gems which are individually and distinctively cut. Eno's 'Miss Shapiro' is tooled through agreeably, the whole sounding more Floydish, and his vocals sounding more like Syd Barratt than ever. Eno's dissonant double-tracking of his vocal line and the obscenely filthy guitar sound Manzanera dredges from his amps both feature heavily. 'Big Day' is an inconsequential if rather funny and singularly chart-worthy pop novelty about a disillusioned Peruvian immigrant abroad in Britain. 'The Flex' is a piece of meretricious mid-1970s formula instrumental funk – the ensemble becomes the Very Average White Band; 'Same Time Next Week' is a misfire of a satire on pop vocal duos, a classic duet of disillusioned lovers enlivened by John Wetton's vocals and lyrics but ruined by Doreen Chanter's superfluous screeching, an eardrum-battering mélange of streetwalker and fishwife. The best of the novelties, however, and perhaps the stand-out track of Manzanera's career, has to be 'Lagrima'; even without the ear-deceiving reverse echo of his subtly picked classical guitar, which some felt to be a technocrat's conceit, this tender duet with Mackay's oboe is a beauty.

Manzanera's next project concerned Quiet Sun, whose reconstitution had first been mooted during the recording of *Diamond Head*. With the album's success, Quiet Sun temporarily re-formed, and Manzanera's new-found reputation ensured a degree of public interest. The new album that resulted could have been hobbled by the amateur's instinctive fear of the spotlight, but was instead unanimously hailed as a masterpiece. Posterity and maturity have maybe moderated that opinion, but there is little doubt that *Mainstream* is a superlative piece of work. Effectively, its loudly emphasized 'group project' status excludes it from consideration within the Manzanera canon and so it lies outside of this book's remit, but its sheer *joie de vivre* and balance of instrumental technique and sheer gutsiness are almost unmatched in the Progressive rock canon. There is a flavour of epigonism – the thematic floridity ('East of Echo') and stuttering time-signatures – which pays homage to the Canterbury(-rock) mythology surrounding Manzanera's adolescent heroes Soft Machine. But not for nothing did *Melody Maker*'s Steve Jones recommend it with unabashed enthusiasm as one of the albums of the year. Manzanera's guitar, he claimed, came on like a 'Messerschmitt with all guns blazing'.[2]

Thereafter, an exhausted and chastened Manzanera toured and recorded with Roxy Music, but also found time for further out-of-school activities. He also produced *Mental Notes*, the début album of Split Enz, a quirky and very original New Zealand band who had supported Roxy Music on the Antipodean legs of their 1975 tour. Enz, the brainchild of the Finn brothers Tim and Neil, were purveyors of a particularly craftsmanlike and convoluted form of classical Progressive rock, among the more unsung and endearingly odd of its kind, a little like a cross between the Enid and Roxy Music themselves. The project would also present Manzanera with a future friend and collaborator in the shape of Tim Finn, later the brains behind colourless Australasian AOR-pedlars Crowded House. Meanwhile, Manzanera, whose music often strays deep into Progressive territory, was also co-opted into the extraordinary Go project initiated by the Japanese percussionist and composer Stomu Yamashta in 1976. An ill-advised supergroup conceived in an era when even well-advised supergroups were *personae non gratae*, this bizarre aggregation featured German synthesizer star Klaus Schulze, Stevie Winwood and poll-winning Santana drum sideman Michael Shrieve, and paired Manzanera with one of the world's most touted guitarists, Al DiMeola, in addition to the workhorse Pat Thrall, a colleague of Shrieve in 1976's great white recording hope that wasn't, Automatic Man. Incomparably gifted in terms of precision and fleetness of execution, DiMeola's work with Chick Corea's Return to Forever was none the less an exercise in the aridity of tonal consonance and time-trial speed. The band had the potential to be one of the greatest ensembles of the rock era, but seemed to be burdened with the notion that history was simply against them.

Two more albums, *Go Too* and *Go Live from Paris*, followed, by which time Manzanera had wisely jumped ship. If nothing else, he had his own supergroup to take care of, the infuriatingly mercurial 801.

If there is a more tantalizing and endearingly useless parlour game in rock than making up supergroups that never were, it is predicting the future for supergroups that happened, and better still imagining futures for the few that worked. Manzanera's 801 were, conceivably, the most artistically successful British supergroup since Cream. This may have had something to do with their vigorous denial of their 'supergroup' status, but that their often highly refined music made any musical and critical impression at all in the 1976–7 winter of Punk is an honour indeed.

The band took their name indirectly from an Eno lyric. Deep in a mescaline-induced sleep in his girlfriend Randi's New York apartment, Eno had dreamed of sailors singing 'We are the 801/we are the central shift' (as one does), a couplet which would provide Eno with the first of the random snatches of text which would serve him as impromptu songwords. Manzanera's friendship with the garrulous Eno and his own burgeoning reputation – particularly after *Diamond Head* – made this a gig to be in on. Francis Monkman, Eddie Jobson's predecessor as Curved Air keyboardist, resumed his *Diamond Head* duties but Manzanera's hand was strengthened and his muso credentials enhanced by the presence of the brilliant young drummer Simon Phillips, as well as slide-guitarist Lloyd Watson and old friends Ainley, McCormick and Eno. Manzanera's ploy from the start was to pool the musicians and then play three concerts – at Cromer's

West Runton Pavilion, the Reading Festival, and a final farewell at London's Queen Elizabeth Hall – which would also be taped for release as a live document of the band's fleeting existence.

Clearly Manzanera, a clever musician, had understood the logic of Eno's own discongruent pairings of players from different backgrounds to construct sounds on his own albums. This time, however, it seems that Manzanera had hedged his bets; unlike Eno, he seems to have selected these musicians to create random frictions to produce the necessary sparks to ignite a very personal and goal-oriented musical vision, whereas Eno's technique predicted an outcome only vaguely heard or conceptualized.

On paper it seems – and on vinyl it sounds – like a better bet than the original line-up Manzanera conceived. In December 1975 he had regrouped and at Basing Street Studios had convened a band of awesome potential – himself, McCormick, Eno, Jobson and ex-King Crimson drummer Bill Bruford, then hawking himself as a session player through gigs with Genesis, Gong and National Health. This would have been the only time that Eno and Jobson ever played together for a recording, and is definitely in the first rank of 'what-if' supergroups. Bruford, a tirelessly exploratory drummer and percussionist particularly taken with sonority, the dependable and occasionally inspired McCormick and the lip-smacking potential of the conflict between Eno's and Jobson's approaches. If anything, however, there is simply too much potential for over-elaboration and self-indulgence, and the results of Jobson and Bruford working together (on 1978's *UK* album) suggest that egocentricity, however benign or unintentional, might have fouled the works. There seems to be too much swish and seductive promise in this line-up, too little apparent risk of dissonance, even with the wild-card of the eclectic Manzanera in the ranks (this quality must surely have appealed to Yamashta), which the final 801 line-up managed to turn to creative input. A trio format featuring Manzanera,

McCormick and Bruford also misfired in the coming months; the three decided that recording backing tracks to form the bases of melodies and lyrics was unworkable. Writing material and then performing it live on to tape didn't work either, especially when McCormick suddenly took it upon himself to rewrite his extant lyrics *and* music. Bruford had, by that time, shipped himself off to a lucrative series of gigs with Genesis, and Manzanera was busy overseeing the end of Roxy Music's first incarnation, and a potentially exciting and abrasive new turn in mainstream rock was wasted. How Eno would have dealt with the joint forces is a moot point, although one is tempted to imagine that he would have found these musicians, taken collectively, simply too institutionalized to common musical goals to be worthy of manipulation and exploitation for sonic experiment. The pall of missed chances will hang over the idea, but the iron-pumping energy of the music will forever do its best to blow such doubts away. One critic called it the most dynamic live recording of the 1970s, and *801 Live*, even twenty years on, does little to refute that.

Save, of course, for the fact that most of *801 Live* was almost classical mid-1970s jazz rock of a kind that would, under the title of any other band, have driven most hacks to homicidal rage. Eno had told reporters, 'For me, projects aren't really interesting if you can predict the outcome. One of the most encouraging aspects...of our recent rehearsals is that something has been happening which nobody could have predicted.'[3] What was heard was actually highly predictable, given the musicians involved, but none the less compelling. The fizz and pop of McCormick's bass on the Lennon/McCartney revamp 'TNK (Tomorrow Never Knows)' is as blatant a giveaway as ever; the logarithmic precision of the thematic contrasts in the hybrid 'East of Asteroid' (half 'East of Echo' and half 'Mummy was an Asteroid, Daddy was a Small Non-stick Kitchen Utensil') wouldn't be out of place in Brand X's repertoire. Phillips's double bass drum technique, deployed with blanket-bombing intensity, only power-drills the message home. Monkman's rhythmic support consists mostly of highly academic (if original) triplets and arpeggios on Fender Rhodes piano (saved only by a colourful harmonic choice).

The album's real plus – its hair-raising intensity – surfaces in 'Sombre Reptiles', raw, funky, with an almost angrily executed Manzanera solo; 'Baby's on Fire' also radiates brutish power and 'Third Uncle', the encore, is the Clash with drop-beats and syncopations, a furious ensemble vamp on a ten-note theme which would not have shamed Miles Davis's mid-1970s band for the sheer savagery of its groove.

Did this mercurial outfit have any intention of staying together? Possibly not – Monkman's and Phillips's diaries were crammed with top-dollar session work (Monkman would later join John Williams's Sky, and Phillips would record with, among others, Mike Rutherford, Jack Bruce, Gordon Giltrap and – ironically – Roxy Music). Watson was only a semi-professional player and Eno was close to collapse, rescued only by a timely phone call from David Bowie, closeted in his hermitage of drugs and deviancy in Berlin.

The 1975 Basing Street tapes were reworked with the help of a battery of other musicians, including Kevin Godley and Lol Creme, recent refugees from 10cc, who were loudly touting their proto-sampler, the Gizmo, around the music business to whomsoever would listen.

Manzanera expressed considerable interest, and this was to lead to a short-lived period of co-operation which, like so much of Manzanera's work, held more promise than it delivered. Pairing musicians of a harmonic literacy and lateral compositional conception with a pop sensibility as acute as that of these three promises a king's ransom, but little happened.

Listen Now!! takes a dive. It's perhaps one of the most anaemic follow-ups in rock history. The constituent musicians from 1976 are there, but dissipated throughout nine tracks of almost uniformly straightforward pop music whose only interest seems to be what its warm textures and leisured rhythms prefigure for Roxy Music's *Manifesto*, which would follow in 1979. If this was, as contemporary legend had it, a concept album with a social conscience, its moral stance has wilted with the years. Given Manzanera's superb trio of preceding albums, it's sadder and soppier than anything Ferry dredged up in the Roxy Music interregnum. The problem with *Listen Now!!* is that it is simply too consonant for its own good. Given the album's creative genesis (bassist and political activist McCormick's sufferance of heavy manners from the ascendant National Front in the mid-1970s), it's a funker. The decentred and decentring marriage of fulminating lyrics with the smooth sessioneers' sound of the studio and drive-time melodic profiles jars rather than amuses, and the tunes lack sufficient strength to overcome this hurdle or invest the project with sufficient popular appeal to make it anything but an exercise in misplaced verisimilitude. History makes the record difficult to judge. One must try to evaluate it independently of Punk, according to its creators' wishes; yet the social conditions which inform it cannot be separated from those which inform Punk. It wishes to be populist yet cannot achieve such status without incurring accusations of derivation, and as such concedes to the tyranny of the studio, of good production, of airplay potential. Perhaps as a compromise one can say that the record would have worked just as well in its historical time-frame using music of the kind that Eno was cutting on *Before and After Science* and *Another Green World*. Instead, *Listen Now!!* smacks of effort dissipated and adulterated by time, indifference, misfortune and the vagaries of fashion.

'I suppose you could call it drone-like, the tranquillity of people who are totally drugged and conditioned. The type of people who whiz along on castors...also you normally associate heavy lyrics with quite uptempo music, but that gives the impression that violence is the only way out. That's the vibe I get from the Clash. I like their music a lot, but I think their approach can be dangerous.'[4]

Or interesting – at least in comparison with Manzanera's music on *Listen Now!!*

The sessions did at least provide some pointers towards Roxy Music's future. The soundstage incorporated the work of keyboardist Dave Skinner, with whom Manzanera had first worked on sessions for Ferry's *These Foolish Things* and who had stalwartly slogged the Transit van circuit with jobbing also-rans like Clancy and Uncle Dog. Paul Thompson was also in tow – the fact that Manzanera chose him to play Simon Phillips' parts on-stage proved his worth, and these two, alongside Ainley, proved a rhythm section of prehensile steel, reliable yet pliable. Ainley was no fool either, and without demeaning the able Tibbs, that Ferry didn't take the three of them into Roxy Music upon its reconstitution in 1978 suggests that he did not wish Manzanera to have a power base within the band. That is not to judge Ferry; given that he'd reconvened the band, the last thing he would have desired was the possibility for further schism, even in the name of benign despotism.

The following year, Manzanera wisely returned to safer, more musically sophisticated ground, although *K-Scope*, released in September, almost simultaneously with band-mate Andy Mackay's *Resolving Contradictions*, failed to convince press or public. Its lingering sense of malaise is difficult to dispel even twenty years later. It's never less than good, and occasionally exceptional. The closing track, 'You Are Here', is absolutely mesmerizing, a gorgeous appetizer for Manzanera's *Primitive Guitars* four years hence, all slithering, multi-tracked and delayed guitars and synthesizers, with Manzanera's brooding extemporization on classical guitar jewelling the musical night with gloomily shining notes. The title track is a bracing, muscle-bound piece of feel-good up-tempo Progressive pop, whose instrumental pyrotechnics and rhythmic *élan* cleverly disguise a traditional verse–chorus structure using hooks of pure pop infectiousness. Pure pop was overtaken by pure corn on 'Remote Control', however, with the proto–punk of *Listen Now!!* taken to extremes. This is not without merit, but its shrill they're–coming–to–get–you urban paranoia and martial law themes, allied to a nursery–school backbeat, err a little on the side of self–parody.

Manzanera didn't record another solo record until 1981. This, however, was a triumph, from its beautiful minimalistic cover (a red Gibson Thunderbird as seen through pastel–coloured water) to its splendid music. His explicitly stated remit was to treat the guitar as an orchestra, which he did with admirable spirit. The music, as usual, often proceeds by cycles of fifth chords, but rogue or strangely constructed fifth chords also occur, as they had done since 'Frontera', the opening track on Manzanera's first solo album, *Diamond Head*, in 1975. In an extensive sleeve note, Manzanera wrote:

> The idea of absorbing a great amount of technique specifically related to the guitar never appealed to me. As a pursuit in its own right it seemed boring; it simply did not suit my temperament.
>
> Instead, I looked for other avenues and in particular for a way of creating atmospheres in music through means other than conventional guitar techniques. This meant the exploration of various devices (echo, feedback and so forth), since my interests were not particularly angled towards the blues (despite a considerable interest in the pioneering jazz guitarist Charlie Christian). The results were often somewhat abstract, dealing in unfamiliar sounds and note clusters.
>
> ...since I achieved the results through empirical means and since I went back to sources of my inspiration, the word 'primitive' seems appropriate. *Primitive Guitars* sets out to expose all the methods I have tried over the past dozen or so years and to put them into a personal chronological context.[5]

Manzanera went on to define this album as a definitive answer to those interviewers who had asked him to talk about his guitar style. It is a magisterial statement, its individual tracks seemingly too beautifully and lovingly crafted to warrant overlong analysis. 'Criollo', for starters, is a beautiful instrumental song; it's theme is stated on *tiple*,★ its sampled voices and fuzz-guitar textures hinting at the quiet technocratic storm which will overtake the album from 'Caracas' onwards. The subtle accumulation of textures, by now a favourite Manzanera device, leads to chancy and devilish interplay of short lines, the basic melodic figure once again subtly altered much in the manner of Andy Mackay's original compositions.

It's hard to know where to lavish the most praise on *Primitive Guitars*. It is perhaps the most musically successful of all Roxy Music solo albums, so consummate is its mastery of instrumental technique, composition, contemporary *zeitgeist* and knowingness. The Chic-style strummed high strings of 'Caracas', doubly highlighted by the beautiful guitar solo and key change which follow, would be worth the album's price alone, but there's more; the utterly authoritative use of up-to-the-minute technique (the Depeche Mode-style rhythmic textures on 'La Nueva Ola', the steely slashing of the guitars at the opening of 'Bogotá', the subtle interplay of synthesizer, guitar and drumbox at the start of 'El Ritmo de Los Angeles', the macho Punk riff which dominates 'Impossible Guitar') is unparalled in the solo output of Manzanera's contemporaries. Perhaps only the brief effulgence of ex-Focus guitarist Jan Akkerman's solo excursions into synthesized funk (*Heavy Pleasure*, 1981, *It Could Happen to You*, 1982) measure up. The harsh dance rhythms and repetition of 'Big Dome', which take wing so radiantly into a beautifully rich and ingenious sequence of chords with a suitably lovely solo accompaniment, echo Akkerman's 'Funkology' (1982).

★A small guitar-like Latin American stringed instrument.

'Impossible Guitar' and, on side two, 'Big Dome' are photofit impressions of what Roxy Music would have sounded like had they retained the edge of their first three albums. 'Big Dome' has the textural elements of new pop, but none of the tinker toy melodic simplicity; it better recalls the reconstituted contemporary King Crimson which made such admirable steps forward for Progressive rock music with the albums *Discipline* (1981) and *Beat* (1982). The non-synchronous *Pointillisme* of clashing and consonant lines throughout, and the percussive edge to the synthesizer contributions, not to mention the sheer *jouissance* of the whole event, make this a mirror-image of Roxy Music at their best, only with the application of the sheen of the contemporary. It is one of the most cohesive statements of Progressive rock ideology of the early 1980s.

Manzanera has never matched it. His 1984 project which reunited him with Andy Mackay, the Explorers, earned far more media attention than its musical qualities warranted. Perceptive observers noted that his choice of vocalist, one James Wraith, sounded not unlike Bryan Ferry, but despite goodly coverage on radio and TV, the resultant album flopped – unsurprisingly, when one listens to the derivatively consonant music. There are beauties, notably the use of electronics and the starry instrumental line-up – Tony Levin on bass and Chapman Stick, Steve Gadd and Jerry Marotta on drums, suggesting that this was indeed a high-profile project. There are meltingly lovely moments, such as Manzanera's amazing choice of chords in the middle-eight interlude of the opener, 'Ship of Fools'. Mackay's renewed recourse to Wagner – he heralds 'Lorelei' with a clever reference to the *motif* of Siegfried's Horn Call from *The Ring* – is also memorable. But despite a well-hyped and well-received concert at the Camden Palace in London, duly taped for video and audio (the band are tauter and tougher altogether in a live setting), the 'new Roxy' tag sank the band. Wraith simply couldn't lift his voice above accusations that he sounded nothing so much as an imitation of Ferry imitators like Martin Fry and David Sylvian.

The partnership would be renewed in 1989 by which time the music the three were producing was resembling little more than a pleasant and competent if somewhat outdated pastiche of Nik Kershaw. In effect, it is little more than a musical calling card for two songwriters – unfortunately, a normal calling card would probably have possessed more personality than *Manzanera and Mackay*.

Manzanera was busy at the end of the 1980s, but the quality of his output was variable. His eponymous duet with John Wetton in 1987, four years after Roxy Music's demise, was an embarrassment, a terrible folly recorded for Geffen Records, where Wetton had earned a crust as a quarter of the horrific AOR supergroup Asia. Few of the tracks on this truly nasty album make it as either rock or pop; strophic sophistries of lost or laboured love which even the dullest recesses of American FM radio might have found predictable.

The album none the less marked a brief convulsion of activity. In April 1987, a superb compilation of solo work, *Guitarissimo*, was put on the market; in 1988, a more than passable venture into New Age/New Instrumental music under the name Nowamowa had Manzanera's name again in the public eye. *The Wasted Lands* was sometimes a little too prototypical (the syndicated orchestral samples from the Kurzweil and Kawai synthesizers dominated the masses of New Instrumental fluff issued at the end of the 1980s). But the surfeit of the style – caused largely by the market bubble created by the new wave boom for prettily homophonic instrumental music and the relative inaction of suitably qualified ex-Progressive 1970s musicians for producing same – didn't stop *The Wasted Lands* from showing its class. Manzanera still had style and wasn't afraid to showcase it. There's a broken, deliciously familiar *Pointilliste* character about the arrangement on '801 Urbania Street'; the titular acknowledgement of the past is echoed in the fruitily suggestive juxtaposition of classical and blues voicings, counterposed as much as combined. This is still, palpably, the creator of *Diamond Head* and *801 Live* at work.

The flurry would be completed with *Southern Cross*, conceived partly in collaboration with Tim Finn, who had flown in to help get Manzanera's 'lyric ideas' in order. This entailed Finn co-writing most of the tracks. These didn't always work; the latter half of the album slackens off in favour of predictable hooks and progressions and dull melodies, only the live-wire Dr Fidel' (presumably an impression of the young Manzanera's view of the 1959 Cuban revolution) shining through with its taut and obsessive ostinati. Finn's beautiful 'Astrud' is, however, a winner, seductively sung by the young Ana María Velez. The album was, in Manzanera's words, an attempt to create a new musical style, crossing Finn's Antipodean pop with Latin American elements. The first side of the LP works remarkably well; the commercial consonance doesn't count against the socially restive sentiment of a song like 'Tambor' (the drum symbolized as signifier both of carnival and of war), for Manzanera simply and bravely tries to displace himself into another musical context. His increasing love for and involvement in Latin American pop – which manifested itself in a lucrative sideline recording and producing artists from that continent at his Gallery Studios in Surrey and on his own Expression record label – led him to try to create a pop commodity comparable to that produced in Latin America. Manzanera had grown up with and retained a love for a popular musical context in which the most opulent trappings of admass pop production could be unashamedly harnessed to pungent, poetic and pertinent social commentary. This preoccupation underscores – and also sometimes under-mines – *Southern Cross*, whose ultimate failing is its swift exhaustion of good melodies and the colourless plaint of Finn's voice, which takes over the soundstage of the album at a crucial mid-point. The album as a whole is satisfactory, how-ever, and there are enough contact points with contemporary pop trends – 'Astrud', for example, chimes neatly with the wine-bar cod-Hispanicism of Matt Bianco and Basia, and 'Blood Brother' and 'The Great Leveller', with their big-biceped pop hooks, sweaty soul fanfares and synthesized rhythmic pulses, master a gamut of throwaway chart-fodder styles from George Michael to Climie Fisher.

Manzanera's talents as a guitarist weren't forgotten, however. He was assigned the post of musical director for the 1991 Guitar Legends Festival in Seville, Spain; as well as acting as general facilitator for a week's worth of fretboard frenzy, Manzanera also performed himself, in a conventional but expectably exciting line-up with bassist Pino Palladino and old friend Simon Phillips. The results – or a fraction of them – can be heard on the Expression CD reissue of *Southern Cross* as *A Million Reasons Why*.

Manzanera, who borrowed money to set up Gallery Studios as a commercial concern after his split with Roxy Music, has continued to cement his relationship with the stimulating sphere of Latin American pop. Thirteen albums have so far been released on his own Expression label. Among the artists he has produced have been Heroes del Silencio, a Spanish band who were for a time 'EMI's most successful band on the Continent of Europe'.[6] The singer,' explains Manzanera, 'looks like Jim Morrison, and they're rock but sing in Spanish.'[7] Another, Paralamas do Succeso, a Brazilian band, are cleaning up in Argentina. Manzanera's own forays into the field are recorded on an excellent CD, *Moncada and Manzanera Live at the Karl Marx*. Released on Expression/Voiceprint in 1997, it features a highly charged and often quite enchanting collaboration between the Cuban band Grupo Moncada and Manzanera onstage at the Karl Marx Theatre, Havana, in March 1992. The material is a selection of traditional and standard pop Cuban tunes, and originals from both Moncada and Manzanera. Manzanera has also worked with Fito Paez, a Spanish singer-songwriter in the Elvis Costello mould.

With Mackay continuing his TV and film work, both men

have been busy, and both relatively content with life's bounty. Reviewing their work is, however, an often bittersweet experience. It connotes something quite different to a retrospective hearing of Ferry's albums, and one which reflects less on their abilities as on the nature of commercial music, which, it is tempting to say, has prematurely abandoned them. *Resolving Contradictions* and *Primitive Guitars* were two albums by unusually skilled musicians, but musicianly abilities, whether by way of composition or interpretation, are not enough to guarantee reputations and pay cheques, save as bankable back-catalogue figures. A re-formation of Roxy Music, one feels, would not be enough to compensate for this, and would perhaps only confirm an unfair public perception of obsolescence. Ferry's continued success, though erratic, has been guaranteed; as charismatic, photogenic and accredited pop legend, that could hardly have been otherwise. Alas, the commercial worth of Mackay's and Manzanera's talents does not seem to have had the same durability. A shame.

11: ROXY FOR EVER? (1982 – THE PRESENT)

TARA…?

Of the eighth and, to date, final Roxy Music studio album, *Avalon*, Pete Sinfield, the urbane producer of their first and most influential LP, says 'There's certainly a lot of paranoia in there …There are no mistakes that one can hear.'[1] And there aren't.

The critical consensus that Roxy Music had become a corporate hit-factory was borne out with rather alarming precision by *Avalon*. Scrutiny of the band's media profile suggests that the overall impression of fans and hacks was that the band had fulfilled the remit of its comeback but now risked over-emphasizing the terms of that comeback. They had survived Punk better than perhaps any of their contemporaries; they had at least a memorial respect in the hearts and minds of a new, vicious breed of rock reviewers; contemporary stars openly acknowledged their debts. Yet, with *Flesh + Blood* and now *Avalon*, they seemed monomaniacally determined to continue ploughing the commercial furrow they'd stumbled upon in the labours of *Manifesto*. The sparse but well-earned praise garnered by Manzanera's sparkling solo album *Primitive Guitars* in 1982 affirmed that the band and their constituent members still had a place in the vanguard of rock creativity. On *Avalon*, however, this tendency was less than obvious.

'By the time you get to *Avalon*,' observes Andy Mackay, '90 per cent of it was being written in the studio...For the last three albums, quite frankly, there were a lot more drugs around as well, which was good and bad. It created a lot of paranoia and a lot of spaced-out stuff.'[2]

True enough; but who, having absorbed the most recent Roxy Music output with anything but approval, could resist the trebly, undulating of the first track, 'More Than This'? The drugs Mackay spoke of were, presumably, downers. The album is often so relaxed as to be almost inert. It undermines some of the band's best melodies for years. The uncertain, coy interplay of saxophone, bass, drums and keyboards from which the chords of 'Take a Chance with Me' assume their form are quite forgotten once the song starts, mostly because the listener is yearning for some infusion of energy into a melody line which craves it. Only on 'The Main Thing' does the ensemble even hint at rousing itself from a lassitude apparently imposed by the mixing desk. Even as interesting a melody as the non-album 'Always Unknowing' – the B-side to the single 'Avalon' – is neutered by the Horlicks-mix. Manzanera and Mackay contribute their quota of incidental graces, sneaking in surprise gifts of mini-solos as of yore (Manzanera particularly effective on 'Avalon' or at the start of 'To Turn You On').

'To Turn You On' is a fine tune with a lovely arrangement, a beautifully accomplished piece of confection; only the melody sounds distinctly second-hand. No disgrace; its progressions and resolutions just don't sound like Roxy Music, although the band do it proud. It sounds like a superior Ferry cover version of someone else's song. 'Tara', Roxy Music's last-ever studio track, would stand up for itself were it given the time; Ferry and Manzanera's chords are as restless and suggestive as the ocean waves which underlie the track, and Mackay's ruminative saxophone solo recalls some of the key relationships he tapped into when soloing in Roxy Music's glory days. Then, however, as if snuffed out by some spoilsport, the party, the album and the band's recording career are over, leaving only wistful speculation on what *Avalon* could have been like had it been recorded by a healthy unit.

Press comments on the album are revealing; they are merely somewhat ambivalent, indifferent acknowledgements of a stylistic given, almost of a music preserved in amber. They don't *try* to meet the intellectual challenge which, prior to *Flesh + Blood*, the band had always given them: go on, describe our music! Hitherto, Roxy Music had made hacks *think* like few other bands. That *Avalon* inspired so little memorable writing, just a series of wordy analogues of luxuriance, was evidence enough that this was one of the least successful albums in Roxy Music's canon. Lynn Hanna of the *NME* made do with saying that 'the music rolls in like glittering fog',[3] a nice comment of a creativity some of the music definitely didn't deserve. *Melody Maker* strewed clichés instead of praise – what else could they do, given Ferry's apparent intent to live his current musical persona to the hilt? – 'immaculate, out of reach...precision-honed...upholstered with velvet'.[4] Pete Sinfield said it best of the album, indeed of the whole trajectory of post-Eno Roxy Music: 'They ran out of naïveté.'[5] They'd run out of love; for each other and for the music. There is no sense of adventure, of discovery.

Meanwhile, Ferry, much to the mixed delight and dismay of the gossip columnists, finally married twenty-one-year-old Lucy Helmore on 26 June 1982. Helmore, the daughter of a Lloyd's insurance broker, was young enough to cast Ferry's comments to *19* magazine the previous September in an interesting light: 'I don't think marriage is for me...you find yourself seeing younger and younger girls and becoming a kind of Svengali figure to someone who will change tremendously between the ages of, say, twenty and twenty-three.'⁶ Lucy had also had the misfortune to fall victim to Fleet Street sloth; so routine was the appearance of a new girl on Ferry's arm to the gossipmongers that facts weren't checked and Helmore became Lucy Hellmann, unwitting heiress to a mayonnaise fortune.

In 1998 Ferry and Helmore are still together. Perhaps significantly, she was the first and only Roxy Music cover girl whose face was never seen (on the cover of *Avalon*, photographed by Neil Kirk) – perhaps this one was not for public consumption, and to be known better by Ferry than anyone else.

The band resumed work later in the summer, with Robert Fripp's excitingly reconstituted King Crimson (Fripp on guitar, Bill Bruford on drums, Adrian Belew on guitar and vocals and Tony Levin on bass) providing stark and possibly sometimes bewildering support on one of the strongest bills in rock history. Roxy Music also toured the US and the Far East, and in the March of the following year a recording taken from the European leg entitled *The High Road* charted as a mini-LP. A commercial video recording of a gig from Fréjus, in the south of France, was later released under the same title. One of the earliest full-length live rock videos, it sold well, and showed how many fond memories Roxy Music had (profitably) inspired.

That European tour was followed up in May 1983 with a short US tour. The land that had always given them the hardest and cruellest ride ironically turned out to be that which hosted Roxy Music's swansong. In an age gearing up for the lionization of rockist maturity and of definitive statements, of *Q* and *Mojo* magazines, this last hurrah of one of the most influential bands from the era which Live Aid helped revitalize as the dominant force in mainstream rock music was largely overlooked and was never officially announced to the press. When two and two were put together, the only confirmation was a tell-tale silence.

The band had played its last hand – or at least the only hand that the current format of Mackay, Manzanera and Ferry could play, given the increasing management pressures being brought to bear upon them. There were few arguments; Mackay and Manzanera were increasingly preoccupied with solo projects that might extricate them from the financial mire that they found that Roxy Music had suddenly landed them in. There were, as with the devolution of 1976, no real arguments, despite Manzanera's bitter claim twelve years later that 'disgusting things were done to make us fight each other'.[7]

There was the added difficulty that with their longevity had come a raft of younger imitators, which inevitably blunted their competitive edge. They might have been able to blow Duran Duran off-stage, but could they compete with the cheekbones and the hairstyles? Ten years ahead of the Q magazine generation, the wrinkled élite couldn't cut the mustard, and had no prospect of so doing. Roxy Music stood to see their legacy usurped.

For Manzanera:

'There was no big meeting, just a general dissatisfaction with the management, EG. There came a point where you could not take it any more. I was in the red financially right up until *Avalon*. We'd done so much touring that me, Bryan and Andy had paid for, investing in the future. And I owed EG a lot of money, so I had to toe the line...I didn't want any more of that manipulation. Eventually Andy, then Bryan, followed suit. Bryan thought he was part of the team, but in the end he realized he wasn't.'[8]

THE STUDIO MUSICIAN

Ferry, of course, had never been entirely dependent on the band. They had been 'something to hide behind' for the best part of eleven years, and speculation as to his first solo album was a matter of rock-hack course in the months following the announcement of the latest suspension of Roxy Music activity.

Ferry fathered two sons, Otis (b.1983) and Isaac (b.1985), in the hiatus between *Avalon* and his next solo effort, *Boys and Girls* (1985). This period also deprived him of his father,

Frederick, whose death in 1984 was a blow which devastated the singer enough to have him dedicate his first post-Roxy Music solo album to his father's memory.

Boys and Girls is a highly competent affair. Predictable, maybe, given the capital invested in its creation; its music gleams with the costly allure of a sales package. The textures are multinational factory fresh, its players masters of their craft. The album was perhaps as talked about for its roll-call of sessioneers as anything else. These sessioneers included Weather Report drummer Omar Hakim, Dire Straits guitarist Mark Knopfler, Pink Floyd's David Gilmour, Chic's Nile Rodgers, vocalist Ruby Turner, Chapman-Stick virtuoso Tony Levin (late of EG stablemates King Crimson), David Sanborn (alto saxophone) and Jim Maelen (percussion). Discreetly veiled was the total absence of Roxy Music personnel (save for Andy Newmark and Neil Hubbard), the whole ensemble limousining Ferry's sound into the new league of globalized pop-musical architecture of the 1980s.

The music isn't bad, unaffected by the dissipation one might expect from the above musicians, the hesitancy and displacement intimated by the use of six studios and the continuing employment of the washes-whiter brilliance of Bob Clearmountain's mixdown. One or two tracks – the deserved hit 'Slave to Love' and 'Don't Stop the Dance' – were Ferry's best originals for five years, the latter worthy of a place in his best-ever canon.

It's silly to ignore the Roxy Music comparisons, for they are there in surprising numbers. 'Sensation' hammers the now archetypal New Pop texture of funk bass/rhythm guitar interplay and wide-open, echoic keys that Roxy Music had perfected on 'Same Old Scene' and, for their pains, had seen appropriated by innumerable New Romantics. There's a mountainous, almost pompous grandeur about the track that sits a little uneasily with Ferry's fragile vocals, although the strength of the melody (with a verse-chorus duality but no actual chorus) compensates. There's also a maybe unconscious

311

nod to Heaven 17's similarly titled gay anthem 'Temptation' which is bothersome. Bass, drums and guitar are the granitic anchor for the entire album. Contemporary techniques are also followed on the similarly heavy-duty romp 'Chosen One', with its thumbed bass and stentorian, almost judgemental Greek-chorus-style backing vocalists (a particular strength of the album, the best backing vocal performance on any Roxy Music-related disc since *These Foolish Things*).

'Slave to Love', on the other hand, has Ferry back commanding the imagistic and lyrical territory he knows best – obsession and regret, a seen-it-all, love-hate reflection on the endless cyclical nature of love and loss. The glitter and tinsel of the soundstage, with its chiming piano, is especially apparent here, as it is on the strange little instrumental interlude, 'A Waste Land', which is moody, hauntingly Eno-ish synthesizer, voices and guitar but with a neat twist; instead of the titularly suggested overcast despair, the harmonies are sunny and friendly, reminiscent of the mood-music of the Swedish guitarist Janne Schaffer. Ferry actually confessed to the BBC's Richard Skinner of a hankering to make more instrumental music and this – rather like the end of his 1993 album, *Taxi* – suggests he would make a very creditable fist of it. Good taste prevails throughout, although rarely is it *too* good, too spotless. This is not the musical equivalent of a *Hello!* centrespread, although the porno-movie alto sax skirling of David Sanborn which utterly sabotages the otherwise sweet title track is truly nightmarish. This sounds like shagging music, and someone's faking it.

Harmonic lustre is also the name of the game for 'Don't Stop the Dance', perhaps a little prefatory of the harmonic language of Norwegian pop craftsmen A-ha, whose fame would shortly follow, but a delightful track none the less, sensitively and authoritatively phrased, a sweetly simple melody paired with lovely rising chords, the nimbly danceable pulse supplied by pin-sharp snare-drum rimshots.

Just as it would be remiss to downplay Roxy Music comparisons, it would be wrong to suggest that there isn't a feeling of unnecessary musical caution here. It's not that the music lacks Ferry's usual open-endedness and is so nakedly commercial. Far from it; but at times its textural sumptuousness simply overwhelms. As with *Avalon*, the Ferry trademarks are polished to within an inch of their life and as a result gain a more tawdrily commercial air than they might otherwise possess. A shift in emphasis on texture and arrangement would make *Taxi* (1993) an infinitely more successful musical statement. *Boys and Girls*, despite its cleverness and complexity, is non-threatening; the details are often too differentiated, and each seems to have a place. The little acoustic guitar flourishes on the otherwise fine dub-styled 'Windswept', for example, recall the *Pointilliste* techniques of early Roxy Music, but there are no overlaps with any other solo lines to confuse the listener. Too often the details, while ingenious, fill a merely rhythmic, propulsive role, which would be fine if, by 1985, this was not starting to sound a little hackneyed. Ferry made somewhat presumptuous Duke Ellington comparisons with his desire to direct and arrange. 'I thought I'd retired from the stage and…now I'm a studio musician. I will create studio masterpieces in the studio. This will be my life.'[9]

Success was considerable. 'Slave to Love' was rightfully a hit in the UK and did good business worldwide. 'Don't Stop the Dance', perhaps because of its fidelity to contemporary sounds, failed to make the grade. Later in 1985 Ferry appeared at the US Live Aid, and the following year, in the midst of recording what was to become his next solo album, *Bête Noire*, recorded the singularly uninspired 'Is Your Love Strong Enough' for the risible Ridley Scott sci-fantasy flop *Legend*. This was more evidence of his co-option into the globalized marketplace of hit-machinery. One of his opt-outs, however, has rather dubiously entered rock legend as a blooper.

In 1985, Ferry turned down Keith Forsey's 'Don't You (Forget About Me)', which, recorded by Simple Minds, scored massively on the soundtrack to John Hughes's depressingly popular cinematic ode to the self-obsession of young bourgeois America, *The Breakfast Club*. Why this was and is still regarded as an oversight is a mystery; a passable song, it none the less lends itself to the corporatized rock din later applied to it by Simple Minds and effectively becomes the kind of admass commodity the film's 'individualist' protagonists pretend to stand apart from.

Better by far to concentrate on the 1987-vintage Ferry, *Bête Noire*. It's a let-down, despite its pedigree. If *Boys and Girls* wasn't a flagrant enough membership card of rock's aristocracy, the liner notes of *Bête Noire* certainly suggested Ferry was royalty. It's recorded in yet costlier studios in yet wealthier locations and with a yet starrier guest list (all the *Boys and Girls* from 1985 are here, and they've brought their even more talented little brothers, new kids on the muso block, like drummer Vinnie Colaiuta, muscular miracle of the paradiddle; voguish, Coltrane-wannabe Courtney Pine; Chester Kamen; and big-thumbed, hard-fonkin' session bassist Abraham Laboriel; Pat Leonard, Madonna's musical mentor, produced). The square peg in the list was ex-Smiths guitarist Johnny Marr; despite the fact that his band had been produced through their campus-conquering glory by ex-Roxy Music bassist John Porter, Marr had gone public with sometimes venomous attacks on Ferry,[10] not least his accusation that the singer had used Live Aid as a commercial platform.

However, according to Ferry:

'Someone at Warners thought it would be a good idea for me to work with Johnny and sent me a cassette of some of his music. I liked it very much. And then when I met him we got on very well. It just went from there. He seems very lively. He seems very genuine as well. There's a kind of Northern honesty about the cut of his jib which I like.'[11]

The result is rather like the album itself: resolutely curate's-eggy. Sadly, the good parts rarely rise above good, whereas the bad parts are depressingly ordinary. Ferry wasn't always in the most upbeat form when discussing it. To Chris Salewicz, he said his aim was:

'to turn it into a musical. That's what I need…playing to full houses in twelve different cities. I could have the songs sung by eight different survivors of an airplane crash, in a life-raft in the sea. They'd each tell their own story. Perhaps they'd be in the stomach of a whale. That's what audiences go for – surrealism.'[12]

Bête Noire was very late. 'I thought it was going to be a very quick record to do,' said Ferry. 'Now it seems I spend most of the time in the studio, creating songs from source. I go in with less of a comprehensive idea than I used to.'[13] Doesn't constant refinement, asked Chris Salewicz, end up depriving the song of something? 'That,' replied Ferry, 'is where you win or lose, where your skill or taste or whatever comes into play. It's a question as to whether you can work on it for a long time without losing that stuff.'[14]

Often, too much was lost. Things start brightly: 'Limbo' is a balls-out curtain-raiser of the kind (if not the degree) of 'Do the Strand'. Its lyrical allusions – tango, lush life, moonlight, bamboo – hint at Ferry's old colonial days in the land of palm-fringed decadence. Its opening is a flurry of haunting guitar chords and its verse melody a delight, the 'down in Limbo' line wrongfooting the listener, and Ferry still stylizes peerlessly. The middle eight is adeptly arranged and beautifully played. 'Kiss and Tell', however, is belt-feeder 1980s funk, which might explain its greater success in the US singles chart than in the UK on its release in early 1988. Reaching No. 31, it was Ferry's biggest breakthrough there for some years. Lyrically, however, the barometer remains high; the words euphonically sound perfect in the melody, despite the inevitable concessions to banality that induces. Images such as that which conjures up a 'public face' in a 'private limousine' are none the less magnificent.

The album is almost relentlessly nugatory; the sun never shines on *Bête Noire*, the world lit only by intrusive flashbulbs. The imagery of 'New Town', despite its sprightly hairpin-bend melodic profiles and beautiful guitar playing, is dyspeptically pessimistic. The singer often still takes Ferry's favourite persona of the High Romantic solitary observer, commenting in the abstract as opposed to narrating experience within one; he sings of 'burning skies'; 'shooting stars'; the 'mystery of life'.

Ferry seems uncertain again. Why, as Dave Rimmer commented in a peevish review of the album in Q magazine, is the album so dominated by guitar, and a peculiarly ordinary guitar sound also?[15] Why does he feel he has to play the game of blue-eye British soul on 'The Right Stuff', which sounds little better than Simply Red (whether this is due to the 'Northern' cut of co-author Johnny Marr's jib is a moot point, but the song is scarcely interesting enough to bother arguing about). Why the appalling quality of the backing vocalists, whose banshee squalling on the aforementioned track and, unforgivably, on 'The Name of the Game', is so tasteless, and far too boilerplate a device to carry any intended soul into any song it is applied to? Why does Ferry's voice dart around all over the mix?

'All this,' charges Rimmer, 'simply serves to remind us that Ferry once had a talent for inspired juxtaposition. These days the element of surprise is drowned in a rich and sophisticated aural soup – it's tasty enough, but the individual elements, including the lyrics, are virtually indistinguishable.'[16] Ferry's solo material, for Sinfield, has suffered because of the lack of a group dynamic: 'His solo work is more indulgent, and he has people around him saying, "Yes, Bryan, that's wonderful", whereas Phil and Andy were more abrasive.'[17] That was rarely truer than on *Bête Noire*.

Rimmer suggests, pertinently, that while Ferry had always played fast and loose with outright commercialism, he had strayed a little too close to the corporate mincer this time.

'Seven Deadly Sins' is too anonymous; the strophic verse-chorus structures, the syndicated mega-studio *klang* of the ensemble. He even sounds a little like Robert Palmer, who was attempting his own stab at stardom late in the day with a cheesecake-laden lounge-lizard image, and doing rather well out of it too. That Ferry should see fit to try and steal some of this very muted thunder is sad indeed. His comment on the dire 'Name of the Game' is revealing; it was, Rimmer writes, 'the absolute nadir…Ferry doing a sort of mega-MTV scarf-waver'.[18] He does, however, reserve praise, just as deservedly, for the title track and album closer, an enchanting thing. A lone fiddle solos over inventive chords and double-tracks into a delightful mid-tempo acoustic dance number. The provenance is doubtful; the melody slightly gypsy-like, with some Portuguese Fado overtones. The accordion-soundalike lends a snapshot of the tango. It's a passionate, imploring paean to a beloved, and, long after the sessioneers have all jetted off, Ferry is at his best; simultaneously sultry, querulous, vulnerable and arrogant, and musically adventurous. One is tempted to wonder how much Latin American pop he has heard; the likes of Milton Nascimento and Ivan Lins of Brazil are two among hundreds whose ingenious use of the rules of commercial pop often mirrors Ferry's methods.

'I think,' Ferry told Salewicz in an excellent and very lengthy interview in *Q*, 'that if you're creating something it's good to do something that has been plucked out of the air.'[19] That's just what 'Bête Noire' sounds like.

The album was successful enough in America for Ferry to be asked to perform on *Saturday Night Live* (NBC) on 5 December 1987, a success which the single 'Kiss and Tell' would bolster the following spring. In the end, however, *Bête Noire* did no better in the States than had *Boys and Girls*. Both reached the upper sixties of the *Billboard* chart. The inevitable global tour followed.

Ferry's life, though comfortably upholstered, still had its edges abraded by work. He split with his and EG's erstwhile mastermind Mark Fenwick in 1987 and joined Dire Straits' manager Ed Bicknell, having previously been in contact with him over the employment of that band's guitarist-leader Mark Knopfler on 1985's album, *Boys and Girls*. Papers were filed on Ferry by an irate Fenwick the minute the singer landed back at London's Heathrow Airport, inaugurating a bitter legal battle which left Ferry dismayed and hurt. The final negotiations were conducted over five hours with neither party speaking to the other save through legal representatives.

By 1990 Ferry had become a father for the third time with the birth of his first daughter, Tara, and for the fourth time the following year with the arrival of his son Merlin. He would also lose his mother, Mary Ann, that same year, and once more dedicated his next album to his parent's memory.

On 21 June 1992, Channel Four broadcast an excellent and enlightening documentary in their *Without Walls* arts strand entitled 'This is Tomorrow'. It subtly and sensitively (if somewhat long-windedly) teased out the relationships between the work of Richard Hamilton and Bryan Ferry. In it, Hamilton finally, and with considerable generosity, acknowledged his most famous pupil as his 'greatest creation'.

For Ferry, it was a creatively fallow period, streaked with nostalgic pain and gain. In March 1990 a video of his 1988 venture into continental Europe, *New Town*, was released. Later that year, 'Heart Still Beating', a laudable live concert from 1982, was belatedly released on LP. It was Roxy Music's last album. In June 1992, Ferry appeared on stage on behalf of EarthPledge in a special concert for that charity held on the Great Lawn of New York City's Central Park. But people began to wonder just how many more past glories Ferry could live on; in 1991 he had even been included in a *Spectator* article about declining creativity being caused by advancing years.[20]

In a *Radio Times* profile in June 1992 timed to coincide with Channel Four's documentary, Ferry comes across as a Roxy Music throwback; he muses on art, slates press intrusion, beefs about the chippiness of others. The press had predictably picked up on his sending his sons to Eton. 'What am I supposed to do?' Ferry snapped. 'Send them to Washington Grammar?'[21]

The fiasco that was unfolding at the time seemed to confirm informed opinion that Ferry was a rudderless relic. A new album of originals, tentatively entitled *Horoscope*, had been recorded in 1991–2 on a cyclopean fifty-six-track console. The thing swelled to monstrous proportions, however, and after the sessions finished in 1992 the traumatic decision was taken to shelve the whole project. Ferry's supporters suggested that he had simply vacillated too long and expended more effort than the end product justified. 'It suffered,' proposed *Q*'s Mat Snow, 'because Ferry wouldn't leave it alone.'[22]

'*Bête Noire* was the start of the Dark Ages for me,' Ferry said later. 'I finished the tour exhausted but really buzzing and thought, "I'm going to make an album and it's going to be wrapped up in six months...but then I hit the old lyrical brick wall.'[23] Also, lacking a producer, he found himself 'running amok' in the studio, inducing a mental indigestion that quickly became a serious creative blockage.[24]

TAXI TO THE MILLENNIUM

The solution was almost too simple, and was initially treated as such, an album of cover versions. Lucy Ferry, it was said, had told her husband to go back to his record collection for solace and inspiration.[25] Ferry met ex Procul Harum guitarist Robin Trower and appointed as producer. David Enthoven, out of Ferry's life for nigh on a decade, gave the singer new hope and new impetus as manager. Trower, said Ferry, made him realize how much he'd missed having a 'real producer'.[26] He also became a 'soulmate', obvious enough from the sensitivity of touch with which Trower orders *Taxi* and *Mamouna*. These new accretions to his personal and professional life gave him the courage to lay aside *Horoscope* and devote his energies to an album which could be done and dusted in a trice. 'Therapy' was Ferry's description of *Taxi*,[27] an album which indeed sounds like a long-overdue check-up and tune-up.

What, cover versions again?! Sell-out, cop-out, moaned the hacks. The comfort blanket of the very finest sessioneers in the world seemed to verify this. Nathan East (bass), Greg Phillinganes (keyboards) and Steve Ferrone (drums) were an imperium of seasoned session talent who'd shone for Michael Jackson, Anita Baker and Eric Clapton, among scores of others. David Williams was an ex-Michael Jackson rhythm guitarist. Yet the album is probably the most successful and, given the circumstances and the musicians playing on it, the most adventurous of all Ferry's latter-day solo works.

'There wasn't a single on it, a radio play record,' Ferry admitted later, and he's right.[28] *Taxi* is a thoroughly off-the-wall record, but a thoroughly successful one. It was disgracefully underestimated and upholds his dignity after the premature abortion of *Horoscope*. 'I'd put my heart and soul into it, as I tend to do, and it just snowballed. This was fun after the difficult time I'd had working on my own songs, and I did more and more.'[29] Somewhat shockingly, Ferry later added, 'I wouldn't actually care much at the moment whether I never wrote another song.'[30]

Taxi isn't remarkable just for its employment of Phillinganes et al. but for its use of them. The four are subsumed – although not anonymously – into a surprisingly bold and contemporary-sounding Ambient wash at odds with megabuck chart fodder. This is music of sonic restraint but thunderous underlying power, as though a great swell is surging within. If Ferry hadn't been listening to Eno, someone close to the mixing desk had, and guitarist Michael Brook, a long-time Eno associate, might be chief suspect.

Mel Collins, an old friend of the EG stable, was used for some saxophone lines ('Rescue Me'), as was Andy Mackay and Maceo Parker. David Sancious ('Amazing Grace') and Chris Stainton ('Just One Look') added the enjoyable incongruities of sandpaper-rough analogue sound to the mix with some sterling Hammond organ work. David Williams was retained from the *Bête Noire*, as was the trusty Hubbard. Trower also played guitar. Andy Newmark played drums, as did Mike Giles (ex-King Crimson). The album was taped in its entirety at one studio, London's Matrix, which indicates something about its considerable coherence as a musical unit.

The album was almost entirely of cover versions, only the outlandish semi-instrumental 'Because You're Mine' a Ferry original and this clocked in, disappointingly, at little over a minute. 'The ultimate cop-out,' thundered John Aizlewood of *Q* magazine in a bitchy and mean-spirited hatchet-job on the album.[31] In fact it's one of the strangest and most inventive albums by any mainstream rock star yet released in the 1990s, laudable for its very daring as much as for anything else. Its treatment of pop standards, in the wake of *These Foolish Things*, is sedate, but hardly respectful. 'The older you become, the more interested you become in laid-back rhythms,' says Ferry with admirable honesty.[32] Predictable? Expectable? Possibly, but the haunting understatements that he brought to bear on such staples of the pop legacy as Fontella Bass's 'Rescue Me' and Elvis Presley's 'The Girl of My Best Friend' were neither.

The clincher is the ingenious change in emphasis of certain elements of each song, retaining their melodic strength but recasting them as quite different sonic artefacts with a wholly different grain. Pop songs are often remembered as a sonic package, as much for their timbres as their hooklines, and this was where Ferry went to work on *Taxi*. The 'mystery' element of the 'spell' in 'I Put a Spell on You' is played up by harmonic tinkering; there's a slightly unsettling quality about the way the chords are voiced here which is quite unlike the original. 'Will You Still Love Me Tomorrow' cleverly brings the Sam Cooke soulfulness into relief. Taken against the bubbly liquidity of the texture, the effect is all the more mesmerizing. Ferry is particularly affecting here; Carole King's anxious teenager wants and expects assurance. Ferry, weary and mature, asks but expects little. It is a peculiarly vulnerable and touching performance.

'Answer Me' has Ferry pumping away at a garage-band organ and delivering the lines with curiously deadpan anonymity. Again, the melody holds up, but its textural relations mean it is remembered as a wholly different entity. One can hardly call it a cover version. The method doesn't work quite so effectively on 'Just One Look', although the makeover of 'Rescue Me' reduces its swagger to an amble. Only the melody and chords remain here; Ferry has taken the song to experiment on. He is once again the Pop Art magpie of early Roxy Music days. There are more straightforward *hommages*: Lou Reed's 'All Tomorrow's Parties' (uninspired) and 'The Girl of My Best Friend' (excellent, with Ferry in top vocal form, capably sneering and crooning in Tupelo accents). It's an almost tender treatment, given the slight restrain in the rhythm.

Taxi's title track was a little-regarded soul number by J. Blackfoot which Ferry had heard on John Peel's late-night Radio 1 show one evening in 1984, driving back to his Sussex home, and transcribed at the wheel at 100 m.p.h. Here it is made thunderous and threatening; funky guitar licks sit uneasily with Ambient guitar, synthesizer and treatments. Unusual, though not as bizarre as 'Amazing Grace', which, from the moment its melody emerges, unrecognizably distorted by the dissonance offered by the opening chords, is a very odd piece of work indeed, with the loose funk of the Phillinganes rhythm section and further Ambient sound-scaping a piquant counterpoint to one of the most overused melodies in musical history. This leaves only 'Because You're Mine', a short, elemental Ambient workout on one chord, with Carleen Anderson repeating the title with shamanistic possession while an electrical storm whirls round the soundstage and the album dissolves in a jangling mist. It's a stunning end to a splendid album, and the most robust recall of Roxy Music's glories. It's certainly a vast improvement on the maundering what-does-this-switch-do synthesizer experiment from the *Flesh + Blood* sessions entitled 'South Downs' that Ferry once tried to pass off as a B-side. Michael Brook's random squirts of Ambient guitar and treatments, as well as his lead work on 'All Tomorrow's Parties', undoubtedly take the laurels, along with the Philliganes rhythm section. All are worthy of high praise, however.

Dates were arranged for a worldwide tour, which sold respectably. Of playing live again, Ferry said, 'I dread it, really. It's the preparation and the commitment to doing it every night I can't handle.'[33]

Horoscope could hardly be thrown in the bin, however. Refreshed by *Taxi*, Ferry recovered the fifty-six-track rushes from the shelf and set about one more tampering session. This time he had a goal, and a purpose, and his rewriting and recording of vocal and percussion tracks, as well as the penning of entirely new numbers that the galvanizing ecstasy of creativity had engendered, made the whole a quite different album. The result was eventually released in 1994 with the interpolation of many other skilled studio hands, as the seemingly seamless offering *Mamouna*. David Williams, Carleen Anderson, Hubbard, East and Ferrone were recalled from the backbone of the *Taxi* sessions. Nile Rodgers, Fonzi Thornton and Yannick Etienne were among those older acquaintances recalled for the new record. But also among those skilled studio hands were those of Brian Eno, moving once more within hailing frequency of Ferry after over two decades apart. While Trower still held the production reins, Eno, now globally fêted as enabler to the stars, to the greats (U2) as well as the guttersnipes (James), was now a big enough player in the global studio game to feature once more within Ferry's line of sight. Once Ferry had signed him because he'd lugged a tape-recorder up the stairs of a terraced house in Battersea. Now he called him in because of a reputation in the superhighways of corporate leisure as a pop technocrat. He plays on all tracks of *Mamouna* bar one, although his contribution is credited with infuriating tweeness as 'sonics', 'sonic emphasis' and so on.

According to Sinfield:

'They got on splendidly. It's come full circle. Bryan was happy to go back and try and find something from then that perhaps he's since lost – a little madness or naïveté or randomness. And Eno would certainly provide some randomness. What they both have in common is a great ear. They both hear how things should be, the mood, the temperature and the colours.'[34]

For his part, Ferry says of Eno's role in *Mamouna*, 'We had such fun when we worked together last year. I hadn't seen such energy for such a long time. It gave me something to react to. That's what I still miss about group projects. The interaction and the friction that comes with shared responsibility.'[35]

The reunion with Eno, tentative as it was, was not the only one Ferry enjoyed on *Mamouna*. Mackay and Manzanera were in attendance also.

For Manzanera:

'It was very enjoyable to do. I had a great day there. I played on quite a few tracks, though I can't hear myself on any of them. But there are so many guitarists on there. I saw one of his Hammersmith shows where he sang very well, but everyone round him was wrong. He's surrounded by so much baggage.'[36]

If Manzanera can't hear himself in there (for the record, he appears on two songs), he's not alone. Andy Mackay crops up on two tracks, 'Gemini Moon' and the Eno co-authored 'Wildcat Days', a presence one can only guess at given the relative absence of any sax playing (similarly, Mackay, a fine oboist, can't have been flattered by Ferry's use of something called a 'syn-oboe' on one of the tracks on which he appears). At times, the listener might be forgiven for thinking that Ferry himself is on vacation. He is once again playing Ellington, and often to good effect. The album has an urban hurly-burly to its arrangements which is singularly unconventional – one can conceive of few tracks as fodder for pub CD players; the sonic democracy of *Taxi* is again operative, only even more actively so. There are many more layers to be accounted for on *Mamouna*; there's an agreeable lack of convention and continuity to the soundstage, many-hued and with much fanciful, spatially minded illustrative relief – the percussion on 'NYC' and the beguiling electronic fancies introducing 'Your Painted Smile' are just two examples. The seasick swell of electronics which prowl the songs, intimating undeployed power, is another hangover from *Taxi*, but loses its charm. This may have something to do with the forbidding misanthropy of the album, which is almost unrelievedly gloomy. 'The Only Face' is particularly mournful, with the sampled 'I Want to be Alone' sounding throughout and the song's arrangement making the music rise and fall with the impetuous passion of a breast rent by sobs.

Only the place of the rhythm section – Nathan East and Steve Ferrone for the most part – is well balanced within the mix; they are less explicitly funky or leaden-footed an anchorage for Ferry's music than usual. They don't want to scream *soul*; they want the listener to dance and forget they're even there. The problem is, one can overlook everyone, so dense is the mix. This worked for Roxy Music when Ferry had strong melodies and strong ideas of how to treat them, but these two latter are often missing on *Mamouna*.

In Q magazine, Stuart Maconie wrote that *Mamouna* was an exercise in 'refining the tenor of sophisticated, etiolated rootlessness that has preoccupied Ferry since *Avalon*'.[37] *Mamouna* is never less than good, but, as Maconie says elsewhere, it funks greatness. Timbral complexity doesn't disguise a lack of variation and relief in Ferry's melodic language. For *Mojo*'s perceptive Cliff Jones, they are 'variations on a single groove.'[38] 'Chain Reaction' and 'Which Way to Turn' are genuinely original, stylist melodies which sound like outtakes from Roxy Music sessions of old, wired-into past *zeitgeists* which had always powered Ferry's inspirations.

The former is Ferry at his best; a pop song which sounds conventional enough until further study. The notes, the progressions, the riffs, the bass line, the lyrical sentiments are pure pop, but new forms have still been wrought from them. 'Wildcat Days', co-authored with Eno, has playful tricks in its verse melodies which catch out the unsuspecting listener.

The title track is another track whose chord progressions are obviously Ferry, and it is with this distinctiveness that the individual beauties of the arrangements are best heard. But too often there is a lugubrious uniformity about the music. If Ferry purveys moods rather than melodies, this is an unrelentingly depressive album, with Ferry's lyrical and vocal gifts sulking in a corner.

Ferry often speaks purely of a state of mind − 'Which Way to Turn' deals entirely in describing feelings − and elsewhere randomly mixes and matches boilerplate lyrical cliché as though to inaugurate some kind of pop Esperanto which lacks narrative continuity but which still creates a 'pop song'. It sounds like nonsense, at least, unless this apparently aimless free association is read as a postmodern satire on pop standardization. 'Chain Reaction' again stands out, the obsolete 'lovey-dovey' and self-consciously juvenile 'pass it on' betraying the lyricist as a human being with heart and memory.

TARA (AGAIN?)

The fact that the presence on the same record of four ex-members of what by the standards of the voraciously nostalgic 1990s would have been termed the 'classic' Roxy Music line-up − Ferry, Eno, Manzanera and Mackay − was overlooked says a lot for the changing profile of the band. Roxy Music, it seemed, just didn't matter any more. Their commercial day had passed, their influence gernerously acknowledged. The extraordinary obsession with 1970s retro chic in British popular culture during the 1990s, with its sudden Technicolor rashes of 'Glam Nights' and 'seventies discos', seemed to pass Roxy Music by. There were few Roxy Music theme events in the provincial nitespots of the band's native land. Two compilations, *Streetlife* (April 1986) and *The Ultimate Collection* (November 1988), which bundled Ferry and Roxy Music material together, sold in vast quantities. But at the same time, and very mystifyingly, the media manifestations of rocks multi-stranded reinvention of its own past – the preponderance of thirty-something retro-sheets like *Q* and *Mojo* – largely ignored Ferry after 1988's *Bête Noire*. Dave Simpson of *Mojo* wrote a lengthy tribute to the band in 1995 to which (almost) all former members contributed, but there was little else.

Rather like their heyday when their very unclassifiability, their evasion of easy estimation, attracted media attention, in the dumbed-down 1990s these qualities repelled attention. The sheer complexity of Roxy Music, in an era which demanded copy that was easy on the eye and the mind, was presumably a turn-off. Fair enough to devote columns to the conundrums when the records were in the charts, but why bother when a few more pages could be filled with overwrought speculations on the unfulfilled promise of Syd Barrett/Nick Drake/Jimi Hendrix (delete where appropriate) and sixth-form postmodern humour?

This had little perceptible effect on the material circumstances of the band members, whose lives retain the majority of the benefits that stardom and its rewards bestowed on them. All live comfortably; Ferry in particular lives well, basing himself in Sussex and west London. Of the five men that piled into Mr Mackay senior's Transit van for those first outlandish gigs in 1971, presently the most luminous has to be Eno. Manzanera and Mackay continue to record as sidemen and as solo artists. Paul Thompson has all but vanished into the twilight world of Newcastle upon Tyne. He was last heard on record in the mid-1980s, thrashing hell out of his long-suffering drums for the hoary Tyneside Punk aggregation the Angelic Upstarts, whose booze-and-tattoos, did-you-spill-my-pint machismo and rowdy laments for lost squaddie pals and working-class heroes were about as far from High Roxy as one could imagine. John Porter, Eddie Jobson, Gary Tibbs, Dave Skinner and John Wetton continue to make good money in music. Porter in particular won many plaudits for his production work in the 1980s, notably with the Smiths. Rik Kenton and Sal Madia have disappeared.

Onetime producer Pete Sinfield sums up the Roxy Music legacy best: 'Eno was always an anti-star who became a star, whereas Bryan Ferry wanted to be a star. Eno is a contented chap these days, whereas I think Ferry is at a bit of a loose end. I don't think he's had much fun in the last few years.'[39]

'I think,' Sinfield continues, 'that he [Ferry] should write a few songs for other people. I'm sure he would write a very interesting song for Tina Turner.'[40]

Ferry replied, 'No way. It's hard enough writing for myself. I wish somebody would write one for me actually.'[41]

Takers, anyone?

BIBLIOGRAPHY

Amaya, Mario, *Pop Art and After*, Viking Press, New York, 1965

Amis, Martin, *Success*, Penguin, Harmondsworth, 1978

– *Money*, Penguin, Harmondsworth, 1984

Balfour, Rex, *The Bryan Ferry Story*, Blandford, London, 1976

Berman, Marshall, *All That is Solid Melts into Air*, Verso, London 1983

Bracewell, Michael, *England is Mine: Pop Life in Albion from Wilde to Goldie*, HarperCollins, London, 1997

Burdon, Eric, *I Used to be an Animal But I'm All Right Now: An Autobiography*, Faber and Faber, London, 1986

Burn, Gordon, *Alma Cogan*, Secker and Warburg Ltd, London, 1991

Carlos Clarke, Robert, *Obsessions*, editions AMP editeur, Paris, 1981

Chambers, Iain, *Urban Rhythms: Pop Music and Popular Culture*, Macmillan, London, 1985

Cohen, Philip, and Dave Robinson, *Knuckle Sandwich*, Penguin, Harmondsworth, 1978

Eno, Brian, and Russell Mills, *More Dark Than Shark*, Faber and

Faber, London, 1986

Frame, Pete, *Rock Family Trees. Vol. 1*, Omnibus, London, 1980

– *Rock Family Trees. Vol. 2*, Omnibus, London, 1983

Frith, Simon, *Sound Effects: Youth, Leisure and the Politics of Rock and Roll*, Constable, London 1983

– *Music for Pleasure*, Polity, London, 1987

Frith, Simon, and Howard Horne, *Art into Pop*, Methuen, London, 1987

Gabor, Mark, *A Modest History of the Pin-up*, Pan, London, 1973

Gambaccini, Paul, et al. (eds.), *The Guinness Book of British Hit Albums*, Guinness Publishing, London, various dates

– *The Guinness Book of British Hit Singles*, Guinness Publishing, London, various dates

Garner, Ken, *In Session Tonight*, BBC Books, London, 1993

Gaunt, William, *The Aesthetic Adventure*, Jonathan Cape, London, 1945

Green, Jonathon (ed.), *Days in the Life: Voices from the English Underground, 1961–1971*, Heinemann, London, 1988

Hall, Jerry (with Christopher Hemphill), *Jerry Hall's Tall Tales*, Boxtree, London, 1985

Hamilton, Richard, *Collected Words*, Thames & Hudson, London, 1982

Hebdige, Dick, *Subculture: The Meaning of Style*, Routledge, London, 1979

– *Hiding in the Light*, Comedia, London, 1988

Hounsome, Terry (ed.), *New Rock Record. Vol. II*, Blandford, London, 1984

Howell, Georgina, *In Vogue: Six Decades of Fashion*, Allen Lane, London, 1979

Hughes, Robert, *Nothing If Not Critical: Selected Essays on Art and Artists*, Harvill, London, 1991

Hulanicki, Barbara, *From A to Biba*, Comet, London, 1984

Hunter, Ian, *Diary of a Rock and Roll Star*, Panther, London, 1974

Knobler, Peter, and Greg Mitchell, *Very Seventies: A Cultural History of the 1970s*, Fireside/Simon & Schuster, New York, 1995

Lanza, Joseph, *Elevator Music: A Surreal History of Muzak, Easy Listening and Other Moodsong*, Quartet, London, 1995

Larkin, Colin (ed.), *The Guinness Encyclopedia of Popular Music*, Guinness Publishing, London, 1992

Logan, Nick, and Bob Woffinden (eds.), *The NME Illustrated Encyclopedia of Rock*, Salamander Books, London, 1977

McRobbie, Angela (ed.), *Zoot Suits and Second-hand Dresses*, Macmillan, London, 1989

Melly, George, *Revolt into Style: The Pop Arts*, Allen Lane, London, 1970

Moore, Allan F., *Rock: The Primary Text*, OUP, Milton Keynes, 1992

Mungham, Geoff, and G. Pearson (eds.), *Working-class Youth Culture*, Routledge, London, 1976

Newton, Helmut, *White Women*, Quartet, London, 1979

– *47 Nudes*, Thames & Hudson, London, 1982

– *World Without Men*, Quartet, London, 1984

Palmer, Tony, *All You Need is Love*, Futura, London, 1976

Parkin, Molly, *Moll: The Autobiography of Molly Parkin*, Victor Gollancz, London, 1992

Pop Art: An Illustrated Dictionary, Methuen, London, 1977

Rees, Dafydd, and Barry Lazell, *Bryan Ferry and Roxy Music*, Proteus, London, 1982

Rogan, Johnny, *Style with Substance: Roxy's First Ten Years*, Star, London, 1982

– *Morrissey and Marr: The Sad Alliance*, Omnibus Press, London, 1992

Roxy Music Songbook, EG Music, London, 1973

Sandford, Christopher, *Bowie: Loving the Alien*, Little, Brown, New York, 1996

St Clair, Lindi, *It's Only a Game*, Piatkus, London, 1992

Strong, M. C., *The Great Rock Discography* (third edition), Canongate, Edinburgh, 1996

Stump, Paul, *The Music's All That Matters: A History of Progressive Rock*, Quartet, London, 1997

Tamm, Eric, *Brian Eno: His Music and the Vertical Colour of*

Sound, Faber and Faber, London, 1989

Vahimagi, Tise, *British Television*, BFI, London, 1994

Wale, Michael, *Voxpop*, Harrap, London, 1972

Williamson, Judith, *Consuming Passions*, Fontana, London, 1985

Willis, Paul, *Profane Culture*, Routledge, London, 1978

York, Peter, *Style Wars*, Faber and Faber, London, 1983

REFERENCES

CHAPTER 1: THE MAKING OF
SUPERGEORDIE
1   *Guardian (Weekend)*, 14
     June 1997.
2   *Melody Maker*, 12 July
     1975.
3   Ibid.
4   Rogan, J., *Roxy: Style with
     Substance*, Star, London,
     1982, p. 9.
5   *New Musical Express*, 4
     March 1978.
6   Burn, G., *Alma Cogan*,
     Secker and Warburg,
     London, 1991, p. 8.
7   *Melody Maker*, 12 July
     1975.
8   Q, March 1993.
9   *New Musical Express*, 19
     June 1982.
10   Frame, P. and Howlett, K.,

     The Bryan Ferry Story,
     BBC Radio 1 Broadcast,
     September–October 1994.
11   Q, March 1993.
12   Ibid.
13   Ibid.
14   Ibid.
15   Frame and Howlett, op.
     cit.
16   Ibid.
17   *Melody Maker*, 12 July
     1975.
18   Hamilton, R., *Collected
     Words*, Thames & Hudson,
     London, 1982, p. 8.
19   Ibid., p. 20.
20   Quoted in Amaya, M.,
     Pop Art and After, Viking,
     New York, 1965, p. 33.
21   Ibid.
22   Hamilton, op. cit., p. 43.

23 Amaya, op. cit., p. 21.
24 Ibid., p. 1.

CHAPTER 2: IDEAS MEN
1 *Melody Maker*, 12 July 1975.
2 Ibid.
3 Ibid.
4 Ibid.
5 *New Musical Express*, 30 August 1975.
6 Ibid.
7 Frame and Howlett, op. cit.
8 Tamm, E., *Brian Eno: His Music and the Vertical Colour of Sound*, Faber and Faber, London, 1989, p. 40.
9 *New Musical Express*, 26 November 1977.
10 Tamm, op. cit., p. 41.
11 Quoted ibid.
12 Ibid., p. 18.
13 Ibid., p. 17.
14 Ibid.
15 Ibid.
16 Ibid.
17 Ibid.
18 *Esquire*, December 1982.
19 Tamm, op. cit., p. 18.
20 *Guardian (Weekend)*, 14 June :1997.
21 Ibid.
22 *Mojo*, December 1995.
23 *Guardian (Weekend)*, 14 June 1997.
24 *Without Walls: This is Tomorrow*, Channel Four Television, June 1992.
25 Hamilton, op. cit., p. 38.
26 Howell, G., *In Vogue: Six Decades of Fashion*, Allen Lane, London, 1979, p. 322.
27 *Guardian (Weekend)*, 14 June 1997.
28 Rogan, op. cit., p. 20.
29 Interview with Pete Sinfield, May 1997.
30 Ibid.
31 *New Musical Express*, 9 September 1972.
32 Ibid.
33 Frame and Howlett, op. cit.
34 *New Musical Express*, 25 November 1978.
35 Ibid.
36 Interview with Tom Newman, June 1998.
37 Rogan, op.cit., p. 21.
38 Ibid.
39 Ibid., p. 23.
40 Ibid., p. 24.
41 Frame and Howlett, op. cit.
42 Quoted in sleeve notes, *The Thrill of It All*, Virgin Records, 1995.
43 Rogan, op. cit., p. 25.
44 Frame and Howlett, op. cit.
45 *Guardian (Weekend)*, 14 June 1997.
46 Frame and Howlett, op. cit.
47 Garner, K., *In Session Tonight*, BBC Publications,

London, 1994, p. 87.

48 Frame and Howlett, op. cit.

49 Garner, op. cit., p. 87.

50 *Mojo*, December 1995.

51 Ibid.

52 Ibid.

53 Frame and Howlett, op. cit.

54 *Mojo*, December 1995.

55 Frame and Howlett, op. cit.

56 Melly, G., *Revolt into Style: The Pop Arts*, Allen Lane, London, 1970, p. 117.

57 Fripp, R., sleeve notes, *King Crimson: The Great Deceiver*, Virgin Records, 1993.

58 Ibid.

59 Frame and Howlett, op. cit.

60 Ibid.

61 Tobler, J., *The Island Records Story*, BBC Radio 1 broadcast, 1987.

62 Ibid.

CHAPTER 3: THE VERB 'TO ROXY'

1 *Mojo*, December 1995.

2 Frame and Howlett, op. cit.

3 Ibid.

4 Rogan, op. cit., p. 30.

5 York, P., *Style Wars*, Faber and Faber, London, 1983, p. 54.

6 *Mojo*, December 1995.

7 Frame and Howlett, op. cit.

8 *New Musical Express*, 16 June 1980.

9 *Guardian (Weekend)*, 14 June 1997.

10 Hughes, R., *Nothing If Not Critical: Selected Essays on Art and Artists*, Harvill, London, 1991, p. 196.

11 Rogan, op. cit., p. 25.

12 Frame and Howlett, op. cit.

13 Ibid.

14 Ibid.

15 *New Musical Express*, 9 September 1972.

16 Ibid.

17 Garner, op. cit., p. 87.

18 *Mojo*, December 1995.

19 Interview with Pete Sinfield, May 1997.

20 *Melody Maker*, 12 July 1975.

21 *Rolling Stone*, 24 April 1975.

22 *New Musical Express*, 12 June 1972.

23 *The Face*, April 1985.

24 *New Musical Express*, 10 March 1979.

25 Rogan, op. cit., p. 36.

26 Frame and Howlett, op. cit.

27 Moore, Allan F., *Rock: The Primary Text*, OUP, Milton Keynes, 1992, p. 110.

28 Ibid.

29 Ibid.

30 Ibid.
31 Frame and Howlett, op. cit.
32 Moore, op. cit., p. 111.
33 Ibid.
34 Ibid.
35 Ibid.
36 Quoted in Rogan, op. cit., p. 24.
37 Frame and Howlett, op. cit.
38 Rogan, op. cit., p. 34.
39 Ibid.
40 *Mojo*, December 1995.
41 Sleeve notes, *Roxy Music: The Thrill of It All*, Virgin Records, 1995.
42 Quoted in Rogan, op. cit., p. 36.
43 Ibid., p. 37.
44 Ibid.
45 *Melody Maker*, 3 July 1976.

CHAPTER 4: GAY(-ISH) BLADES
1 *Melody Maker*, 12 July 1975.
2 Rogan, op. cit., p. 46.
3 *New Musical Express*, 19 January 1974 .
4 *Melody Maker*, 6 July 1974.
5 *Mojo*, December 1995.
6 Hunter, Ian, *Diary of a Rock and Roll Star*, Panther, London, 1974, p. 87.
7 Ibid.
8 BBC Radio 1 interview, 1985.
9 *New Musical Express*, 16 August 1980.
10 Rogan, op. cit. p. 43.
11 Ibid., p. 38.
12 Quoted in Palmer, T., *All You Need is Love*, Futura, London, 1977, p. 265.
13 *New Musical Express*, 9 September 1972.
14 *Guardian (Weekend)*, 14 June 1997.
15 Ibid.
16 *Melody Maker*, 8 July 1976.
17 Ibid.
18 *Melody Maker*, 29 January 1977.
19 Frame and Howlett, op. cit.
20 Melly, op. cit., p. 117.
21 York, op. cit., p. 54.
22 Melly, op. cit., p. 117
23 Palmer, op. cit., p. 265.
24 *Mojo*, December 1995.
25 Quoted in Hughes, op. cit., p. 248.
26 Ibid., p. 249.
27 *Guardian (Weekend)*, 14 June 1997.
28 *Mojo*, December 1995.
29 Frame and Howlett, op. cit.
30 *New Musical Express*, 26 November 1977.
31 *New Musical Express*, 2 October 1982.
32 *Guardian (Weekend)*, 14 June 1997.
33 Lanza, J., *Elevator Music: A Surreal History of Muzak,*

Easy Listening and Other Moodsong, Quartet, London, 1995, p. 68.

34 Quoted in Rogan, op. cit., p. 39.
35 *Melody Maker*, 29 December 1973.
36 Ibid.
37 Ibid.
38 Ibid.
39 Ibid.
40 Quoted in Rogan, op. cit., p. 38.
41 Amaya, op. cit., p. 20.
42 Ibid.
43 Ibid.
44 Quoted in Melly, op. cit., p. 177.
45 York, op. cit., p. 116.
46 Ibid.
47 Sandford, C., *Bowie: Loving the Alien*, Little, Brown, New York, 1996, p. 62.
48 Ibid., p. 47.
49 *New Musical Express*, 26 November 1977.
50 *New Musical Express*, 9 September 1972.
51 *Record Mirror*, 7 April 1979.
52 Ibid.
53 Rogan, op. cit., p. 61.
54 *Trouser Press*, No. 32.
55 Frame and Howlett, op. cit.
56 *New Musical Express*, 26 November 1977.
57 Rogan, op. cit., p. 65.
58 Frame and Howlett, op. cit.
59 Ibid.
60 Ibid.
61 Ibid.
62 *Guardian (Weekend)*, 14 June 1997.

CHAPTER 5: UNDERWEAR AND UNDERGROWTH
1 *Record Collector*, June 1995.
2 Ibid.
3 *Hot Press*, August 1981.
4 Moore, op. cit., p. 111.
5 *New Musical Express*, 26 November 1977.
6 Quoted in Tamm, op. cit., p. 55.
7 *New Musical Express*, 19 January 1974.
8 *Zoo World*, May 1974.
9 *Melody Maker*, 6 July 1974.
10 Quoted in sleeve notes, *The Thrill of It All*, Virgin Records, 1995.
11 *Hot Press*, August 1981.
12 Palmer, op. cit., p. 279.
13 Quoted in sleeve notes, *The Thrill of It All*, Virgin Records, 1995.
14 *Melody Maker*, 29 December 1973.
15 Ibid.
16 *Melody Maker*, 12 July 1975.
17 *Melody Maker*, 3 November 1973 . The *naif* in question was Steve Lake.
18 Interview with Pete Sinfield, May 1997.

19 *Mojo*, December 1995.
20 Frame and Howlett, op. cit.
21 *Guardian (Weekend)*, 14 June 1997.
22 Rogan, op. cit., p. 86.
23 *Guardian (Weekend)*, 14 June 1997.
24 *New Musical Express*, 19 October 1974.
25 Rogan, op. cit., p. 86.
26 Frame and Howlett, op. cit.
27 Ibid.
28 Ibid.
29 *Melody Maker*, 6 July 1974.
30 Frith, S., *Sound Effects: Youth Leisure and the Politics of Rock and Roll*, Constable, London, 1983, p. 54.
31 *Sounds*, 19 January 1974.
32 *New Musical Express*, 19 May 1979.
33 Ibid.
34 Ibid.
35 *Melody Maker*, 29 December 1973.
36 *Rolling Stone*, 24 April 1975.
37 *Melody Maker*, 29 December 1973.
38 *Melody Maker*, 12 July 1975.
39 Ibid.
40 *Melody Maker*, 29 December 1973.
41 Ibid.
42 Ibid.
43 Ibid.
44 *New Musical Express*, 30 August 1975.
45 *New Musical Express*, 21 December 1974.
46 Hughes, op. cit., p. 246.
47 Ibid., p. 247.
48 *Melody Maker*, 12 July 1975.
49 *Guardian (Weekend)*, 14 June 1997.
50 Ibid.
51 *Melody Maker*, 12 July 1975.
52 Ibid.
53 Ibid.
54 Ibid.
55 Ibid.
56 Ibid.
56 Rogan, op. cit., p. 78.
57 *Melody Maker*, 8 July 1976.
58 *Rolling Stone*, 24 April 1975.
59 Ibid.
60 Berman, M., *All That is Solid Melts into Air*, Verso, London, 1983.
61 Ibid., p. 161.
62 Ibid., p. 162.
63 Ibid.
64 *Rolling Stone*, 24 April 1975.
65 *Melody Maker*, 12 July 1975.
66 *New Musical Express*, 19 June 1982.
67 Ibid.
68 *Melody Maker*, 12 July 1975.

69 Ibid.
70 *Sun,* 8 June 1979.
71 *Melody Maker,* 6 July 1974.
72 Ibid.
73 *Melody Maker,* 12 July 1975.
74 *Melody Maker,* 6 July 1974.
75 Ibid
76 *New Musical Express,* 19 June 1982.
77 *New Musical Express,* 5 October 1974.
78 Ibid.
79 Ibid.
80 *New Musical Express,* 21 December 1974.
81 *New Musical Express,* 22 February 1975.
82 *New Musical Express,* 19 October 1974.
83 Ibid.
84 Ibid.
85 Quoted in Frame and Howlett, op cit.
86 *New Musical Express,* 6 March 1976.
87 *New Musical Express,* 21 December 1974.
88 *New Musical Express,* 5 October 1974.
89 Frame and Howlett, op. cit.
90 *Melody Maker,* 8 July 1976.
91 *Record Collector,* June 1995.
92 *New Musical Express,* 9 November 1974.
93 Ibid.
94 *Melody Maker,* 8 July 1976.
95 Ibid.
96 *New Musical Express,* 9 November 1974.
97 *New Musical Express,* 21 December 1974.
98 Ibid.

CHAPTER 6: THE TIMES OF THEIR LIVES

1   *Mojo,* December 1995.
2   Frame and Howlett, op. cit.
3   Ibid.
4   Hughes, op. cit., p. 247.
5   Melly, op. cit., p. 103.
6   Ibid.
7   Ibid., p. 94.
8   Interview with Pete Sinfield, May 1997.
9   Melly, op. cit., p. 165.
10 Ibid., p. 161.
11 Ibid., p. 192.
12 Ibid.
13 York, op. cit., p. 112.
14 Parkin, M., *Moll: The Autobiography of Molly Parkin,* Victor Gollancz, London, 1992, p. 166.
15 Ibid., p. 201.
16 Frame and Howlett, op. cit.
17 Ibid.
18 Interview with Pete Sinfield, May 1997.
19 Ibid.
20 Sandford, op. cit., p. 125.
21 Ibid.
22 Ibid., p. 86.
23 Ibid.

24 Ibid.
25 *New Musical Express*, 30 August 1975.
26 Ibid.
27 Hebdige, D., *Subculture: The Meaning of Style*, Routledge, London, 1979, p. 61.
28 Sandford, op. cit., p. 107.
29 Frame and Howlett, op. cit.
30 Sandford, op. cit., p. 77.
31 York, op. cit., p. 9.
32 Amis, M., *Success*, Penguin, Harmondsworth, 1978, p. 41.
33 Ibid., p. 72.
34 Ibid., p. 151.
35 Fell, D., quoted in Knobler, P. & Mitchell, G., *Very Seventies: A Cultural History of the 1970s*, Fireside/Simon & Schuster, New York, 1995.
36 *Guardian (Weekend)*, 14 June 1997.
37 Ibid,
38 Rogan, op. cit., p. 122.
39 Ibid., p. 123.
40 York, P., *Harpers & Queen*, October 1976.
41 Garnier, P., quoted in Newton, H., *White Women*, Quartet, London, 1979.
42 Newton, H., *White Women*, Quartet, London, 1979.
43 Garnier, P., in Newton, op. cit.
44 *Mojo*, December 1995.
45 Logan, N., and Woffinden, B., *The New Musical Express Encyclopedia of Rock*, Salamander Books, London, 1977, p. 176.
46 *New Musical Express*, 22 November 1975.
47 Ibid.
48 *New Musical Express*, 2 November 1974.
49 *Melody Maker*, 8 July 1976.
50 Frame and Howlett, op. cit.
51 Ibid.
52 *Melody Maker*, 8 July 1976.
53 Frame and Howlett, op. cit.
54 Ibid.

CHAPTER 7: GLOBAL COOLING

1 *Guardian (Weekend)*, 14 June 1997.
2 *Record Mirror*, 7 April 1979.
3 Ibid.
4 Quoted in Rogan, op. cit., p. 157.
5 Ibid., p. 157.
6
7 *Miss London*, 30 May 1978.
8 *Melody Maker*, 16 September 1978.
9 Logan and Woffinden, op. cit., p. 81.
10 *New Musical Express*, 26 February 1977.
11 *Melody Maker*, 12 February 1977.

12   Ibid.
13   Frame and Howlett, op. cit.
14   *Melody Maker*, 19 February 1977.
15   *Record Mirror*, 3 September 1977.
16   *New Musical Express*, 4 March 1978.
17   Rogan, op. cit., p. 160.
18   Amis, M., *Money*, Penguin, Harmondsworth, 1984, p. 124.
19   *Sun*, 23 September 1977.
20   Hughes, op. cit., p. 247.
21   *Melody Maker*, 16 September 1978.
22   Rogan, op. cit., p. 162.
23   *Melody Maker*, 12 July 1975.
24   *OK*, September 1977.
25   Hall, J. (with Hemphill, C.), *Jerry Hall's Tall Tales,* Boxtree, London, 1985.
26   Ibid.
27   Frame and Howlett, op. cit.
28   Ibid.
29   *Daily Mirror*, 14 March 1980.
30   *Daily Mirror*, 20 October 1978.
31   *Sunday Mirror*, 22 March 1981.
32   Rogan, op. cit., pp. 95–6.
33   Ibid.
34   *New Musical Express*, 19 June 1982.
35   Ibid.
36   *Melody Maker*, 29 December 1973.
37   York, op cit., p. 67.
38   *New Musical Express*, 19 June 1982.
39   *Melody Maker*, 16 September 1978.
40   *Miss London*, 30 May 1978.
41   *Daily Mirror*, 20 October 1978.
42   *Melody Maker,* 12 March 1977.
43   Frame and Howlett, op. cit.
44   *Melody Maker*, 16 September 1978.
45   Frame and Howlett, op. cit.
46   *Melody Maker*, 16 September 1978.
47   Frame and Howlett, op. cit.
48   *New Musical Express*, 19 June 1982.
49   Ibid.
50   *Rolling Stone*, 24 April 1975.
51   Hughes, op. cit., p. 245.
52   Ibid., p. 254.
53   *Melody Maker*, 5 August 1978.
54   *Melody Maker*, 16 September 1978.
55   Ibid.
56   Ibid.

CHAPTER 8: HAIRDRESSER'S DELIGHT

1   Frame and Howlett, op. cit.
2   *New Musical Express*, 19 May 1979.

3   Ibid.
4   Ibid.
5   Frame and Howlett, op. cit.
6   *New Musical Express*, 10 March 1979.
7   *Melody Maker*, l0 March 1979.
8   Ibid.
9   *New Musical Express*, 10 March 1979.
10 Frame and Howlett, op. cit.
11 *New Musical Express*, 16 August 1980.
12 Ibid.
13 Ibid.
14 Ibid.
15 *Mojo*, December 1995.
16 *New Musical Express*, 16 August 1980.
17 *New Musical Express*, 28 June 1980.
18 Frame and Howlett, op. cit.
19 *Mojo*, December 1995.
20 Quoted in *The Thrill of It All* sleeve notes, Virgin Records, 1995.
21 *New Musical Express*, 19 June 1982.
22 Frame and Howlett op. cit.
23 *Hot Press*, August 1981.
24 *Melody Maker*, 25 July 1981.
25 Rogan, op. cit., p. 210.
26 Frame and Howlett, op. cit.
27 *New Musical Express*, 16 August 1980.
28 Ibid.
29 *New Musical Express*, 19 June 1982.
30 *Guardian (Weekend)*, 14 June 1997.
31 *Melody Maker*, 25 July 1981.
32 *Guardian (Weekend)*, 14 June 1997.
33 Frith, S, and Horne, H., *Art into Pop*, Methuen, London, 1987, p. 87.
34 Ibid.
35 Ibid.
36 Ibid.
37 *New Musical Express*, 19 June 1982.
38 Ibid.

CHAPTER 9 ENO: BALD MAN SEEKS MUSICIANS, VIEW TO SOMETHING DIFFERENT

1   Tamm, E. op. cit., p. 5.
2   *Guardian*, 8 May 1998.
3   Tamm, op. cit., p. 23.
4   Ibid.
5   Ibid., p. 24.
6   Ibid., p. 151.
7   *New Musical Express*, 26 November 1977.
8   Rogan, op. cit., p. 129
9   *New Musical Express*, 26 November 1977.
10 Ibid.
11 Rogan, op. cit., p. 131.
12 *New Musical Express*, 26 November 1977.
13 Ibid.
14 Ibid.
15 Ibid.

16 Quoted in Tamm, op. cit.,
    p. 103.
17 *New Musical Express*, 26
    November 1977.
18 Ibid.
19 Quoted in Tamm, op. cit.,
    p. 81.
20 Ibid.
21 *New Musical Express*, 26
    November 1977.
22 Quoted in Tamm, op. cit.,
    p. 57.
23 *New Musical Express*, 26
    November 1977.
24 *New Musical Express*, 3
    December 1977.
25 Quoted in Rogan, op. cit.,
    p. 168.
26 Ibid., p. 171.
27 Quoted in Tamm, op. cit.,
    p. 100.
28 Ibid., p. 77.
29 Eno, B. and Schmidt, P.,
    Oblique Strategies, London,
    1977.
30 Quoted in Tamm, op. cit.,
    p. 79.
31 *New Musical Express*, 3
    December 1977.
32 Quoted in Tamm, op. cit.,
    p. 158.
33 *New Musical Express*, 3
    December 1977.
34 Quoted in Tamm, op. cit.,
    p. 107.
35 Rogan, op. cit., p. 178.
36 Quoted in Tamm, op. cit.,
    p. 27.

37 Ibid., p. 27.
38 Quoted in Tamm, op. cit.,
    p. 30.
39 Ibid., p. 31.
40 Ibid.
41 Ibid., p. 109.
42 Quoted in ibid., p. 65.
43 Ibid., p. 49.
44 Ibid., p. 64.
45 Quoted in ibid., p. 19.
46 Quoted in ibid., p. 20.
47 Quoted in ibid., p. 20.
48 Quoted in Rogan, op. cit.,
    p. 180.
49 Quoted in Tamm, op. cit.,
    p. 32.
50 Ibid., p. 37.
51 *Without Walls: This is
    Tomorrow*, Channel Four
    TV documentary,
    London, June 1992.
52 Tamm, op. cit., p. 98.
53 Quoted in ibid., p. 37.
54 Lanza, op. cit., p. 196.
55 Ibid., p. 197.
56 Ibid., p. 198.
57 *Mojo*, May 1998.
58 Ibid.
59 Ibid.
60 Ibid.
61 Ibid.
62 *Guardian*, 8 May 1988.
63 Ibid.
64 *Mojo*, December 1995.
65 *Guardian*, 8 May 1998.
66 Ibid.
67 Ibid.
68 Ibid.

69 Ibid.
70 Ibid.
71 Ibid.
72 Ibid.

CHAPTER 10: M & M, OR THE
ROXY SOLOS

1   Mackay, A., sleeve note, *Resolving Contradictions,* Polydor Records, 1978.
2   *Melody Maker,* 30 August 1975.
3   *Melody Maker,* 7 August 1976.
4   *New Musical Express,* 12 November 1977.
5   Manzanera, P., sleeve note, *Primitive Guitars,* Polydor Records, 1982.
6   *Record Collector,* June 1995.
7   Ibid.

CHAPTER 11: ROXY
FOREVER?

1   *Mojo,* December 1995.
2   Ibid.
3   *New Musical Express,* 19 June 1982.
4. *Melody Maker,* 19 May 1982.
5. *Mojo,* December 1995.
6. *19,* August 1981.
7. *Record Collector,* June 1995.
8   Ibid.
9. *Mojo,* October 1994 (Andy Gill).
10 Rogan, J., Morrissey and Marr: *The Sad Alliance,* Omnibus Press, London, 1992, p. 174.
11 *Q,* February 1988 (Chris Salewicz).
12 Ibid.
13 Ibid.
14 Ibid.
15. Ibid.
16 *Mojo,* December 1995.
17 *Q,* February 1988 (Dave Rimmer).
18 *Q,* February 1988 (Chris Salewicz).
19. Ibid.
20 Quoted in *Radio Times,* 20–26 June 1992.
21 Ibid.
22 *Q,* March 1993. (Mat Snow).
23 *Q,* October 1994.
24 *Mojo,* October 1994.
25 Ibid.
26 *Q,* March 1993 (Mat Snow).
27 Ibid.
28 Ibid.
29 Ibid.
30 Ibid.
31 *Q,* March 1993 (John Aizlewood).
32 BBC Radio 1 interview, 1985.
33 *Mojo,* December 1995.
34 Ibid.
35 Ibid
36 *Record Collector,* June 1995.
37 *Q,* October 1994.

38   *Mojo*, October 1994 (Cliff
     Jones).
39   *Mojo*, December 1995.
40   Ibid.

41   Ibid.

DISCOGRAPHY

★ Omitted on early copies

Man'/'Grey Lagoons'/'For Your Pleasure'
Bryan Ferry: vocals, keyboards/Andy Mackay: oboe, saxophones/
Paul Thompson: drums/Phil Manzanera: guitars/Brian Eno:
synthesizer, tapes
Guest artiste: John Porter: bass guitar
Recorded: February 1973, AIR Studios, London
Engineers: John Middleton, John Punter
Producer: Chris Thomas and Roxy Music
Released: March 1973
UK LP: Island ILPS9232, reissued Polydor 1978
Chart Position UK: 4 (27weeks)

Stranded

'Street Life'/'Just Like You'/'Amazona'/'Psalm'/'Serenade'/'A Song
for Europe'/'Mother of Pearl'/'Sunset'
Bryan Ferry: voices, piano/Andy Mackay: oboe, saxophones,
treatments/Paul Thompson: drums, timpani/ Phil Manzanera:
guitar, treatments/Eddie Jobson: violin, synthesizer, keyboards/
Johnny Gustafson: bass guitar/Chris Lawrence: double bass (on
'Sunset')
Recorded: September 1973, AIR Studios, London
Engineer: John Punter
Producer: Chris Thomas
Released: November 1973
UK LP: Island ILPS9252, reissued Polydor 1978
Chart Position UK: 1 (17 wks)

Country Life

The Thrill of It All'/'Three and Nine'/'All I Want is You'/'Out of
the Blue'/'If It Takes All Night'/'Bitter-Sweet'/'Triptych'/
'Casanova'/'A Really Good Time'/'Prairie Rose'
Bryan Ferry: vocals, keyboards/Andy Mackay: oboe, saxophones/
Paul Thompson: drums/Phil Manzanera: guitars/Eddie Jobson:
violin, electric violin, synthesizer, keyboards/Johnny Gustafson:
bass guitar
Recorded: summer 1974 AIR Studios, London
Engineer: John Punter
Producer: Chris Thomas and Roxy Music
Released: November 1974

UK LP: Island ILPS9303, reissued Polydor 1978
Chart Position UK: 3 (10 weeks)

Siren

'Love is the Drug'/'End of the Line'/' Sentimental Fool'/
  'Whirlwind'/'She Sells'/'Could It Happen to Me?'/'Both Ends
  Burning'/'Nightingale'/'Just Another High'
Bryan Ferry: vocals, keyboards/Andy Mackay: oboe, saxophones/
  Paul Thompson: drums/Phil Manzanera: guitar/Eddie Jobson:
  strings, synthesizer, keyboards/Johnny Gustafson: bass guitar
Recorded: summer 1975, AIR Studios, London
  Engineer: Steve Nye
  Producer: Chris Thomas.
  Released: October 1975
  UK LP: Island ILPS9344, reissued Polydor 1978
  Chart Position UK: 4 (17 wks)

Viva! Roxy Music

'Out of the Blue'/'Pyjamarama'/'The Bogus Man'/'Chance
  Meeting'/'Both Ends Burning'/'If There Is Something'/'In
  Every Dream Home a Heartache'/'Do the Strand'
Bryan Ferry: vocals, keyboards/Andy Mackay: oboe, saxophones/
  Paul Thompson: drums, percussion/Eddie Jobson: strings,
  synthesizer, keyboards/John Wetton: bass guitar/Sal Madia: bass
  guitar/Johnny Gustafson: bass guitar/Rick Wills: bass guitar/
  The Sirens: backing vocals
Recorded: Glasgow Empire Theatre (November 1973), Newcastle
  City Hall (November 1974), Wembley Arena (October 1975)
  Engineer: Steve Nye
  Producer: Chris Thomas:
  Released: July 1976
  UK LP: Island ILPS9400, reissued Polydor 1978
  Chart Position UK: 6 (12 weeks)

Manifesto

Manifesto'/'Trash'/'Angel Eyes'/'Still Falls the Rain'/'Stronger
  Through the Years'/'Ain That So'/'My Little Girl'/'Dance
  Away'/'Cry Cry Cry'/'Spin Me Round'
Bryan Ferry: voices, piano/Andy Mackay: oboe, saxophones,

treatments/Paul Thompson: drums, timpani/Phil Manzanera: guitar, treatments

Guest artistes: Alan Spenner: bass guitar/ Paul Carrack: keyboards/ Gary Tibbs: bass guitar/Richard Tee: piano/Rick Marotta: drums/Steve Ferrone: drums/Luther Vandross: backing vocals

Recorded: November 1978, Ridge Farm, Surrey, and Basing Street Studio, London; also Atlantic Studios, New York, January 1979.

Engineers: Rhett Davies, Jimmy Douglass, Phil Brown, Randy Mason.

Producer: Roxy Music,

Released: March 1979

UK LP: Polydor-EG POLH001, reissued 1983

UK LP: Picture disc; Polydor-EG PBB001

Chart Position UK: 7 (34 weeks)

Flesh + Blood

'In the Midnight Hour'/'Oh Yeah'/'Same Old Scene'/'My Only Love'/'Over You'/'Eight Miles High'/'Rain Rain Rain'/'No Strange Delight'/'Running Wild'

Bryan Ferry: vocals, keyboards/Andy Mackay: saxophones/Phil Manzanera: guitar

Guest artistes: Allan Schwartzberg: drums/Andy Newmark: drums/ Simon Phillips: drums/Alan Spenner: bass/Neil Jason: bass/Gary Tibbs: bass/Neil Hubbard: guitar/Paul Carrack: keyboards

Recorded: spring 1980, Basing Street and Gallery Studios, London

Engineer: Rhett Davies

Producer: Rhett Davies and Roxy Music

Mixed at Power Station, New York City, by Bob Clearmountain

Released: June 1980

UK LP; Polydor-EG POLH002

Chart Position UK: 1 (80 weeks)

Avalon

'More Than This'/'The Space Between'/'Avalon'/'India'/'While My Heart is Still Beating'/'The Main Thing'/'Take A Chance With Me'/'To Turn You On'/'True to Life'/'Tara'

Bryan Ferry: vocals, keyboards/Andy Mackay: saxophones/Phil Manzanera: guitars

Guest artistes: Neil Hubbard: guitar/ Alan Spenner: bass/ Andy
Newmark: drums/Jimmy Maelen: percussion/Fonzi Thornton:
backing vocals/Yannick Etienne: backing vocals/Kermit
Moore: cello/Guy Fletcher: keyboards
Recorded: 1981-2 at the Compass Point, Nassau, New York, and
the Power Station, New York City
Engineers: Rhett Davies, Bob Clearmountain
Producers, Rhett Davies and Roxy Music
Released: June 1982
UK LP: Polydor-EG EGH 50
Chart Position UK: 7

Heart Still Beating
'India'/'Can't Let Go'/'While My Heart is Still Beating'/'Out of the
Blue'/' Dance Away'/'Impossible Guitar'/'A Song for Europe'/
'Love is the Drug'/'Like a Hurricane'/'My Only Love'/'Both
Ends Burning'/'Avalon'/'Editions of You'/'Jealous Guy'
Recorded: live at Fréjus, France, August 1982
Released: October 1990
UK LP: Polydor – EGLP 77

ROXY MUSIC COMPILATION ALBUMS
Roxy Music: Greatest Hits'
Virginia Plain'/'Do the Strand'/'All I Want is You'/'Out of the
Blue'/'Pyjamarama'/'Editions of You'/'Love is the Drug'/
'Mother of Pearl'/'A Song for Europe'/'The Thrill of It All'/
'Street Life'
Released: November 1977
UK LP: Polydor 2302 073
Chart Position UK: 20 (11 weeks)

Roxy Music: The First Seven Albums Box Set
Released: 1981
UK LP: Polydor-EG EGBS 1 (7LP)
Chart Position UK: n/a

The Atlantic Years
'Dance Away'/'Angel Eyes'/'Over You'/'Love is the Drug'/'Oh
yeah'/'Ain't That So'/'My Only Love'/'In the Midnight

Hour'/'Still Falls the Rain'/'Do the Strand'
Released: November 1983
UK LP: Polydor-EG EGLP54
UK CD: Polydor-EG 815 849 2
Chart Position UK: 23 (25 weeks)

The Thrill of It All

'Remake/Remodel'/'Ladytron'/'If There is Something'/'2HB'/
'Chance Meeting'/'Sea Breezes'/'Do the Strand'/'Beauty
Queen'/'Strictly Confidential'/'Editions of You'/'In Every
Dream Home a Heartache'/'The Bogus Man'/'For Your
Pleasure'/'Street Life'/'Just Like You'/'Amazona'/'A Song for
Europe'/'Mother of Pearl'/'Sunset'/'The Thrill of It All'/
'Three and Nine'/'All I Want is You'/'Out of the Blue'/
'Bitter-Sweet'/'Casanova'/'A Really Good Time'/'Prairie
Rose'/'Love is the Drug'/'Sentimental Fool'/'Could It
Happen to Me?'/'Both Ends Burning'/'Just Another
High'/'Manifesto'/'Trash'/'Angel Eyes'/'Stronger Through the
Years'/'Aint That So'/'Dance Away'/'Oh Yeah'/'Same Old
Scene'/'Flesh and Blood'/'My Only Love/Over You'/'No
Strange Delight'/'More Than This'/'Avalon'/'While My Heart
is Still Beating'/'Take A Chance With Me'/'To Turn You On'/
'Tara'/'Virginia Plain'/'The Numberer/ 'Pyjamarama'/'The
Pride and the Pain'/'Manifesto' (Remake)/'Hula Kula'/'Trash
2'/'Your Application's Failed'/'Love'/'Sultanesque'/'Dance
Away'(extended remix)/'South Downs'/'Angel Eyes' (extended
remix)/'Always Unknowing'/'The Main Thing' (extended
remix)/'India'/'Jealous Guy'
Released: December 1995
UK CD: Virgin CDBOX5 (4CD)

ROXY MUSIC MINI-ALBUMS
The High Road (Live)
'Can't Let Go'/'My Only Love'/' Like a Hurricane'/'Jealous Guy'
Released: March 1983
UK LP: Polydor EG MLP 1

ROXY MUSIC SINGLES
UK releases (label, date, chart placing)

'Virginia Plain'/'The Numberer' (Island, June 1972, 4)

'Pyjamarama'/'The Pride and the Pain' (Island, March 1973, 10)

'Street Life'/'Hula-kula' (Island, November 1973, 9)

'All I Want is You'/'Your Application's Failed' (Island, October 1974, 12)

'Love is the Drug'/'Sultanesque' (Island, October 1975, 2)

'Both Ends Burning'/'For Your Pleasure' (Island, March 1976, 25)

'Virginia Plain'/'Pyjamarama' (Polydor-EG, October 1977, 11)

'Do the Strand'/'Editions of You' (Polydor-EG, November 1978)

'Trash'/'Trash 2' (Polydor-EG, Febuary 1979, 40

'Dance Away'/'Cry Cry Cry' (Polydor-EG, March 1979, 2)

'Angel Eyes' (edited disco version)/'My Little Girl' (Polydor-EG, July 1979, 4)

'Angel Eyes' (full disco version)/'My Little Girl' (Polydor-EG, July 1979)

'Over You'/'Manifesto' (Polydor-EG, May 1980, 5)

'Oh Yeah'/'South Downs' (Polydor-EG, July 1980, 5)

'The Same Old Scene'/'Lover' (Polydor-EG, November 1980, 12)

'Jealous Guy'/'To Turn You On' (Polydor-EG, January 1981, 1)

'More Than This'/'India' (Polydor-EG, April 1982, 6)

'Avalon'/'Always Unknowing' (Polydor-EG, June 1982, 13)

'Take A Chance With Me'/'The Main Thing'(Polydor-EG August 1982, 26)

'Jealous Guy'/'Love'/'South Downs' (EP) (Polydor-EG) (June 1988)

'Love is the Drug' (Live) 'Editions of You' (Live) December 1990)

'Love is the Drug' (Live) 'Editions of You'(Live) (12") as above)

'Love is the Drug' (Live) 'Editions ofYou' (Live) 'Do the Strand' (Live) (CDS) (as above)

'Love is the Drug' (re-mix) (Polydor-EG VSCDT 1580, March 1996, 33)

BRYAN FERRY & ROXY MUSIC COMPILATIONS
Compilation records bearing the material of both Roxy Music and
Bryan Ferry. An asterisk denotes Ferry tracks.

Streetlife
'Virginia Plain'/'A Hard Rain's a–Gonna Fall'★/'Pyjamarama'/'Do
   the Strand'/'These Foolish Things'★/'Street Life'/'Let's Stick
   Together'★/'Smoke Gets in Your Eyes'★/'Love is the Drug'/
   'Sign of the Times'★/'Dance Away'/'Angel Eyes'/'Oh Yeah'/
   'Over You'/'Same Old Scene'/'In the Midnight Hour'/'More
   Than This'/'Avalon'/'Slave to Love'★/'Jealous Guy'
   Released: April 1986
   UK LP: EG TV-1
   UK CD: EG CTV-1

The Ultimate Collection
'Let's Stick Together'(1988 remix)★/'The In Crowd'★/'Angel
   Eyes'/'He'll Have to Go'★/'Tokyo Joe'★/'All I Want is
   You'/'Jealous Guy'/'The Price of Love'★/'Don't Stop the
   Dance'★/' Love is the Drug'/'This is Tomorrow'★/'Slave to
   Love'★/'Help Me'★/'Avalon'/'Dance Away'
   Released: November 1988
   UK LP: EG TV-2
   UK picture LP: EG PIXTV-2
   UK CD: EG CTV-2

More Than This
'Virginia Plain'/'A Hard Rain's a–Gonna Fall'/'Street Life'/'These
   Foolish Things'/ 'Love is the Drug'/'Smoke Gets in Your
   Eyes'/'Dance Away'/'Let's Stick Together'/'Angel Eyes'/'Slave
   to Love'/'Oh Yeah'/'Don't Stop the Dance'/'Same Old
   Scene'/'Is Your Love Strong Enough'/'Jealous Guy'/'Kiss and
   Tell'/'More Than This'/'I Put a Spell on You'/'Avalon'/'Your
   Painted Smile'
   Released: December 1995
   UK LP: Virgin V-2791
   UK LP: Virgin CDV-2791

SOLO DISCOGRAPHIES
UK releases only. An asterisk denotes compositional input to collaboration. Only Roxy Music members, temporary or permanent, who have recorded 'solo' material under their own names are included here.

Brian Eno
Albums
Here Come the Warm Jets (EG, 1973, 26)
Taking Tiger Mountain By Strategy (EG, 1974)
Another Green World (EG, 1975)
Discreet Music (EG/Obscure, 1975)
Before and After Science (Fourteen Pictures) (EG, 1977)
Music for Films (EG/Obscure, 1978, 55)
Ambient Music 1: Music for Airports (EG, 1979)
Ambient Music 4: On Land (EG, 1982, 93)
Apollo: Atmospheres and Soundtracks (EG, 1983)
Music for Films Vol. 2 (EG, 1983)
Thursday Afternoon (EG, 1985)
Nerve Net (Opal, 1992)
The Shutov Assembly (Opal, 1993)
Neroli (All Saints, 1993)
The Drop (All Saints, 1997)

OTHERS (selective)
Sparrowfall: incidental music to lay by Alan Drury, Hampstead Theatre, London, 1976 (see also *Music for Films*)
Sebastiane: OST to feature film by Derek Jarman, UK, 1976 (see also *Music for Films*, 'Inland Sea', 'Quartz', 'Final Sunset')
Science Report: 'Alternative Three': Anglia TV incidental music commission (see also *Music for Films*)
Jubilee: feature film by Derek Jarman, UK, 1978: contribution, 'Slow Water' to OST (Virgin, 1978) (see also *Music for Films*)
'Silk Cut': UK TV commercial for Collett, Dickinson and Pearce, 1982 (unreleased)
Great River Journeys of the World: The Nile: incidental music to BBC TV documentary, BBC TV, UK, 1984 (unreleased)
Dune: feature film by David Lynch, US, 1985: contribution, 'Prophecy Theme' (unreleased)

Creation of the Universe: PBS documentary, US, 1985: contribution, 'Theme' (unreleased)

Glint: East of Woodbridge (Artforum International Magazine, Inc. Evatone Soundsheets, 861222XS, 1986): tear-out disc

Another Green World/Dover Beach/Deep Blue Day/2/1 (EG–cd singles, 1987)

Mr Wroe's Virgins: incidental music to BBC TV drama series, 1993 (with Roger Eno) (unreleased)

Glitterbug: incidental music to TV film by Derek Jarman, UK, 1994, for BBC TV's *Arena* (unreleased)

Compilations

Fripp + Eno ((*No Pussyfooting*) and *Evening Star,* double cassette) (EG 1982)

Rarities (EG) (EP released only in ten-album EG boxed set, 'Working Backwards 1983-1973' EG–, 1983)

More Blank Than Frank: Songs from the Period 1973–1977 (EG – l986)

Desert Island Selection (Virgin, 1987)

Island Various Artists (with others, triple album featuring *Another Green World, Before and After Science, Apollo*) (EG, 1989)

Brian Eno (collaborations, triple album compilation) (Virgin, 1993)

Brian Eno 2 (as above) (1993)

The Essential Fripp and Eno (Venture, 1993)

The Compact Collection (Virgin, 1994)

Singles

'Seven Deadly Finns'/'Later On' (Island, March 1974)

'The Lion Sleeps Tonight (Wimoweh)'/(Island, – August 1975)

'King's Lead Hat'/'RAF'(B-side credited to 'Eno and Snatch') (Polydor, January 1978)

'The Jezebel Spirit'/'Regiment' (with David Byrne) (EG, May 1981)

'One World'/'Grandfather's House'/Palaquin (EP) (with John Cale) (Land, October 1990)

'Fractal Zoom'/'('A'-Moby mix) (12"- 4 mixes) (Opal, July 1992)

'Fractal Zoom'/'The Roil, The Choke' (CDS) (with another 'A' mix) Opal, July 1992)

'Ali Click (Beirut Mix)'/('A' rural mix) (12" with ('A' Markus

Draws and Grid mix) (October 1992)
'Ali Click (Beirut Mix)'/('A' trance long darkly mad mix)/ ('A' trance instrumental) (October 1992)

Collaborations

Cornelius Cardew & The Scratch Orchestra, *The Great Learning* (Deutsche Grammophon, 1971), voice

Matching Mole, *Matching Mole's Little Red Record* (CBS, 1972), synthesizer

Robert Fripp & Brian Eno, *(No Pussyfooting)* (EG, 1973), synthesizer loops

Kevin Ayers, John Cale, Brian Eno, Nico, *June 1st 1974* Island, 1974), synthesizer, vocals

Robert Calvert, *Captain Lockheed and the Starfighters* (UA, 1974), unspecified

Genesis, *The Lamb Lies Down on Broadway* (Charisma, 1974), 'Enossification'

Lady June, *Lady June's Linguistic Leprosy* (Virgin/Caroline, 1974), unspecified

Nico, *The End* (Island, 1974), synthesizer

John Cale, *Slow Dazzle* (Island, 1975), synthesizer

John Cale, *Helen of Troy* (Island, 1975), synthesizer

Robert Calvert, *Lucky Leif and the Longship*s (UA, 1975) (unspecified)

Robert Fripp & Brian Eno, *Evening Star* (EG, 1975) synthesizer, loops

Phil Manzanera, *Diamond Head* (EG, 1975), synthesizer

Quiet Sun, *Mainstream* (EG, 1975), synthesizer

801, *801 Live* (Polydor-EG, 1976), vocals, synthesizer, tapes, guitar

David Bowie, *Low* (RCA, 1977), general studio collaboration

David Bowie, *"Heroes"* (RCA, 1977), synthesizer, keyboards, guitar treatments

Camel, *Rain Dances* (Decca, 1977), Mini Moog, electric and acoustic piano, random notes, bells

Cluster & Eno, *Cluster & Eno* (Sky, 1977), instruments

Phil Manzanera & 801, *Listen Now!!* (Polydor-EG, 1977), musician

Harold Budd, *The Pavilion of Dreams* (Obscure, 1978), voices,

Eno, Moebius, Roedelius, *After the Heat* (Sky, 1978), instruments

John White and Gavin Bryars, *Machine Music* (Obscure, 1978), bottle, electric guitars

David Bowie, *Lodger* (RCA, 1979), Ambient drone, prepared piano and cricket menace, synthesizers, guitar treatments, horse trumpets, Eroica horn, piano

Robert Fripp, *Exposure* (EG, 1979), synthesizer

Robert Sheckley, *In a Land of Clear Colours* (limited edition of 1,000 copies with book), Galeria el Mensajero, lbiza (unspecified)

Harold Budd & Brian Eno, *Ambient Music No. 2: The Plateaux of Mirrors* (EG, 1980), instruments and treatments

Jon Hassell & Brian Eno, *Fourth World No. 1: Possible Musics* (EG, 1980), Prophet 5 synthesizer, other synthesizers

Talking Heads, *Remain in Light* (Sire, 1980), bass, keyboards, percussion, voices

David Byrne, *The Catherine Wheel* (Sire, 1981), bass, 'prophet scream', vibes

David Byrne & Brian Eno, *My Life in the Bush of Ghosts* (Sire, 1981), guitars, basses, synthesizers, drums, percussion and found objects★ (29)

Jon Hassell, *Dream Theory in Malaya: Fourth World No. 2* (EG, 1981), drums, bowl gongs, bells, mixing

Material, *One Down* (Elektra/Celluloid, 1982), unspecified

John Cale, *Caribbean Sunset* (Island, 1984), AMS Pitch changer

Eno, Moebius, Roedelius and Plank, *Begegnungen* (Sky, 1984), electronics

Michael Brook, Brian Eno, Daniel Lanois, *Hybrid* (EG, 1985), unspecified

Eno, Moebius, Roedelius and Plank, *Begegnungen II* (Sky, 1985), unspecified

Roger Eno, *Voices* (EG, 1985), treatments

Cluster and Eno, *Old Land* (Sky, 1986), unspecified

He Said, *Hail* (Mute, 1986), unspecified

Harold Budd, *The White Arcades* (Land, 1988), unspecified

Various Artists, *Music for Films III* (Virgin, 1988), unspecified

Daniel Lanois, *Acadie* (Opal, 1989), unspecified

The Neville Brothers, *Yellow Moon* (A&M, 1989), unspecified

U2, *Rattle and Hum* (Island, 1989), unspecified

Eno/Cale, *Wrong Way Up* (Land, 1990), vocals, instruments

Michael Brook, *Cobalt Blue* (4AD, 1992), unspecified
Bryan Ferry, *Mamouna* (Virgin, 1994), unspecified
Eno/Jah Wobble, *Spinner* (All Saints, 1995), unspecified
James, *Whiplash* (Mercury, 1996)
Harmonia, *Harmonia & Eno* (Sony, 1998), instruments★

★Recorded 1976

Bryan Ferry
Albums
These Foolish Things (Island, 1973, 5)
Another Time, Another Place (Island, 1974, 4)
Let's Stick Together (Island, 1976, 19)
In Your Mind (Polydor-EG, 1977, 5)
The Bride Stripped Bare (Polydor-EG, 1977, 13)
Boys and Girls (Polydor-EG, 1985,1)
Bête Noire (Virgin, 1987, 9)
Taxi (Virgin, 1993, 2)
Mamouna (Virgin, 1995, 11)

Singles
'A Hard Rain's a–Gonna Fall'/'2HB'(Island, September 1973, 10)
'The In Crowd'/'Chance Meeting'(Island, May 1974, 13)
'Smoke Gets in Your Eyes'/'Another Time, Another Place' (Island, August, 1974)
'You Go to My Head'/'Remake/Remodel' (Island, July 1975, 33)
'Let's Stick Together'/'Sea Breezes' (Island, May 1976, 4)
'This is Tomorrow'/'As the World Turns' (Polydor, February 1977, 9)
'Tokyo Joe'/'She's Leaving Home' (Polydor, May 1977, 15)
'What Goes On'/'Casanova' (Polydor, May 1978, 67)
'Sign of the Times'/'Four Letter Love' (Polydor, July 1978, 37)
'Carrickfergus'/'When She Walks in the Room' (Polydor, October 1978)
'Sign of the Times'/'Can't Let Go' (Polydor, November 1978)
'Slave to Love'/' Valentine' (EG, May 1985, 10)
'Slave to Love'/'Slave to Love' (Instrumental, 12″)
'Don't Stop the Dance'/'Nocturne' (EG, August 1985, 21)
'Don't Stop the Dance'/'Windswept' (instrumental, 12")

'Windswept'/'Crazy Love' (EG, November 1985, 46)

'Windswept'/'Crazy Love'/'Broken Wings'/'Feel the Need' (12")

'Is Your Love Strong Enough?'/'Windswept'(instrumental) (EG, March 1986, 22)

'Is Your Love Strong Enough?'/'Windswept' (instrumental) ('A' remix, 12") (EG, as above)

'Help Me'/'Broken Wings' (EG, July 1986)

'The Right Stuff'/'The Right Stuff' (instrumental) (Virgin, October 1987, 37)

'The Right Stuff'/'The Right Stuff'(instrumental)/('A' extended)/ ('A' dub version) (cassette single, also CD single) (EG)

'Kiss and Tell'/'Zamba'(Virgin, February 1988, 41)

'Kiss and Tell'/'Zamba' ('A' and 'B' remixes) (12" and CD single) (EG)

'Limbo' (Latin Mix)/'Bête Noire' (instrumental) (EG)

'Limbo' (Latin Mix)/'Bête Noire' (instrumental)/ Limbo ('A' mix) (12" and CD single) (EG, June 1988)

'The Price of Love' (R & B remix) 'Lover' (EG, March 1989, 43)

'The Price of Love' (R & B remix) 'Lover'/'Don't Stop the Dance' (remix)/'Nocturne' (12") (EG)

'The Price of Love' (R & B remix)/'Lover'/'Don't Stop the Dance' (remix)/'Slave to Love' (remix) (CD single) (EG)

'He'll Have to Go'/'Carrickfergus' (EG, April 1989, 49)

'He'll Have to Go'/'Carrickfergus'/'Windswept'/'Is Your Love Strong Enough?' (12") (EG)

'He'll Have to Go'/'Take Me to the River'/'Broken Wings' (CD single) (EG)

'I Put a Spell on You'/'These Foolish Things' (Virgin, March 1993, 18)

'I Put a spell on You'/'These Foolish Things'/'Ladytron' (live)/ 'While My Heart is Still Beating' (live) (CD single) (EG)

'Will You Love Me Tomorrow?'/'A Hard Rain's a–Gonna Fall' (Virgin, May 1993, 23)

'Will You Love Me Tomorrow?'/'A Hard Rain's a–Gonna Fall'/'A Wasteland' (live)/'Windswept' (live) (CD single) (EG)

'Girl of My Best Friend'/'Noctune'/'Are You Lonesome Tonight?'/ 'Valentine' (CD single) (Virgin, September 1993, 57)

'Your Painted Smile'/'Don't Stop the Dance' (Virgin, October 1994, 52)

'Your Painted Smile'/'Don't Stop the Dance'/'In Every Dream
   Home a Heartache' (live)/ 'Bête Noire' (live) (CD single with
   bonus tracks) (Virgin)
'Mamouna'/'The 39 Steps' (Brian Eno Mix) (Virgin, February
   1995, 57)
'Mamouna'/'The 39 Steps' (Brian Eno Mix)/'Jealous Guy' (live)/
   'Slave to Love' (live) (CD single with bonus tracks) (Virgin)

Others
Extended Play EP: 'Price of Love'/'Shame, Shame, Shame'/'Heart
   On My Sleeve'/'It's Only Love' (Island, July 1976, 7)
'Is Your Love Strong Enough?' contributed to Legend OST, 1986, 22
'Let's Stick Together'/'Shame, Shame, Shame'/'Chance Meeting'/
   'Sea Breezes' (CD EP) (EG, June 1988)
'Let's Stick Together'('88 remix)/' Trash' (EG, October 1988, 12)
'Let's Stick Together' ('88 remix)/'Trash'/'Shame, Shame,
   Shame'/'Angel Eyes'/(12") (EG)
'Let's Stick Together'('88 remix)/' Trash'/'Casanova'/'Sign of the
   Times' (CD single) (EG)
'Are You Lonely Tonight?' contributed to Honeymoon in Vegas
   OST, 1993

Edwin (Eddie) Jobson
Albums
The Green Album: Zinc (Polydor EG, 1983)
Theme of Secrets (Private Music, 1988)

Singles
not known

Collaborations
Curved Air, *Air Cut* (Warner Brothers, 1973)
Bryan Ferry, *These Foolish Things* (Island, 1973)
Amazing Blondel, *Mulgrave Street* (DJM, 1974)
Dana Gillespie, *Ain't Gonna Play No Second Fiddle* (RCA, 1974)
Roger Glover, *The Butterfly Ball* (Purple, 1974)
Andy Mackay, *In Search of Eddie Riff* (Island, 1974)
King Crimson, *USA* (Polydor-EG, 1974)
John Entwistle, *Mad Dog* (Track, 1975)

Flash Fearless, *Flash Fearless vs. The Zorg Women* (Chrysalis, 1975)★
    (various artists under a pseudonym)
Mike Heron, *Reputation* (Neighbourhood, 1975)
Phil Manzanera, *Diamond Head* (Island, 1975)
Frank Zappa, *Zoot Allures* (DiscReet, 1976)
Jason Martz, *The Pillory* (All Ears, 1978)
UK, *UK* (Polydor-EG, 1978)
UK, *Danger Money* (Polydor-EG, 1979)
UK, *Night After Night* (Polydor-EG, 1979)
Jethro Tull, *A* (Chrysalis,1980)
Frank Zappa, *Shut Up 'n' Play Yer Guitar* (CBS, 1981)
Frank Zappa, *You Are What You Is* (CBS, 1982)

Andy Mackay
Albums
In Search of Eddie Riff (Island, 1974)
Resolving Contradictions (Bronze, 1978)

Singles
'Wild Weekend'/'Walking the Whippet'(EG, August 1974)
'A Song of Friendship'/'Skill and Sweat' (Polydor, October 1978)

Collaborations
Mott, *The Hoople* (CBS, 1973)
Brian Eno, *Here Come the Warm Jets* (EG, 1974)
Brian Eno, *Taking Tiger Mountain By Strategy* (EG, 1975)
Phil Manzanera, *Diamond Head* (Island, 1975)
Pavlov's Dog, *The Sound of the Bell* (CBS, 1976)
Rock Follies, *Rock Follies OST* (Island, 1976)
Rock Follies, *Rock Follies 77 OST* (Polydor-EG, 1977)
Ray Russell, *Ready or Not* (DJM, 1977)
Johnny Cougar, *Biography* (Riva, 1978)
Godley and Creme, *L* (Mercury, 1978)
Mickey Jupp, *Long Distance Romancer* (Chrysalis, 1979)
Godley and Creme, *Freeze Frame* (Mercury, 1979)
Paul McCartney, *Tug of War* (Parlophone, 1981)
Paul McCartney, *Pipes of Peace* (Parlophone, 1982)
Yukihiro Takahashi, *Neuromantic* (Alfa, 1982)
Arcadia, *So Red the Rose* (EMI, 1985)

The Explorers, *The Explorers,* (Virgin, 1985)
Pet Shop Boys, *Please* (Parlophone, 1986)
Mike Oldfield, *Islands* (Virgin, 1987)
Manzanera and Mackay, *Manzanera and Mackay* (Relativity, 1988)
Tim Wheater, *Art of Landscape* (Theta, 1988)

Books
Electronic Music, Phaidon Press, Oxford, 1981

Phil Manzanera
Albums
Diamond Head (EG, 1975, 40)
K-Scope (Polydor, 1978)
Primitive Guitars (Polydor, 1982)
Southern Cross (Expression, 1991)
A Million Reasons Why (Expression, 1992)

Singles
'Flight 19'/'Car Rhumba' (Polydor-EG, September 1977) (credited
    to 801)
'Remote Control'/'K-Scope' (Polydor, October 1978)

Compilations
Guitarissimo! (EG, 1991)
The Complete Collection (Virgin, 1995)

Collaborations
Bryan Ferry, *These Foolish Things* (Island, 1973)
John Cale, *Fear* (Island, 1974)
Brian Enoe, *Here Come the Warm Jets* (EG, 1974)
Andy Mackay, *In Search of Eddie Riff* (Island, 1974)
Nico, *The End* (Island, 1974)
John Cale, *Slow Dazzle* (Island, 1975)
Brian Eno, *Taking Tiger Mountain By Strategy* (EG, 1975)
Quiet Sun, *Mainstream* (Island, 1975)
801, *801 Live* (Island, 1976)
Bryan Ferry, *Let's Stick Together* (Polydor-EG, 1976)
Stomu Yamashta, *Go* (Island, 1976)
801, *Listen Now!!* (Polydor, 1977)

Bryan Ferry, *In Your Mind* (Polydor-EG, 1977)
Andy Mackay, *Resolving Contradictons* (Bronze, 1978)
Godley and Creme, *Freeze Frame* (Mercury, 1979)
Yukihiro Takahashi, *Neuromantic* (Alfa, 1982)
Arcadia, *So Red the Rose* (EMI, 1985)
The Explorers, *The Explorers* (Virgin, 1985)
Manzanera and Wetton, *Manzanera and Wetton* (Geffen, 1987)
Nowamowa, *The Wasted Lands* (Coda, 1988)
Manzanera and Mackay, *Manzanera and Mackay* (Relativity, 1988)

APPENDIX 1
Other solo recordings by erstwhile members of live or studio Roxy Music line-ups

Richard Tee
Albums
Strokin' (CBS, 1978)
Natural Ingredients (CBS, 1979)
Inside You (CBS, 1984)

John Wetton
Albums
Caught in the Crossfire (Polydor-EG, 1980)
King's Road (Polydor-EG, 1982)

APPENDIX 2
The Explorers (Manzanera and Mackay)
Albums
The Explorers (Virgin, 1985)
The Explorers Live at the Palace (Camden) (Expression, 1997)

Singles
'Lorelei'/'You Go Up in Smoke' (7" & 12") (Virgin, June 1984)
'Falling for Nightlife'/'Crack the Whip'★ (7" & 12") (Virgin, October 1984)
'Two Worlds Apart'/'It Always Rains in Paradise' (7") (Virgin, April 1985)
'Venus de Milo'/'Another Lost Soul on the Run'★ (7" & 12") (Virgin, June 1985)

★ Non-album tracks: 'Crack the Whip' is featured on the live 'Camden Palace' album

VIDEOTAPES
Musique/The High Road
Released: April 1986 (VHS), October 1988 (CDV)
Recorded: Fréjus, France, 27 August 1982
Duration: 75 minutes
UK release (CDV): PolyGram Video CDV 080 438 1
UK release (VHS): Channel 5 CFV00012 (also reissued 1991 on 4 Frank 0835763

Total Recall
'Remake/Remodel'/'The Bob: (Medley)'/'Ladytron'/'If There is Something'/'Virginia Plain'/'Would You Believe?'/'For Your Pleasure'/'In Every Dream Home a Heartache'/'Do the Strand'/'Editions of You'/'These Foolish Things'/'The Paw Paw Negro'/'Blowtorch' (Eno solo)/'Wild Weekend'(Mackay solo)/'A Hard Rain's a-Gonna Fall'/'Street Life'/'A Song for Europe'/'Smoke Gets in Your Eyes'/'It Ain't Me Babe'/'A Really Good Time'/'All I Want is You'/'Diamond Head' (Manzanera solo)/'You Go to My Head'/'Whirlwind'/'Love is the Drug'/'Both Ends Burning'/'Let's Stick Together'/ 'Baby's On Fire '(801/Manzanera)/'The Price of Love'/'In Your Mind'/'Trash'/'Dance Away'/'Angel Eyes'/'Ain't That So'/'Same Old Scene'/'Oh Yeah'/ 'Jealous Guy'/'Avalon'/'The Main Thing'/'Can't Let Go'/'Slave to Love'
Released: (VHS) March 1990
Duration: 90 minutes
UK release: Virgin Vision VVD 649

More Than This
'Your Painted Smile'/'Same Old Scene'/'Limbo'/'These Foolish Things'/'Remake/Remodel'/'Will You Still Love Me Tomorrow'/'Let's Stick Together'/'Windswept'/'A Hard Rain's a-Gonna Fall'/'Slave to Love'/'The Right Stuff'/'What Goes On'/'Is Your Love Strong Enough'/'The Price of Love'/'Angel Eyes'/'Don't Stop the Dance'/'You Go to My Head'/'I Put a Spell on You'/'The Main Thing'/'Girl of My Best Friend'/ 'Kiss and Tell'/'Jealous Guy'/'Don't Want to Know'/'Mamouna'

INDEX